DISCARDED

ADVANCES IN
THE ECONOMICS
OF ENERGY
AND RESOURCES

Volume 1 • 1979

THE STRUCTURE OF
ENERGY MARKETS

ADVANCES IN THE ECONOMICS OF ENERGY AND RESOURCES

A Research Annual

Editor: ROBERT S. PINDYCK
Sloan School of Management
Massachusetts Institute of Technology

VOLUME 1 • 1979

THE STRUCTURE OF ENERGY MARKETS

Ai JAI PRESS INC.
Greenwich, Connecticut

Copyright © 1979 JAI PRESS INC.
165 West Putnam Avenue
Greenwich, Connecticut 06830
All rights reserved. No part of this publication may be reproduced, stored on a retrieval system, or transmitted in any form or by any means, electronic, mechanical, photocopying, filming, recording or otherwise without prior permission in writing from the publisher.

ISBN NUMBER: 0-89232-078-8

Manufactured in the United States of America

CONTENTS

INTRODUCTION
Robert S. Pindyck — 1

ENERGY-ECONOMY INTERACTIONS: THE FABLE OF THE ELEPHANT AND THE RABBIT?
William W. Hogan and Alan S. Manne — 7

INPUT PRICES, SUBSTITUTION, AND PRODUCT INFLATION
John R. Moroney and Alden L. Toevs — 27

SUBSTITUTION AMONG ENERGY, CAPITAL, AND LABOR INPUTS IN U.S. MANUFACTURING
Robert Halvorsen and Jay Ford — 51

THE STANFORD PILOT ENERGY/ECONOMIC MODEL
T. J. Connolly, George B. Dantzig and S. C. Prikh — 77

NEW CAR EFFICIENCY STANDARDS AND THE DEMAND FOR GASOLINE
James L. Sweeney — 105

FACTORS LEADING TO STRUCTURAL CHANGE IN THE U.S. OIL-REFINING INDUSTRY IN THE POSTWAR PERIOD
Stephen C. Peck and Scott Harvey — 135

INTEGRATION AND INNOVATION IN THE ENERGY MARKETS
David J. Teece — 163

THE ECONOMICS OF THE THROWAWAY NUCLEAR FUEL CYCLE
John B. Gordon and Martin L. Baughman — 213

PROSPECTS FOR NUCLEAR POWER IN THE DEVELOPING
COUNTRIES
Alan M. Strout 257

FINANCIAL MARKETS AND THE ADJUSTMENT TO HIGHER
OIL PRICES
Tamir Agmon, Donald Lessard and James L. Paddock 291

ADVANCES IN THE ECONOMICS OF ENERGY AND RESOURCES

Volume 1 • 1979

THE STRUCTURE OF ENERGY MARKETS

INTRODUCTION

Robert S. Pindyck

Advances in the Economics of Energy and Resources brings together new research results covering a wide spectrum of problems in energy and resource economics and policy. In this first volume, *The Structure of Energy Markets*, ten papers have been assembled that cover aspects of energy markets ranging from the behavior of individual firms to the behavior of the entire energy sector to the interactions between the energy sector and the macroeconomy. In addition, the coverage ranges from domestic (U.S.) energy markets and energy policy to international problems in energy. In editing *Advances in the Economics of Energy and Resources*, this breadth of coverage was an objective in inviting papers. The other objective, of course, was obtaining new and significant research results of high quality. I believe that the papers here have succeeded in meeting both of these objectives.

The first paper in this volume, "Energy-Economy Interactions: The Fable of the Elephant and the Rabbit?" by William Hogan and Alan Manne, looks at the interactions between the energy sector and the rest of the economy. In most energy studies, the energy sector is viewed by itself, so that GNP and other macroeconomic variables are taken as exogenous inputs to the determination of energy demand and supply—i.e., as though they themselves were unaffected by the energy sector. Hogan and Manne show that in fact there could be a significant interdependence between the energy sector and the macroeconomy. They develop a simple aggregate model of energy-economy interaction, and use it to show the possible range of impacts that energy policy can have on the economy as a whole. They show how the size of these impacts depends on two important empirical parameters: the relative size of the energy sector, and the elasticity of substitution between energy and other factors of production.

As illustrated in the paper by Hogan and Manne, the impact of higher energy prices on the cost of production depends critically on the elasticity of substitution between energy and the other factors of production. The next two papers in the volume provide an empirical focus on the size of this elasticity and its variation across industries. "Input Prices, Substitution, and Product Inflation," by John Moroney and Alden Toevs, begins by demonstrating that fixed-coefficient (no factor substitution) and Cobb-Douglas (unitary elasticity of substitution) production functions are inappropriate in describing industrial production, and then goes on to estimate generalized translog cost functions for several natural resource using industries. These cost functions provide unrestricted estimates of the elasticities of substitution for capital, labor, and natural resource inputs for each of these industries. Using these estimates, Moroney and Toevs go on to determine the influence of factor substitution on inflation, and they find that prolonged resource price increases would indeed lead to sharp inflation of the output prices of these industries.

A second empirical study of factor substitution is provide by Robert Halvorsen and Jay Ford in "Substitution Among Energy, Capital, and Labor in U.S. Manufacturing." Halvorsen and Ford also apply the translog cost function at the industry level (eight two-digit industries), but they disaggregate energy inputs, so that their factors of production are capital, labor, and individual fuels. Furthermore, they test for, rather than assume, separability of energy inputs from capital and labor (they find that separability can be accepted for four of the eight industries). Thus they obtain unrestricted estimates of the elasticies of substitution between factors, and the demand elasticities for energy and for individual fuels.

The next paper, by Thomas Connally, George Dantzig, and Shailendra

Parikh, provides an overview of "The Stanford PILOT Energy/Economic Model," and demonstrates its application to the analysis of energy policy. PILOT is a model of the energy sector as a whole, together with its relationship to the national economy and to the foreign sector. The energy sector is described in the model in considerable detail, and is linked to a less detailed model of the economy (which in turn is linked to the foreign sector through trade balance relations) and to an estimated inventory of raw energy resources. The model is an optimizing model (essentially in linear programming form), and its solution maximizes the sum over time of discounted aggregate consumption. As a result, the model provides a vehicle for analyzing the impacts of alternative energy policy options not only on the energy sector, but also on the economy as a whole, and on total consumer welfare. To illustrate the model's use, the authors present the results of three alternative policy scenarios, which differ in terms of allowed imports, allowed nuclear capacity, and coal use. The PILOT model is still in its development stage, and the authors conclude with a discussion of their ongoing work in expanding and improving the model.

James Sweeney, in his paper, "New Car Efficiency Standards and the Demand for Gasoline," evaluates the likely impact of the Energy Policy and Conservation Act of 1975 (EPCA) on gasoline demand. This Act was passed to reduce the growth rate in gasoline consumption, and requires that manufacturers meet a new car efficiency standard of 20 miles per gallon in 1980 and 27.5 mpg in 1985. A penalty is imposed on manufacturers failing to meet this standard, and this penalty can be viewed as a price for inefficiency (the price is positive for average efficiency below the standard, and zero for average efficiency above).

James L. Sweeney examines the economics of this penalty, and in particular determines the rational pricing response of the manufacturer and the subsequent response by consumers. In addition, he identifies and examines the incentives toward modification of industrial structure resulting from the penalty, and suggests an alternative penalty structure that would eliminate these incentives. Finally, Sweeney calculates empirical estimates of the response to the efficiency standard, and uses these to determine the impact of the standard on gasoline demand.

The next two papers in the volume deal with issues in the industrial organization of the oil industry. In "Factors Leading to Structural Change in the U.S. Oil Refining Industry in the Postwar Period," Stephen Peck and Scott Harvey begin by examining the implications of a number of changes in the technological and institutional environment of the industry, including the introduction of market demand prorationing in the 1930s, catalytic cracking in the late 1930s, large-diameter pipelines in the postwar period, the Pipeline Consent Decree of 1941, and finally the oil import quota introduced in 1959. Next, they consider aspects of industry concentration, including barriers to entry in the industry, and the effects of mergers on concentration. In the second section of their paper, Peck and Harvey use data on the capacity of surviving firms in the U.S. oil-refining industry over the period 1950 to 1974 to study the relationship between firm growth rate and firm size. They find that small firms typically grew faster than larger firms owing to a combination of the hypothesized unwillingness of large firms to upset market equilibrium, the set of government policies in effect during the period, and the technical and institutional changes in the industry environment. And they find that the steady-state probability distribution of firm sizes is lognormal with constant mean and variance, so that there should not be a tendency for continually increasing concentration.

David Teece, in his paper, "Integration and Innovation in the Energy Markets," looks at a different aspect of the petroleum and other energy industries. He attempts to identify an economic rationale for the existing organization of U.S. energy industries and the changes in that organization that are now occurring. Teece argues that traditional measures of market structure (in particular the degree of monopoly power and the form of government regulation) are not sufficient to explain economic performance, but rather the more important criteria are the manner in which firms span different markets and the nature of firms' internal organization. Teece singles out petroleum companies as the empirical test case for his approach, and after describing the structure and organization of the petroleum industry, he relates that organization to the technological performance of the industry. In so doing, he provides a basis for assessing public policy options regarding the structure of the industry, and regarding energy research.

According to the conventional wisdom, the economic viability of nuclear power in the long run requires that the nuclear fuel cycle ultimately be closed, i.e. that spent fuel be recovered, refabricated, and reintroduced into the system. The reprocessing of the fissionable material in spent fuel is viewed as economically desirable for light water reactors, and is inherent to the breeder reactor. However, the implementation of a closed nuclear fuel cycle has been impeded by a number of factors, and this has reduced the commitment to nuclear power plants by the electric utility industry. In their paper, "The Economics of the Throwaway Nuclear Fuel Cycle," John Gordon and Martin Baughman argue that the conventional wisdom has been misguided, and that a "throwaway" fuel cycle offers an economically viable, and in some ways more attractive, fuel cycle concept to support a nuclear industry. They demonstrate that the "throwaway" fuel cycle would result in total fuel costs lower than those for a closed fuel cycle prior to 1985, and would result in fuel costs only 12–15 percent higher than those for a closed cycle up to the year 2000. They argue that in view of the urgent need for non-petroleum resources, and in view of the fact that the "throwaway" fuel cycle offers an institutionally simpler alternative than the closed fuel cycle, a needless reliance on a closed fuel cycle should not stand in the way of the transition to nuclear power over the next ten years.

"Future Prospects for Nuclear Power in the Developing Countries," by Alan Strout, examines the importance of nuclear power to developing countries over the next 25 years, and attempts to project the number of developing countries likely to have nuclear capacity (and the extent of that capacity) by the year 2000. In order to determine the importance of nuclear power to the developing countries, it is first necessary to project energy demand for those countries, and then to assess the costs and supplies of nonnuclear energy that will be available. Strout begins with a discussion of energy demand and energy use in developing countries, and shows why and how energy demand elasticities are likely to differ from those for developed countries. He then projects the demand for electricity in the developing countries, and projects alternative sources of energy supply, as well as the costs of these sources. He then estimates and discusses the costs of delivered electricity for a typical generating plant in a typical developing country for three alternative fuels—nuclear, coal, and oil. Strout finds the nuclear-fueled plant to be more expensive under most assumptions—but not very much more expensive. He concludes that significant financial losses would be incurred by "going nuclear," but he argues that many developing countries might view these losses as a reasonably price to pay for joining the Nuclear Club.

The last paper in the volume, "Financial Markets and the Adjustment to Higher Oil Prices," by Tamir Agmon, Donald Lessard, and James Paddock, looks at three important aspects of the role of financial markets in the adjustment—of both producing and consuming countries—to higher oil prices. First, the authors analyze the extent to which financial markets can change the adjustment to higher oil prices, and the extent to which they can absorb the shock of that adjustment. They show that financial markets did absorb much of the shock of the 1973-74 oil-price increases, both on the producer side and consumer side of the market. In addition, they argue that as a result of the oil-price increases, there is today a much greater demand for financial intermediation. Agmon, Lessard and Paddock then go on to look at the financial problem of a typical OPEC country. They contend that higher oil prices increased the risk of the financial portfolio of such a country because the major component of that portfolio is now unsold oil in the ground. They argue that this produces an incentive to *reduce* oil prices relative to what they would be if the financial portfolio were completely diversified. Finally, they examine the financial stress that higher oil prices place on less-developed countries and they speculate on the implications of this stress for world financial markets and the financial portfolio of the OPEC countries.

ENERGY-ECONOMY INTERACTIONS: THE FABLE OF THE ELEPHANT AND THE RABBIT?*

William W. Hogan, STANFORD UNIVERSITY
Alan S. Manne, STANFORD UNIVERSITY

I. INTRODUCTION

In most energy policy studies, the energy sector is viewed in isolation from the remainder of the economy, and the analysis is performed without consideration of the broader impacts. Typically, the GNP and other macroeconomic indices are taken as given—as though they were unaffected by the energy sector. This is not fully satisfactory, for there could be two-way interdependence with the remainder of the economy.

As a rough measure of the cost (or benefit) of a given energy policy, it often is sufficient to calculate the impact upon the aggregate consumption or the GNP. The dollar magnitude of this impact may be significant and highly relevant to energy policy. Nonetheless, even a large absolute amount may constitute only a small fraction of the GNP. It is in this sense that there may be virtually one-way linkage—that the GNP growth rate may affect the energy sector but not vice versa. With one-way linkage, there would be no need to couple the energy sector with an economy-wide analysis. Approximate estimates of economic impacts would be adequate for energy policy evaluations. If it turns out, however, that two-way linkages are significant, we cannot treat the energy sector in isolation but must consider the full interdependence effects.

Before undertaking a complex analysis of the interdependence effects, it would appear useful to make a rough assessment of their magnitude. That is the purpose of this paper. We present a simple model for organizing the central concepts and the parameters that might underlie a more realistic study. This aggregative model provides insights and indicates the possible range of energy policy impacts upon the economy as a whole.

II. THE ELEPHANT AND THE RABBIT?

For simplicity, we represent the economy in terms of just two inputs—energy and all other items. Note that energy is only a small component of the U.S. economy. As of 1970, the value of primary energy inputs did not exceed 4 percent of the GNP. At 1970 or even at current prices, this is something like an elephant-rabbit stew. If such a recipe contains just one rabbit (the energy sector) and one elephant (the rest of the economy), won't it still taste very much like elephant stew?

If prices had not risen after 1970, it is likely that energy demands would have grown at about the same rate as the GNP. The 4 percent ratio then would continue into the future. But what if energy costs double, *and* there is sufficient time for the economy to adapt to this change? A naïve estimate of the impact may be obtained by assuming a constant input mix. On this basis, an additional 4 percent of the GNP must be allocated to cover the costs of energy. Other input-mix options are, in fact, available, and some would lead to lower costs. Thus, the first doubling of energy costs would produce, at most, a 4 percent loss in GNP.

Reductions in the physical availability of energy also can be interpreted in terms of higher costs. However, for questions phrased in terms of the physical availability rather than dollar costs, an alternative application of the value share is useful. The elephant-rabbit analogy still is applicable, if there is sufficient time for the economy to respond smoothly to changes in the availability of energy relative to other inputs. The value share of the energy sector determines the incremental effect upon the GNP. *If* the 4 percent value share remained constant, this would mean that a 10 percent reduction in energy inputs would produce only a 0.4 percent drop in total output. Thus, for small changes in energy availability, there need not be a proportional impact upon the economy as a whole.

For large reductions in the availability of energy, the value share need not remain constant. If the value share rises, the GNP effects may become more pronounced. To evaluate large changes, we must proceed beyond the metaphor of the elephant and the rabbit.

III. SUBSTITUTION

The processes for future production and utilization of energy are not fixed immutably. Insulation, engine efficiency improvements, and "input juggling" in production processes can all alter the energy requirements for a fixed level of output. Such substitution modifies the economic impacts of changes in the energy system. This flexibility in energy utilization is the next essential element, after the value share of energy, in measuring the magnitude of the energy-economic feedback. It also characterizes the key difference among many energy models. In economists' jargon, different assessments of this flexibility of energy utilization can be phrased as a disagreement over the numerical value of the "elasticity of substitution." This is a measure of the ease or difficulty of replacing energy with other inputs.

The discussion is simplified here by restricting attention to the long run, when energy equipment and processes can be changed substantially. Not that the short run is unimportant, but the character of the problem is different. A sudden shock may create far more serious problems than the gradual long-run pressures of resource exhaustion. Here we focus only on these long-run adjustments.

The elasticity of substitution concept is illustrated in Figure 1. The point identified as "current input mix" represents one possible combination of the inputs of energy and other factors (capital and labor) used to produce a given level of total output. The lines drawn through this point indicate alternative combinations of inputs that could be used to produce the same level of output. These constant output curves summarize the potential for substitution between energy and other inputs. Except for the explicit assumption that energy and other inputs are substitutes (i.e., that the slopes of these curves are negative), the general shape of these curves might be quite varied. Three alternatives are shown in Figure 1—with elasticities of substitution equal to zero, one, and infinity.

If the energy-GNP ratio were an immutable constant, this would imply a *zero* elasticity of substitution. It would mean that total output could not be increased without increases in both energy and nonenergy inputs. This fixed proportions assumption flies in the face of common sense. It is reminiscent of the theories that led the U.S. and its allies to attempt to destroy the

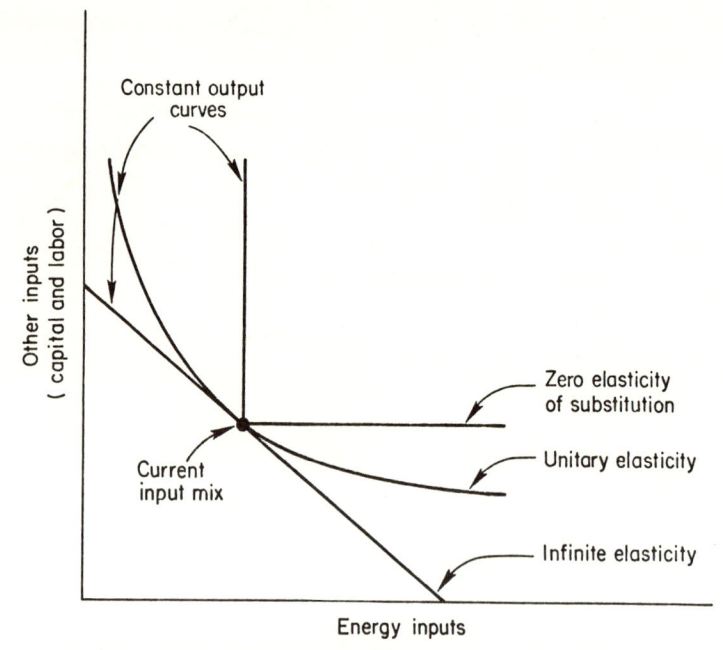

Figure 1. The elasticity of substitution concept.

German ball-bearing industry during World War II, and thereby to knock out the entire German economy.

At the opposite extreme, if all inputs to the economy were completely fungible, there would be an *infinite* elasticity of substitution. This also flies in the face of common sense. It would mean that machinery could run without energy, or that energy would be useful without machines.

Still another hypothesis is that the elasticity of substitution is *unity*. This would imply that as the relative price of energy increased, the optimal value share of energy inputs would still remain constant at, say, 4 percent of GNP.

The elasticity of substitution need not be zero or unity or infinity. If we restrict ourselves to a constant elasticity of substitution, we can construct a simple model of energy-economy linkages. In examining the implications of this model, however, it is not necessary to rely on altogether arbitrary judgments as to the appropriate elasticity. For this aggregate model, the numerical values of the long-run price elasticity of demand and of the long-run elasticity of substitution are virtually identical. Therefore, many econometric and engineering studies of the price elasticity of energy demand can be applied directly to the measurement of the elasticity of substitution. Unfortunately, a variety of defects can be found in each such empirical study. Unlike the value share of the energy sector, no definitive estimate of the elasticity of demand/substitution is available. The weight of the evidence would suggest that the elasticity lies between 0.2 and 0.6.[1] In presenting the economic impacts of alternate energy availabilities, we encompass this range of elasticities—partly because of the empirical evidence and partly because the results do not vary significantly for elasticities that are either much higher or much lower.

For the present purposes, it is reasonable to assume that energy demand would grow at a rate close to that of the total economy *if* relative energy prices were to remain constant. A 3 percent year growth over 1970 would imply a GNP in 2010 of approximately $4,400 billion (1975 dollars) and a total primary energy input of 220 quads. Suppose that for reasons of resource

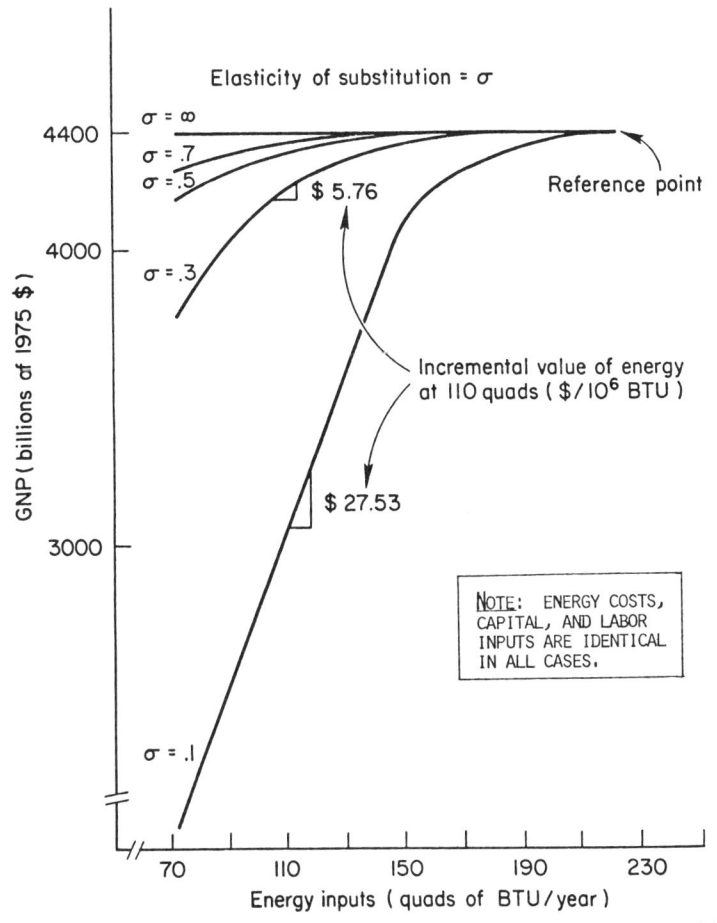

Figure 2. Economic impacts of energy reductions in the year 2010.

conservation, environmental protection, or national security, there is a need for reduced energy consumption. Suppose, further, that there is no reduction in the economic inputs other than energy. One way to achieve a reduction in energy consumption would be through an energy conservation tax with the tax revenues fully redistributed. Other policy measures (e.g., auto efficiency standards) also could achieve much the same goal, but for illustrative purposes we shall simply describe all of these as a BTU tax. This tax represents the incremental value of energy at the various consumption levels. Under these assumptions, the feedback issue can be posed through two questions: (1) What is the size of the necessary BTU conservation tax? (2) What is the resulting impact on GNP?

For alternative values of the elasticity of substitution, the answers to these questions are illustrated in Figure 2. This graph depicts the GNP that would result at various levels of energy input, ranging from the reference value of 220 quads down to 70 quads, if the inputs of capital and labor are held constant, and if energy costs remain constant. The results are shown for elasticities of substitution between 0.1 and 0.7. The slope at each point indicates the "BTU tax" needed to achieve the specified level of energy consumption. Thus, if the elasticity of substitution is 0.3, a tax of $5.76/10^6

Table 1. Alternative estimates of economic impact in the year 2010 (with constant energy costs and constant capital and labor inputs).

| E = quads of energy in 2010 | \multicolumn{5}{c}{Elasticity of demand/substitution} |
	0.1	0.2	0.3	0.5	0.7
	\multicolumn{5}{c}{Percent reduction in GNP}
220	0	0	0	0	0
190	0.6	0.3	0.2	0.1	0.1
160	4.5	1.3	0.8	0.4	0.3
110	27.7	9.2	4.3	1.9	1.2
70	53.8	30.8	14.3	5.2	3.0
	\multicolumn{5}{c}{Incremental value of energy ($/10^6 BTU)}
220	0	0	0	0	0
190	2.40	.80	.48	.26	.18
160	10.37	2.69	1.38	.67	.44
110	27.53	13.69	5.76	2.17	1.26
70	29.05	34.52	19.24	5.94	2.99

Note: Developed using base case assumptions and approximations discussed in the Appendix. Throughout, it is assumed that if 220 quads of energy were available, the GNP would be $4,400 billions in 2010 (when expressed at 1975 prices). The cost of energy in all cases is the 1970 price: $.80 per million BTU. The incremental value represents the *excess* over this amount.

BTU would be needed to reduce energy consumption from 220 quads to 110 quads. The resulting GNP would be reduced from $4,400 billion to $4,213 billion (4.3 percent). For convenience, the same information is repeated in tabular form in Table 1.

According to this simple model, the long-run elasticity can have a startling effect. A 50 percent reduction in energy utilization would produce a 28 percent reduction in GNP if the elasticity is 0.1, but only a 1 percent reduction in GNP if the elasticity is 0.7. The taxes required to achieve these reductions display a corresponding variation. Most existing estimates of the price elasticity of demand for primary energy would fall within the range of 0.2 to 0.6. This issue certainly has not been resolved, and there is some evidence for both higher and lower values. It is essential, therefore, that any improved analysis of the energy-economy link provide a careful specification of the elasticity of demand/substitution. Most modeling efforts can be characterized in terms of their treatment of this important concept.

IV. EXTENSIONS OF THE ANALYSIS

The estimate of economic impact is sensitive to simplifying assumptions, one of the most questionable being that changes in energy availability do

Table 2. Alternative estimates of economic impact in the year 2010 (with constant energy costs, constant labor inputs, and a constant rate of return on capital).

E = quads of energy in 2010	Elasticity of demand/substitution				
	0.1	0.2	0.3	0.5	0.7
	Percent reduction in GNP				
220	0	0	0	0	0
190	4.0	2.0	1.4	1.0	1.0
160	12.0	5.7	3.5	2.1	1.8
110	33.4	19.2	11.3	5.5	3.9
70	55.6	39.9	25.8	11.7	7.2
	Incremental value of energy ($/$10^6$ BTU)				
220	0	0	0	0	0
190	1.41	.67	.42	.24	.17
160	4.26	2.00	1.19	.62	.41
110	11.94	7.41	4.32	1.95	1.18
70	19.63	16.79	11.69	5.06	2.76

Note: Developed using base case assumptions and approximations discussed in the Appendix. Throughout, it is assumed that if 220 quads of energy were available, the GNP would be $4,400 billions in 2010 (when expressed at 1975 prices). The cost of energy in all cases is the 1970 price: $.80 per million BTU. The incremental value represents the *excess* over this amount.

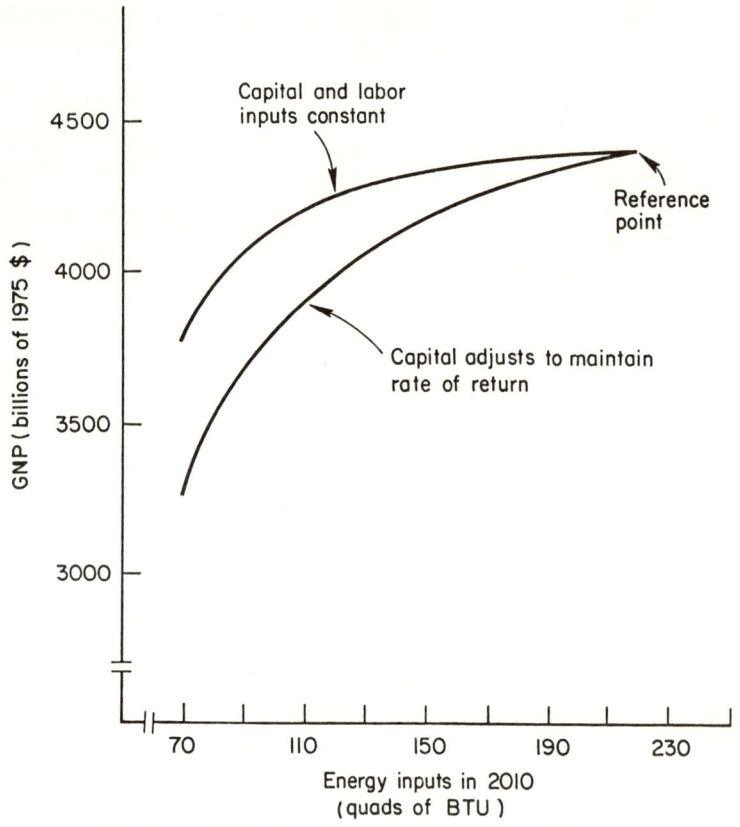

Figure 3. Economic impact of energy scarcity in the year 2010 for alternate capital assumptions (elasticity of substitution $\sigma = 0.3$).

not affect the pattern of investment and the long-run inputs of capital services. The effect of this assumption can be illustrated by extending the initial framework to include three inputs to the economy: energy, capital, and labor. Instead now of holding capital and labor constant as energy changes, let capital adjust to maintain its rate of return.[2] The impact of this change in assumption is displayed in Figure 3 for an elasticity of 0.3. At an energy input reduction of 50 percent, the adjustment of capital from a constant input to a constant rate of return increases the economic impact. Instead of 4 percent, the impact now becomes 11 percent. The energy tax needed to achieve this reduction in energy use is $4.32/10^6$ BTU. But the potential for substitution still preserves the basic qualitative results. Reductions in energy input need not produce proportional reductions in total economic output. The economic impact of energy conservation is quite sensitive to the assumptions—either explicit or implicit—on the elasticity of substitution. (See Table 2.)

Other objections can be raised against this analysis. First, the aggregation may disguise distinctly different behavior in individual sectors. The specific processes for energy substitution are varied and intricate. The morass of detail may be approached gradually by expanding the simple model for improved description of the elasticities through the separate analysis of more representative groupings. Second, the aggregate substitution parameter does not provide an engineering description of the new processes and the technologies that must be adopted. A more disaggregated analysis is needed in order to provide the detail to lend credibility to the simple analysis. A large part of the motivation for the construction of more sophisticated models can be viewed as the need for overcoming these difficulties by improving the aggregate estimate of the elasticity of demand/substitution or by providing a demonstration of energy utilization flexibility at a verifiable level of detail.

V. POLICY AND ANALYTIC IMPLICATIONS

The implications of substitution are significant for the energy-economic interface. If there is no substitution, reductions in energy use produce corresponding reductions in economic activity. But if the higher estimates of the elasticity of energy demand are accepted, it follows that major changes in energy utilization can be achieved without corresponding changes in total economic activity. Even in the latter case, we are not freed from difficult energy policy trade-offs. The absolute impacts of the change in GNP may be significant. A small proportion of a large number still remains a large number. A given reduction in energy supplies may produce only a 1 percent reduction in GNP each year, but this can be a large loss in dollar terms. If the economy is growing at 3 percent in real terms, and we discount future consumption at 6 percent, a 1 percent reduction in annual GNP corresponds to a present value of nearly half a trillion dollars. Such a figure would justify a substantial research investment aimed at developing low-cost technologies which expand energy supply or improve the efficiency of energy utilization.

At a more technical level, the implications for energy modeling may be more conclusive. If there is little energy substitution, the feedback effect is significant, and energy models must account for this effect in representing the energy system. However, if the substitution effects are significant, the feedback effect on the evaluation of the energy system is relatively small. In this case, the energy sector may be analyzed by itself. The changes in energy utilization and economic costs can be represented adequately by the first-order effects contained in traditional microeconomic demand curve analyses. This permits important modeling simplifications and expanded detail for the improved description of the energy system.

VI. SUMMARY

A simple aggregative model can illustrate some key concepts in determining the economic impacts of energy policies. The small relative size of the energy sector motivates the metaphor of the elephant and the rabbit. It indicates that small changes in energy availability do not produce proportional changes in economic activity. The elasticity of substitution determines the economic impacts for large changes in energy availability. A low elasticity implies significant interactions. Higher elasticities may yield important economic impacts, but these may be represented adequately in an isolated analysis of the energy sector.

FOOTNOTES

*Presented at ORSA/TIMS Meeting, San Francisco, May 9–11, 1977. The authors are solely responsible for the views expressed here. They gratefully acknowledge suggestions received from Ernst Berndt, Dale Jorgenson, Tjalling Koopmans, Lester Lave, William Nordhaus, Shailendra Parikh, James Sweeney, David Wood, and members of the CONAES Modeling Resource Group and the Energy Modeling Forum Working Group. The calculations were performed by Dennis Fromholzer.

1. The elasticity of demand is defined here in terms of primary energy prices. This complicates the direct comparison of elasticity estimates from other studies due to definitional and aggregation problems. However, representative estimates for energy demand can be found in (1, 2, 3).

2. Examining the relationship between capital and energy leads to the debate about complementarity versus substitution and the proper measurement of the Allen partial elasticities of substitution. Because of our aggregation to the level of the total economy and our range of elasticities, the resolution of this debate does not affect our qualitative results about the impacts of reduced energy on capital. The conflicting empirical arguments are found in (4, 5, 6).

REFERENCES

1. Baughman, M. L., and P. L. Joskow, "Energy Consumption and Fuel Choice by Residential and Commercial Customers in the United States," MIT Energy Laboratory, Cambridge, Mass., May 20, 1975.
2. Federal Energy Administration, *National Energy Outlook* (Washington, D. C.), February 1976, Appendix C.
3. Nordhaus, W. D., "The Demand for Energy: An International Perspective," Cowles Foundation Discussion Paper No. 405, Yale University, September 1975.
4. Berndt, E. R., "Technology, Prices, and the Derived Demand for Energy," *Review of Economics and Statistics* (August 1975): 259–268.

5. Griffin, J. M., and P. R. Gregory, "An Intercountry Translog Model of Energy Substitution Responses," *American Economic Review*, vol. 66, no. 5 (December 1976).
6. Hudson, E. A., and D. W. Jorgenson, "U.S. Energy Policy and Economic Growth, 1975–2000," *Bell Journal of Economics and Management Science* (Autumn 1974): 461–514.

APPENDIX

A.1 Introduction

The metaphor of the elephant and the rabbit applies to an aggregate view of the economy with a single output and two inputs. If this approximation is accepted and if certain accounting conventions are adopted, it is straightforward to manipulate static comparisons of this model. This Appendix records the aggregation and accounting conventions, summarizes the development of the two-factor model, and develops its application. An extension is presented to illustrate the possible relationship between energy and capital inputs.

A.2 Accounting Conventions

A basic accounting structure is needed to proceed toward a quantitative analysis of energy-economic interactions. To focus on the essentials, we distinguish initially between only two types of economic inputs—energy, denoted by E with price P_E, and all other inputs, denoted by R with price P_R. Here, the symbol R denotes the aggregate economic value of inputs, such as capital and labor, assuming that their relative prices do not change significantly. Later we examine one disaggregation of R into its capital and labor constituents.

With this notation, the economic transactions of Table A-1 summarize the accounting conventions for the production and use of energy and nonenergy goods. Energy is treated as an intermediate product contributing to the ultimate production of goods and services for final demand. This might be the case, for example, if the consumer is viewed as demanding

Table A-1. Interindustry Transaction Flows.

FROM \ TO	Energy	Nonenergy	Final Demand
Energy	0	$P_E E$	0
Nonenergy	$P_E E$	0	GNP
Primary Factors	0	$P_R R$	

Fable of Elephant and Rabbit?

transportation services rather than gasoline. Attention is focused here on the gross output of the nonenergy sector, denoted as Y. This output is measured in the same units as GNP. As the only consumer good, it is assumed throughout to have a price of 1. From the standard identity relating the value of inputs and outputs, we have

$$Y = P_E E + P_R R \tag{1}$$

and also,

$$Y = P_E E + GNP. \tag{2}$$

The heart of the model is the assumed aggregate production function relating gross output (Y) to the inputs of energy (E) and all other factors (R):

$$Y = F(E, R). \tag{3}$$

It is assumed that F is a positive, differentiable, concave function exhibiting constant returns to scale. Each of these assumptions is supported by plausible economic intuition.

A.3 Efficient Solutions and the Value Share

If producers are making efficient choices, they are, in effect, solving the problem:

$$\text{Max} \quad F(E, R) - P_E E - P_R R. \tag{4}$$

Then for an economically efficient solution, the price of energy must equal its marginal productivity:

$$\frac{\delta F}{\delta E} = P_E. \tag{5}$$

The importance of the relative size of the energy sector can be demonstrated without any additional information about the production function. From equation (5), it follows that

$$\frac{\delta F}{\delta E} \cdot \frac{E}{Y} = \frac{P_E E}{Y}. \tag{6}$$

The left-hand side of equation (6) is the elasticity of output as the input of E varies, assuming that R is held constant. The right-hand side of equation (6) is the value share of the energy input as a proportion of total output. If $P_E E/Y = s$, then a 1 percent change in the energy input produces an s percent change in gross output. If we assume that the value share s remains approximately constant over a wide range of E, then

$$\frac{Y}{Y_0} \approx \left(\frac{E}{E_0}\right)^s. \tag{7}$$

Under these conditions, with the 1970 level of s = .04, a 50 percent reduction in E would lead to only a 2.7 percent reduction in Y. Even with s = 0.1, a 50 percent reduction in E would produce only a 6.6 percent reduction in Y.

This observation is the motivation for the fable of the elephant and the rabbit. This analogy would be persuasive if the energy value share did indeed remain constant. Even major changes in energy inputs then could be accommodated over the long run with a small effect on output. But constancy of s is a strong assumption, and it depends crucially upon the degree of potential substitution between energy and other inputs. If the substitution possibilities are quite limited, then one effect of a change in energy availability is to increase the energy value share. There then could be large impacts upon the economy.

The importance of the elasticity of substitution is a main theme of this paper. (Recall Figure 2.) The next section of this Appendix develops a two-factor model on the basis of different elasticities of substitution, but drops the assumption of a constant value share, s.

A.4 Elasticity of Substitution

The elasticity of substitution provides a dimensionless index of the relationship between the relative use of the two inputs and their relative marginal productivities. Formally, the elasticity of substitution is defined as:

$$\sigma = -\frac{\delta \ln (E/R)}{\delta \ln \left(\frac{\delta F/\delta E}{\delta F/\delta R}\right)}. \tag{8}$$

A constant elasticity of substitution implies that a given percentage change in the ratio of the two inputs (holding output constant) produces a constant but opposite percentage change in their marginal rate of substitution. This somewhat awkward definition provides the minimal approximation of the substitution potential in any production function with adequate flexibility for analysis of the feedback issue. Excluding three special cases (that is, for $\sigma \neq 0, 1, \infty$), equation (3) now becomes

$$Y^{(\sigma-1)/\sigma} = aE^{(\sigma-1)/\sigma} + bR^{(\sigma-1)/\sigma} \tag{9}$$

where a and b are two constants.

For given prices, the input mix must satisfy the first-order optimality condition in equation (5) above,

$$\frac{\delta F}{\delta E} = a\left(\frac{Y}{E}\right)^{1/\sigma} = P_E. \tag{10}$$

At constant prices, equation (10) implies that E/Y will be constant (ap-

Fable of Elephant and Rabbit? 21

proximately a constant energy-GNP ratio). For changing prices, however, this ratio will change.

For the present discussion, observe that equation (10) may be inverted to relate energy use to output and prices,

$$E = Ya^{\sigma}(P_E)^{-\sigma}. \tag{11}$$

Note that the marginal productivity function equation (11) is the approximate form of many empirical studies of energy demand as a function of output and prices. Now, if Y is *approximately* independent of E, equation (11) implies that the price elasticity of demand for energy remains nearly constant and is virtually identical to the elasticity of substitution. Hence, the more familiar concept of the aggregate price elasticity of energy demand can be used to estimate σ.

The production function in equation (9) and the demand function in equation (11) are the center of the aggregate analysis. The importance of the σ parameter is indicated when we interpret equation (11) in the context of value shares. Analogous to the discussion of the previous section, equation (6) can be restated as,

$$s = \frac{P_E E}{Y} = a^{\sigma}(P_E)^{1-\sigma}. \tag{12}$$

This means that s (the value share of energy) is a function of the real price of energy. If the elasticity of substitution or demand is one, the value share is constant. However, if σ is less than one, an increasing price of energy implies an increasing value share associated with a reduced availability of energy. At small values of σ, s increases rapidly, and energy reductions produce large reductions in GNP.

The price elasticity of the demand for energy in equation (11) no longer is constant once we account for the adjustments in output induced by the price changes. At any point, the exact elasticity is $-\sigma/(1-s)$. The impact of rising shares is to reduce demand further through the feedback.

A.5 Production Function Analysis

The production function analysis utilizes the constant elasticity production function and the associated demand curve. Figure A-1 illustrates the relationship between Y, GNP, and P_E. Given σ and base estimates of Y_0, E_0, R_0, and $P_{E,0}$, equations (9) and (11) determine the parameters a and b. Variations in E then determine variations in P_E, Y, and GNP with R_0 held constant. In moving from E_0 to E_1, there is an increase in P_E, a decrease in Y, and a larger decrease in GNP.

If the increase in energy price is a real resource cost (e.g., all energy is imported from OPEC), then the increase in price and decrease in output

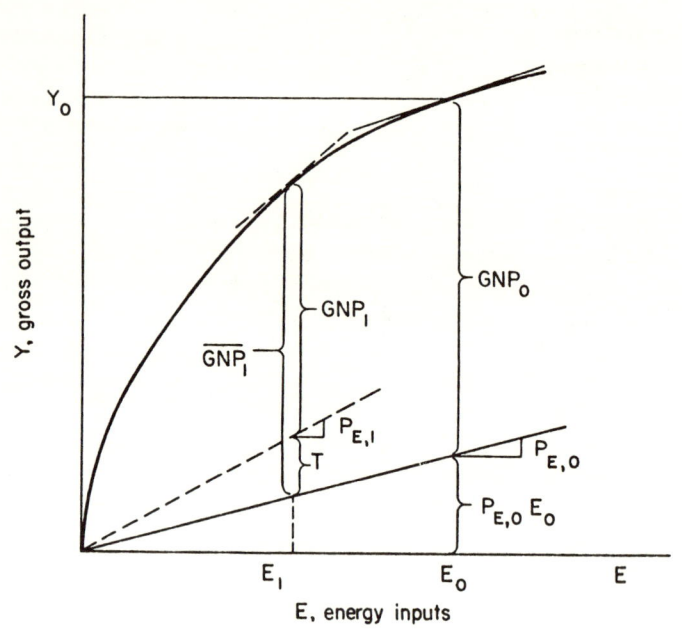

Figure A-1. Output as a function of energy input.

reduces the GNP to GNP_1. However, if the price increase and reduced demand are achieved through a tax, the tax revenue is T. If this revenue is returned to consumers and transferred to nonenergy uses, the new GNP or real income level is $\overline{GNP}_1 = GNP_1 + T$. The magnitude of each of these changes depends on the curvature of the function as determined by σ, the elasticity of substitution.

To illustrate these calculations, recall from (11) that

$$E_0 = Y_0 a^\sigma (P_{E,0})^{-\sigma}. \tag{13}$$

Therefore,

$$a = \left(\frac{E_0}{Y_0}\right)^{1/\sigma} P_{E,0}. \tag{14}$$

From the assumption of constant returns to scale and the accounting conventions, we know that

$$Y = P_R R + P_E E \tag{15}$$

and $P_{R,0} R_0 = GNP_0$. By appropriate choice of units, we can define $R_0 = 1$. Since R_0 must satisfy optimality condition corresponding to (11), it follows that

$$R_0 = Y_0 b^\sigma (P_{R,0})^{-\sigma}, \tag{16}$$

Fable of Elephant and Rabbit? 23

Table A-2. Economic impacts of energy reductions (with constant energy costs and constant capital and labor inputs).

σ	E	Energy price to consumers, including BTU tax $P_E(\$10^6\ BTU)$	GNP change (billions of 1975 dollars) GNP^a (based on BTU tax)
.10	220	.80	0
	190	3.10	− 27
	160	11.17	− 197
	110	28.33	− 1220
	70	29.85	− 2366
.20	220	.80	0
	190	1.60	− 11
	160	3.49	− 59
	110	14.49	− 405
	70	35.32	− 1351
.30	220	.80	0
	190	1.28	− 7
	160	2.18	− 33
	110	6.56	− 187
	70	20.04	− 630
.50	220	.80	0
	190	1.06	− 5
	160	1.47	− 18
	110	2.97	− 82
	70	6.74	− 230
.70	220	.80	0
	190	.98	− 4
	160	1.24	− 12
	110	2.06	− 52
	70	3.79	− 131

[a] Energy tax-induced change in GNP in the year 2010. Base value at 220 quads is $4,400 billions.

or
$$b = GNP_0(Y_0)^{-1/\sigma}. \qquad (17)$$

Given a and b, equation (9) determines Y for any E_1 with $R = 1$. Equation (11) determines the associated price $P_{E,1}$, which then yields GNP_1 and GNP_1 as in Figure A-1.

In Table A-2, prices and GNP values are presented for different values of energy demand in the year 2010. These results are obtained by assuming that the equilibrium E and GNP would have grown at a 3 percent annual rate from 1970 to 2010, *if* energy prices had remained at their 1970 level of $.80 per million BTU. (This represents the 1970 U.S. wellhead price of crude oil, expressed in terms of the 1975 general price level.)

Table A-2 shows the importance of the elasticity of substitution. If this parameter is as high as 0.5, there is a substantial decoupling of energy and the GNP, even at energy consumption levels as low as 110 quads in the year 2010. But if the elasticity of substitution is 0.1, the effects of reduced energy input could be large. A 70 quad scenario would then imply that the growth in real GNP would have to be held to virtually zero over the years 1970 through 2010!

A.6 Accommodating Capital and Energy

The analysis of substitution identifies an important element of the energy-economic interaction and illustrates the limits of the analogy of the elephant and rabbit stew. Several other deficiencies can be found in this model. The most serious may be the relationship between changed inputs of energy and the inputs of all other factors. It might be a reasonable first approximation to assume that labor inputs are undiminished by the changed availability of energy, even though their productivity declines. But the same may not be true for capital inputs. Reduced energy inputs will lower the marginal productivity of capital. This, in turn, may depress the rate of saving and the level of investment. This energy-induced capital reduction will further reduce the level of output and GNP. Such indirect effects may be the most important component of the economic impact of energy scarcity.[1]

There are several paths to follow in complicating the analysis to accommodate the roles of capital, labor, and energy. Following a popular approach in the literature, we adopt the natural extension of the two-factor production function by assuming that R is a Cobb-Douglas function of the inputs of capital (K) and labor (L),

$$R = cK^{\alpha}L^{1-\alpha}, \qquad (18)$$

where α is the share of payments to capital and $1 - \alpha$ is the share of payments to labor. This yields a new production function of the form

$$Y = F(K,L,E) = \left[aE^{(\sigma - 1)/\sigma} + b(cK^{\alpha}L^{1-\alpha})^{(\sigma - 1)/\sigma} \right]^{\frac{\sigma}{\sigma - 1}}. \qquad (19)$$

Given base values of K_0 and L_0 for an assumed α, the natural extensions of equations (15)–(17) determine b and c by equating the marginal productivities of capital and labor with their respective prices.

If K and L are held constant as E varies, this three-factor model duplicates the analysis of the previous section. As an alternative assumption, however,

Table A-3. Economic impacts of energy reductions (production function analysis of BTU tax) (with constant energy costs, constant labor inputs, and a constant rate of return on capital).

σ	E	Energy price to consumers, including BTU tax $P_E(\$/10^6\ BTU)$	GNP change (billions of 1975 dollars) $\overline{GNP^a}$ (based on BTU tax)
.10	220	.80	0
	190	2.21	−177
	160	5.06	−526
	110	12.74	−1471
	70	20.43	−2447
.20	220	.80	0
	190	1.47	−88
	160	2.80	−251
	110	8.21	−844
	70	17.59	−1755
.30	220	.80	0
	190	1.22	−60
	160	1.99	−155
	110	5.12	−496
	70	12.49	−1136
.50	220	.80	0
	190	1.04	−44
	160	1.42	−91
	110	2.75	−244
	70	5.86	−516
.70	220	.80	0
	190	.97	−43
	160	1.21	−77
	110	1.98	−170
	70	3.56	−316

[a] Energy tax-induced change in GNP in the year 2010. Base value at 220 quads is $4,400 billions.

it may be assumed that P_k, rather than K, is held constant and the level of capital input is adjusted as the availability of energy changes. This maintains the return on capital and is a long-run proxy for the adaptation in capital that might be induced by the reduced use of energy. It should represent a lower bound for the level of capital input and an upper bound for the energy-capital-induced economic impact.

In Table A-3 we present the relevant GNP and energy price estimates assuming that P_k is constant. The value of α is set at 0.35, L_0 is set at 1, and the initial input of capital stock is assumed to be 2.5 times the GNP. Figure 3 illustrates the same calculations for the alternate capital assumptions, assuming the elasticity of substitution is 0.3. The reductions in capital input produce significant reductions in GNP. For $\sigma = 0.3$ and $E = 110$ quads, the reduction in GNP increases from 4 percent to 11 percent. The required tax, however, is reduced from $5.76 to $4.32. But the qualitative conclusion of the two-factor analysis is preserved. Reductions in energy availability produce less than proportional reductions in GNP. The changes in capital can be important, but the economic impact is most sensitive to the index of flexibility, the elasticity of substitution.

FOOTNOTE

1. We are indebted particularly to Dale Jorgenson for calling our attention to this issue and for his assistance in developing the argument. See footnote 2 (main text) regarding the closely related issue of energy-capital complementarity.

INPUT PRICES, SUBSTITUTION, AND PRODUCT INFLATION

John R. Moroney, TULANE UNIVERSITY
Alden L. Toevs, UNIVERSITY OF OREGON

I. INTRODUCTION

A resurgent interest in natural resources has swept the economics profession in recent years. This renascence is attributable in part to the widely publicized (and roundly criticized) visions of a natural resource-based Armageddon [Forrester (9), Meadows *et al.* (13)], as well as to the realization that certain natural resources upon which modern industrial societies currently depend shall be seriously depleted within a generation or so. Accordingly, the classical tendency to amalgamate natural resources (or "land") and capital has given way to models incorporating natural resources, capital, and labor as distinct inputs [Nordhaus and Tobin (15); Dasgupta and Heal (7); Solow (25, 26);

Sweeney (30)]. These models have been used to analyze questions of optimal resource depletion paths, the roles of competitive markets and uncertainty in diverting an economy from such paths, and the weighty importance of factor substitution and technological progress in sustaining intertemporal per capita consumption.

A related question that has not been analyzed, but deserves to be, is the influence of factor substitution on inflation. If natural resource shortages appear, the prices of natural resource products will inevitably rise. The facility with which one can substitute now relatively less-expensive inputs for natural resource products will help to determine the output price increases in natural resource-using manufacturing industries. In turn, these output price increases bear importantly on: (a) the substitution among materials, capital and labor in manufacturing at higher levels of fabrication, (b) the product substitution taking place in consumption, and (c) the general rate of inflation in the economy.

A statistical examination of the effect rising input costs have on output price in natural resource-using manufacturing industries is, therefore, the major purpose of this paper. A necessarily related purpose is to present some evidence on capital, labor, and natural resource input substitution for production. In particular, output price increases are simulated for alternative price paths in seven natural resource-using industries. The simulations are performed under three assumptions on input substitution: no substitution is possible, substitution follows the Cobb-Douglas production function, and substitution follows the production function dual to the industry-specific translog cost function. The translog technology model is more likely to yield reliable estimates of commodity inflation than those derived from the a priori more restrictive Cobb-Douglas and fixed-coefficients models. Disclosing the results obtained from the alternative substitution technologies permits us to examine the sensitivity of changes in output price to input substitution.

The paper is organized as follows. Changes in prices and usage of labor, capital, and natural resource inputs during the period 1954–1971 are described in section II. Section III is devoted to estimating the parameters of a general translog cost function. Much of the material in this section is necessarily technical, and will be of interest chiefly to applied econometricians. The remaining portion of the paper, however, may be understood independently of these issues. Section IV reports and interprets the relations existing between commodity prices and input prices under alternative technologies, and presents the simulation results. Section V summarizes and concludes the paper.

II. TRENDS IN FACTOR COSTS, FACTOR USE, AND REAL OUTPUT, 1954–1971[1]

A. Sample Selection

We wish to select manufacturing industries satisfying two criteria: (i) The industry must make intensive use of a comparatively homogeneous natural resource input, thus permitting a microscopic focus on input substitution; (ii) labor and capital must also be important elements in total cost. The sample industries are therefore selected such that each input accounts for at least 5 percent, and the three inputs together for at least 50 percent, of the value of industry shipments. The Direct Requirements Input-Output Table for 1963 (Office of Business Economics, 17) reveals that many industries do not make direct purchases of natural resource inputs. Indeed, direct natural resource purchases account for less than 1 percent of total cost in most industries. It is possible in six industries satisfying criteria (i) and (ii) both to construct constant dollar capital stock series and to obtain accurate coverage of natural resource usage for a period of 18 years. In the seventh industry, petroleum refining, the sample period excludes the last two years because our resource input series terminates in 1969. A complete discussion of data sources and series construction is given in Appendixes A and B.

B. Definition of Variables

Labor input is reported by industry as production worker man-hours and nonproduction worker man-years.[2] They are combined in a single man-hour series using the standard (and accurate) assumption that a nonproduction worker man-year converts to 2,000 man-hours.

The industry capital series are combined stocks of plant and equipment deflated for changes in capital goods prices. The use of constant dollar stocks, as opposed to stocks valued at acquisition prices, is imperative in a time-series study: if capital goods were measured in historical costs, pure inflation in their prices—on the average about three percent per year during the sample period—would cause a serious overstatement in the apparent use of capital.

Natural resource inputs used in manufacturing are not pristine natural resources, but instead the outputs of primary industries, which are in turn purchased as direct inputs by manufacturing.[3] Three industries (petroleum refining, gypsum processing, and primary zinc manufacturing) each use a single, homogeneous resource input. The other four (meat packing, dairy products, flour milling and cereals, and hydraulic cement) each employ a constant dollar aggregate of resource inputs.

Output is measured as the sum of constant dollar value added plus the constant dollar value of natural resource inputs. Value added is deflated by the respective industry wholesale price index, and in each industry the natural resource component is valued at its base period price. This definition of net output relies on the assumption that capital (K), labor (L), and natural resource inputs (N) are weakly separable from the remaining intermediate inputs (I). Hence we assume the gross output function in each industry can be written

$$V = F(K, L, N, I) = G[f(K, L, N); I]$$

where V is gross real output attributable to K, L, N, and I, and $f(K, L, N)$ is net output. This separability assumption seems justifiable on two grounds. First, the major criterion for selecting sample industries is that they use primarily K, L, and N: Any intermediate input necessarily plays a minor role in total cost; and the aggregate of individually unimportant intermediates should not affect the internal relations among K, L, and N. Second, the indirect, but related, evidence presently available does not contradict it.[4] Accordingly, the wage bill, gross quasi-rents, and natural resource input costs exhaust the value of net output.

The average annual wage rate, P_L, is computed in each industry by dividing the total wage bill by the estimated man-hours worked.

The cost of capital, P_K, is obtained annually in each industry by dividing the current value of gross quasi-rent by the estimated real capital stock. Capital cost computed in this way embodies several influences. First of all, it mirrors cyclical variations in an industry's activity, because one divides moderately sensitive quasi-rent by a cyclically sluggish capital stock. Fortunately the cyclical variation in P_K is inconsequential relative to long-term trend. Second, P_K reflects inflationary trends in capital goods prices. This is as it should be: entrepreneurs must weigh the rising prices of real plant and equipment against trends in wages and resource input costs in selecting their optimal technique. Third, P_K embodies both debt and equity costs, because gross quasi-rent includes all nonlabor components of value added. One final point should perhaps be made explicit: P_K is, by computation, the average rate of return on real capital. In order that it also be strictly interpreted as the normal cost of capital, one must assume the observations occur at points of tangency between average revenue and average cost for firms constituting the industry. Although this strict interpretation is generally unwarranted, it seems reasonable that the observations are generated by forces tending toward equilibrium.[5]

In the three industries employing one resource input, P_N is its average annual market price. If the resource is purchased on more than one market,

Input Prices, Substitution, and Inflation 31

the price is an average of the market prices. In the industries using more than one resource input, P_N is a Laspeyres price index (see Appendix B). It bears emphasizing that all of the P_N series closely follow regular trends, and cyclical variance was hardly detectable in any of them.

C. Trends in Factor Costs and Factor Use

The relative changes in factor costs shown in Table 1 refer to the average value in the last three years divided by that of the three earliest years. By making this adjustment for the specific influences present in the base or terminal years, one obtains a more accurate picture of sample period trends. Note that in every industry wages increase relative to resource costs. In the first four, capital costs also rise in comparison with resource costs. Indeed, the three industries in which P_N increases relative to P_K share a common characteristic: all use nonrenewable resource inputs. Two industries appear to have experienced excessive inflation in capital costs, which is attributable in part to short-period disequilibria. The meat-packing industry (2011) was suffering an industry-specific recession during the base years. By contrast, petroleum refining (2911) experienced an output boom and above-normal short-run quasi-rents during the late 1960s.

Because of the significance accorded to alleged natural resource scarcities in this country, trends in resource input prices merit further comment. Between 1954 and 1971 the price index for Gross National Product increased 58 percent. Throughout this period, slaughtered meat is the only resource input whose price rose as rapidly. The prices of all other resource inputs analyzed here decreased relative to the cost of goods in general, and fell quite sharply relative to labor costs. These patterns of declining resource

Table 1. Percentage changes in the costs of labor, capital, and natural resource inputs in seven U.S. manufacturing industries.

	Percent Δ in P_L	Percent Δ in P_K	Percent Δ in P_N	Time Period
Industries using renewable resources				
2011: Meat packing	+ 95	+ 148	+ 57	1954–1971
202: Dairy products	+ 91	+ 98	+ 40	1954–1971
2041, 43: Flour milling and cereals	+ 102	+ 88	− 24	1954–1971
Industries using nonrenewable resources				
2911: Petroleum refining	+ 68	+ 193	+ 7	1954–1969
3241: Hydraulic cement	+ 122	− 29	+ 12	1954–1971
3275: Gypsum	+ 92	− 28	+ 22	1954–1971
3333: Primary zinc	+ 78	− 16	+ 29	1954–1971

Sources: See text, section IIB, and Appendixes A and B.

Table 2. Percentage changes in input use and output among seven U.S. manufacturing industries.

	Percent Δ in labor employment	Percent Δ in constant dollar capital stock	Percent Δ in natural resource input	Percent Δ in output	Time period
Industries using renewable resources					
2011: Meat packing	−27	−20	+28	+27	1954–1971
202: Dairy products	−32	−10	+12	+10	1954–1971
2041, 43: Flour milling and cereals	−22	+30	+12	+28	1954–1971
Industries using non-renewable resources					
2911: Petroleum refining	−29	+37	+37	+53	1954–1969
3241: Hydraulic cement	−28	+111	+35	+15	1954–1971
3275: Gypsum	−12	+64	+5	+17	1954–1971
3333: Primary zinc	−23	+6	+8	+2	1954–1971

Sources: See text, sections IIA and IIB, and Appendixes A and B.

input costs, reckoned against those of labor, are entirely consistent with the longer historical trends documented by Potter and Christy (18).[6]

The percentage changes in factor use and real output are shown in Table 2. Output was remarkably stable in most industries. Although it increased by nearly 4 percent per year in petroleum refining, it expanded more than 1 percent per year in only two other industries, meat packing and flour milling and cereals.

It is striking that employment declined absolutely in all industries. And by comparing columns 1 and 4, one confirms in each industry a substantial decrease in labor per unit of output. Five industries experienced increases in real capital stocks, and the capital/labor ratio increased in every industry, reflecting a pervasive substitution of machines and structures against labor.

Resource input use closely paralleled changes in output in most industries. In only two, petroleum refining and hydraulic cement, did output per unit of resource input change by as much as 1 percent per year. The most remarkable fact of all is that in every industry resource inputs were substituted against labor. From a descriptive viewpoint, this pattern of factor use appears to be perfectly consistent with the declining relative costs of resource inputs. But an adequate analysis requires a comprehensive three-input model of cost and production. Accordingly, we now turn to a formal framework designed to analyze these facts.

III. THEORETICAL AND STATISTICAL MODELS

The models that follow are grounded on principles of duality developed by Samuelson (20), Shephard (22, 23), Uzawa (37), and Diewert (8). The spirit of our effort is to estimate elasticities of substitution from cost-minimizing factor demand equations. To this end, assume that for each industry there exists a cost function:

$$C = C(P_i, q) \qquad i = K, L, N \qquad (1)$$

where C and q are total cost and output, and P_i is the price of the i-th input. We assume that C is (a) a positive, continuous function in q and P_i that tends to infinity as q tends to infinity; and (b) concave and linearly homogeneous in P_i.

If C is minimized with respect to P_i, which are predetermined, the principles of duality insure the existence of a production function dual to the cost function (1). Though the parametric form of the production function may not be known, its technological properties can be determined from certain parameters of the cost function. In particular, Uzawa (37) showed that under the postulate of cost minimization the partial elasticity of substitution between inputs i and j is

$$\sigma_{ij} = C(\partial^2 C/\partial P_i \partial P_j)/(\partial C/\partial P_i)(\partial C/\partial P_j). \qquad (2)$$

One must specify a parametric form for (1) in order to estimate its substitution elasticities. To this end, a transcendental logarithmic (translog) form proposed originally by Christensen, et al. (5) seems quite suitable for three reasons. First, it may be regarded as a general log-quadratic local approximation to any arbitrary cost function. Second, it enables the direct estimation of elasticities of substitution and permits tests of their statistical significance.[7] Third, it entails no *a priori* restrictions respecting their values or constancy.

A translog cost function pertaining to three inputs may be written

$$\ln C = a_o + \theta_1 \ln q + \frac{1}{2}\theta_2 (\ln q)^2 + \sum_i \beta_i \ln P_i$$

$$+ \frac{1}{2}\sum_i\sum_j \varepsilon_{ij} \ln P_i \ln P_j + \sum_i \delta_i \ln P_i \ln q, \quad i = K, L, N \qquad (3)$$

where a_o, θ_1, θ_2, β_i, ε_{ij}, and δ_i are technologically determined parameters. To insure that $\sigma_{ij} = \sigma_{ji}$, a symmetry condition is imposed: $\varepsilon_{ij} = \varepsilon_{ji}$ for $i \neq j$. The assumption of linear homogeneity in factor prices entails the additional restrictions:

$$\sum_i \beta_i = 1 \qquad (4a)$$

$$\sum_j \varepsilon_{ij} = \sum_i \varepsilon_{ji} = \sum_i\sum_j \varepsilon_{ij} = 0 \qquad i, j = K, L, N \qquad (4b)$$

$$\sum_i \delta_i = 0 \tag{4c}$$

The assumption that C is strictly concave in factor prices yields the three equations:

$$\partial \ln C/\partial \ln P_K = \beta_K + \varepsilon_{KK} \ln P_K + \varepsilon_{KL} \ln P_L + \varepsilon_{KN} \ln P_N + \delta_K \ln q > 0 \tag{5a}$$

$$\partial \ln C/\partial \ln P_L = \beta_L \varepsilon_{LK} \ln P_K + \varepsilon_{LL} \ln P_L + \varepsilon_{LN} \ln P_N + \delta_L \ln q > 0 \tag{5b}$$

$$\partial \ln C/\partial \ln P_N = \beta_N + \varepsilon_{NK} \ln P_K + \varepsilon_{NL} \ln P_L + \varepsilon_{NN} \ln P_N + \delta_N \ln q > 0 \tag{5c}$$

Equations (5a), (5b), and (5c) may be interpreted as derived input demand equations with the use of a lemma due to Samuelson (20, pp. 67–68) and Shephard (23, p. 171): Along the minimum cost expansion path the equilibrium employment of the i-th input is

$$X_i^*(q, P_L, P_K, P_N) = \partial C/\partial P_i \qquad i = K, L, N \tag{6}$$

But relative shares in total cost are, by definition,

$$M_i = P_i X_i / C \tag{7}$$

Substituting X_i^* from (6) into (7), relative shares on the minimum cost locus are

$$M_i^* = (\partial C/\partial P_i)(P_i/C) \equiv \partial \ln C/\partial \ln P_i \qquad i = K, L, N \tag{8}$$

Hence for all points of cost minimization M_i^* may be substituted for $\partial \ln C/\partial \ln P_i$ in equations (5a) – (5c).

Entrepreneurs plainly are not able to minimize cost in any exact sense. Under circumstances of varying input prices and technical innovation, to say nothing of employment and raw material contracts, capital in place, and sheer entrepreneurial inertia, we may expect factor usage to be tending toward optimal combinations. Thus the observed shares, M_i, are

$$M_i = M_i^* + e_i \qquad i = K, L, N \tag{9}$$

where e_i is the disturbance from cost minimization. Substituting equations (8), (5a), (5b), and (5c) in equations (9) yields the stochastic input demand functions:

$$M_K = \beta_K + \varepsilon_{KK} \ln P_K + \varepsilon_{KL} \ln P_L + \varepsilon_{KN} \ln P_N + \delta_K \ln q + e_K, \tag{10a}$$

$$M_L = \beta_L + \varepsilon_{LK} \ln P_K + \varepsilon_{LL} \ln P_L + \varepsilon_{LN} \ln P_N + \delta_L \ln q + e_L, \tag{10b}$$

$$M_N = \beta_N + \varepsilon_{NK} \ln P_K + \varepsilon_{NL} \ln P_L + \varepsilon_{NN} \ln P_N + \delta_N \ln q + e_N. \tag{10c}$$

Two classes of estimation problems are present in the system (10a) – (10c). The first is overidentification. Linear homogeneity in factor prices, (4a) – (4c), and the symmetry restrictions $\varepsilon_{ij} = \varepsilon_{ji}$ for $i \neq j$, insure that the parameters of any two equations exactly identify all parameters of the system. Consider,

Input Prices, Substitution, and Inflation 35

for example, equations (10a) and (10b). Symmetry requires that $\varepsilon_{KN} = \varepsilon_{NK}$ and $\varepsilon_{LN} = \varepsilon_{NL}$. Restriction (4a) insures that $\beta_N = 1 - \beta_K - \beta_L$; (4b) implies that $\varepsilon_{NN} = -(\varepsilon_{KN} + \varepsilon_{LN})$; and (4c) insures that $\delta_N = -(\delta_K + \delta_L)$. Furthermore, a set of unique parameters cannot be estimated by applying least squares to (10a) and (10b) individually, because the estimates ε_{KL} and ε_{LK} will not generally be equal. One may incorporate the *a priori* restrictions $\varepsilon_{LN} = \varepsilon_{NL} = -(\varepsilon_{LL} + \varepsilon_{KL})$ and $\varepsilon_{KN} = \varepsilon_{NK} = -(\varepsilon_{KK} + \varepsilon_{KL})$ by writing (10a) and (10b) as

$$\begin{bmatrix} M_L \\ M_K \end{bmatrix} = \begin{bmatrix} 1 & 0 & \ln(P_L/P_N) & \ln(P_K/P_N) & 0 & \ln q & 0 \\ 0 & 1 & 0 & \ln(P_L/P_N) & \ln(P_K/P_N) & 0 & \ln q \end{bmatrix} \begin{bmatrix} \beta_L \\ \beta_K \\ \varepsilon_{LL} \\ \varepsilon_{KL} \\ \varepsilon_{KK} \\ \delta_L \\ \delta_K \end{bmatrix} + \begin{bmatrix} e_L \\ e_K \end{bmatrix} \quad (11)$$

The second class of problems is computational. One might initially suspect that the disturbances in the individual e_L and e_K series would be autocorrelated, perhaps because of lagged adjustment to changes in relative factor prices. To check this possibility, we performed the Swed-Eisenhart tests for independence among the ordinary least squares residuals in each series.[8] In every case the hypothesis of autocorrelation is rejected at $p \leq .05$. On the other hand, the elements in e_L and e_K are contemporaneously correlated because random disturbances affect all input demand functions simultaneously. Hence, the two-stage estimation method suggested by Zellner (39) yields (asymptotically) more efficient estimates. The estimates obtained by applying Zellner two-stage least squares to the constrained regression may be sensitive to the two equations selected from (10a) – (10c). We therefore estimate parameters by the iterative Zellner efficient (IZEF) method, which has been shown by Kmenta and Gilbert (12) and by Ruble (19) to yield maximum likelihood estimates.

It should be emphasized that although each manufacturing industry in our sample is the principal domestic purchaser of its resource input, the industry is a price taker either if the resource-producing industry is domestically competitive or a price-setting cartel, or if the resource is traded on an internationally competitive market. The assumption that resource input prices are predetermined therefore seems reasonable in our sample industries.

The estimates and asymptotic t ratios under the null hypothesis that the

Table 3. Translog cost function estimates in seven U.S. manufacturing industries

Parameter Est.	2011	202	2041, 43	Industry Code 2911	3241	3275	3333
β_K	.324	−.182	1.345	−2.602	−1.448	−.988	1.101
	(.860)	(−.218)	(.994)	(−5.527)	(−2.892)	(−1.385)	(2.972)
β_L	2.040	−4.956	.340	.583	2.146	1.621	1.344
	(4.805)	(−4.529)	(1.042)	(1.555)	(4.703)	(3.805)	(3.512)
β_N	−1.364	6.138	−.685	3.019	.302	.367	−1.445
	(−1.830)	(3.931)	(−.480)	(5.198)	(1.099)	(1.199)	(−2.864)
ε_{KL}	−.001	.010	.038	−.006	−.038	−.060	−.024
	(−.010)	(.642)	(2.107)	(−1.813)	(−4.373)	(−5.934)	(−3.037)
ε_{KN}	−.022	−.084	−.217	−.034	.025	−.034	−.104
	(−1.426)	(−4.242)	(−9.017)	(−4.878)	(2.332)	(−4.267)	(−9.211)
ε_{LN}	−.053	.188	−.033	.022	.024	−.064	−.005
	(−2.275)	(6.510)	(−5.657)	(1.211)	(2.656)	(−8.437)	(−.222)
ε_{KK}	.023	.075	.179	.040	.013	.094	.127
	(2.779)	(3.763)	(5.950)	(5.544)	(1.158)	(5.631)	(16.142)
ε_{LL}	.053	−.197	−.005	−.017	.014	.124	.029
	(2.359)	(−8.240)	(−.323)	(−.985)	(1.660)	(16.963)	(1.341)
ε_{NN}	.075	−.103	.250	.012	−.049	.098	.109
	(2.256)	(−2.536)	(9.867)	(.548)	(−.277)	(9.394)	(3.543)
δ_K	−.015	.028	−.075	.173	.154	.140	−.056
	(−.639)	(.523)	(−.809)	(6.175)	(4.085)	(2.424)	(−1.914)
δ_L	−.123	.335	−.015	−.030	−.143	−.123	−.099
	(−4.602)	(4.804)	(−.688)	(−1.254)	(−4.170)	(−3.563)	(−3.260)
δ_N	.138	−.363	.090	−.143	−.011	−.017	.155
	(2.977)	(−3.649)	(.924)	(−3.984)	(−.528)	(−.687)	(3.867)
F	25.45	4306.45	260.75	527.43	1482.42	99779.90	64.36

Sources: See text, section II; and Appendixes A and B.
Notes: Asymptotic t statistics for testing the null hypothesis that a parameter is zero are listed in parentheses beneath the parameter estimates.

parameter is zero appear in Table 3. In assessing the estimates it may be helpful to note the following points. First, substituting the translog derivatives into equation (2) yields the cross elasticities

$$\sigma_{ij} = (\varepsilon_{ij}/M_i M_j) + 1 \quad i \neq j \tag{12}$$

and own elasticities

$$\sigma_{ii} = (\varepsilon_{ii} + M_i^2 - M_i)/M_i^2. \tag{13}$$

Thus, it may occur simultaneously that ε'_{ii} is significantly positive and σ'_{ii} is either significantly negative or not different from zero. Indeed, 12 of the 21 ε'_{ii} are significantly positive, yet none of the σ'_{ii} is statistically positive. Since the constant-output elasticity of demand for input i is $E_{ii} = M_i \sigma_{ii}$, each σ_{ii} must be nonpositive as a stability condition [Allen (1, pp. 508–509)]. Local stability is satisfied by all of the estimates.

Consider now the estimates of δ_i. Note that δ'_K is significantly positive in three industries, but insignificant in the other four. By contrast, the estimates of δ_L are significantly negative in four industries, but positive in only one. The significant estimates of δ_N are divided with two positive and two negative. In these time-series regressions, the logarithm of output accounts for cyclical variations in M_i, and leads to more reliable estimates of the long-run elasticities.

These elasticities generally vary with the values of relative input shares,

Table 4. Cross and own substitution elasticities estimated from translog cost functions in U.S. manufacturing industries.

Industry Code	σ_{KL}	σ_{KN}	σ_{LN}	σ_{KK}	σ_{LL}	σ_{NN}
2011	.847	.602*	.335†	−8.796*	−3.592	−.085*
	(1.568)	(.278)	(.287)	(1.755)	(2.556)	(.045)
202	1.256*	.370*†	2.803*†	−2.005*	−11.625*	−.918*
	(.399)	(.149)	(.276)	(.417)	(.690)	(.108)
2041, 43	2.495*†	−.320*†	.490*†	−.173	−9.519*	.050
	(.729)	(.149)	(.103)	(.455)	(1.958)	(.062)
2911	.413	.625*†	1.330*	−4.770*	−13.251*	−.227*
	(.289)	(.073)	(.268)	(.513)	(1.615)	(.019)
3241	.755*†	1.292*†	1.643*†	−.630*	−2.682*	−8.384*
	(0.57)	(.125)	(.251)	(.046)	(.151)	(.854)
3275	.629*†	.565*†	−.864*†	−.399*	−1.004*	−.853
	(.063)	(.105)	(.252)	(.048)	(.104)	(.697)
3333	.265†	.059†	.954*	−.508*	−3.504*	−.295*
	(.242)	(.110)	(.205)	(.293)	(.647)	(.077)

Sources: See text, section II, and Appendixes A and B.
Notes: Estimated asymptotic standard errors are listed in parentheses.
  *Denotes elasticities significantly different from zero at P ≤ .05.
  †Denotes cross elasticities significantly different from one at P ≤ .050.

as shown by equations (12) and (13). The best summary evidence concerning substitution is conveyed by point estimates at sample means.[9] The asymptotic variances of the mean substitution elasticities are estimated by expressing the relative shares in terms of the regressors and the estimated parameters and expanding in a Taylor series that includes explicitly all variances and covariances.

The estimated elasticities, at sample means, and their asymptotic standard errors appear in Table 4. The statistical tests are conducted at $P \leq .05$, although one is reminded that these finite-sample tests are conducted with asymptotic t statistics. Consider first the own elasticities in the last three columns. Twenty of the 21 estimates are negative, 15 being statistically significant. The only positive estimate appears in industry 2041, 43; and it is obviously insignificant.

The estimated cross elasticities appear in the first three columns of Table 4. Two general points are noteworthy: All industries exhibit at least one significant positive cross elasticity, so the general fixed coefficients hypothesis is rejected. Similarly, all industries exhibit at least one cross elasticity different from one, so the underlying production functions are not of the Cobb-Douglas form.

IV. INFLATION UNDER ALTERNATIVE TECHNOLOGIES

Having estimated the structure of input substitution, we now wish to assess the influence of alternative substitution technologies on commodity price inflation. The relation between input prices and commodity price, in the absence of technological change, is straightforward. First, write the commodity price as

$$P = \sum_i P_i(X_i/q) \qquad (14)$$

where P_i is the price of input i and (X_i/q) is the physical input-output coefficient. Differentiating (14) with respect to time, one obtains

$$dP/dt = \sum_i [P_i d(X_i/q)/dt + (X_i/q)dP_i/dt] \qquad (15)$$

For a constant rate of output, equation (15) may be rewritten

$$\hat{P} = \sum_i M_{i(t)} \hat{P}_i + \sum_i M_{i(t)} \hat{X}_i \qquad (16)$$

where a circumflex denotes the percentage change of a variable. Thus the proportional rate of commodity inflation is the weighted sum of percentage changes in input prices, plus the weighted sum of relative changes in input use. If technology were described by fixed-coefficient production functions, the

Input Prices, Substitution, and Inflation 39

second set of terms would plainly be zero. But somewhat surprisingly, this set vanishes even in the general case when input substitution occurs. To establish this result, totally differentiate the cost-minimizing input demand equations, such as (6), with respect to time, and substitute $M_i \sigma_{ij}$ for E_{ij}, to obtain

$$\hat{X}_1 = M_1\sigma_{11}\hat{P}_1 + M_2\sigma_{12}\hat{P}_2 + M_3\sigma_{13}\hat{P}_3 \tag{17a}$$

$$\hat{X}_2 = M_1\sigma_{21}\hat{P}_1 + M_2\sigma_{22}\hat{P}_2 + M_3\sigma_{23}\hat{P}_3 \tag{17b}$$

$$\hat{X}_3 = M_1\sigma_{31}\hat{P}_1 + M_2\sigma_{32}\hat{P}_2 + M_3\sigma_{33}\hat{P}_3 \tag{17c}$$

Second-order conditions for cost minimization require that

$$M_1\sigma_{i1} + M_2\sigma_{i2} + M_3\sigma_{i3} = 0 \quad (i = 1,2,3)$$

as shown, for example, by Allen (1938, p. 504). Thus one may substitute $-(M_2\sigma_{12} + M_3\sigma_{13})$ for $M_1\sigma_{11}$, $-(M_1\sigma_{21} + M_3\sigma_{23})$ for $M_2\sigma_{22}$, and $-(M_1\sigma_{31} + M_2\sigma_{32})$ for $M_3\sigma_{33}$, and obtain

$$M_1\hat{X}_1 = M_1M_2\sigma_{12}(\hat{P}_2 - \hat{P}_1) + M_1M_3\sigma_{13}(\hat{P}_3 - \hat{P}_1) \tag{18a}$$

$$M_2\hat{X}_2 = M_2M_1\sigma_{21}(\hat{P}_1 - \hat{P}_2) + M_2M_3\sigma_{23}(\hat{P}_3 - \hat{P}_2) \tag{18b}$$

$$M_3\hat{X}_3 = M_3M_1\sigma_{31}(\hat{P}_1 - \hat{P}_3) + M_3M_2\sigma_{32}(\hat{P}_2 - \hat{P}_3) \tag{18c}$$

Hence $\sum_i M_i\hat{X}_i = 0$ for all conceivable classes of input substitution. And equation (16) becomes

$$\hat{P} = \sum_i M_{i(t)}\hat{P}_i \tag{19}$$

Suppose $\hat{P}_i$ are constants, but distinct for each input. In this instance, the crucial determinant of commodity inflation is the behavior of relative shares. We shall consider and simulate three cases. If technology is characterized by fixed production coefficients, the relative share of the most (least) rapidly inflating input increases (decreases), and the proportional rate of commodity inflation accelerates. Asymptotically, the cost share of the input whose price rises most rapidly approaches unity, and the rate of commodity inflation approaches the rate of input price inflation.

Second, if technology is distinguished by a Cobb-Douglas production function, the relative cost shares are constant, as is the rate of inflation. Substitution against the increasingly costly inputs, however, insures that commodity inflation is strictly less than that occurring with a fixed-coefficients technology.

Finally, consider the general translog cost technology. If it differs from the Cobb-Douglas, then relative shares and the rate of inflation vary through time. But since input substitution cannot possibly be less flexible than the fixed coefficients technology, intuition suggests that the rate of commodity inflation cannot be greater than that occurring in a regime of fixed coefficients.

We proceed to analyze two questions. First, if the time paths of input prices are given, what are the rates of product inflation experienced under the alternative substitution models? Second, how sensitive is product inflation with respect to alternative rates of input inflation? Numerous combinations of factor price growth and time periods could be investigated. To keep the presentation manageable, we use equation (19) together with several assumptions to simulate inflation for the period 1971–1981. In all simulations the price of capital is assumed to grow at five percent annually. We specify a broad range of wage and natural resource price increases. Zero wage growth is used as a benchmark, 7.5 percent growth seems to be realistic in light of wage settlements since 1970, and 10 percent is a liberal upper limit. Similarly, a stable resource price serves as a benchmark, 5, and 10 percent growth are included as reasonable brackets for inflation in most resource markets, and 15 percent is a hyperinflationary standard.

The following cost shares are those fitted by the translog estimation for 1971; they are used to initiate the simulations:

Industry	M_K	M_L	M_N
2011	.0705	.0742	.8553
202	.2303	.1489	.6208
2041	.3729	.1169	.5102
2911	.1886	.0670	.7445
3241	.5867	.2631	.1502
3275	.5783	.3104	.1112
3333	.1388	.2085	.6527

In the exercises based on fixed-coefficient production functions, new cost shares are calculated each year, as follows. By definition,

$$M_{i(t)} = M_{i(t-1)} + \Delta M_{i(t-1)} = M_{i(t-1)}[1 + \hat{M}_{i(t-1)}], \qquad (20)$$

$$M_{i(t-1)} = P_{i(t-1)} X_{i(t-1)} / P_{(t-1)} q_{(t-1)}. \qquad (21)$$

Because $\hat{X}_i = \hat{q} = 0$,

$$\hat{M}_{i(t-1)} = \hat{P}_{i(t-1)} - \hat{P}_{(t-1)} \qquad (22)$$

is used in (20) to construct the $M_{i(t)}$ series. The Cobb-Douglas simulations treat the initial shares as constant through time. In the translog simulations, the series of relative shares are constructed from

$$M_{i(t)} = \beta_i' + \sum_i \varepsilon_{ij}' \ln P_{i(t)} + \delta_i' \ln q(1971). \qquad (23)$$

The simulation results appear in Table 5. The percentage commodity inflation rates for the last year in the simulations are reported. This was done

Input Prices, Substitution, and Inflation 41

to maximize the differences in the results obtained from the alternative production technologies. The reported inflation rates are strikingly unresponsive to the substitution assumptions. If the results from the fixed-coefficients and Cobb-Douglas technologies are compared, with natural resource inflation of 5 and 10 percent *and the full range of wage changes*, only one case is found (industry 3333 for $\hat{P}_N = 10$ percent and $\hat{P}_L = 0$ percent) in which the simulations differ by more than one percentage point. The more accurate simulations obtained from the translog technology model are very close to those of the *a priori* more restrictive models. Here the only instance of price sensitivity to the substitution assumption is in the dairy products industry with $\hat{P}_N = 10$ percent and $\hat{P}_L = 0$ percent, a circumstance similar to the previously mentioned exception in that it is unlikely to be encountered factually.[10]

Only when natural resource prices inflate at annual rates of 15 percent

Table 5. Simulated commodity inflation rates under alternative substitution technologies.

Industry 2011: Meat Packing

	Fixed coefficients			Cobb-Douglas			Translog		
$\hat{P}_L =$	0%	7.5%	10%	0%	7.5%	10%	0%	7.5%	10%
$\hat{P}_N = 0$	0.5%	1.5%	2.0%	0.4%	0.9%	1.1%	0.4%	1.2%	1.6%
5	4.8	5.2	5.6	4.6	5.2	5.4	4.7	5.2	5.5
10	9.4	9.6	9.8	8.9	9.5	9.6	9.4	9.5	9.7
15	14.4	14.4	14.5	13.2	13.7	13.9	14.4	14.2	14.2

Industry 202: Dairy Products

	Fixed coefficients			Cobb-Douglas			Translog		
$\hat{P}_L =$	0%	7.5%	10%	0%	7.5%	10%	0%	7.5%	10%
$\hat{P}_N = 0$	1.6%	3.1%	4.0%	1.2%	2.3%	2.6%	1.3%	1.5%	1.4%
5	4.5	5.4	6.1	4.3	5.4	5.7	3.8	5.3	5.3
10	8.4	8.8	9.2	7.4	8.5	8.8	5.9	8.6	9.0
15	13.0	13.1	13.3	10.5	11.6	12.0	7.6	11.4	12.2

Industry 2041, 43: Flour milling and cereals

	Fixed coefficients			Cobb-Douglas			Translog		
$\hat{P}_L =$	0%	7.5%	10%	0%	7.5%	10%	0%	7.5%	10%
$\hat{P}_N = 0$	2.4%	3.5%	4.2%	1.9%	2.7%	3.0%	2.3%	3.4%	3.7%
5	4.6	5.4	5.9	4.4	5.3	5.6	4.4	5.3	5.6
10	7.9	8.3	8.6	7.0	7.8	8.1	7.6	8.3	8.5
15	12.2	12.3	12.5	9.5	10.4	10.7	11.8	12.3	12.5

Table 5 (*Contd.*)

Industry 2911: Petroleum Refining

	$\hat{P}_L =$	Fixed coefficients 0%	7.5%	10%	Cobb-Douglas 0%	7.5%	10%	Translog 0%	7.5%	10%
$\hat{P}_N =$	0	1.3%	2.1%	2.6%	0.9%	1.4%	1.6%	1.0%	1.4%	1.5%
	5	4.8	5.2	5.5	4.7	5.2	5.3	4.6	5.2	5.3
	10	9.0	9.2	9.4	8.4	8.9	9.1	8.3	9.0	9.1
	15	13.8	13.8	13.9	12.1	12.6	12.8	12.0	12.8	13.0

Industry 3241: Hydraulic cement

	$\hat{P}_L =$ (Percent)	Fixed coefficients 0%	7.5%	10%	Cobb-Douglas 0%	7.5%	10%	Translog 0%	7.5%	10%
$\hat{P}_N =$	0	3.5%	5.3%	6.4%	2.9%	4.9%	5.6%	3.0%	4.8%	5.4%
	5	4.1	5.8	6.8	3.7	5.7	6.3	3.7	5.7	6.3
	10	5.4	6.7	7.6	4.4	6.4	7.1	4.3	6.4	7.1
	15	7.5	8.5	9.2	5.2	7.2	7.8	4.6	6.9	7.6

Industry 3275: Gypsum

	$\hat{P}_L =$	Fixed coefficients 0%	7.5%	10%	Cobb-Douglas 0%	7.5%	10%	Translog 0%	7.5%	10%
$\hat{P}_N =$	0	3.4%	5.6%	6.8%	2.9%	5.2%	6.0%	3.1%	5.6%	6.7%
	5	3.9	5.9	7.1	3.4	5.8	6.6	3.7	5.8	6.8
	10	4.9	6.6	7.7	4.0	6.3	7.1	4.8	6.5	7.3
	15	6.6	8.0	8.8	4.6	6.9	7.7	6.2	7.5	8.2

Industry 3333: Primary Zinc

	$\hat{P}_L =$	Fixed coefficients 0%	7.5%	10%	Cobb-Douglas 0%	7.5%	10%	Translog 0%	7.5%	10%
$\hat{P}_N =$	0	1.0%	3.2%	4.5%	0.7%	2.3%	2.8%	1.0%	2.5%	3.1%
	5	4.3	5.6	6.5	4.0	5.5	6.0	4.0	5.5	6.1
	10	8.5	9.1	9.5	7.2	8.8	9.3	7.5	9.0	9.5
	15	13.3	13.4	13.6	10.5	12.0	12.6	11.5	12.9	13.5

do some, but by no means all, technology comparisons differ noticeably. Note that a 10-year experience with $\hat{P}_N = 15$ percent would be a period over which natural resource prices quadruple. This rapid rate of input inflation has happened extremely infrequently, as illustrated by the recent unsettling experiences with crude-oil prices.

Consider now the response of commodity inflation to alternative rates of factor-price growth. If we initially focus on the rows depicting natural resource inflation of 5 and 10 percent, we confirm that commodity inflation is rather insensitive to alternative wage paths. The greatest impact of wage growth is understandably registered in the more labor-intensive industries 3241, 3275, and 3333. On the other hand, commodity inflation rates are quite responsive to alternative natural resource price paths, except in the least resource-intensive industries 3241 and 3275.

Natural resource inputs used in several of the sample industries are subject to one or more of the following: seriously declining estimated reserves, government price-influencing programs and foreign cartel manipulations. Future adjustments in these forces could generate sustained yearly rates of natural resource price inflation at or above 10 percent. One must conclude that, barring substantial technical progress, the result would be large yearly price increases in the sample industries, with the possible exceptions of industries 3241 and 3275.[11]

This section has demonstrated that the significant input substitution found in the sample industries and reported in Table 4 is generally insufficient to prevent the transmission of large natural resource price rises into large price increases in manufactured outputs using these resources. Indeed, use of the available substitutions leads to results little different from those obtained under the pessimistic assumption of fixed-coefficients technology.

Rapid increases in resource input prices would provide incentives to substitute among capital, labor, and materials in industries at higher levels of fabrication and to substitute final demand goods in consumption. Given these inducements will be present, if the future holds these price movements for us, investigative efforts are imperative on these secondary types of substitution. Without this knowledge it is impossible to determine whether or not natural resource price increases will dramatically affect the general price level of the economy.

V. SUMMARY AND CONCLUSIONS

This paper is intended to cast light on several questions. We began by describing changes in relative input costs and use in seven manufacturing industries that depend strongly on natural resources. Trends in factor use plainly show that none of the industries are characterized by fixed-coefficient production functions. Instead, most sectors demonstrate much latitude for input substitution, the dominant pattern being substitution of natural resources and capital for labor. We then proposed a framework for estimating partial elasticities of substitution. The estimates obtained from translog cost-minimizing input demand relations indicate that the unitary elasticity of substitution Cobb-Douglas model is not appropriate in any of these industries.

Having rejected both the fixed-coefficient and Cobb-Douglas hypotheses in favor of generalized translog cost functions, we inquire as to what influence these technologies exert on inflation, given the paths of input prices. Our salient finding is that for a wide range of input price changes the three technologies yield quite similar 10-year commodity inflation rates. The shorter-term rates are even more homogeneous. It would appear that factor substitution is far less important in the analysis of inflation than in models of optimal resource depletion or intertemporal consumption.

Commodity inflation rates are understandably found to be sensitive to changes in natural resource input prices. We conjecture that a prolonged period of resource inflation would lead to sharply rising output prices in these industries, irrespective of technically feasible options for input substitution.

FOOTNOTES

Moroney's research was supported by the National Science Foundation under Grant No. AER77-14568, and Toevs's by NSF Grant No. HES75-19933. Any opinions, findings, and conclusions or recommendations expressed in this publication are those of the authors, and do not necessarily reflect the views of the National Science Foundation.

1. This descriptive section, and an extended version of section III, appear in Moroney and Toevs (14).
2. These series are published annually either in U.S. Bureau of the Census, *Census of Manufactures* (32), or for the intercensal years in the *Annual Survey of Manufactures*.
3. One may refer to Schultz (21), Potter and Christy (18), Vanek (38), and Humphrey and Moroney (11) for further details distinguishing natural resources from natural resource products. The central conclusions from these studies are (1) abstract natural resources are not well suited for analytical purposes, and (2) natural resource products are the economically relevant inputs in manufacturing and other nonprimary sectors. The second point follows from the method used by the Department of Commerce to classify industries: All industries that make direct use of land or other natural resources are *defined* to be primary sectors, and their products are termed natural resource products.
4. Humphrey (10) found in a study of six manufacturing sectors that capital and labor are weakly separable from an aggregate of all intermediate inputs.
5. This method of calculating P_K is a natural consequence of product value exhaustion, and has been used in virtually all other studies. Cf. Berndt and Christensen (3), Berndt and Wood (4), and Humphrey and Moroney (11).
6. Although systematic evidence is not yet available for more recent years, from the documentary series used to construct resource input costs in Table 1, casual evidence points to comparatively sharp increases in many resource input prices since 1973. Whether they are permanent or transitory remains to be established.
7. Straightforward tests of significance are not possible for the estimated elasticities of the translog production function, because they are complex, nonlinear combinations of the estimated production parameters. See Berndt and Christensen (3) and Humphrey and Moroney (11).
8. The nonparametric Swed-Eisenhart test applies independently of the parametric

distribution of the disturbances, and is therefore preferable to the more familiar Durbin-Watson test, whose interpretation is ambiguous when applied to residuals obtained from restricted regressions. The Swed-Eisenhart test and tables for its statistical significance are found in Siegel (24).

9. The estimated elasticities never vary so much within an industry as to reverse an inference concerning substitution or complementarity based on elasticities evaluated at sample means.

10. Note that within industries 2011, 2041–43, and 3275 the fixed-coefficient and translog technologies yield essentially identical results. Industry 2011 is characterized econometrically by one small, positive elasticity of substitution, while industries 2041–43 and 3275 each possess a significant input complementarity sufficient to produce time paths of relative shares similar to those in the fixed-coefficients model.

11. In a recent article Toevs (31) shows that technical change was insignificant in all the sample industries used in this paper.

REFERENCES

1. Allen, R. G. D., *Mathematical Analysis for Economists*. The Macmillan Company, London, 1938.
2. American Petroleum Institute, *Petroleum Facts and Figures*. Port City Press, Baltimore, 1969.
3. Berndt, Ernst R., and Laurits Christensen, "The Translog Function and the Substitution of Equipment, Structures, and Labor in U.S. Manufacturing, 1929–1968." *Journal of Econometrics* 1 (March 1973), 81–114.
4. Berndt, Ernst R, and David Wood, "Technology, Prices, and the Derived Demand for Energy." *Review of Economics and Statistics* 57 (August 1975), 259–268.
5. Christensen, L. R., D. Jorgenson, and L. Lau, "Conjugate Duality and the Transcendental Logarithmic Production Function." Unpublished paper presented at the Second World Congress of the Econometric Society, Cambridge, England, 1970.
6. Creamer, Daniel, S. Dobrovolsky, and I. Borenstein, *Capital in Manufacturing and Mining*. Princeton University Press, Princeton, N. J., 1960.
7. Dasgupta, P., and G. M. Heal, "The Optimal Depletion of Exhaustible Resources." *Review of Economic Studies* (Symposium, 1974), 3–28.
8. Diewert, W. E., "An Application of the Shephard Duality Theorem: A Generalized Leontief Production Function." *Journal of Political Economy* 79 (May/June 1971), 481–507.
9. Forrester, Jay W., *World Dynamics*. Wright-Allen Press, Cambridge, Mass, 1971.
10. Humphrey, David B., "Estimates of Factor-Intermediate Substitution and Separability." *Southern Economic Journal* 41 (January 1975), 531–534.
11. ———, and J. R. Moroney, "Substitution Among Capital, Labor, and Natural Resource Products in American Manufacturing." *Journal of Political Economy* 83 (February 1975), 57–82.
12. Kmenta, J., and R. Gilbert, "Small Sample Properties of Alternative Estimators of Seemingly Unrelated Regressions." *Journal of the American Statistical Association* 63 (December 1968), 1180–1200.
13. Meadows, D., et al., *The Limits to Growth*. Universe Books, New York, 1972.
14. Moroney, J. R., and Alden Toevs, "Factor Costs and Factor Use: An Analysis of Labor, Capital, and Natural Resource Inputs." *Southern Economic Journal* 44 (October 1977), 222–39.
15. Nordhaus, William, and James Tobin, "Is Economic Growth Obsolete?" in

Economic Growth (Fiftieth Anniversary Colloquium, V, National Bureau of Economic Research, New York, 1972).
16. Office of Business Economics, *National Income and Product Accounts of the United States, 1929-1965.* U.S. Government Printing Office, Washington, D.C., 1966.
17. ———, *Input-Output Structure of the U.S. Economy, 1963.* Vol. 1 *Transactions Data for Detailed Industries.* U.S. Government Printing Office, Washington, D. C., 1969.
18. Potter, N., and F. T. Christy, Jr., *Trends in Natural Resource Commodities.* The John Hopkins Press for Resources for the Future, Baltimore, 1962.
19. Ruble, William L., "Improving the Computation of Simultaneous Stochastic Linear Equation Estimates." Ph.D. dissertation, Michigan State University, 1968.
20. Samuelson, P. A., *Foundations of Economic Analysis.* Harvard University Press, Cambridge, Mass., 1947.
21. Schultz, T. W., *The Economic Organization of Agriculture.* McGraw-Hill, New York, 1953.
22. Shephard, R. W., *Cost and Production Functions.* Princeton University Press, Princeton, N. J., 1953.
23. ———, *Theory of Cost and Production Functions.* Princeton University Press, Princeton, N. J., 1970.
24. Siegel, Sidney, *Nonparametric Statistics.* McGraw-Hill, New York, 1956.
25. Solow, R. M., "The Economics of Resources or the Resources of Economics." *American Economic Review Papers and Proceedings* 64 (May 1974), 1-14.
26. ———, "Intergenerational Equity and Exhaustible Resources." *Review of Economic Studies* (Symposium, 1974). 29-45.
27. Stigler, George J., *Capital and Rates of Return in Manufacturing Industries.* Princeton University Press, Princeton, N. J., 1963.
28. Stiglitz, Joseph E., "Growth and Exhaustible Natural Resources: Efficient and Optimal Growth Paths." *Review of Economic Studies* (Symposium, 1974), 123-37.
29. ———, "Growth with Exhaustible Natural Resources: The Competitive Economy." *Review of Economic Studies* (Symposium, 1974), 139-52.
30. Sweeney, James L., "Economics of Depletable Resources: Market Forces and Intertemporal Bias." *Review of Economic Studies* 44 (February 1977), 125-41.
31. Toevs, Alden, "Technical Change in Manufacturing Industries Using Natural Resource Products." *Southern Economic Journal* 44 (January 1978).
32. U. S. Bureau of the Census, *Census of Manufactures,* Volumes for 1954, 1958, 1963, and 1967. U.S. Government Printing Office, Washington, D. C.
33. ———, *Annual Survey of Manufactures,* yearly volumes for 1947-1971. U.S. Government Printing Office, Washington, D.C.
34. U.S. Department of Agriculture, *Agricultural Statistics,* yearly volumes for 1954-1972. U.S. Government Printing Office, Washington, D.C.
35. U.S. Department of the Interior, Bureau of Mines, *Minerals Yearbook,* yearly volumes for 1954-1971. U.S. Government Printing Office, Washington, D.C.
36. U.S. Department of the Treasury, Internal Revenue Service. *Tax Information on Depreciation* U.S. Government Printing Office, Washington, D.C., 1972.
37. Uzawa, Hirofumi, "Production Functions with Constant Elasticities of Substitution." *Review of Economic Studies* 29 (1962), 291-99.
38. Vanek, Jaroslav, *The Natural Resource Content of United States Foreign Trade.* The M.I.T. Press, Cambridge, Mass., 1963.
39. Zellner, Arnold M., "An Efficient Method of Estimating Seemingly Unrelated Regressions and Tests for Aggregation Bias." *Journal of the American Statistical Association* 57 (June 1962), 585-612.

DATA APPENDIX

A: Derivation of the Constant Dollar Gross Book Value Series

The gross book value of capital assets in historical acquisition costs for many four-digit manufacturing industries are published in U.S. Bureau of the Census, *Annual Survey of Manufactures*, beginning in 1962 (except for the years 1965, 1966, and 1967). Comparable gross book value figures for 1957 and 1967 are published in U.S. Bureau of the Census, *Census of Manufactures* for 1958 and 1967. Continuous series for the sample manufacturing industries over the time period 1954–1971 necessitates the approximation of gross book value for 1954–1956, 1958–1961, and 1965–1966.

Data on new capital expenditures, generally available in the *Annual Survey of Manufactures*, and a computed adjustment for fully depreciated capital, permitted the approximation of gross book value in all of these years for six industries. This method is best described using a specific application, for example the approximation of capital stocks for 1958–1961. (i) For each industry, the reported 1957 gross book value was added to the sum of new capital expenditures for the years 1958 through 1962. (ii) This aggregate was compared to the 1962 reported gross book value. The two numbers would be equal only if none of the initial (1957) capital stock had been completely depreciated. (iii) The observed difference was averaged over the five year period; this figure is the annual adjustment for fully depreciated capital. (iv) For each year in the interval 1958–1961 the new capital expenditure was reduced by this annual adjustment. The result approximates the actual addition to gross book value made during each year. For all industries, yearly investment data are reported from 1955 through 1957. These expenditures were reduced by the annual adjustment for depreciated capital noted above. The resulting figures were subtracted from the 1957 gross book value benchmarks to yield a gross book value series for 1954 through 1956. The unreported gross book values for the years 1965 and 1966 were approximated using the methodology employed for the years 1958–1961.

The gross book value for an industry can be usefully separated into two components: Structures (plant and structures) and nonstructures (machinery and equipment). This disaggregation permits the consideration of the separate price movements in new structural additions and in new nonstructural investments. In addition, structures have substantially longer useful lives than nonstructures, so it is necessary to employ a different deflator for structures than for nonstructures.

Consider first the method used to obtain a gross book value deflator for nonstructures in a specific manufacturing industry. A nonstructure that is in service less than n years is included in gross book value, where n is the average useful life of a nonstructure. (These life expectancies, which average twelve years, are obtained from the U.S. Department of the Treasury publication, *Tax Information on Depreciation*.) The formula used to calculate the deflator for the nonstructure component of gross book value in year T, D_{NT}, is:

$$D_{NT} = \sum_{t=T-n}^{T} \frac{NI_t d_{Nt}}{\sum_{t=T-n}^{T} NI_t}$$

where d_{Nt} is the Implicit Price Deflator for Producers' Durable Equipment in year t (compiled and reported by the Department of Commerce in the Survey of Current Business) and NI_t is constant dollar nonstructure investment in year t. Thus the weights are determined by the relative importance of each year's investment in total nondepreciated investment of nonstructures.

Since nonstructure investment is reported for four-digit manufacturing industries beginning in 1947, a less-precise method of computing D_{NT} for the years 1954 to 1947 + (n − 1) was employed. It is assumed that the annual industry investment in nonstructures for years prior to 1947 is in the same proportion to total manufacturing investment in nonstructures as its average for the years 1947 through 1965. Total manufacturing investment in nonstructures is known for the years prior to 1947. It is computed as the sum of lines 8, 9, 10, 15, 16, 17, 20, 21, 23, 29, and 30 in Table 5.4 of Office of Business Economics, *National Income and Product Accounts of the United States, 1929–1965*. Thus one can approximate industry-specific investment for these years. In each industry the reliability of this proportionality assumption is investigated by regressing the known ratios of industry investment to total manufacturing investment on time. In no industry is there a significant time trend, so the assumption seems reasonable.

Consider now the structures component of gross book value. We assume that structures have a useful life of forty years. A deflation procedure similar to that just developed is unfruitful because yearly investment in structures is reported for four-digit industries only since the year 1947. The only workable alternative is to assume that for each industry the ratio of investment in structures to total manufacturing investment in structures has been constant since 1913. This assumption, although somewhat restrictive, has a precedent in the literature. For example, George J. Stigler (1963) and Daniel Creamer, et al. (1960) used it to derive gross book value deflators for specific industries.

The construction price index, d_S, used to build a deflator for the gross book value of structures is the American Appraisal Company's Price Index of Construction Costs. The measure used for total manufacturing investment in structures is the "Industrial and Commercial Construction Put in Place" series. Both are reported in the *Statistical Abstract of the United States*. The deflator for gross book value of structures in year T, D_{ST}, is:

$$D_{ST} = \sum_{t=T-n}^{T} \frac{SI_t d_{St}}{\sum_{t=T-n}^{T} SI_t}$$

where SI_t is the constant dollar investment in structures undertaken by all manufacturing industries in year t. Given the assumption made above, the resulting deflator will be applicable to all the sample industries.

The two components of gross book value cannot be individually deflated because reported gross book value is not always disaggregated into structures and nonstructures. Therefore, a composite deflator is calculated as a weighted average of the nonstructures deflator and the structures deflator. In each manufacturing industry the weights are the average relative shares of structures and nonstructures in gross book value during the period 1967–1971. The resulting figures are used industry by industry to deflate the series on the gross book value of capital assets, forming the constant dollar gross book value series that serve as our measures of capital stocks.

B. Derivation of the Natural Resource Product Input Series

The annual outputs of renewable natural resource products are obtained from *Agricultural Statistics*, a statistical yearbook published by the Department of Agriculture. The dispositions of natural resource product outputs are given for relatively large purchasers of these products. These disposition figures permit the imputation of input usage by our sample manufacturing industries.

Minerals Yearbook, a publication of the U.S. Department of the Interior, Bureau of Mines, is the source for the output of nonrenewable natural resource products except petroleum. Crude petroleum production and imports are obtained from the American Petroleum Institute, *Petroleum Facts and Figures*. The end uses of yearly output flows are published for major purchasers of these nonrenewable resource products.

The following lists the natural resource product inputs used by each manufacturing industry. The first three industries process renewable resource products, and the remaining industries fabricate nonrenewable resource products.

Natural Resource Products Included in the Sample Industries

Meat Packing (2011): Slaughtered cattle, calves, lambs, and hogs
Dairy Products (202): Cream and fluid milk sold to plants and dealers
Flour Milling and Cereals (2041, 43): Wheat, rye, oats, and corn sold to produce foodstuffs

Petroleum Refining (2911): Crude petroleum imported and domestically produced

Hydraulic Cement (3241): Cement rock, limestone, clay, shale, crude gypsum, sand and sandstone

Gypsum Products (3275): Crude gypsum domestically produced and imported

Primary Zinc (3333): Mined zinc ores, domestic and imported

In the four industries using more than one resource product input, the resource product aggregate is constructed as the sum of constant dollar resource products embodied in the aggregate. The prices of all resource products are published in the cited yearbooks. The imputed usage of the resource input is precisely correct if the value of shipments coverage ratio for the manufacturing industry is one. In fact, five of the seven coverage ratios exceed 0.9, and the remaining two exceed 0.8. The imputed annual use of resource inputs would also differ from actual use according to changes in resource product inventories held. Marked inventory changes do not appear to be a problem in any of the industries for the time period reviewed.

The annual price indexes of the resource product aggregates are Laspeyres indexes, in which 1958 quantities are used as the base. The resulting series are used for illustrative purposes in section II and for estimating the translog cost parameters in section IV. The use of a price index, rather than an actual input price, does not affect the estimate of any parameter of interest. The only parameter whose estimate is affected is a_o, the regression constant. For a proof, see Berndt and Christensen (3).

The data used in this paper will be provided by the authors upon appropriate request.

SUBSTITUTION AMONG ENERGY, CAPITAL, AND LABOR INPUTS IN U.S. MANUFACTURING

Robert Halvorsen, UNIVERSITY OF WASHINGTON*

Jay Ford, UNIVERSITY OF WASHINGTON

I. INTRODUCTION

Manufacturing industries account for approximately one-fourth of total energy consumed for power and heat in the United States. As shown in Table 1, the contribution of individual industries to total manufacturing demand varies widely. Industry 28, chemicals and allied products, accounted for 21.9 percent of total manufacturing demand in 1974 while industry 21, tobacco products, accounted for only 0.2 percent. Differences in energy consumption are due both to differences in total output and to differences in the energy intensiveness of production. Expenditure on energy as a percentage of value added is also shown in Table 1. By this measure, energy

Table 1. Energy consumption by two-digit industries, 1974[a].

Industry	Energy Consumption[b]	Percent of Total	Energy Intensiveness[c]
20 Food and kindred products	280.2	7.14%	3.22%
21 Tobacco products	5.9	0.15	1.21
22 Textile mill products	94.5	2.41	5.24
23 Apparel, other textile products	19.0	0.48	1.15
24 Lumber and wood products	79.6	2.03	4.17
25 Furniture and fixtures	17.1	0.44	1.84
26 Paper and allied products	390.0	9.94	10.05
27 Printing and publishing	26.5	0.68	1.03
28 Chemicals, allied products	858.1	21.86	7.71
29 Petroleum and coal products	459.4	11.70	12.68
30 Rubber, misc. plastics products	74.7	1.90	3.63
31 Leather and leather products	6.7	0.17	1.70
32 Stone, clay and glass products	391.5	9.98	10.67
33 Primary metal industries	774.0	19.72	11.24
34 Fabricated metal products	120.7	3.08	2.33
35 Machinery, except electrical	107.8	2.75	1.48
36 Electrical equipment and supplies	73.5	1.87	1.64
37 Transportation equipment	109.9	2.80	1.84
38 Instruments and related products	20.8	0.53	1.20
39 Miscellaneous manufacturing industries	15.0	0.38	1.68
Total	3924.7[d]	100.00%[d]	

[a]Source, U.S. Bureau of the Census, *Annual Survey of Manufactures 1974*.
[b]Billions of kilowatt-hours equivalent.
[c]Energy cost as percent of value added.
[d]Detailed figures may not add to totals because of independent rounding.

intensiveness varied from 12.7 percent for industry 29, petroleum and coal products, to 1.0 percent for industry 27, printing and publishing.

The differences in energy intensiveness across industries suggest that the underlying determinants of energy demand also vary across industries. Therefore it is desirable to examine energy demand on an industry-by-industry basis, rather than at the level of aggregate manufacturing.

Since the characteristics of demand can also be expected to differ across types of energy, it is desirable to examine demand for individual types of energy rather than for aggregate energy. In estimating the demand equations for different types of energy, the restrictions on demand interrelationships implied by economic theory should be taken into account. Doing so requires that the systems of demand equations be estimated simultaneously.

The demand for each type of energy will depend on the possibilities for substitution among types of energy and among energy and non-energy inputs. If energy inputs are separable from non-energy inputs, substitution among types of energy can be studied separately from substitution among energy and non-energy inputs. In the absence of separability, this simplification is not appropriate, and substitution among all types of inputs should be examined simultaneously.

Previous studies of industrial energy demand have generally considered the demand for only one type of energy, usually electric energy,[1] or have provided results only for total manufacturing rather than for individual industries.[2] In this study, complete systems of energy demand equations are estimated for individual two-digit industries. Duality theory is used to derive the systems of demand equations from flexible cost functions which impose only those restrictions on the estimated elasticities of demand and substitution that are implied by economic theory.

Rather than assuming separability of energy inputs from non-energy inputs, we examine substitution among energy and non-energy inputs directly. This procedure makes it possible to perform statistical tests for separability and provides estimates of the cross elasticities of demand between energy and non-energy inputs. The cross elasticities have considerable potential interest for policy analysis. For example, the cross elasticities of demand for energy inputs with respect to the cost of capital indicate the effect of investment incentives on demand for each type of energy. For those industries for which separability is accepted, own and cross elasticities of demand for aggregate energy are also estimated.

The systems of demand equations are estimated with data from the 1958 *Census of Manufactures*. While the use of more recent data would have been desirable, the 1958 Census is the last to report adequate data on the quantity and cost of capital. A sufficient number of observations is available to estimate the systems of demand equations for eight two-digit industries, which together account for approximately three-fourths of total energy demand in manufacturing.

The results include estimates of own price elasticities of demand for electricity, oil, gas, capital, production workers, and non-production workers. Almost all of the estimated own price elasticities are significant and indicate considerable price responsiveness of demand. The range of the estimated energy own price elasticities is $-.50$ to -2.55 for electricity, -1.56 to -2.40 for fuel oil, and -1.21 to -2.90 for gas. Estimated cross price elasticities between energy inputs, and between energy and non-energy inputs, indicate that the predominant relationship is that of substitutes rather than complements.

Separability of energy inputs from capital and labor is accepted for four industries, which together account for approximately two-thirds of total energy consumption by the group of eight industries. Estimated own price elasticities of demand for aggregate energy for these four industries range from $-.66$ to -2.56.

The next section of the paper describes the derivation of the systems of demand equations and the estimation procedures used. Section III discusses data sources and the definition of each variable. Empirical results are presented in section IV. The final section contains concluding comments.

II. THE MODEL

A twice differentiable aggregate production function is assumed to exist at the state level for each two-digit industry,

$$Y = f(K,B,W,E,O,G,X), \qquad (1)$$

where W is total cost of the aggregate input, Z, and the P_i are the prices of production and non-production workers, respectively, E is electricity, O is fuel oil, G is gas, and X is a vector of all other inputs. Assuming that the production function is homothetically weakly separable in K,B,W,E,O, and G, it can be written,

$$Y = g[h(K,B,W,E,O,G),X], \qquad (2)$$

where h is an input aggregator function.

Dual to the input aggregator function is a cost function,

$$W = e(Z, P_K, P_B, P_W, P_E, P_O, P_G),$$

where W is total cost of the aggregate input, Z, and the P_i are the prices of the inputs.[3] If the aggregator function is a positive, nondecreasing, positively linear homogeneous, concave function, then the cost function can be written

$$W = Z \cdot V(P_K, P_B, P_W, P_E, P_O, P_G),$$

where V is a unit cost function satisfying the same regularity conditions, Diewert (11).

Demand functions for the inputs can be obtained from the unit cost function using Shephard's lemma,

$$X_i = Z \frac{\partial V}{\partial P_i}, \quad i = K, B, W, E, O, G,$$

where X_i is the cost minimizing quantity of input i, Diewert (11). Thus the characteristics of industrial demand for energy and other inputs can be examined by specifying an appropriate functional form for the unit cost function and differentiating it to obtain a system of demand equations.

A convenient functional form for the cost function is the transcendental logarithmic (translog),

$$\ln V = \alpha_0 + \sum_i \alpha_i \ln P_i + 1/2 \sum_i \sum_j \gamma_{ij} \ln P_i \ln P_j, \quad i,j = K, B, W, E, O, G, \quad (3)$$

where $\gamma_{ij} = \gamma_{ji}$. The translog form, which was introduced by Christensen, et al. (8,9), provides a second order approximation to an arbitrary twice continuously differentiable unit cost function. The translog unit cost function does not satisfy the regularity conditions globally unless all $\gamma_{ij} = 0$, i.e., unless it collapses into a Cobb-Douglas form. However, the estimated cost function can be checked to determine if the regularity conditions are satisfied in the relevant region.

Demand equations are obtained by logarithmic differentiation of the unit cost function,

$$\frac{\partial \ln V}{\partial \ln P_i} = \frac{\partial V}{\partial P_i} \cdot \frac{P_i}{V} = \alpha_i + \sum_j \gamma_{ij} \ln P_j, \quad i,j = K, B, W, E, O, G. \quad (4)$$

By Shephard's lemma, $\partial V/\partial P_i = X_i/Z$. Since the cost function is linear homogeneous in prices, $W = \Sigma P_i X_i$ by Euler's theorem. Therefore, $V = \Sigma P_i X_i/Z$. Substituting in (4),

$$\frac{\partial \ln V}{\partial \ln P_i} = \frac{P_i X_i/Z}{\Sigma P_i X_i/Z} = \frac{P_i X_i}{\Sigma P_i X_i} = M_i, \quad i = K, B, W, E, O, G,$$

where M_i is the cost share for input i. Thus demand equations for the inputs in Z can be estimated even though Z itself is not observed.

Because the cost shares sum to unity at each observation, the parameters must satisfy adding-up restrictions,

$$\sum_i \alpha_i = 1,$$

$$\sum_i \gamma_{ij} = 0, \quad i,j = K, B, W, E, O, G. \quad (5)$$

The adding-up restrictions, together with the restrictions $\gamma_{ij} = \gamma_{ji}$, impose linear homogeneity in prices on the cost function.

Imposition of the restrictions results in the following set of cost share equations:

$$M_K = \alpha_K + \gamma_{KB}(\ln P_B - \ln P_K) + \gamma_{KW}(\ln P_W - \ln P_K) + \gamma_{KE}(\ln P_E - \ln P_K)$$
$$+ \gamma_{KO}(\ln P_O - \ln P_K) + \gamma_{KG}(\ln P_G - \ln P_K) + u_K,$$

$$M_B = \alpha_B + \gamma_{KB}(\ln P_K - \ln P_B) + \gamma_{BW}(\ln P_W - \ln P_B) + \gamma_{BE}(\ln P_E - \ln P_B)$$
$$+ \gamma_{BO}(\ln P_O - \ln P_B) + \gamma_{BG}(\ln P_G - \ln P_B) + u_B,$$

$$M_W = \alpha_W + \gamma_{KW}(\ln P_K - \ln P_W) + \gamma_{BW}(\ln P_B - \ln P_W) + \gamma_{WE}(\ln P_E - \ln P_W)$$
$$+ \gamma_{WO}(\ln P_O - \ln P_W) + \gamma_{WG}(\ln P_G - \ln P_W) + u_W,$$

$$M_E = \alpha_E + \gamma_{KE}(\ln P_K - \ln P_E) + \gamma_{BE}(\ln P_B - \ln P_E) + \gamma_{WE}(\ln P_W - \ln P_E)$$
$$+ \gamma_{EO}(\ln P_O - \ln P_E) + \gamma_{EG}(\ln P_G - \ln P_E) + u_E,$$

$$M_O = \alpha_O + \gamma_{KO}(\ln P_K - \ln P_O) + \gamma_{BO}(\ln P_B - \ln P_O) + \gamma_{WO}(\ln P_W - \ln P_O)$$
$$+ \gamma_{EO}(\ln P_E - \ln P_O) + \gamma_{OG}(\ln P_G - \ln P_O) + u_O,$$

$$M_G = \alpha_G + \gamma_{KG}(\ln P_K - \ln P_G) + \gamma_{BG}(\ln P_B - \ln P_G) + \gamma_{WG}(\ln P_W - \ln P_G)$$
$$+ \gamma_{EG}(\ln P_E - \ln P_G) + \gamma_{OG}(\ln P_O - \ln P_G) + u_G, \quad (6)$$

where the additive disturbance terms, u_i, are included to reflect random errors in cost minimizing behavior.

Since the dependent variables in (6) are cost shares, the disturbance terms can be expected to exhibit joint covariance. Therefore the equations are estimated with the procedure suggested by Zellner (22). The sum of the disturbances across the share equations is zero at each observation and the disturbance covariance matrix is singular. Therefore one equation must be omitted from the system of equations. Estimates of the parameters of the omitted equation can be obtained from (5). The choice of equation to be omitted is arbitrary. Use of an iterative Zellner-efficient procedure, which is equivalent to maximum likelihood estimation, insures that the parameter estimates are invariant to the choice of equation to be omitted.[4]

Previous studies of industrial demand for energy have assumed that energy inputs are separable from all other inputs. Inclusion of capital and labor inputs in the systems of equations make it possible to test for the separability of energy inputs from these inputs. Since intermediate inputs are not included in the systems of equations, separability of energy inputs from the included inputs is a necessary but not sufficient condition for separability of energy inputs from all non-energy inputs.

Weak separability of the (homogeneous) input aggregator function in E, O, and G implies weak separability of the unit cost function in P_E, P_O, and P_G. However, the translog approximation of a weakly separable cost function is not necessarily weakly separable. Restrictions on the parameters of the translog unit cost function corresponding to weak separability of the true unit cost function in P_E, P_O, and P_G from P_K, P_B, and P_W are,

$$\gamma_{EK} = \theta_K \alpha_E, \quad \gamma_{EB} = \theta_B \alpha_E, \quad \gamma_{EW} = \theta_W \alpha_E,$$
$$\gamma_{OK} = \theta_K \alpha_O, \quad \gamma_{OB} = \theta_B \alpha_O, \quad \gamma_{OW} = \theta_W \alpha_O,$$
$$\gamma_{GK} = \theta_K \alpha_G, \quad \gamma_{GB} = \theta_B \alpha_G, \quad \gamma_{GW} = \theta_W \alpha_G. \quad (7)$$

Explicit separability of the translog function itself requires the further restriction, $\theta = 0$, in (7).[5]

If the input aggregator function is homothetically weakly separable in the energy inputs, it can be written

$$h[K, B, W, d(E, O, G)]$$

where d is an energy input function. In this case, the unit cost function can be written

$$V(P_K, P_B, P_W, P_F)$$

where P_F is the price of the aggregate energy input.

For those industries for which weak separability in energy inputs is accepted, a four-input model incorporating aggregate energy is also estimated. The price of the aggregate energy input is constructed from the prices of the individual energy inputs using a discrete Divisia index, which is exact for the translog functional form.[6]

In order to test for separability, the systems of equations are estimated with and without the corresponding restrictions imposed. The results are compared by computing $-2 \log \lambda$ where λ is the ratio of the maximum value of the likelihood function for the restricted equations to the maximum value of the likelihood function for the unrestricted equations. Under the null hypothesis this test statistic is distributed asymptotically as chi-squared with degrees of freedom equal to the number of restrictions being tested. Explicit separability is tested conditional on the acceptance of implicit separability.

The Cobb-Douglas functional form is a special case of the translog form. Therefore it is also possible to test whether the more restrictive Cobb-Douglas form is appropriate for the cost function. Since the Cobb-Douglas form is self-dual, this is equivalent to a test of whether the input aggregator function is Cobb-Douglas. The translog unit cost function reduces to the Cobb-Douglas form when all $\gamma_{ij} = 0$, and this set of restrictions is also tested using the log-likelihood ratio procedure.

As noted above, the translog unit cost function does not satisfy the regularity conditions globally. Imposition of the adding-up restrictions together with the restrictions $\gamma_{ij} = \gamma_{ji}$ insures that the unit cost function is linear homogeneous in the input prices. However, the fitted unit cost function may or may not satisfy the conditions that it be nondecreasing and concave.

The fitted unit cost function is nondecreasing in the input prices if the fitted shares are non-negative, since

$$M_i = \frac{\partial V}{\partial P_i} \cdot \frac{P_i}{V} \quad i = K, B, W, E, O, G,$$

and P_i and V are always positive. Concavity of the unit cost function requires that the Hessian matrix be negative semidefinite for each observation. This will be true if the first $n-1$ ordered principal minors alternate in sign. The nth order principal minor will be zero due to the imposition of linear homogeneity in input prices. Concavity is checked for each observation by calculating the values of the principal minors. Since it is not determined if the principal minors are statistically significant, this procedure does not constitute a statistical test of concavity.

An appropriate measure of goodness of fit of the estimated equations is the "pseudo-R^2," which states the proportion of generalized variance in the system of equations explained by variation in the right-hand variables.[7] The pseudo-R^2 is calculated as $1 - |r_1|/|r_2|$ where $|r_1|$ is the determinant of the estimated residual moment matrix and $|r_2|$ is the determinant when the coefficients of all right-hand variables are constrained to equal zero. The value of the pseudo-R^2 is invariant to the choice of equation to be omitted from the system.

Estimates of own and cross price elasticities of demand are calculated from the estimated cost share equations. The own price elasticity of demand for energy input i is defined as

$$E_{ii} = \frac{\partial X_i}{\partial P_i} \cdot \frac{P_i}{X_i}.$$

Applying Shephard's lemma to obtain expressions for X_i and $\partial X_i/\partial P_i$ in terms of derivatives of the unit cost function, the own price elasticity can be written,

$$E_{ii} = \frac{P_i \cdot \partial^2 V/\partial P_i^2}{\partial V/\partial P_i} = \frac{M_i^2 - M_i + \gamma_{ii}}{M_i}, \quad i = K, B, W, E, O, G. \quad (8)$$

Similarly, the cross price elasticity of demand for input i with respect to the price of input j is,

$$E_{ij} = \frac{\partial X_i}{\partial P_j} \cdot \frac{P_j}{X_i} = \frac{P_j \cdot \partial^2 V/\partial P_i \partial P_j}{\partial V/\partial P_i} = \frac{M_i M_j + \gamma_{ij}}{M_i}, \quad i,j = K, B, W, E, O, G. \quad (9)$$

Allen partial elasticities of substitution are equal to[8]

$$\sigma_{ii} = \frac{1}{M_i} E_{ii} = \frac{M_i^2 - M_i + \gamma_{ii}}{M_i^2},$$

$$\sigma_{ij} = \frac{1}{M_j} E_{ij} = \frac{M_i M_j + \gamma_{ij}}{M_i M_j}, \quad i,j = K, B, W, E, O, G. \quad (10)$$

Thus the Allen elasticities can be interpreted as normalized price elasticities, where the normalization is chosen such that the elasticity of substitution is invariant to the ordering of the factors. Accordingly, $\sigma_{ij} = \sigma_{ji}$, although, in general, $E_{ij} \neq E_{ji}$.

Because the elasticities of demand are functions of the cost shares, they will vary across the sample.[9] Rather than report the estimated elasticities for each observation, the elasticities are evaluated at the means of the data and only these values are reported here. The data are scaled so that the means of the prices are equal to unity. Therefore the estimated α_k; k = K, B, W, E, O, G, are equal to the fitted cost shares at the means, and the formulas for the elasticities at the means are given by (8), (9), and (10) with M_k replaced by α_k.

Since the elasticities at the means are functions only of the estimated parameters, the calculation of their estimated standard errors is considerably simplified. A first-order Taylor series approximation to the variance of the estimated elasticities can be computed as

$$S_B' V(B) S_B$$

where S_B is the column vector of first partial derivatives of the elasticities with respect to the parameters α_k and γ_{km} and $V(B)$ is the estimated variance-covariance matrix of the parameter estimates.[10]

III. DATA SOURCES AND VARIABLE DEFINITIONS

The *Census of Manufactures, 1958* was distinguished by the publication of detailed data on the quantity and the cost of owning and maintaining capital equipment and structures. This information is reported at infrequent intervals and the 1958 census is the most recent source of complete data on capital.[11] These data, along with information from which may be inferred the prices of production and non-production workers and energy inputs, are sufficient to estimate the systems of cost share equations.

The prices of energy inputs are calculated by dividing the reported expenditures on electricity, oil, and gas by the quantity at each observation.[12] These prices are then transformed into cents per kilowatt-hour equivalent. The price of capital services cannot be developed in this straightforward manner, because the transaction normally takes place within the firm. Hence we have adopted with some modification the procedure used by Christensen and Jorgenson (7), inferring the rental price of capital from the price of investment goods, the rate of return on corporate property, and the rates of taxation, depreciation, and capital gains.

The rental price of capital to industry i in state j is calculated as follows:

$$P_{ij} = \left[\frac{1 - u_{ij}Z_{ij}}{1 - u_{ij}}\right][q_{t-1}r + q_t w_{ij} - (q_t - q_{t-1})] + q_t d_{ij},$$

where q is the asset price of capital, u is the effective rate of combined Federal and state corporate income taxes, Z is the present value of depreciation deductions for tax purposes on a one-dollar investment in producers' durables, w is the rate of depreciation, and d is the effective property tax rate.

As is indicated by the absence of state and industry subscripts on q and r, it is assumed that a single market exists for new investment goods and capital so that these prices are equalized across states and industries. The value of q_t is set equal to one in 1958. The value of $q_t - q_{t-1}$ is equal to the change in the price index for producers' durables from 1957 to 1958. The value of r is the rate of return in the corporate sector in 1958. Data on the price index for producers' durables and the rate of return in the corporate sector are from Christensen and Jorgenson (7).

The remaining elements of the rental price of capital are constructed in the following manner:

u_{ij} = the sum of the effective Federal corporate profits tax rate by industry and the state corporate profits tax by state,

$Z_{ij} = \frac{1}{rL_{ij}}\left[1 - \left(\frac{1}{1+r}\right)^{L_{ij}}\right]$, where r is the discount rate and L_{ij} is an estimate of the lifetimes of depreciable assets used for tax purposes,

w_{ij} = annual depreciation charges in 1957 divided by the gross book value of depreciable assets as of December 31, 1957, and

d_{ij} = property taxes paid during 1957 divided by the gross book value of depreciable assets as of December 31, 1957.

This procedure amounts to the calculation of the annual user cost of one dollar's worth of capital equipment.

The available 1958 employment data by state and two-digit industry consist of total payroll and number of employees and, for production workers, the number of workers, man-hours, and total wages. The price of production workers' services is total wages divided by man-hours. The price for non-production workers is based on the residual payroll and number of employees and the assumption that white-collar workers are employed forty hours per week. The wage rate for both production and non-production workers is augmented to reflect the reported cost of supplementary employee benefits.

IV. EMPIRICAL RESULTS

A sufficient number of observations is available for estimation of the system of cost share equations for industries 20, 26, 28, 32, 33, 34, 35, and 37. These eight industries account for approximately three-fourths of total energy consumption in manufacturing.

Monotonicity of the unit cost function for each industry is checked by determining if the fitted values of the cost shares are positive. As shown in Table 2, all but nine of the 978 fitted cost shares are positive, and no one industry has more than three fitted cost shares with the incorrect sign. It is not determined whether or not the negative fitted cost shares are significantly different from zero, so this check does not provide a statistical test of monotonicity. However, a statistical test is available at the means of the data where the fitted cost shares are equal to the estimated α_i. All α_i are significantly positive at the five percent level for all industries. Therefore, monotonicity is accepted at the means of the data.[13]

Concavity of the unit cost function is checked by examining the signs of the principal minors at each observation. The number of observations with principal minors of the incorrect sign are shown in Table 2. Although it is not determined if the principal minors with incorrect signs are statistically significant, the existence of incorrect signs for more than a few percent of the observations is considered to cast doubt on the satisfaction of the concavity condition.[14] As shown in Table 2, industries 26, 32, 35, and 37 do not appear to satisfy the concavity condition and the performance of the model has to be considered suspect for these four industries. However, the model appears to perform very well for industries 20, 28, 33, and 34, which together account for more than two-thirds of total energy consumption by the group of eight industries.

Table 2. Monotonicity and concavity checks: six-input model

Industry	Number of Fitted Shares Total	With incorrect sign	Number of Observations Total	With incorrect sign
20	228	2	38	0
26	108	3	18	10
28	132	2	22	2
32	120	0	20	14
33	114	0	19	0
34	120	0	20	2
35	78	1	13	12
37	78	1	13	13
Total	978	9	163	53

Table 3. Parameter estimates[a]
Six-input model

Parameter	\multicolumn{7}{c}{Industry}
	20	26	28	32	33	34	35	37
α_K	.258	.356	.372	.300	.364	.207	.230	.214
	(.004)	(.019)	(.014)	(.011)	(.018)	(.009)	(.009)	(.018)
α_B	.415	.438	.315	.459	.432	.532	.480	.514
	(.007)	(.011)	(.008)	(.008)	(.011)	(.007)	(.005)	(.019)
α_W	.293	.160	.244	.167	.146	.239	.276	.256
	(.009)	(.007)	(.013)	(.010)	(.007)	(.004)	(.010)	(.014)
α_E	.020	.022	.049	.031	.034	.014	.011	.012
	(.001)	(.002)	(.016)	(.002)	(.005)	(.0002)	(.001)	(.001)
α_O	.006	.014	.007	.015	0.13	.003	.001	.002
	(.001)	(.004)	(.001)	(.003)	(.002)	(.0004)	(.0002)	(.001)
α_G	.008	.008	.012	.028	.012	.004	.001	.002
	(.001)	(.001)	(.002)	(.005)	(.001)	(.0003)	(.0002)	(.0001)
γ_K	.016	−.288	−.084	−.031	−.142	−.061	−.089	−.273
	(.027)	(.171)	(.063)	(.042)	(.133)	(.121)	(.067)	(.116)
γ_{KB}	−.081	.174	−.014	−.004	.130	.067	−.017	.169
	(.034)	(.099)	(.031)	(.034)	(.081)	(.090)	(.038)	(.119)
γ_{KW}	.063	.151	.064	−.006	.020	−.0006	.097	.115
	(.052)	(.070)	(.063)	(.042)	(.049)	(.064)	(.080)	(.114)
γ_{KE}	.007	.002	.124	−.010	.002	−.007	.003	−.005
	(.004)	(.023)	(.024)	(.009)	(.031)	(.004)	(.004)	(.006)
γ_{KO}	−.001	−.040	.009	.019	−.002	.005	.001	−.004
	(.005)	(.030)	(.006)	(.011)	(.012)	(.006)	(.002)	(.004)
γ_{KG}	−.005	−.0001	.012	.032	−.009	−.004	.005	−.002
	(.005)	(.014)	(.008)	(.019)	(.008)	(.006)	(.002)	(.001)
γ_{BB}	.135	−.037	.056	.045	−.184	.026	.078	.144
	(.081)	(.063)	(.055)	(.057)	(.069)	(.080)	(.158)	(.221)

γ_{BW}	−.037 (.104)	−.213 (.044)	−.081 (.055)	−.047 (.067)	.025 (.057)	−.111 (.042)	−.088 (.165)	−.308 (.239)
γ_{BE}	−.008 (.007)	.004 (.014)	.023 (.015)	.001 (.014)	.019 (.020)	.008 (.003)	.021 (.014)	.006 (.011)
γ_{BO}	−.013 (.008)	.026 (.019)	.006 (.010)	−.003 (.013)	.016 (.013)	−.001 (.004)	.008 (.007)	−.015 (.007)
γ_{BG}	.004 (.010)	.046 (.009)	.010 (.010)	.007 (.021)	−.006 (.010)	.111 (.004)	−.004 (.005)	.003 (.002)
γ_{WW}	−.039 (.146)	.045 (.051)	.0001 (.089)	.090 (.101)	−.083 (.064)	.132 (.064)	.021 (.196)	.185 (.305)
γ_{WE}	−.001 (.009)	.009 (.011)	.040 (.024)	.0003 (.020)	.027 (.013)	−.008 (.004)	−.023 (.015)	−.014 (.013)
γ_{WO}	.015 (.011)	.013 (.014)	−.021 (.011)	−.028 (.016)	−.010 (.013)	−.004 (.005)	−.008 (.007)	.021 (.008)
γ_{WG}	−.0003 (.014)	−.006 (.012)	−.003 (.012)	−.010 (.030)	.021 (.010)	−.009 (.005)	.001 (.005)	.002 (.002)
γ_{EE}	.001 (.003)	−.009 (.006)	−.079 (.027)	.002 (.007)	−.053 (.012)	.007 (.001)	.001 (.004)	.012 (.003)
γ_{EO}	.002 (.002)	.006 (.006)	.004 (.002)	.004 (.004)	.008 (.005)	−.0004 (.0007)	.001 (.001)	.002 (.002)
γ_{EG}	−.002 (.002)	−.012 (.003)	−.001 (.003)	.003 (.008)	−.004 (.003)	.0004 (.0006)	−.002 (.001)	−.001 (.001)
γ_{OO}	−.009 (.003)	−.002 (.011)	−.004 (.003)	.001 (.006)	−.016 (.006)	−.002 (.001)	−.002 (.001)	−.005 (.001)
γ_{OG}	.005 (.002)	−.004 (.004)	.005 (.003)	.006 (.007)	.004 (.004)	.002 (.001)	.0002 (.0004)	.001 (.0003)
γ_{GG}	−.002 (.003)	−.023 (.005)	−.024 (.004)	−.039 (.016)	−.006 (.004)	−.001 (.001)	−.0003 (.001)	−.001 (.0003)
Pseudo R^2	.704	.971	.898	.738	.960	.847	.966	.984
Number of Observations	38	18	22	20	19	20	13	13

[a]Figures in parentheses are asymptotic standard errors.

Parameter estimates and asymptotic standard errors for each of the industries are shown in Table 3, together with the value of the pseudo-R^2 for each system of equations. The values of the pseudo-R^2's range from .70 for industry 20 to .98 for industry 37. Results shown are for the initial regressions, there was no sequential estimation.

The estimates of the α_i parameters are equal to the fitted cost shares at the means of the data. Since the cost shares are equal to the elasticity of the unit cost of the aggregate input, Z, with respect to the price of each input, $\partial \ln V/\partial \ln P_i$, the estimates of α_i show the responsiveness of the price of the aggregate input to the prices of each input at the means of the data. As shown in Table 3, the elasticity of the price of the aggregate input with respect to the price of production workers is generally the largest. The prices of energy inputs have the least effect on the price of the aggregate input. The average values of the estimated α_i parameters are, $\alpha_K = .29$, $\alpha_B = .45$, $\alpha_W = .22$, $\alpha_E = .02$, $\alpha_O = .01$, $\alpha_G = .01$.

The estimates of the γ_{ij} parameters can be interpreted as estimated share elasticities. The cost share of input i is equal to $\partial \ln V/\partial \ln P_i$. The cross partial derivative

$$\frac{\partial^2 \ln V}{\partial \ln P_i \partial \ln P_j} = \gamma_{ij}$$

can be defined as a constant share elasticity summarizing the response of cost share M_i to a change in $\ln P_j$. Alternatively the share elasticity can be defined as

$$\frac{\partial \ln M_i}{\partial \ln P_j} = \frac{\gamma_{ij}}{M_i}.$$

In the latter case, the estimated share elasticities at the means of the data will be equal to the estimates of γ_{ij}/α_i.

Estimates of the own and cross price elasticities of demand at the means of the data are shown in Table 4 for the energy inputs. Because the elasticities are derived from unit cost functions, they show the price responsiveness of demand for individual types of energy holding the quantity of the aggregate input constant.

Estimates of the energy own price elasticities are shown in the first three rows of the table. All but one of the own price elasticities have the correct sign. The exception is the estimated own price elasticity for electricity in industry 37. The incorrect sign for this estimate reflects the apparent failure of this industry to satisfy the concavity condition.

The approximate standard errors of the estimated elasticities are also shown in the table. Of the 23 estimated own price elasticities with the correct sign, all but one are significant at the 5-percent level using one-tailed tests

Table 4. Estimates of price elasticities: energy inputs[a]
Six-input model

Elasticity[b]	Industry						
	20	26	28	32	33	34	35	37
E_{EE}	−.919[c]	−1.378[c]	−2.551[c]	−.903[c]	−2.546[c]	−.496[c]	−.909[c]	.042
	(.163)	(.268)	(.817)	(.221)	(.471)	(.095)	(.325)	(.305)
E_{OO}	−2.397[c]	−1.116[d]	−1.561[c]	−.902[c]	−2.283[c]	−1.803[c]	−2.629[c]	−3.296[c]
	(.516)	(.795)	(.545)	(.365)	(.476)	(.420)	(.614)	(.767)
E_{GG}	−1.262[c]	−3.812[c]	−2.902[c]	−2.380[c]	−1.510[c]	−1.209[c]	−1.223[c]	−1.647[c]
	(.374)	(.755)	(.416)	(.665)	(.305)	(.283)	(.441)	(.180)
E_{EO}	.120	.294	.093[d]	.139	.263[d]	−.026	.072	.157
	(.106)	(.257)	(.050)	(.136)	(.144)	(.047)	(.101)	(.149)
E_{EG}	−.078	−.547[c]	−.010	.121	−.094	.028	−.216[c]	−.083
	(.101)	(.159)	(.062)	(.245)	(.085)	(.045)	(.099)	(.057)
E_{OE}	.388	.466	.669[c]	.276	.701[c]	−.135	.626	.791
	(.345)	(.413)	(.291)	(.271)	(.356)	(.242)	(.896)	(.777)
E_{OG}	.888[c]	−.280	.777[d]	.429	.337	.729[c]	.153	.459[c]
	(.367)	(.298)	(.407)	(.464)	(.302)	(.306)	(.326)	(.160)
E_{GE}	−.184	−1.482[c]	−.039	.135	−.255	.106	−1.673[c]	−.492
	(.240)	(.493)	(.247)	(.272)	(.233)	(.167)	(.786)	(.338)
E_{GO}	.652[c]	−.478	.432[c]	.241	.345	.531[c]	.136	.543[c]
	(.276)	(.511)	(.220)	(.257)	(.308)	(.216)	(.291)	(.140)

[a]Figures in parentheses are asymptotic standard errors.
[b]E_{ij} indicates the elasticity of demand for input i with respect to the price of input j.
[c]Significant at the 5-percent level.
[d]Significant at the 10-percent level.

and the remaining estimate is significant at the 10 percent level. The one estimate with an incorrect sign is not significant.

There is considerable variation across industries in the estimated own price elasticities for energy. Omitting the four industries for which concavity appears not to be satisfied, the range of estimated own price elasticities is −.50 to −2.55 for electricity, −1.56 to −2.40 for fuel oil, and −1.21 to −2.90 for gas.

The estimated cross price elasticities between energy inputs are generally not statistically significant,[15] but the pattern of results is suggestive. The relationship between different types of energy appears to be predominantly that of substitutes rather than complements. All but 16 of the 48 estimated cross elasticities are positive, and only four of the negative estimates are statistically significant at the 10-percent level. As would be expected, the estimates of the cross price elasticities tend to be smaller in absolute magnitude than the estimates of own price elasticities.[16]

Estimated own price elasticities for capital, production workers, and non-production workers, as well as the cross elasticities of these inputs with the energy inputs, are shown in Table 5. All of the estimated own price elasticities for capital are significant at the five percent level using one-tailed tests. Five of the eight own price elasticities for production workers and three of the own price elasticities for non-production workers are significant at this level.

All of the estimated own price elasticities for the capital and labor inputs have the correct sign with the exception of the estimated elasticity for non-production workers in industry 26, which is not statistically significant. Industry 26 is one of the industries for which the concavity condition appears not to be satisfied. Omitting the four industries for which concavity appears not to be satisfied, the range of estimated own price elasticities is −.68 to −1.08 for capital, −.26 to −1.00 for production workers, and −.18 to −1.30 for non-production workers.

The estimated cross price elasticities between energy inputs and non-energy inputs are generally not significant,[17] but the pattern of results indicates that the relationship between energy inputs and non-energy inputs is predominantly that of substitutes rather than complements. All but 25 of the 72 estimated cross price elasticities are positive, and only three of the negative estimates are significant at the 10-percent level. Previous studies have indicated that capital and aggregate energy are complements for aggregate manufacturing.[18] However, only nine of the 24 estimated cross price elasticities between capital and individual energy inputs for two-digit industries are negative, of which only one is statistically significant.

As noted above, price elasticities estimated with a unit cost function for the aggregate input, Z, show the extent of price responsiveness holding the aggregate input constant. This is clearly not equal to the total price re-

Table 5. Estimates of price elasticities: capital and labor inputs[a]
Six-input model

Elasticity[b]	20	26	28	32	33	34	35	37
E_{KK}	−.679[c]	−1.452[c]	−.853[c]	−.802[c]	−1.025[c]	−1.085[c]	−1.156[c]	−2.060[c]
	(.103)	(.482)	(.173)	(.141)	(.368)	(.584)	(.294)	(.566)
E_{BB}	−.260[d]	−.647[c]	−.508[c]	−.442[c]	−.996[c]	−.419[c]	−.358	−0.205
	(.196)	(.144)	(.173)	(.123)	(.162)	(.150)	(.329)	(.430)
E_{WW}	−.652[c]	.371	−.543[c]	−.272	−1.302[c]	−.183	−.304	.448
	(.383)	(.265)	(.277)	(.538)	(.495)	(.182)	(.592)	(.933)
E_{KE}	.048[c]	.029	.083	−.002	.039	−.021	.022	−.010
	(.017)	(.056)	(.066)	(.031)	(.085)	(.018)	(.019)	(.028)
E_{KO}	.003	−.097	.032[c]	.079[c]	.007	.029	.005	−.014
	(.019)	(.084)	(.015)	(.035)	(.034)	(.029)	(.008)	(.019)
E_{KG}	−.013	.008	.045[c]	.134[c]	−.011	−.014	.024[c]	−.012[c]
	(.021)	(.038)	(.022)	(.063)	(.022)	(.028)	(.007)	(.005)
E_{BE}	−.0004	.031	.123[c]	.032	.078[d]	.029[c]	.056[d]	.024
	(.016)	(.031)	(.048)	(.030)	(.046)	(.005)	(.030)	(.022)
E_{BO}	−.026	.073[d]	.025	.010	.050[d]	.001	.019	−.026[d]
	(.020)	(.043)	(.031)	(.028)	(.026)	(.008)	(.014)	(.014)
E_{BG}	.019	.114[c]	.045	.043	−.002	.025[c]	−.005	.007[c]
	(.024)	(.021)	(.033)	(.046)	(.024)	(.008)	(.011)	(.004)
E_{WE}	.016	.080	.215[c]	.033	.220[c]	−.018	−.073	−.045
	(.030)	(.068)	(.097)	(.122)	(.091)	(.016)	(.055)	(.051)
E_{WO}	.056	.097	−.078[d]	−.151	−.057	−.013	−.029	.083[c]
	(.035)	(.089)	(.045)	(.097)	(.086)	(.022)	(.026)	(.032)
E_{WG}	.007	−.030	.001	−.030	.154[c]	−.034	.004	.008
	(.047)	(.073)	(.050)	(.178)	(.071)	(.023)	(.019)	(.009)

[a]Figures in parentheses are asymptotic standard errors.
[b]E_{ij} indicates the elasticity of demand for input i with respect to the price of input j.
[c]Significant at the 5-percent level.
[d]Significant at the 10-percent level.

sponsiveness since a change in the price of an input will affect the price of the aggregate input and thus will affect demand for the aggregate input. Treating the aggregate input as variable, the effect of a change in the price of input j on the quantity of input i is

$$E_{ij}^T = E_{ij} + E_{iZ} \cdot E_{Zj}$$

where E_{ij} is the price elasticity holding the aggregate input, Z, constant, E_{iZ} is the elasticity of demand for input i with respect to the quantity of the aggregate input, and E_{Zj} is the elasticity of demand for the aggregate input with respect to the price of input j.

Since the input aggregator function is assumed to be linear homogeneous, E_{iZ} is equal to one. Also,

$$E_{Zj} = \frac{\partial \ln Z}{\partial \ln V} \cdot \frac{\partial \ln V}{\partial \ln P_j} = E_{ZV} \cdot M_j,$$

where E_{ZV} is the elasticity of demand for the aggregate input with respect to the price of the aggregate input. Therefore

$$E_{ij}^T = E_{ij} + E_{ZV} \cdot M_j.$$

Allowing the aggregate input to vary increases the absolute magnitudes of the (correctly signed) own price elasticities. Since the estimated α_j are equal to the fitted cost shares, M_j, at the means of the data, the estimated effect

Table 6. Tests of hypotheses.

Test statistic for industry:	Separability of Energy		Cobb-Douglas functional form
	Weak separability	Explicit separability	
20	7.38	8.68	46.29[c]
26	23.62[c]	a	63.71[c]
28	11.35	21.81[c]	50.18[c]
32	21.01[c]	a	26.81
33	10.15	36.78[c]	60.88[c]
34	10.22	12.56[c]	37.58[c]
35	23.33[c]	a	44.25[c]
37	20.78[c]	a	56.27[c]
Degrees of freedom	6	3	15
χ^2 Critical value[b]	16.81	11.34	30.58

[a]Explicit separability is tested conditional on the acceptance of weak separability.
[b]Significance level = .01.
[c]The null hypothesis is rejected.

Table 7. Parameter estimates[a]
Four-input model

Parameter	Industry 20	Industry 28	Industry 33	Industry 34
α_K	.258 (.004)	.373 (.013)	.364 (.018)	.207 (.008)
α_B	.414 (.007)	.315 (.007)	.431 (.011)	.532 (.007)
α_W	.293 (.009)	.243 (.013)	.145 (.006)	.240 (.004)
α_F	.034 (.001)	.069 (.014)	.059 (.004)	.021 (.0004)
γ_{KK}	.018 (.026)	−.046 (.063)	−.169 (.132)	−.075 (.112)
γ_{KB}	−.082 (.032)	−.009 (.030)	.141 (.080)	.066 (.082)
γ_{KW}	.065 (.050)	.029 (.060)	.029 (.046)	.018 (.062)
γ_{KF}	−.001 (.007)	.026 (.027)	−.001 (.028)	−.009 (.007)
γ_{BB}	.113 (.076)	.061 (.058)	−.198 (.068)	.033 (.075)
γ_{BW}	−.010 (.097)	−.092 (.056)	.033 (.054)	−.117 (.043)
γ_{BF}	−.021 (.012)	.041 (.017)	.024 (.019)	.017 (.005)
γ_{WW}	−.072 (.139)	.017 (.082)	−.101 (.055)	.115 (.065)
γ_{WF}	.017 (.017)	.046 (.029)	.040 (.014)	−.015 (.007)
γ_{FF}	.005 (.006)	−.113 (.031)	−.063 (.011)	.007 (.004)
Pseudo R^2	.420	.486	.862	.536
Number of Observations	38	22	19	20

[a]Figures in parentheses are asymptotic standard errors.

on the price elasticities at the means is

$$E_{ij}^T - E_{ij} = E_{zv} \cdot \alpha_j.$$

As seen from the estimates of α_j in Table 3, the effect on the estimated own price elasticities of allowing the aggregate input to vary would be greatest for production workers. The estimated own price elasticities for energy inputs would be affected least, with the effect being greater for electricity than for fuel oil or gas.

Inclusion of capital and labor inputs in the systems of equations makes

Table 8. Estimates of price elasticities[a]
Four-input model

	Industry			
Elasticity[b]	20	28	33	34
E_{FF}	−.829[c]	−2.564[c]	−2.004[c]	−.660[c]
	(.165)	(.605)	(.214)	(.171)
E_{KK}	−.674[c]	−.750[c]	−1.099[c]	−1.155[c]
	(.100)	(.171)	(.366)	(.539)
E_{BB}	−.313[c]	−.492[c]	−1.029[c]	−.405[c]
	(.184)	(.184)	(.159)	(.141)
E_{WW}	−.952[c]	−.685[c]	−1.550[c]	−.282
	(.472)	(.336)	(.375)	(.270)
E_{KF}	.031	.139[d]	.057	−.022
	(.027)	(.073)	(.078)	(.034)
E_{BF}	−.016	.199[c]	.115[c]	.054[c]
	(.028)	(.055)	(.044)	(.010)
E_{WF}	.091	.257[c]	.331[c]	−.042
	(.057)	(.118)	(.093)	(.031)
E_{FK}	.237	.752[d]	.351	−.213
	(.204)	(.393)	(.479)	(.338)
E_{FB}	−.201	.907[c]	.841[c]	1.357[c]
	(.348)	(.288)	(.316)	(.252)
E_{FW}	.792	.905[c]	.813[c]	−.484
	(.497)	(.460)	(.239)	(.355)

[a]Figures in parentheses are asymptotic standard errors.
[b]E_{ij} indicates the elasticity of demand for input i with respect to the price of input j.
[c]Significant at the 5-percent level.
[d]Significant at the 10-percent level.

it possible to perform statistical tests of the separability of energy inputs from these inputs. Separability of energy inputs from capital and labor inputs is a necessary but not sufficient condition for separability from all non-energy inputs. Weak separability of the input aggregator function is tested by imposing the restrictions in (7) on the estimated parameters. Explicit separability of the translog cost function is tested conditional on the acceptance of weak separability.

The test statistics for each industry are shown in Table 6. Weak separability of the energy inputs is accepted at the one percent level for industries 20, 28, 33, and 34 and is rejected for industries 26, 32, 35, and 37.[19] Explicit separability conditional on weak separability is accepted at the one percent level for industry 20 only.

The test statistics for the null hypothesis that the Cobb-Douglas functional form is appropriate for the unit cost function are also shown in Table 6.

Substitution among Energy, Capital, and Labor Inputs 71

The restrictions corresponding to the Cobb-Douglas functional form are rejected at the one percent level for all industries except industry 32. Since the Cobb-Douglas form is self-dual, the test results indicate that studies employing Cobb-Douglas production functions for two-digit industries are incorrectly specified.

A four-input model incorporating aggregate energy, F, as an input is estimated for each of the four industries for which weak separability is accepted. Parameter estimates for the four-input model are shown in Table 7. All estimates of α_i, which are equal to the fitted cost shares at the means of the data, are significantly positive.[20] Also, all principal minors have the correct sign. Thus the four-input model appears to satisfy the monotonicity and concavity conditions for all four industries.

Estimates of the own and cross price elasticities of demand at the means of the data are shown in Table 8. All estimates of the own price elasticities have the correct sign and all except the estimate for non-production workers for industry 34 are significant at the five percent level. The range of estimated own price elasticities is $-.66$ to -2.56 for aggregate energy, $-.67$ to -1.16 for capital, $-.31$ to -1.03 for production workers, and $-.28$ to -1.55 for non-production workers.

Ten of the 24 estimated cross price elasticities between energy and the non-energy inputs are significant at the five percent level and an additional

Table 9. Allen cross elasticities of substitution[a]
Four-input model

Elasticity[b]	Industry			
	20	28	33	34
σ_{KF}	.921	2.015[c]	.963	−1.028
	(.790)	(1.041)	(1.311)	(1.630)
σ_{BF}	−.485	2.883[c]	1.950[c]	2.551[c]
	(.841)	(.887)	(.731)	(.475)
σ_{WF}	2.701	3.720[c]	5.590[c]	−2.018
	(1.691)	(1.835)	(1.634)	(1.482)
σ_{KB}	.235	.920[c]	1.898[c]	1.601[c]
	(.300)	(.259)	(.509)	(.747)
σ_{KW}	1.858	1.321[c]	1.540[d]	1.357
	(.654)	(.664)	(.872)	(1.250)
σ_{BW}	.917	−.206	1.525[d]	.082
	(.800)	(.727)	(.862)	(.339)

[a] Figures in parentheses are asymptotic standard errors.
[b] Computed from equation (10) using fitted shares at the means of the data.
[c] Significant at the 5-percent level.
[d] Significant at the 10-percent level.

two are significant at the 10-percent level. Only four of the estimated cross price elasticities are negative, of which none are statistically significant. The results again fail to support previous studies which indicated that capital and energy are complements,[21] since the estimated cross price elasticities between capital and energy are positive for three of the four industries.

Estimates of the Allen partial cross elasticities of substitution for the four-input model are shown in Table 9. The range of the estimated Allen cross elasticities is -1.03 to 2.02 for capital and energy, $-.48$ to 2.88 for production workers and energy, and -2.02 to 5.59 for non-production workers and energy.

The estimated Allen cross elasticities of substitution between the non-energy inputs are also shown in Table 9. Five of the twelve estimated non-energy cross elasticities are significant at the 5-percent level and an additional two are significant at the 10-percent level. Only one of the non-energy cross elasticities is positive, and it is not statistically significant.

V. CONCLUDING COMMENTS

Since the characteristics of energy demand can be expected to vary across industries, we have estimated systems of demand equations for individual two-digit industries. Derivation of the systems of demand equations from translog unit cost functions provides estimates of elasticities of demand and substitution that are subject to only those restrictions that are implied by economic theory. Including non-energy inputs in the analysis provides estimates of the cross elasticities between energy and non-energy inputs and makes it possible to perform statistical tests of energy separability, rather than assuming its existence as done in previous studies.

Almost all of the estimated own price elasticities for energy inputs are statistically significant and indicate considerable price responsiveness of demand. The range of estimated own price elasticities is $-.50$ to -2.55 for electricity, -1.56 to -2.40 for fuel oil, -1.21 to -2.90 for gas, and $-.66$ to -2.56 for aggregate energy. Estimated cross price elasticities are generally insignificant, but the pattern of results indicates that the predominant relationship between energy inputs and between energy and non-energy inputs is that of substitutes rather than complements.

Two points should be noted with respect to the interpretation of the estimated elasticities for analysis of public policies toward energy. First, since cross-section data are used, the estimates presumably reflect the long-run effects of prices on energy demand. Short-run effects can be expected to be considerably smaller. Second, the elasticities do not measure the net effects of price changes on consumption of fuel oil and gas. Because these fuels are inputs in the production of electric energy, the net effects of price changes will include changes in the demand for fuels in electric power generation.[22]

FOOTNOTES

*The authors are Assistant Professor and Doctoral Candidate respectively in the Department of Economics, University of Washington. Financial support for this study was provided by a grant to the NBER from the National Science Foundation RANN Program. This paper is not an official NBER publication since it has not been reviewed by the board of directors.

1. See Fisher and Kaysen (12), Halvorsen (14), and Mount, et al. (20).

2. Berndt and Wood (6) consider the demand for aggregate energy and other inputs by total U.S. manufacturing. Berndt and Jorgenson (5) and Fuss (13) consider the demand for individual types of energy by total U.S. and total Canadian manufacturing respectively. Halvorsen (15) considers the demand for individual types of energy by two-digit industries under the assumption, shared by the other studies noted, that energy inputs are separable from non-energy inputs.

3. Coal is included in "other inputs" rather than considered explicitly because data on coal prices are not available for a sufficient number of observations.

4. See Oberhofer and Kmenta (21).

5. Jorgenson and Lau (17) develop these restrictions in the context of translog utility functions. The test for implicit separability is exact only at the point of approximation. However, the test for explicit separability is invariant to the scaling of the price variables.

6. See Diewert (10).

7. See Berndt (4).

8. See Allen (1, p. 373).

9. Not having the elasticities of demand constrained to be constant is one of the major advantages of the use of a flexible functional form for the unit cost function.

10. See Kmenta (18, pp. 443–444).

11. Data on capital costs were collected as part of the 1963 census but in less detail than in 1958.

12. Thus the price data are equal to average prices. The use of declining block rate schedules for electricity and gas results in a divergence between marginal and average prices for these inputs, but data on marginal prices are not available. See Halvorsen (14, 16) for discussion of the effects of declining block rates on estimated elasticities of demand.

13. The monotonicity test at the means of the data can be interpreted as a local test at the point of expansion, see Jorgenson and Lau (17).

14. A procedure proposed by Lau (19) provides a statistical test of concavity but was not used due to computational difficulties.

15. Thirteen of the 48 estimated cross price elasticities are significant at the 5-percent level and an additional three are significant at the 10-percent level using two-tailed tests.

16. The cross price elasticities should generally be smaller because the sum of the own and cross price elasticities is zero and most of the cross price elasticities are positive.

17. Sixteen of the 72 estimated cross price elasticities are significant at the 5-percent level and an additional six are significant at the 10-percent level using two-tailed tests.

18. See Berndt and Wood (6) and Fuss (13).

19. It should be noted that the industries for which weak separability is rejected are

the same industries for which the performance of the model is questionable with respect to satisfaction of the concavity condition.

20. All other fitted shares are also positive.

21. See Berndt and Wood (6) and Fuss (13).

22. Estimates of the elasticities of demand for fuel oil and gas in electric power generation are reported in Atkinson and Halvorsen (3).

REFERENCES

1. Allen, R. G. D., *Mathematical Analysis for Economists*. St. Martin's Press, New York, 1966.
2. Anderson, Kent P., "Toward Econometric Estimation of Industrial Energy Demand: An Experimental Application to the Primary Metals Industry." Report R-719-NSF, The Rand Corporation, December 1971.
3. Atkinson, Scott E., and Robert Halvorsen, "Interfuel Substitution in Steam Electric Power Generation." *Journal of Political Economy* 84, No. 5 (October 1976), 959–978.
4. Berndt, Ernst R., "Notes on Generalized R^2." University of British Columbia Research Memorandum, 1977
5. ———, and Dale W. Jorgenson, "Production Structure," Chapter 3 in D. W. Jorgenson, E. R. Berndt, L. R. Christensen, and E. A. Hudson, *U.S. Energy Resources and Economic Growth*, Final Report to the Energy Policy Project, Washington, D. C., September 1973.
6. ———, and David O. Wood, "Technology, Prices and the Derived Demand for Energy." *Review of Economics and Statistics* LVII, No. 3 (August 1975), 259–268.
7. Christensen, Laurits R., and Dale W. Jorgenson, "The Measurement of U.S. Real Capital Input, 1929–1967." *The Review of Income and Wealth* 15, No. 4 (December 1969), 293–320.
8. ———, ———, and Lawrence J. Lau, "Conjugate Duality and the Transcendental Logarithmic Production Function." *Econometrica* 39, No. 4 (July 1971), 255–256.
9. ———, ———, and ———, "Transcendental Logarithmic Production Frontiers." *Review of Economics and Statistics* LV, No. 1 (February 1973), 28–45.
10. Diewert, W. E., "Exact and Superlative Index Numbers." *Journal of Econometrics* 4, No. 2 (May 1976), 115–145.
11. ———, "Separability and a Generalization of the Cobb-Douglas Cost, Production and Indirect Utility Functions." Paper 13, Projection Studies Section, Department of Manpower and Immigration, Canada, January 1973.
12. Fisher, Franklin M., and Carl Kaysen, *A Study in Econometrics: The Demand For Electricity in the United States*. North-Holland Publishing Company, Amsterdam, 1962.
13. Fuss, Melvyn A., "The Demand for Energy in Canadian Manufacturing: An Example of the Estimation of Production Structures with Many Inputs." *Journal of Econometrics* 5, No. 1 (January 1977), 89–116.
14. Halvorsen, Robert, "Demand for Electric Energy in the United States." *Southern Economic Journal* 42, No. 4 (April 1976), 610–625.
15. ———, *Econometric Models of U.S. Energy Demand*. Lexington Books, Lexington, Mass., 1978.
16. ———, "Residential Demand for Electric Energy." *Review of Economics and Statistics* LVII, No. 1 (February 1975), 12–18.
17. Jorgenson, Dale W., and Lawrence J. Lau, "The Structure of Consumer Preferences." *Annals of Economic and Social Measurement* 4, No. 1 (January 1975), 49–101.

18. Kmenta, Jan, *Elements of Econometrics*. The Macmillan Company, New York, 1971.
19. Lau, Lawrence J., "Econometrics of Monotonicity, Convexity, and Quasi-Convexity." Technical Report # 123, Institute for Mathematical Studies in the Social Sciences, Stanford University, 1974.
20. Mount, T. D., L. D. Chapman, and T. J. Tyrell, "Electricity Demand in the United States: An Econometric Analysis." Report ORNL-NSF-EP-4P, Oak Ridge National Laboratory, June 1973.
21. Oberhofer, W., and J. Kmenta, "A General Procedure for Obtaining Maximum Likelihood Estimates in Generalized Regression Models." *Econometrica* 42, No. 3 (May 1974), 579–590.
22. Zellner, Arnold, "An Efficient Method of Estimating Seemingly Unrelated Regressions and Tests for Aggregation Bias." *Journal of the American Statistical Association* 57, No. 298 (June 1962), 348–368.

THE STANFORD PILOT ENERGY/ECONOMIC MODEL

T. J. Connolly, STANFORD UNIVERSITY

G. B. Dantzig, STANFORD UNIVERSITY

S. C. Parikh, STANFORD UNIVERSITY

1. INTRODUCTION

PILOT is a target model. It does not predict what the path into the future will be but, rather, suggests what it could be. It assumes that the purpose of the economy is to provide a high standard of living for the people. Thus, what PILOT does is to provide a trajectory which, if followed, would maximize the standard of living over a given time span. This maximum is the target or goal.

Our model is only a first step. In general, a target model to be fully useful requires, in addition, a comparison between actions in progress and those targeted. The differences between them plus incentives considered necessary to close the gap permit identification and development of policy changes.

PILOT is a U.S. national energy/economic model designed to measure the impact on the standard of living of various policy decisions, such as the scheduling of various energy technologies to be built and used, pollution abatement equipment to be installed, the nature and the extent of conversion to equipment types that use energy more efficiently, the required expansion of the general economy and foreign trade to supply an increasing population with a high standard of living, etc. (7). PILOT reflects certain assumptions or scenarios regarding changes in life-styles, embargoes, feasibility of proposed new technologies, restrictions on use of certain technologies, and availability of raw reserves. The growth of population, the available workforce, and labor productivity are key assumptions that provide a setting for the growth of the standard of living. Another important class of assumptions relates to the amounts of raw energy resources available at various levels of extraction effort, or available through imports which, in turn, depend on import limits, prices, and the availability of export markets for U.S. goods.

Main Linkages

The main linkages in PILOT are displayed in Figure 1. The energy supply sector is modeled in great detail. It is linked to raw energy sources, on the one hand, and to the rest of the economy, including the final consumer, on the other. The economy is linked to the rest of the world through imports and exports, which are limited by available markets and balance-of-trade relations. The economy is modeled in a less detailed way. It consists of various industrial sectors, capacity formation, and government. The payoff is the bill-of-goods vector that the economy supplies the population. The popula-

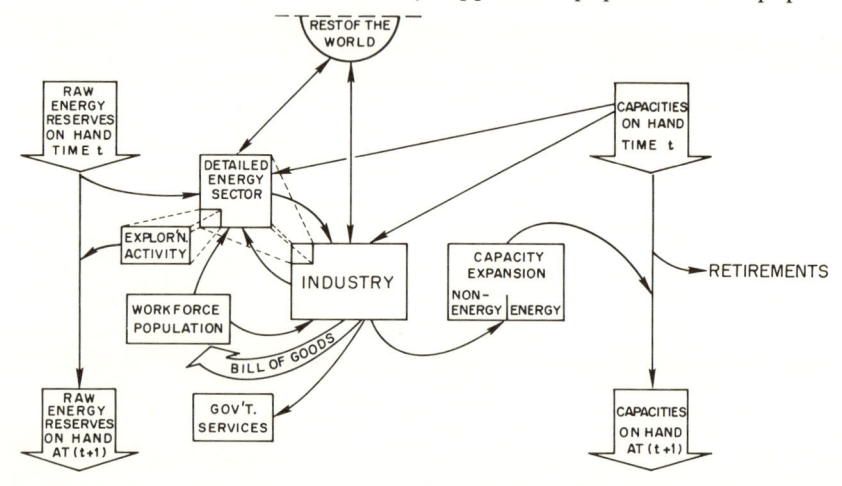

Figure 1. Main linkages of the PILOT model.

tion, in turn, supplies man-hours to the economy. There are four main linkages between the economy and the detailed energy sector:

First, there are the energy demands of the economy upon the energy sector for industrial processing, for consumers, for exports, and for governmental needs. These are supplied in five final energy forms: coal, crude oil, oil products, gas products, and electricity.

Second, there are the energy sector demands upon the economy for capital and material resources, such as crude-oil pipelines, railroad shipments of coal, etc. (provided by the transportation sector of the economy); machinery and construction for capacity expansion (provided by the capital formation sectors of the economy). The latter must compete with capacity formation of the other industrial sectors for expansion or replacement.

Third, the energy sector and the economy use the same workforce pool to obtain the manpower needed for operation, maintenance, and capacity expansion.

Finally, the trade balance constraint, by matching total exports to total imports, links the energy sector and the economy with the rest of the world. Thus, in the model, if the crude oil import price or quantity or both go up, the economy must export more of something else to bring in the foreign exchange needed to pay for the imports.

PILOT is a dynamic model and the linkages through time are shown on the left and on the right side of the diagram (Figure 1)—namely, the carrying forward from one time period to the next of remaining raw energy reserves and of capacity of various facilities in the energy sector and in the economy. Another link between periods is that caused by the time it takes to build new facilities.

Physical Flow Model

PILOT is a physical flow model except for the foreign trade constraint. Insofar as possible, we endeavor to express material balances of various input and output items into the various processes in physical units, for example, BTU's of coal or oil, etc. The several sectors of the general economy each produces a characteristic item. For example, the sector—Textiles, Leather, Clothing, and Shoes—produces a composite item, abbreviated TEX, which is made up of a large variety of textile-related products. It is, of course, impossible to treat this composite except in some aggregated way. This is done by applying weights to the vector of various quantities produced and summing. It is assumed that this industry in the future can produce the same aggregated output using the same aggregated inputs from other industries and the same aggregated facilities. This suggests that the vector of products aggregated into TEX either occurs in the same proportions in the future or that substitutions can occur among them as long as they preserve their aggregated total. The weights most convenient to use are the prices of the products in the base year 1967. Thus, the unit of TEX is the quantity of that composite item (vector of outputs) that could be purchased for $1 in 1967.

Utility Function, Linear Consumption Vector

The standard of living also is expressed in physical terms. The bill-of-goods vector is what the population receives. On a per capita basis, the sum of components of this vector represents the take home or consumption income measured in 1967 dollars. As the consumption income of an individual rises, his consumption vector undergoes changes. For example, people of higher income allocate a higher percentage share of their income to service-type items. What the PILOT model requires is not the consumption vector of a typical individual at a given consumption income level but, rather, the average consumption vector formed by weighting the various vectors by the percentage distribution of people at various consumption income levels. In the future the average consumption income will increase—implying, therefore, that the distribution will shift toward higher income levels. We assume in PILOT that the distribution in the future will be the same as it is currently except translated to the right. This assumption means that lower-income people would get a greater percentage increase in income. It turns out empirically, under fixed base year prices, that the resulting average consumption vector is approximately linear, i.e., consumption of each item can be assumed to be a linear function of consumption income (2). Since future prices as well as average income are expected to vary, we have under test a hierarchical utility function that permits substitutions among components of the consumption vector for a given level of utility (16).

There are many possible choices for the utility function that can be used as a maximand. Up to now we have been using as our maximand a standard-of-living measure, the consumption income, in 1967 dollars, summed for each year from the start of the plan, say 1975, to the end of the planning horizon, say 2010 or 2075. The model permits one to specify any discount factor in forming the sum. In many of our studies we have used a discount factor of unity.[1] In addition, we assume that consumption income in any time period is not less than that of the previous time period.

Time Horizon, End Conditions

The time horizon of our model has been 40 years in five-year periods centered at 1975, 1980, 1985, 1990, 1995, 2000, 2005, 2010. In addition to initial conditions, it also is necessary to provide end conditions at 2010 that reflect post-2010 needs. We do this by means of a variant of the PILOT model (called the "variable time period" model) which allows us to aggregate several time periods into one. For the same computational effort, we solve such a model up to 2075 and extract from the solution the facilities and stocks on hand at end of 2010 and pass these data off-line to the regular PILOT model (17, Appendix H).

2. THE GENERAL ECONOMY

The I/O Tableau

The source of our economic data of industrial processes is the 87 Sector Leontief Input/Output Table, published by the Bureau of Economic Analysis for the year 1967 (19). Because of our limited human and computational resources, we have had to aggregate this down to 23 sectors for regular runs and down to 12 sectors for Sigma Mode runs. These industrial aggregations are displayed in Table 1.

Capital Formation

The dynamic linear programming model formulation allows the modeled economy to endogenously select the allocation of the industrial output to two types of activities: consumption in the current period that provides the country's standard of living, and capital formation in the current period that will provide the future production capacity by replacement of old equipment and structures as well as building of new additional equipment and structures. The capital formation activities, of course, provide the economy with a vehicle for achieving a better standard of living in future years (5).

The PILOT model distinguishes and keeps separate account of the capacities of the 18 non-energy sectors (7 in Sigma Mode). In any given period, the model allows the building of additional capacity for any sector, provided, of course, the industrial output is available for such addition.

In order to keep the initial version of the model relatively simple, the input profile to produce $1 increase in capacity per year for each individual sector is assumed to be the same as the input profile averaged over all sectors. The profile used is the distribution of the total capital formation inputs in the 1967 Input/Output Data Base of the Bureau of Economic Analysis (19). A provision has been made for later inclusion of a detailed capital matrix by sector of destination, developed by Battelle Institute, 1971 (5), which will allow a more realistic description of the capital equipment and structures. Hence at some later stage of development it will be possible either to incorporate such detail directly into the model or to use such data indirectly to check and correct the assumed profiles and then rerun the model.

Table 1. Sectoral aggregations of PILOT.

Sigma Mode (12 sectors)			Standard Mode (23 sectors)		Bea Sectors (87 indstrl. sectors)
Line count	Sector code	Sectors	Sector code	Line count	Industry number
Macroenergy Sectors					
1	COL	Coal	COL	1	7
2	CRO	Crude oil and crude natural gas	CRO	2	8
3	ROP	Refined oil products	ROP	3	31
4	GAS	Gas	GAS	4	68.02
5	ELE	Electricity	ELE	5	68.01, 78.02, 79.02
Macro Nonenergy Sectors					
6	AGR	Agriculture	AGR	6	1–4
7	MNG	Mining and construction			
		Mining	MNG	7	5,6,9,10
		Construction	CON	8	11,12,55
8	EIM	Energy intensive manufacturing			
		Chemicals and plastics	CMP	9	27–30,32
		Foodstuffs	FDS	10	14,15
		Paper products	PPP	11	24,25
		Stone, clay, and glass	SCG	12	35,36
		Primary metals	MET	13	37,38
9	ENM	Energy nonintensive manufacturing			
		Textiles, leather, clothing and Shoes	TEX	14	16–19,33,34
		Lumber	LUM	15	20
		Furniture and appliances	FAP	16	21–23,54
		Miscellaneous manufacturing	MFG	17	13,26,39–42,56, 57, 62–64
10	TAW	Transportation and warehousing	TAW	18	65
11	TRD	Trade and other services			
		Wholesale and retail trade	TRD	19	69
		Finance and real estate	FIN	20	70,71
		Miscellaneous services	SVS	21	66,67,68.03,72, 73,75–79 (except 78.02,79.02),81–87
12	MAC	Machinery and transportation equipment			
		Transportation equipment	TRE	22	59–61
		Machinery	MAC	23	43–53,58

Construction Lags

For the non-energy sectors, a construction lag of two years is assumed. This means that 20 percent of the total capacity addition initiated in any five-year period is completed and becomes available for production in the' same five-year period and the remaining 80 percent in the next five-year period. The construction lags (after the planning and approval stage) for energy facilities typically are three years except for nuclear. For the latter, we use a seven-year lag.

Discard Factors

Discard (depreciation) factors used for the general economy are 4.5 percent, which is slightly lower than that suggested in the 1976 Report of the President (8). For the energy facilities we have adopted a convention used in Brookhaven studies (6), namely, no depreciation for 30 years, followed by a 100 percent discard.

Imports/Exports

PILOT assumes that the United States has a favorable balance of trade over each five-year period. Its import/export activities permit the economy to trade with the rest of the world and to adjust the mix of domestic output to a more desirable one. For example, imports of crude oil and exports of agricultural products allow the United States to trade its excess output from the agriculture sector in order to reduce its shortages in the energy sector.

Preliminary runs indicate that the solution is sensitive to what is assumed about import/export markets available to the United States. Our import/export functions are based on studies by Clopper Almon and his students at the University of Maryland (1, 14). Noncompetitive imports are assumed to be proportional to the domestic output of the respective industry. All imports by the final demand sectors, personal consumption, capital formation, and government services, are treated as noncompetitive. On the other hand, non-energy competitive imports are allowed in the base case to be chosen freely within broad limits. In certain scenarios total energy imports have been limited to a fraction of total domestic energy consumption.

The non-energy exports in the model are assumed to be in accordance with the decreasing returns to scale, i.e., the higher the amount of exports, the lower the average price received per unit. Finally, the growth of the world markets available for U.S. exports, if we choose to use them, is assumed to follow an exogenously given growth profile. In the base case of the model, a 4 percent per year growth of this potential market is assumed. Imports and exports of energy are accounted for in BTU terms. They are bought or sold at prices assumed by the scenario.

Government

The government expenditures, including state and local, are provided for in the model by assuming that the vector of future government consumption is in fixed proportions to what it is currently. In the base case of the model, the total level of government expenditures is assumed to be 34 percent of the total personal consumption expenditures.

Population

The population is assumed to grow in accordance with Series II of the Bureau of the Census (20). The workforce assumption is based on the estimates for 1975-1990 by the Bureau of Labor Statistics (18) and what we believe to be reasonable extrapolations for the period beyond.

Technological Change

Turning now to technological change, new technologies, such as coal synthetics, nuclear reactors, solar energy, etc., are all included in the model. The actual choice of the mix and the intensity of the processes are determined by the model consistent with available resources and facilities.

An important measure of technological change is the growth in labor productivity. An explicit provision is made in the model that allows exogenous specification of the productivity growth profile (which need not follow a constant percentage growth through time). In the base case scenario, we have assumed a constant rate of growth in labor productivity of 2 percent per year.

By specifying the technology available in the energy sector and by specifying the labor productivity in the general economy, we believe that a significant portion of the technological change is captured in the model. What is left out, of course, is the effect of new processes in all sectors that are not known today but will affect the capital, labor, and material inputs for the future production, and the effect of non-energy sector processes, some of which are known today, that will bring about changes in the capital, labor, and material input ratios in the future.

Pollution Abatement

The model includes exogenously given pollution abatement requirements related to level of industrial expansion. Our assumptions concerning these are based on ten-year projections developed by the Environmental Protection Agency (EPA) using the SEAS (Strategic Environmental Assessment System) Model, 1975 (9). Using its reference scenario 1, the capital, operating, and maintenance expenditures for abatement equipment are approximately $200 billion (1975 dollars) over the ten-year period 1975-1985.

The base case of our model assumes the environmental related expenditures to be of the same order of magnitude and spread across the 12 sectors in accordance with the 1967 profile for gross private fixed capital formation as recorded in the input/output transactions table. Beyond 1985, a level of expenditures of $22.5 billion (1975 dollars) annually is assumed.

3. ENERGY CONVERSION

The detailed energy sector includes technological description of the raw material extraction and energy conversion processes. Technical coefficients are defined for

- exploration and production of oil and gas,
- extraction of natural uranium, and
- 18 other energy technologies. (See Figure 2.)

Fossil Fuels

The fossil fuel portion of the model includes various technical options with respect to oil, gas, coal, and oil shale. Exploration drilling for either oil or gas results in additions to the proven reserves of these raw energy forms. The level of drilling effort is endogenously determined, and the resulting oil-in-place and gas reserves are determined in accordance with the

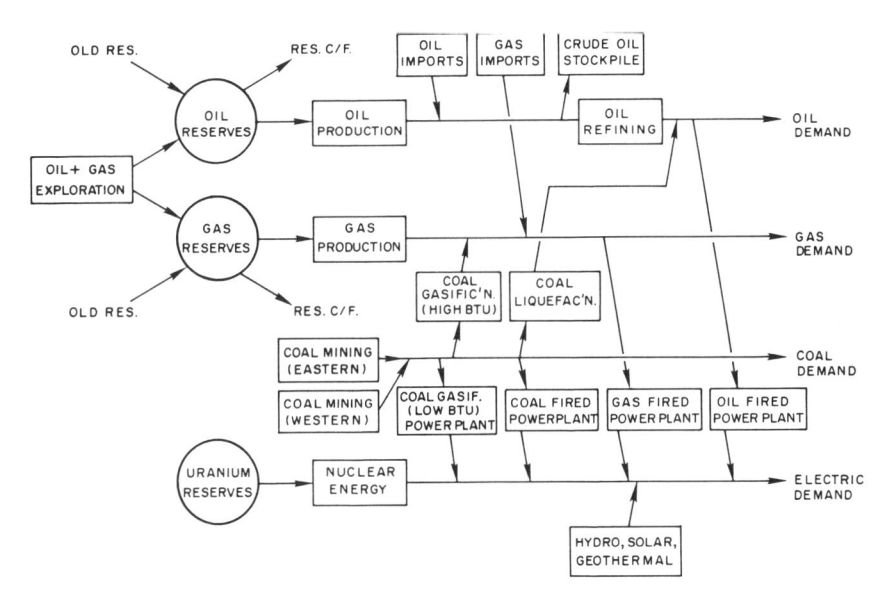

Figure 2. The energy sector of PILOT.

exogenously given finding rate functions. Expensive secondary and tertiary developments are options that can be undertaken to add to proven oil reserves. An oil shale mining, retorting, and upgrading activity also is defined in the model to provide shale oil to complement the crude oil production. Oil and gas production, and coal mining activities provide the raw fossil fuels which are next processed into final energy forms. Oil refining, coal gasification, coal liquefaction, and electric power generation processes are defined in the model for this purpose.

Coal

Steps are under way to correct limitations of the present version of the PILOT model with regard to the mining and shipping of coal—in particular, reclamation activities related to strip mining of coal and pollution control gear, such as sulfur scrubbers, needed for burning high sulfur coal in power plants. We are in the process of investigating various alternative ways of formulating the regional and environmental economics of coal extraction and usage. For now, we limit the Western coal-mine construction to some exogenous limits in the base case and have placed upper limits on the total coal production in any time period, which we dub "the environmental limit on coal production."

Exhaustible Oil and Gas Resources

The domestic oil and gas resources have reached a point where it takes progressively greater and greater amounts of physical effort to find a given amount of additional reserves (10, 12).

Primary Oil Recovery, Finding Rate Functions. In the model the cumulative supply of oil and gas as functions of cumulative amount of effort to extract them, called the "finding rate" functions, are employed. Using these functions, the model endogenously determines, consistent with optimal allocation of resources in the economy, the amount of drilling that should be undertaken in each period to find new reserves. The finding rate functions are consistent with the estimates in the *National Energy Outlook*, 1976 (10), and the U.S. Geological Survey Circular 725 of the U.S. Department of Interior (12). There is, of course, a great deal of doubt regarding the accuracy of these estimates. The approach of the model is flexible in that it allows one who is interested to assess the effect of this uncertainty by assuming different finding rate functions and measuring how sensitive the key economic indicators are to their differences.

Secondary and Tertiary Oil Recovery. As new reserves become progressively more difficult to find, it also becomes attractive to develop additional reserves from the existing unproven reserve base by secondary and tertiary recovery techniques. In any period, the model determines total unproven reserves that are available for development by advanced recovery techniques and within these limits the extent of development undertaken depends on other options and their costs—not only with respect to oil and gas but also coal synthetics, etc., taking into account the short- and long-term interactions with the economy and the rest of the energy sector. The numerical estimates were derived with the aid of data developed by the National Petroleum Council, Federal Energy Administration (FEA) for the Business-as-Usual (BAU) Scenario, and by the Bechtel Corporation.

Electric Power Generation

For electric power generation, the model includes the following activities: LWR (enriched uranium operation), LWR (plutonium operation), LMFBR, coal-fired power plant, gas-fired power plant, oil-fired power plant, low BTU gas-fired power plant (coupled to a low BTU coal-gasification process), hydroelectric power plant (coupled to pumped storage facilities), geothermal power plant, and solar power plant.

Nuclear Fuel Cycle, Uranium Resources

The nuclear portion of the model includes the following processes for the nuclear fuel cycle: the mining and milling of natural uranium, enrichment of natural uranium by gaseous diffusion, fabrication into the fuel elements, electricity generation using light water reactors (LWR). The spent fuel may be stored, or reprocessed to recover plutonium and uranium for recycling, i.e., the recycled uranium may be converted and enriched for use in the light water reactors; also, plutonium can be used together with natural uranium as a fuel for light water reactors dedicated to this mixed oxide operation. Finally, a fast breeder reactor also is defined in the model in which plutonium and tailings from the enrichment unit can be fabricated into the cores for its operation. See Figure 3.

Exhaustible Uranium Resources. Limited reserves of uranium are known to be recoverable with relatively low physical effort. For example, 200 thousand tons of proven uranium reserves (U_3O_8) are identified to be recoverable at a cost of up to $10 per pound (1975 dollars). See BNL Sourcebook, 1975, p. 37 (6). Undiscovered potential reserves at various levels of uncertainty (probable, possible, and speculative) would add another 530 thousand short tons for a total of 730 thousand short tons. In BTU equivalent terms, these reserves amount to approximately 60 quadrillion BTU of proven and 220 quadrillion BTU of total (proven + potential) reserves. The latter amount in light water reactors could produce only enough BTU's

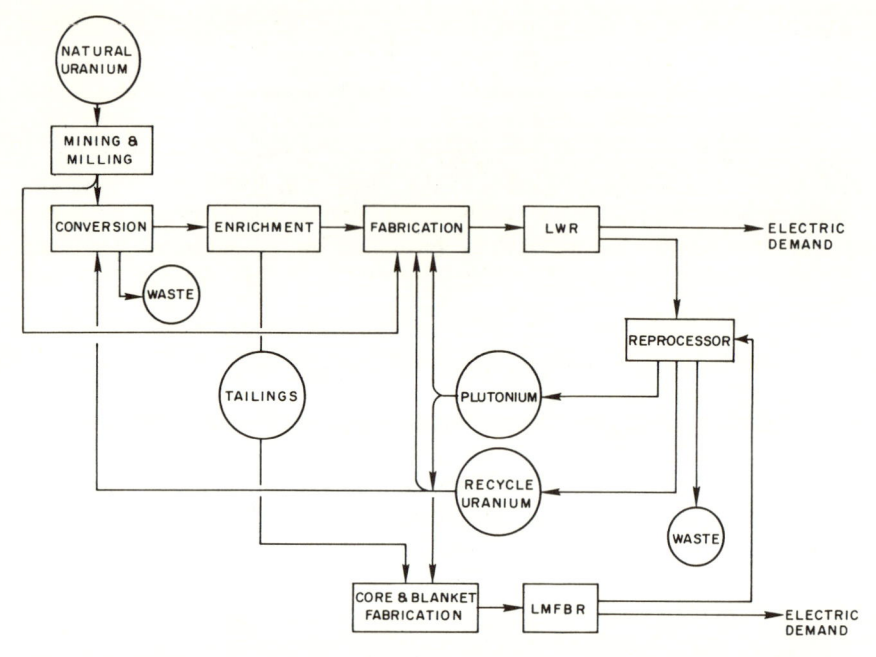

Figure 3. LWR and FBR technology in the energy sector of PILOT.

to cover U.S. total energy demand for approximately three years (assuming the total consumption in any one year is the same as in 1975).

Options within the nuclear sector. There are two methods to augment these extremely limited inexpensive uranium reserves:

- augment natural uranium reserves through greater physical effort and higher production costs, and
- reprocess spent fuel from reactors to recover recycle uranium and plutonium

Plutonium obtained from reprocessed fuels can be used in fast breeder reactors as well as in place of enriched uranium in light water reactors. These, then, are the alternatives available in the model: reprocessing, enrichment of recycled uranium, enriched uranium fueled light water reactors, plutonium fueled light water reactors, fast breeder reactors, and the mining of uranium ore that requires greater and greater effort as more uranium resources are extracted.

4. MATHEMATICAL STRUCTURE

Solution Method

The PILOT model consists of a number of mass balance constraints in the form of linear equations and linear inequalities. The variables are unknown levels of various processes which are constrained to be nonnegative since these activities cannot operate at negative levels. Certain of the relations are nonlinear, such as the finding rate functions for oil or export revenues as a function of the amount physically exported. These we have approximated by broken-line fits. The net result is a mathematical system called a linear program which can be solved using the simplex method.

The matrix structure for the linear program for eight periods takes the form of Figure 4. The coefficients outside the "staircase" blocks are zero (with the exception of a few coefficients). The staircase blocks themselves have an internal structure which is displayed in Figure 5.

The full eight-period 40-year model with 23 industrial sectors has roughly 800 equations and 2,000 variables. We use the Stanford Linear Accelerator Computer System, which consists of a system of three IBM 370 series computers. The Wylbur Text Editing System is used to input and modify data. The relations defining the linear program are inputted using the MAGEN matrix generator developed by Haverly. The optimal solution is obtained using the MPS3 software system developed by Management Sciences and the MINOS software system developed at Stanford's Systems

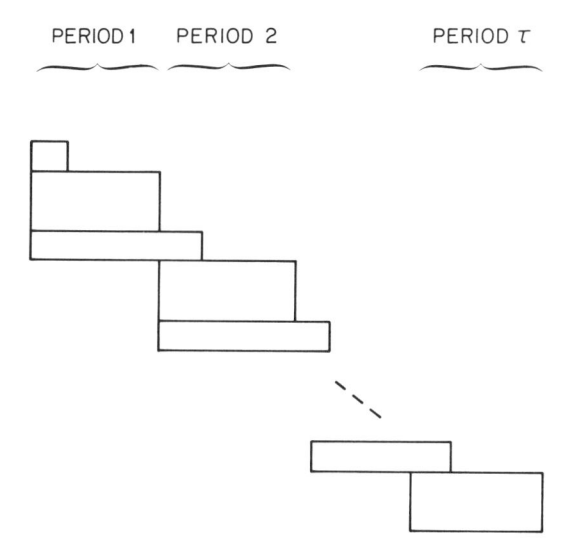

Figure 4. The dynamic staircase structure of PILOT

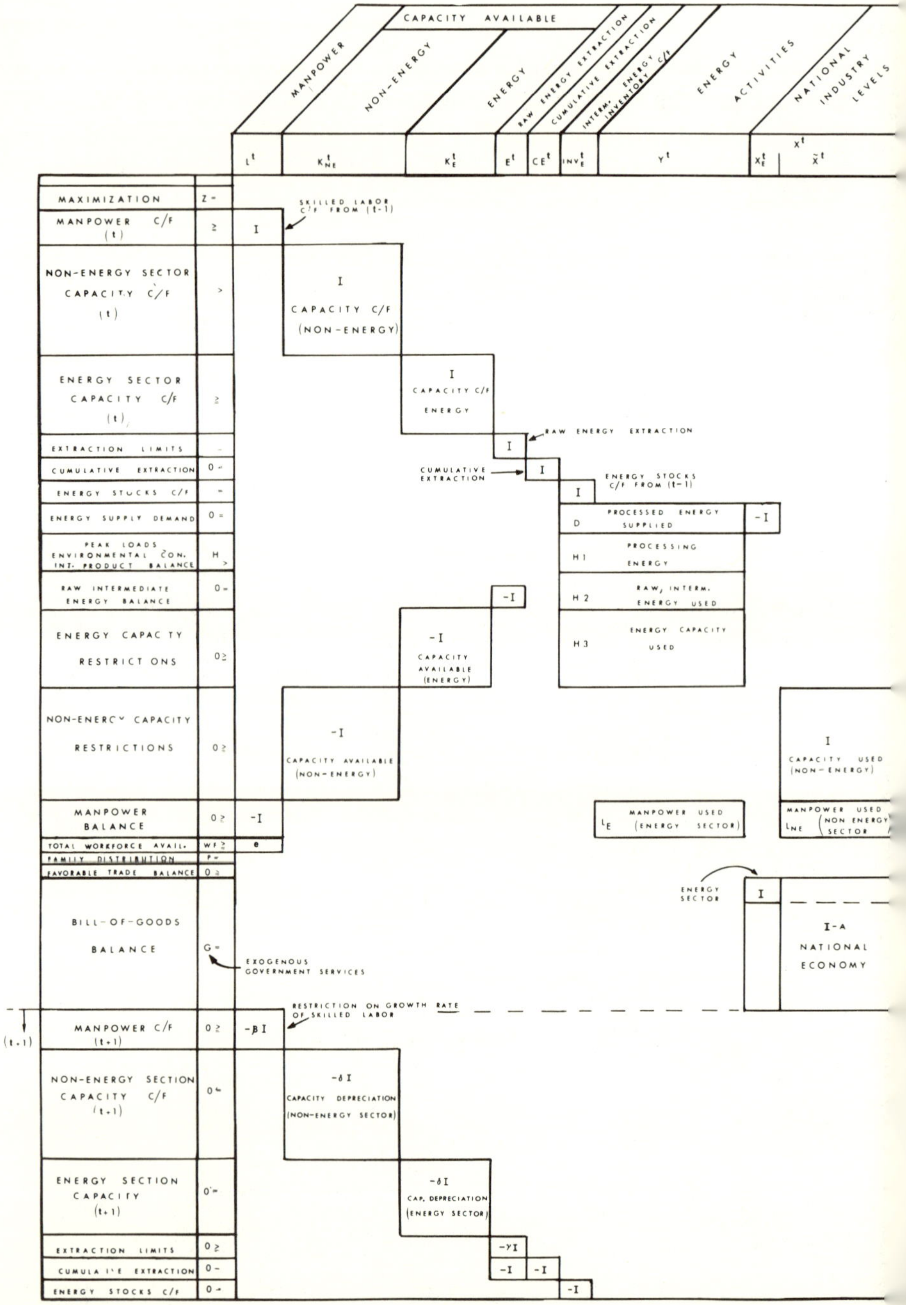
CAPACITY AVAILABLE
MANPOWER
NON-ENERGY
ENERGY
RAW ENERGY EXTRACTION
CUMULATIVE EXTRACTION
INTERM. ENERGY INVENTORY C/F
ENERGY ACTIVITIES
NATIONAL INDUSTRY LEVELS
L^t
K^t_{NE}
K^t_E
E^t
CE^t
INV^t_E
Y^t
X^t
X^t_E
$\tilde{X}^t$
MAXIMIZATION
Z =
MANPOWER C/F (t)
NON-ENERGY SECTOR CAPACITY C/F (t)
ENERGY SECTOR CAPACITY C/F (t)
EXTRACTION LIMITS
CUMULATIVE EXTRACTION
ENERGY STOCKS C/F
ENERGY SUPPLY DEMAND
PEAK LOADS ENVIRONMENTAL CON. INT. PRODUCT BALANCE
RAW INTERMEDIATE ENERGY BALANCE
ENERGY CAPACITY RESTRICTIONS
NON-ENERGY CAPACITY RESTRICTIONS
MANPOWER BALANCE
TOTAL WORKFORCE AVAIL.
FAMILY DISTRIBUTION
FAVORABLE TRADE BALANCE
BILL-OF-GOODS BALANCE
MANPOWER C/F (t+1)
NON-ENERGY SECTION CAPACITY C/F (t+1)
ENERGY SECTION CAPACITY (t+1)
EXTRACTION LIMITS
CUMULATIVE EXTRACTION
ENERGY STOCKS C/F
(t+1)
SKILLED LABOR C/F FROM (t-1)
I
CAPACITY C/F (NON-ENERGY)
CAPACITY C/F ENERGY
RAW ENERGY EXTRACTION
CUMULATIVE EXTRACTION
ENERGY STOCKS C/F FROM (t-1)
D
PROCESSED ENERGY SUPPLIED
-I
H1
PROCESSING ENERGY
H2
RAW, INTERM. ENERGY USED
H3
ENERGY CAPACITY USED
-I
CAPACITY AVAILABLE (ENERGY)
CAPACITY AVAILABLE (NON-ENERGY)
CAPACITY USED (NON-ENERGY)
L_E MANPOWER USED (ENERGY SECTOR)
L_{NE} MANPOWER USED (NON ENERGY SECTOR)
e
WF ≥
P =
0 ≥
G =
EXOGENOUS GOVERNMENT SERVICES
ENERGY SECTOR
I-A NATIONAL ECONOMY
RESTRICTION ON GROWTH RATE OF SKILLED LABOR
-βI
-δI
CAPACITY DEPRECIATION (NON-ENERGY SECTOR)
CAP. DEPRECIATION (ENERGY SECTOR)
-γI

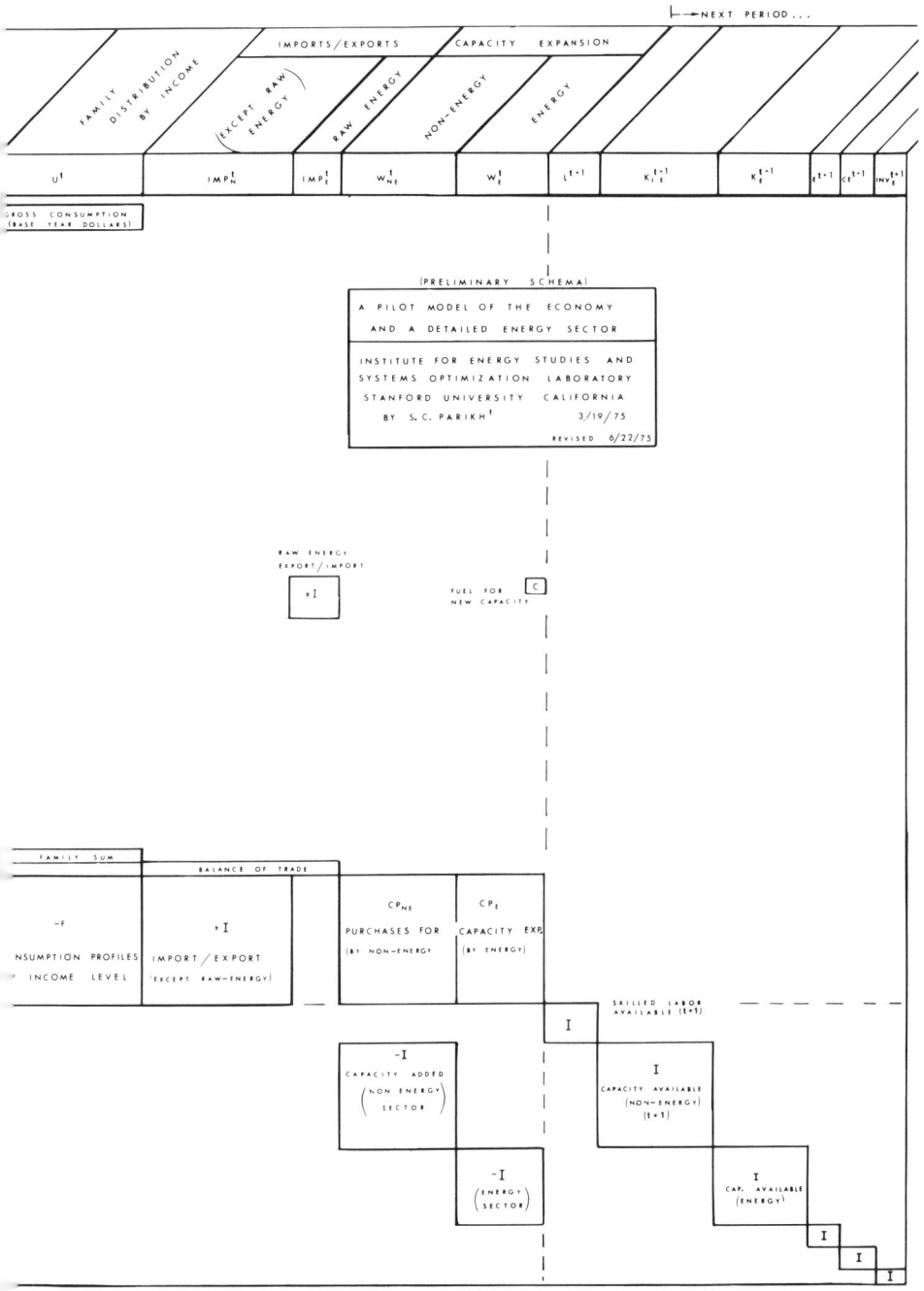

Figure 5. Matrix structure of two successive periods of PILOT.

Optimization Laboratory by Michael Saunders (13). A detailed specification of the relations of the model can be found in (15).

5. THE NATURE OF THE ENERGY CRISIS

Independent of any model, under reasonable assumptions on population, labor force, and labor productivity growth, and continuation of historical energy growth patterns, one easily can calculate that the country will need approximately 6Q ($1Q = 10^{18}$ BTU) units[2] of primary energy over the transition period of the next 40 years for which a major contribution from an ultimate energy source, such as solar or fusion, is not expected. Further, assuming the recoverable oil and gas resources of approximately 2Q units[3], the country will need an additional 4Q units of primary energy.

This situation contrasts from the one for the sixties where approximately two-thirds of the primary energy demand was met by oil and gas (Figure 6). The energy needs in the transition period can be met either by the *supply side options,* such as coal, oil shale, nuclear, and imported energy in addition to contributions from hydroelectric energy, geothermal energy, etc., or by *demand side options,* such as efficiency improvements through redesign and retrofit measures reducing conversion and heat losses, substitutions away from energy, as well as demand reductions through adjustment in life-styles. In addition to demonstrating the nature of the output information from the PILOT model, the preliminary experiments reported in (15) and additional

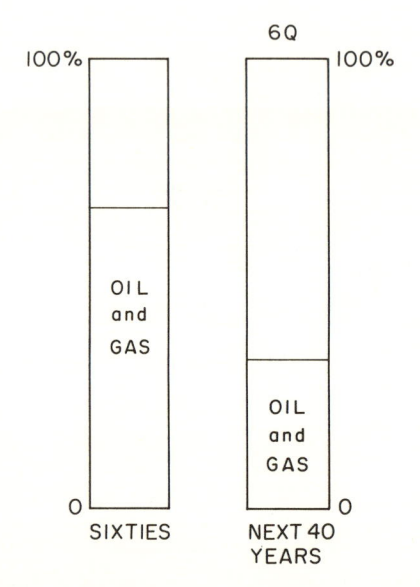

Figure 6. The transition problem of energy needs in the U.S.

experiments reported here are intended to provide scenarios that would help toward some quantification and understanding of answers to the following questions: Given limited availability of oil and gas resources, to what extent does the country's economic growth over the next 35–40 years depend upon new energy technologies? Also, what is the effect of this country's following a policy of independence from foreign energy sources?

6. THREE ILLUSTRATIVE SCENARIOS[4]

Key Assumptions

The following are the key assumptions in PILOT about the future.

- *Consumption patterns* at any given income level in a future period *will be the same* as they are now at the same income level. Conservation, if successful, would represent a change in consumption patterns. This option, available in PILOT, is not part of the three scenarios presented.[5]
- *The price of imported energy will increase by 2 percent per year* in constant dollars. At this rate, the price will double in 36 years.
- *Advances in electrical energy technology* which are in an early stage of development, such as fusion, *are not included* in the scenarios presented.
- Availability of nonconventional *alternative energy systems* (AES) for nonelectric purposes is permitted after 1990. This is a catchall for unspecified new technologies. It is assumed that no more than 10 quads of energy per year, at an average cost of $6 per million BTU, can be developed by 2010 from these sources.
- *Oil shale will be available* after 1995 at a maximum level of 6 quads per year in 2010.
- The *fast breeder reactor* (*FBR*) *will be available* for commercial use by 2000. Its use, however, is excluded in one of the scenarios presented.
- Assumptions about fossil fuel and uranium reserves, population growth, productivity, environmental needs, and government spending are included in PILOT.

Policy Constraints

In addition, several constraints are imposed in all three scenarios. These constraints reflect assumptions about the acceptability of certain policy implications:

- *Imports cannot exceed exports.* The U.S. must have a favorable balance of trade over each five-year period.

- *An upward mobility constraint* prevents a decrease in the standard of living from one five-year period to the next.
- *Nuclear electricity cannot exceed one-half of the total electrical production.*

The base case imposes certain additional policy constraints on imports and coal. These restrictions are removed for the high-energy resource availability scenario. For the low-energy resource availability case, even tighter policy restrictions are placed on coal, nuclear, and imported energy availability than in the base case:

Coal

Base Case — Overall limits are specified on coal development. These limits are not too restrictive, however.
High Case — No limits.
Low Case — Overall limits are set at a lower level than in the base case.

Imports

Base Case — Energy imports cannot exceed 20 percent of total energy consumption, to keep dependence on foreign sources moderate.
High Case — No restrictions.[6]
Low Case — An additional constraint is imposed: energy imports cannot exceed 20 quads per year.

Nuclear Energy

Base Case — Nuclear cannot exceed 50 percent of total electricity.
High Case — Same limit.
Low Case — No *new* nuclear plants can be built.

The low availability case reflects restrictions on the use of nuclear energy (owing, let us say, to fears about plutonium theft or nuclear accident), restrictions on the expansion of coal mining (owing, let us say, to fears about the effect on the environment), and restrictions on foreign energy imports (in order, let us say, to maintain our political independence). The high availability case, by way of contrast, reflects the de-emphasis of these concerns.

Analysis of Scenario Results

The following sections describe the optimum mix of energy sources and conversion activities for each scenario. A comparison of the impact which

The Stanford Pilot Energy/Economic Model

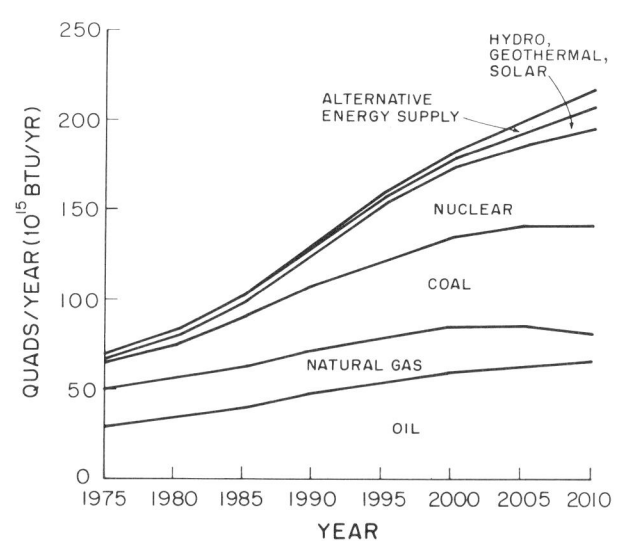

Figure 7. Optimal energy supply mix to maximize the standard of living under *base case* conditions.

each scenario would have on total energy consumption, the Gross National Product, and the standard of living follows this section.

Base Case Scenario Results. The base case is a constrained energy availability scenario. (See Figure 7.) Since coal is economical to use, its production reaches the limits imposed. Despite the lag time needed to build new mines, *twice as much coal is produced per year by 1990 as now.* Use of coal for conversion to pipeline gas becomes moderately economical in the 1990s.

In the base case, the *nuclear power is heavily developed.* The policy constraint which prevents nuclear power production from exceeding 50 percent of total electricity becomes binding. Use of nuclear power to this extent is achieved in this scenario through use of conventional light water reactors as well as reprocessing of nuclear fuel and the fast breeder reactors.

Oil consumption doubles by 2010 with the use of secondary and tertiary recovery techniques, the extraction of oil from shale, Alaskan production, and imports. Much of the growing energy demand is met by increased imports, which are limited to 20 percent of total energy.

Natural gas production is fairly even over the planning horizon, with rise in consumption compensated by a slight rise in imports and coal gasification.

Other technologies, such as hydroelectric and geothermal energy, are developed at the same exogenously specified rate in all cases. In addition, some energy in the base case comes from central station solar plants and alternative energy systems (AES).

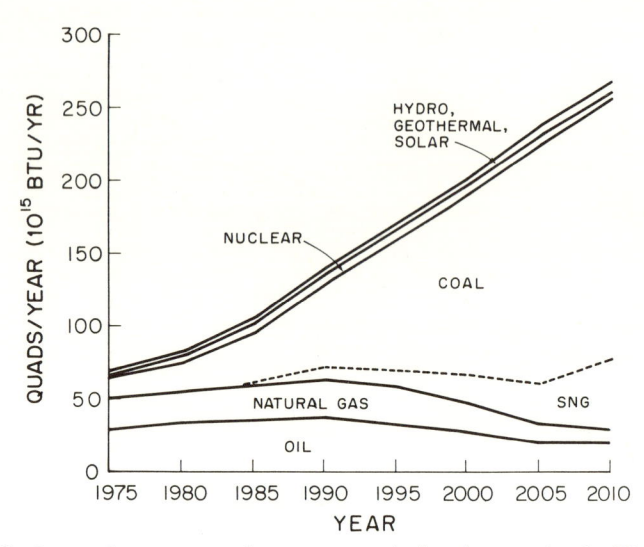

Figure 8. Optimal energy supply mix to maximize the standard of living under high availability of energy resources.

High Availability Scenario Results. The key feature of the high availability case is the use of *coal*. (See Figure 8.) After a substantial period in which investment in coal mines and infrastructure takes place, *the use of coal skyrockets beginning in the late 1980s*. Coal production grows to 12 times present levels by 2000. As a result, total production grows dramatically, nuclear power is not used as extensively, coal conversion activities are very attractive, and imports cease by 1995.

Total *oil consumption and domestic production are similar to that in the base case through 2000, after which* the unrestrained availability of *coal causes oil use to decline.* The use of oil-fired power plants ceases in the late 1990s.

Since *only 14 percent of electricity is generated from nuclear plants* in 2000, the need for the fast breeder reactor is precluded and installation of reprocessing capacity is delayed beyond the 2000s.

The permissibility of the unrestrained development of coal makes synthetic gas even less costly to produce than natural gas. For this reason, *the use of natural gas declines after 1985*.

Use of costly *other technologies*, such as central station solar electricity plants and alternative energy systems, *is not economically competitive* under this scenario.

Low Availability Scenario Results. In this case, the three major energy sources are tightened down to levels significantly below that of the base case.

The Stanford Pilot Energy/Economic Model

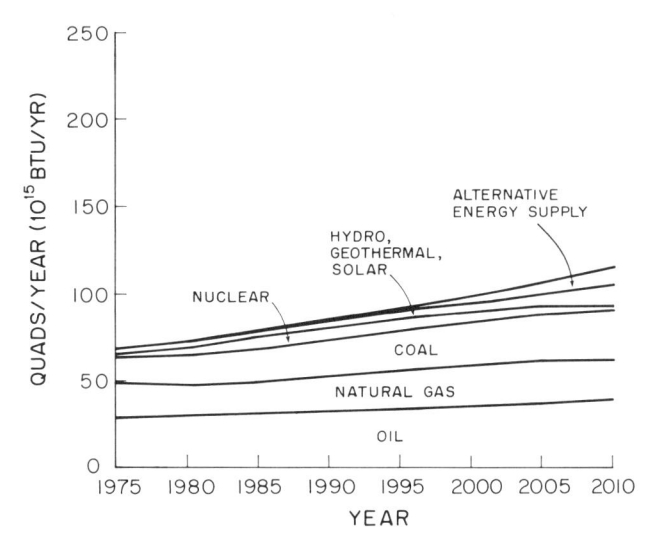

Figure 9. Optimal energy supply mix to maximize the standard of living under *low availability* of energy resources.

(See Figure 9.) *Coal production grows to the limits allowed* — at a rate considerably slower than the base case. These limits are low enough to prevent coal synfuels from playing a significant role.

Oil use is similar to that in the base case scenario. Imports increase more rapidly until 1990, when the additional constraint limiting imports to 20 quads per year becomes binding. Since coal and nuclear energy are tightly restrained, twice as many oil-fired power plants are used in 2000 as in the base case.

Since nuclear plants already under construction are allowed to be completed, *growth in nuclear power does not cease until 1985.* By assumption, the fast breeder reactor and reprocessing technologies also are absent in this scenario.

Natural gas production is similar to that in the base case. Also, the lower coal limits make coal gasification less desirable.

Scenario Comparisons

As mentioned at the outset, supply policies affect total energy consumption, the gross national consumption, and the standard of living. The differences between scenarios are displayed by the following graphs.

Total Energy Consumption. The base case is energy supply oriented in the sense that no demand reduction measures are assumed to be implemented by the consumers and the industry. It is found that growth of the total

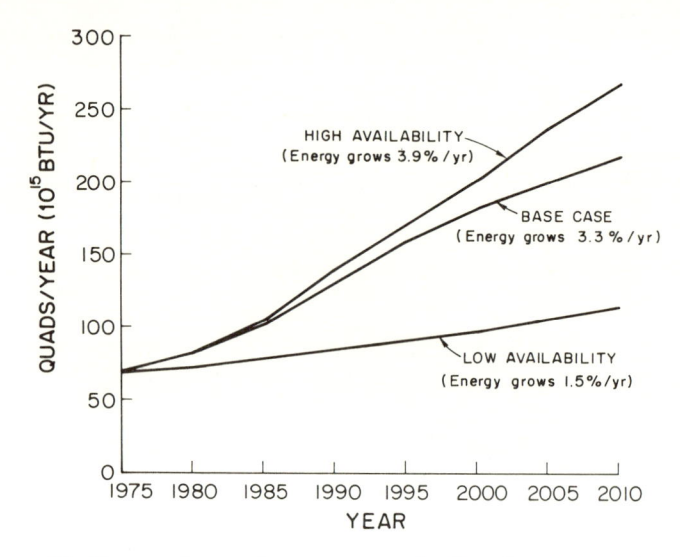

Figure 10. Comparison of energy supply for three scenarios.

energy flow in the base case parallels the historical growth scenario of the Energy Policy Project of the Ford Foundation (11). The growth is about 3.3 percent per year. At this rate, total U.S. energy consumption would double every 21 years. In comparison, the high availability case allows energy consumption to grow at a considerably faster rate of 3.9 percent per year. Energy consumption would then double every 18 years.

Despite the very strict limits imposed on the low availability scenario, energy consumption still would grow but only 1.5 percent per year. At this rate, it would take 46 years for the United States to double its current consumption. (See Figure 10.)

Gross National Consumption. Growth in the U.S. gross national consumption in the base case parallels the growth in the total energy consumption (Figure 11). Energy growth is related to economic growth since these scenarios assume traditional consumption patterns will hold for the future. Conservation measures, if successful in improving the efficiency of our energy use, would permit GNC to grow at a faster rate, or energy use to grow at a slower rate, or both.

Standard of Living. Energy availability can have a great impact on the standard of living. This effect will not be noticed until 1985 when today's energy choices begin to affect the level of personal consumption. Some growth in the personal consumption is achieved under all scenarios but the contrast between the high-energy availability case and the low one is striking.

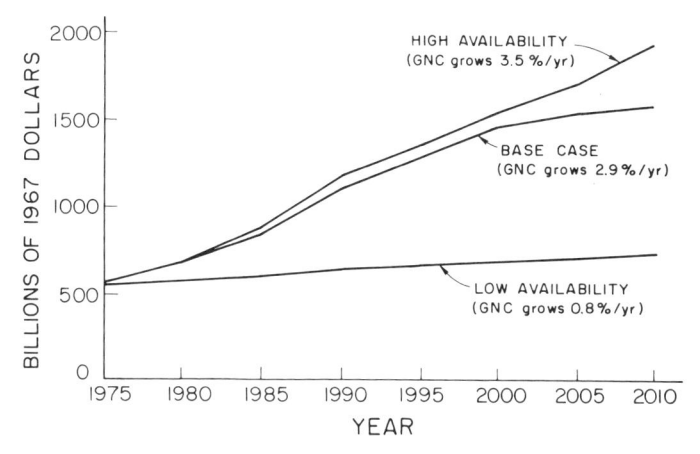

Figure 11. Gross national consumption for three scenarios.

A fuller range of substitution possibilities by the final consumer will be included in future PILOT runs. The estimates above on the gross national consumption attained are conservative, especially in the low energy availability case.

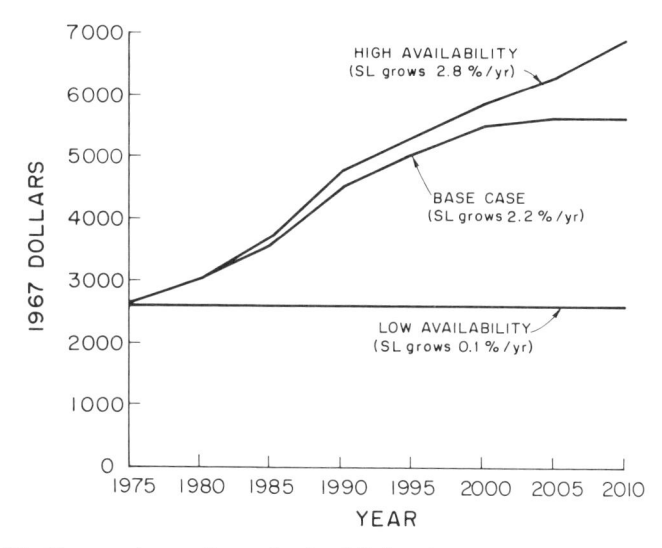

Figure 12. Comparison of standard of living (average per capita consumption) for three scenarios.

The consumption level attained by 2000 under the high-energy availability case is twice as much as that attained under the low availability case. (See Figure 12.)

7. DRAWBACKS AND DEVELOPMENT WORK IN PROGRESS

Deficiencies in Mid-1976 Version of PILOT

In its present form the model includes: detailed description of the energy technologies, explicit description of the exhaustion processes for oil, gas, and uranium, the dynamics of the capital formation and the resource extraction that explicity take into account the intertemporal trade-offs, nonmalleable capital, variable construction lags, endogenous treatment of trade with the rest of the world, and consumption functions that were derived using a procedure that assumes equal absolute additions to income of all income groups and that describe the changing patterns of consumption with the changes in the standard of living as measured by the aggregate level of per capita consumption.

The model also contains a flexibility to experiment with the exogenously specified temporal profiles of consumer fuel mix. This feature makes it possible to examine the effects of the interfuel substitution by consumers especially in those scenarios where initial optimization indicates wide dispersion in the shadow prices of different fuels. There also is a flexibility in the model to examine the effects of reduced energy demand resulting from the conservation and efficiency measures implemented by the consumers and the industry, either voluntarily or through legislative means.

This version of the model, however, does have some weaknesses. It does not contain explicit modeling of the substitution possibilities on the energy demand side. Thus, the possibilities of switches by the consumers and the industry from the scarce forms of fuels to more abundant forms of fuels, non-energy materials, labor, or capital are not endogenously considered in the model. The main disadvantages here consist of the necessity for examination of the solution outputs for bottleneck-reducing substitutions, and reoptimization with appropriate adjustments in the matrix coefficients. Such reoptimizations, however, could be time-consuming and cumbersome.

On the energy supply side, a weakness in the model is an absence of the endogenous descriptions of the requirements for the environmental related hardware particularly with respect to coal usage. The total coal production, therefore, is essentially exogenous in the model. Also, the 40-year planning horizon of the model is not long enough for certain decisions related to energy. Two examples worthy of mention in this regard are the decisions related to the fast breeder reactor and the central station solar technologies.

Main Model Developments

The main model developments are listed below. Naturally, most of them deal with overcoming the deficiencies just outlined.

- *Coal Module* — Physical Supply Curve of Delivered Coal (factors included: water, environment, changing transportation requirements).
- *Longer Planning Horizon* — 100-Year Model with Variable Time Period Aggregation for Computational Efficiency.
- *Potential Interfuel and Capital Fuel Substitution Module* — Incorporates Efficiency Improvements and Constraints Imposed by Existing Stocks of Utilizing Devices.
- *Welfare Equilibrium Variant* — Comprehensive but more Aggregate Substitution Functions for Consumers and Industry.
- *Financial Flow Model* — To Study Market Imperfections.

A coal module is being prepared that takes into account the following considerations related to significant increases in the coal production: water availability constraints, environmental considerations related particularly to high sulfur coal, and shifts as well as increases in transportation requirements related to anticipated increases in the market share of Western coal. While it is true that the supply curve of coal at mine mouth is relatively flat, a more meaningful treatment of coal must take into account the above economic and environmental considerations (17 Appendix D).

An approach is being developed for extending the planning horizon to 100 years. The staircase structure of the PILOT model with 20 five-year periods would take a significantly longer computation time. To ovecome this difficulty, a computer program has been developed and is being tested to aggregate the 20 time periods into a smaller number of time periods of variable length. The length of any time period in the aggregation can be any desired multiple of five years (17, Appendix H).

A major area of development deals with modeling of the substitutions on the demand side. Two approaches are being pursued. The first one concerns process analysis based modeling of the limited area of interfuel and capital fuel substitution, the objective of which is to facilitate studies dealing with the determination of potential substitutions away from the scarce forms of energy that explicitly take into account the fact that the demand in the short run is "locked" into the existing stock of utilizing devices, and either retrofitting or replacement is required to bring forth adjustments (17, Appendix G).

The second approach concerns modeling of a much more comprehensive set of substitutions in the consumer and industrial demand but on a highly aggregated scale. Implementation of substitutions is achieved through a hierarchy of pairwise substitutions. "Hierarchical homothetic functions" are used to mathematically express the choice-making behavior and technological substitutions (16).

Finally, some basic research is being conducted in the area of modeling market imperfections. The key idea here is an observation that the shadow prices from linear programming are marginal prices and do not reflect market prices which may be affected in part by institutional factors (e.g., salaries, taxes, profits, subsidies). The purpose of the Financial Flow Model is to derive a modified set of dual variables which reflect a number of these institutional factors (3).

FOOTNOTES

1. That is, an interest rate of zero.
2. For example, assuming a 3 percent per year growth in the real gross national product, a fixed energy/GNP ratio, and starting with 76 quadrillion BTU in 1976, the energy consumption would add up to 5.9Q over the 1976–2015 period. Commercialization of synfuels would imply a larger amount, and a lower growth rate would imply a smaller amount.
3. According to U.S. Geological Survey (12), the 90 percent confidence intervals for oil and gas resources recoverable with current technology under present economic conditions are: 112–189 billion barrels of oil, 23–34 billion barrels of natural gas liquids, and 761–1094 trillion cubic feet of natural gas. At six million BTU per barrel of oil and one million BTU per thousand cubic feet of gas, one obtains 1.6Q–2.4Q for 90 percent confidence interval on oil and gas.
4. Material in this section drawn from (4).
5. A major weakness of the present version of PILOT is that it does not have any alternative technologies except in the energy sector. Nor does it reflect the full range of possible substitutions by the final consumer due to higher prices. See section 7 for work in progress to overcome these deficiencies.
6. There are two intermediate limits on the quantities of energy which can be imported. The importing of refined oil products is limited to a maximum of 7 quads per year. Natural gas imports are restricted to below 5 quads per year. These policy constraints also apply to the high energy availability scenario.

REFERENCES

1. Almon, C., Jr., et al., *1985: Interindustry Forecasts of the American Economy*. Lexington Books, Lexington, Mass., 1974.
2. Avriel, M., "Modeling Personal Consumption of Goods in the PILOT Energy Model," Technical Report SOL 76-17, Department of Operations Research, Stanford University, August 1976.
3. Avriel, M., and G. B. Dantzig, "Determining Prices and Monetary Flows of the PILOT Energy Model." Technical Report SOL 76-28, Department of Operations Research, Stanford University, October 1976.
4. Barzelay, M., "The National Energy Potential According to PILOT." Technical Report SOL 77-10, Department of Operations Research, Stanford University, May 1977.

5. Battelle Memorial Institute, "An *Ex Ante* Capital Matrix for the United States, 1970–1975," prepared for *Scientific American*, 1971.
6. Brookhaven National Laboratory, "Sourcebook for Energy Assessment," M. Beller, ed., BNL 50483, Upton, New York, December 1975.
7. Dantzig, G. B., and S. C. Parikh, "On a PILOT Linear Programming Model for Assessing Physical Impact on the Economy of a Changing Energy Picture." *Energy: Mathematics and Models*, Fred S. Roberts, ed., Proceedings of a SIMS Conference on Energy, Alta, Utah, July 1975, SIAM, 1976, pp. 1–23.
8. *Economic Report of the President* Transmitted to the Congress, January 1976, together with "The Annual Report of the Council of Economic Advisers," 1976.
9. Environmental Protection Agency, *Strategic Environmental Assessment System* (draft), 1975.
10. Federal Energy Administration, *National Energy Outlook*, 1976.
11. Ford Foundation Energy Policy Project Report, *A Time to Choose*, Ballinger Publishing Company, Cambridge, Mass., 1974.
12. Miller, B. M., et al., "Geological Estimates of Undiscovered Recoverable Oil and Gas Resources in the United States." Geological Survey Circular 725, U.S. Department of the Interior, 1975.
13. Murtagh B. A., and M. A. Saunders, "MINOS: A Large-Scale Nonlinear Programming System (For Problems with Linear Constraints) User's Guide." Technical Report SOL 77–9, Department of Operations Research, Stanford University, February 1977.
14. Nyhus, D., "The Trade Model of a Dynamic Input-Output Forecasting System," Ph.D. Dissertation, University of Maryland, 1975.
15. Parikh, S. C., "Analyzing U.S. Energy Options Using the PILOT Energy Model." Technical Report SOL 76–27, Department of Operations Research, Stanford University, October 1976, a portion to appear in the *Proceedings of the First International Conference on Mathematical Modeling*, Rolla, Missouri, September 1977.
16. ———, "Progress Report on the PILOT Energy Modeling Project," Technical Report SOL 77–11, Department of Operations Research, Stanford University, May 1977, to appear in *Proceedings of an IIASA Workshop on Energy Studies, Conception and Embedding*, Laxenburg, Austria.
17. Systems Optimization Laboratory, "The Stanford PILOT Energy/Economic Model," Department of Operations Research. Prepared for the Electric Power Research Institute, Report No. EA-626, 1977.
18. U.S. Bureau of Labor Statistics, Labor Force Data up to 1990, *Monthly Labor Review*, July 1973.
19. U.S. Department of Commerce, Bureau of Economic Analysis, "The Input-Output Structure of the U.S. Economy: 1967." *Survey of Current Business* 54, No. 2, February 1974.
20. U.S. Department of Commerce, *Population Estimates and Projections*, Current Population Reports, Series P-25, No. 601 (Series II), October 1975.

NEW CAR EFFICIENCY STANDARDS AND THE DEMAND FOR GASOLINE

James L. Sweeney, STANFORD UNIVERSITY*

I. INTRODUCTION

In order to reduce the growth rate of gasoline consumption, new car minimum efficiency standards were mandated as part of the Energy Policy and Conservation Act of 1975 (EPCA). Under the provisions of the EPCA each manufacturer must meet or surpass a new car efficiency standard of 20 mpg in 1980 and 27.5 mpg in 1985. This standard is to be applied to the harmonic mean efficiency of all cars sold by the manufacturer during the model year.[1] EPCA also specifies a non-tax-deductible civil penalty to be imposed on each manufacturer failing to meet the minimum efficiency standard. For such manufacturers, the penalty per automobile increases linearly with the difference between the mandated standard and the mean efficiency obtained. For manufacturers above the standard, no tax is levied. Hence, the penalty can be viewed as imposing a price for inefficiency. The inefficiency price is positive for average efficiency below the standard and is zero for average efficiency above.

The EPCA efficiency standard is qualitatively different from most standards imposed by the Federal government. First, it is applied not to individual automobiles, but rather to the average of all automobiles sold by a given manufacturer. Thus, the manufacturer can sell cars less efficient than the standard, while avoiding all penalties, if enough cars more efficient than the standard are also sold. Second, a penalty structure is imposed with penalties gradually increasing for increasing degrees of noncompliance. Manufacturers are penalized a relatively small amount for small degrees of noncompliance, and a proportionally larger amount for proportionally greater degrees of noncompliance.

This paper examines the economics of the EPCA penalty. The attention is placed on one aspect of the economic response—the pricing response of the manufacturer and the subsequent response by consumers. Relatively little attention is paid to the manufacturer's decision to change the efficiency of automobiles of given characteristics. In addition, incentives toward modification of industrial structure are identified and evaluated. An alternative penalty structure is proposed to eliminate these incentives. Other policy instruments are also examined to determine their impacts in the presence of the EPCA efficiency standard.

The paper is divided into six additional sections.

Section II describes the standard and the existing penalties. An alternative penalty structure is defined for later use. Section III examines the optimal response of firms facing the standard. The two types of responses—technological responses and pricing responses—are identified and described briefly. The theory of optimal pricing under the standard is presented and its implications are explored. Section IV uses quantitative estimates to examine whether automobile manufacturers will meet the standard. Section V examines additional policy instruments in conjunction with the efficiency standard: a gasoline tax and a set of gas-guzzler texes and rebates. Section VI explores issues of industrial structural change encouraged by the standard. The alternative formulation of section II is shown to eliminate some problems associated with the current penalty structure. Finally, section VII presents a summary and conclusion to the paper.

II. THE PENALTY STRUCTURE

The EPCA mandates a minimum efficiency standard applied to the harmonic mean of all automoblies sold by each manufacturer, along with a fine

New Car Efficiency Standards

for noncompliance. The fine is linear in the number of cars sold and linear in the difference between the mileage standard and the harmonic mean miles per gallon, if the former exceeds the latter. The fine is zero if mean efficiency exceeds the standard. Equation (1) describes this relationship more precisely:

$$F = \begin{cases} t(\text{mst} - \overline{\text{mpg}})N & \text{for mst} \geq \overline{\text{mpg}} \\ 0 & \text{for mst} \leq \overline{\text{mpg}} \end{cases} \quad (1)$$

where F is the equivalent-before-tax penalty cost of the fine,

> mst is the standard
> $\overline{\text{mpg}}$ is the harmonic mean efficiency obtained
> N is the number of cars sold, and
> t is the penalty rate.

Under the EPCA, mst equals 20 mpg in 1980 and 27.5 in 1985. t equals $100/mpg-car, under the assumption of a 50 percent marginal corporate tax rate.

The manufacturer offers various automobile models for sale. The particular models will be indicated by the subscript i. The symbol x_i denotes the number of automobiles of model i sold during the model year. The following two equations[2] define the variables N and $\overline{\text{mpg}}$:

$$N = \Sigma x_i \quad (2)$$

$$\overline{\text{mpg}} = \frac{\Sigma x_i}{\Sigma(x_i/\text{mpg}_i)} \quad (3)$$

where mpg_i is the efficiency—the miles per gallon—obtained by the ith model of car.

Several properties of the penalty structure should be noted. The penalty is linear in the numbers of cars sold. Thus, the penalty per car is independent of the number of cars. The magnitude of the penalty depends both on the mix of cars sold and on the efficiency of each model. Thus, the fine can be reduced or eliminated either (a) by increasing the efficiency of the various models (increasing mpg_i) while holding the mix constant (x_i constant) or (b) by holding constant the efficiencies of the various models while increasing the sales of the high-efficiency models and reducing the sales of low-efficiency models.

Alternative penalty structures could be legislated. One, in particular, is proposed and defined here. At a later point in the paper it will be shown that this alternative penalty structure is in some ways preferable to the current structure. Equation (4) will be said to define the "alternative penalty structure."

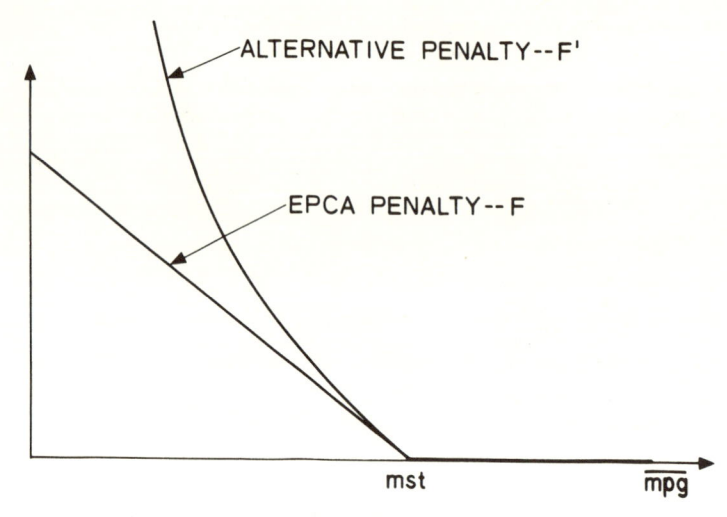

Figure 1. Penalty structure under EPCA and under alternative formula.

$$F' = \begin{cases} t(\text{mst})^2 \left\{ \dfrac{1}{\overline{\text{mpg}}} - \dfrac{1}{\text{mst}} \right\} N, & \text{for } \overline{\text{mpg}} \leq \text{mst} \\ 0 & \text{otherwise} \end{cases} \quad (4)$$

where F' is the alternative penalty structure.

The properties of the alternative structure are similar to those of the current structure. The only difference is in the manner of penalty variation with changes in average efficiency. The current penalty is linear in the mandated value of miles per gallon minus the mean miles per gallon obtained by the new car fleet. The alternative penalty is linear in the *inverse* of mean miles per gallon minus the inverse of the mandated miles per gallon. These inverses can be interpreted as the gallons of gasoline consumed per mile driven. Thus, the alternative penalty is linear in new car fleet gallons per mile obtained minus the mandated value of gallons per mile. For $\overline{\text{mpg}}$ close to mst, the two penalty structures are virtually identical. However, for values of $\overline{\text{mpg}}$ well below the standard, the alternative penalty is greater than the current penalty. Figure 1 graphs the two penalties.

III. INDUSTRY RESPONSE UNDER STANDARDS: THEORY

For a firm faced with the efficiency standard, two types of economically motivated responses may occur. The first may be an improvement in the efficiency of automobiles with given characteristics, an increase in the various mpg_i. Electronic ignitions, better carburetors, more efficient transmissions, and light-weight materials could be chosen by the manufacturer. The manufacturer would adopt those technology changes that would pay for themselves by reducing penalty costs and changing demands. This type of response seems to have captured the most attention in current policy discussions.

A second manufacturer response is possible, a response involving pricing policy of automobiles. The civil penalty imposes a set of marginal costs on the manufacturer, and these costs would be incorporated into automobile prices. In particular, for a manufacturer not meeting the standard, additional sales of low-mpg cars would increase the civil penalty, while sales of high-mpg cars would reduce the penalty. If the manufacturer were to pass on these incremental costs (either positive or negative) to the consumers, consumers would be induced to shift purchases toward the more efficient models. This induced consumer response would increase the mean efficiency of all cars purchased and would reduce the penalty. Thus, the EPCA provides an incentive for pricing so as to increase the market shares of efficient cars and decrease shares of the inefficient. This paper focuses attention on the pricing response of the firm.[3] Consider an automobile manufacturer facing the efficiency standard and its associated civil penalty. The penalty cost imposed upon the firm is given by equation (1). Each x_i depends upon each price, P_j, or, equivalently, each P_j depends upon every x_i. The inverse demand function will be written as:

$$P_i = f_i(x_1, \ldots, x_m) = f_i(x), \text{ for each } i, \tag{5}$$

where x is the vector $x_i, \ldots, x_m$.

The manufacturer faces a cost (excluding the penalty) of C, a cost dependent upon the sales of each model. The profit of the manufacturer, Π, can then be written as follows:

$$\Pi = \Sigma P_i x_i - C - F = R - C - F, \tag{6}$$

where R is the revenue obtained and F is the fine. For the specific tax structure of the EPCA, this expression becomes:

$$\Pi = \begin{cases} R - C - t\left[\text{mst } \Sigma x_i - \dfrac{(\Sigma x_i)^2}{\Sigma(x_i/\text{mpg}_i)}\right], & \text{for } \overline{\text{mpg}} \leq \text{mst} \\ R - C, & \text{for } \overline{\text{mpg}} \geq \text{mst} \end{cases} \tag{7}$$

Profit maximizing requires the marginal revenue of selling one more car of type i to equal the marginal cost, including the penalty. When F is differentiable, the following necessary condition must be satisfied for optimization:[4]

$$MR_i = P_i + \sum_j x_j \frac{\partial P_j}{\partial x_i} = \frac{\partial C}{\partial x_i} + \frac{\partial F}{\partial x_i}, \quad \text{for all } i, \tag{8}$$

where MR_i is the marginal revenue associated with selling one more auto of type i.

When $\overline{mpg}$ = mst, the penalty function is not differentiable. Profit maximization can be written as a constrained maximization problem:

$$\text{Max } \Pi = R - C$$
$$\text{under mst} = \overline{mpg}. \tag{9}$$

To solve problem (9), a Lagrangian can be defined:

$$\mathscr{L} = R - C - \mu[\text{mst} - \overline{mpg}],$$

where μ is a Lagrange multiplier. The necessary conditions for optimization then become:

$$MR_i = \frac{\partial C}{\partial x_i} + \mu \frac{\partial \overline{mpg}}{\partial x_i}, \quad \text{for all i.} \tag{10}$$

Equations (8) and (10) can be evaluated for the specific EPCA penalty structure as given by equation (1). In order to present the results in the most symmetric form, the Lagrange multiplier μ has been scaled by a factor N, to give the multiplier λ. Then the following necessary conditions for optimization emerge:

$$MR_i = P_i + \sum_j x_j \frac{\partial P_j}{\partial x_i} = \frac{\partial C}{\partial x_i} + T_i, \quad \text{for each i} \tag{11}$$

where
$$T_i = \lambda \, \overline{mpg} \, \{(\overline{mpg}/mpg_i - 1) + (mst/\overline{mpg} - 1)\} \tag{12}$$

and where

$$0 \le \lambda \begin{cases} = t, \text{ for } \overline{mpg} < \text{mst}, \\ \le t, \text{ for } \overline{mpg} = \text{mst}, \\ = 0, \text{ for } \overline{mpg} > \text{mst}. \end{cases} \tag{13}$$

The term T_i will be referred to as the marginal penalty cost associated with the standard, or, more simply, the marginal penalty cost. For $\overline{mpg} \neq$ mst, the term T_i is the increased penalty cost of selling one more car of type i. For $\overline{mpg} =$ mst, the term T_i is the shadow price associated with the constraint $\overline{mpg} =$ mst.

The marginal penalty cost expression includes two terms. The first is positive for all autos having an efficiency less than the mean efficiency, and is negative for autos more efficient. This term varies between minus unity and infinity as mpg_i varies between infinity and zero, and it reflects the fact that selling a car more efficient than the mean raises the mean efficiency, while selling a less efficient car lowers the mean.

The second term of equation (12) is positive for $\overline{mpg} <$ mst and is zero for $\overline{mpg}$ = mst. This term reflects the fact that the penalty is proportional to the number of cars sold.

Note that if the mean efficiency is below the standard, then the marginal penalty cost is positive for automobiles with efficiency just equal to the standard. If the mean efficiency just meets the standard, then marginal penalty costs are positive for autos less efficient than the standard and are negative for autos more efficient.

Analogous equations can be obtained for the alternative penalty structure of equation (4). In this case, equations (11) and (13) would remain valid. However, T_i would be replaced by T'_i, where

$$T'_i = \lambda \, \text{mst} \, \{\text{mst}/\text{mpg}_i - 1\}. \tag{14}$$

Under the alternative penalty structure, the marginal penalty cost would always be negative for autos more efficient than the standard, and positive for autos less efficient. Contrary to the current law, the marginal penalty costs would be independent of the mean efficiency obtained. When the standard is just met (mst = $\overline{mpg}$), the marginal penalty costs of the current law are identical to those of the alternative penalty structure.

Equations (11) through (14) can be used to analyze either a competitive model or a monopoly model. For a purely competitive market, equation (11) is simplified, since the term $\partial P_j / \partial x_i$ is identically zero. Hence, in equilibrium, the competitive price of the ith model would equal its marginal production cost plus marginal tax cost:

$$P_i = \frac{\partial C}{\partial x_i} + T_i, \tag{11'}$$

If the firm under question is representative of the industry, then all firms face the same T_i. Hence, in the situation of constant returns to scale, with additively separable cost functions, the equilibrium value of each P_i will change by precisely T_i.

The firm's choice can be depicted graphically. Assume that there are only two types of cars—large and small—denoted by subscripts l and s respectively. Small cars have efficiency greater than the standard, while large cars have efficiency lower.

For x_s fixed, Figure 2 illustrates the optimal choice of x_l both without and with the EPCA standard. At x_l^0, the standard is just met. With the standard, the marginal penalty cost varies discontinuously as $x_l = x_l^0$. For $x_l < x_l^0$, the mean efficiency is above the standard and the marginal penalty cost is zero. For $x_l > x_l^0$, the average efficiency is below the standard and the marginal penalty cost is positive.

In the absence of the efficiency standard, the firm equates marginal cost and marginal revenue. This occurs at Point A for the marginal revenue curve labeled MR_l and at Point C for the marginal revenue curve MR''_l.

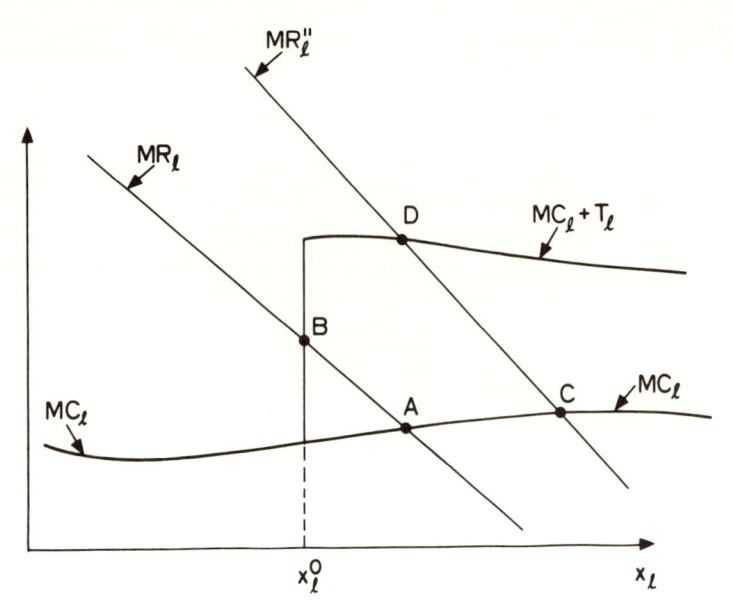

Figure 2. Optimal choice of X_1 for X_s given.

With the efficiency standard, two types of solutions are possible. The first is represented by Point B. In this case, x_1 is reduced to x_1^0; the efficiency standard is just met. Marginal revenue exceeds marginal cost by less than the marginal penalty cost. The second occurs if there is a particularly large demand for large cars or if the demand elasticities are low. In this case, represented by Point D, x_1 may exceed x_1^0, and the mean efficiency would be lower than the standard. The difference between marginal revenue and marginal cost would just equal the marginal penalty cost.

A third case is not possible. If $x_1 \geq x_1^0$ in the absence of the standard, then it will never occur that $x_1 < x_1^0$ in the presence of the standard. The EPCA will not motivate firms to *exceed* the efficiency standard.

Figure 3 illustrates the firm's choice of x_s, the number of small cars sold, for x_1 given. For $x_s = x_s^0$, the standard is just met, for $x_s < x_s^0$ the mean efficiency is below the standard, and for $x_s > x_s^0$ the mean efficiency exceeds the standard. Analogously to the large car result, the imposition of the EPCA standard can be expected to increase the number of small cars sold (shifts from A to B or from C to D).

In each case illustrated, the price of large cars is increased and the price of small cars is reduced in response to the standard. In the move from Point A to Point B, the prices are changed so as to shift demand to just meet the standard. In the change from Point C to Point D, each marginal revenue is changed by roughly the marginal penalty cost. The price changes may be less than or greater than the marginal penalty cost, depending upon the shape of the demand curves. In the special case of pure competition, the new car price would increase (or decrease) by exactly the amount of the marginal penalty cost.

Whether the equilibrium is similar to that of Point B or Point D depends upon the magnitude of the various T_i and upon the responsiveness of demands to price changes. To estimate demand response requires a method of merging existing quantitative evidence into the problem.

One approach would be to use econometric studies that estimate own and cross elasticities of demand for various classes of automobiles. Several such studies exist (1, 2, 3, 4, 7, 8). However, each suffers from serious difficulties. First, each segments the market into a small number (usually three) of automobile classes and estimates changes in market shares among the classes. This approach implicitly assumes away shifts in demand mix within a class and focuses entirely on shifts between classes. However, price changes can be expected to influence *which* cars within a class are purchased and therefore to influence mean efficiency of a given class, even with each mpg_i held constant. This excluded effect may be quantitatively more important than the included effect. Second, the data and econometric problems of estimating market share equations have been overwhelming. For these reasons, models that estimate market shares of auto classes are probably not reliable. Hence, they will not be used for this analysis.

A second method, which will be used, involves establishing an equivalence between the marginal penalty costs and the costs of a gasoline tax.

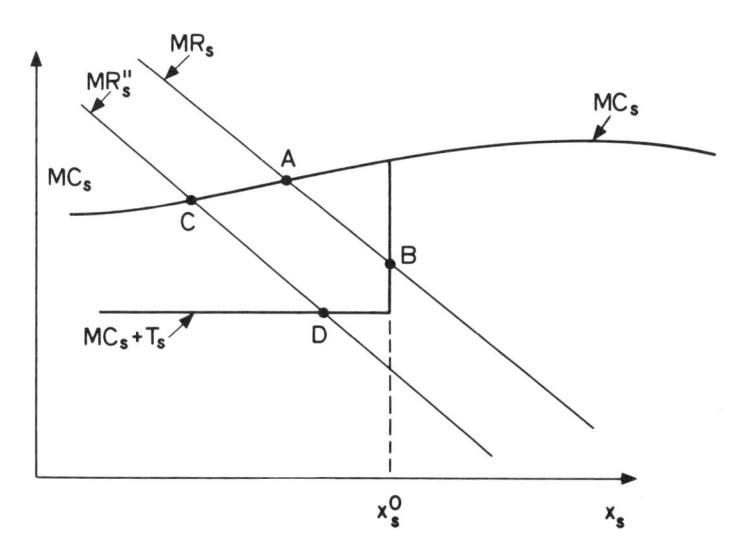

Figure 3. Optimal choice of X_s for X_1 given.

This approach, then, can utilize the existing quantitative estimates of the effects of gasoline taxes on mean new car efficiency.

In order to establish the equivalence, equation (12) can be separated into two terms, S_i^0 and S^1:

$$T_i = S_i^0 + S^1, \text{ where:} \tag{15}$$

$$S_i^0 = \lambda(\overline{mpg})^2/mpg_i, \tag{16}$$

and

$$S^1 = \lambda[\text{mst} - 2\,\overline{mpg}]. \tag{17}$$

The first term, S_i^0, is inversely proportional to the efficiency of the ith type of car. The second term, S^1, is independent of the efficiency of the ith model. S^1 is usually negative.

It will be shown that effects of the term S_i^0 can be related directly to the effects of an equivalent gasoline tax in the following sense: a gasoline tax can be defined that would lead to all x_i identical to those calculated above. The term S^1 is generally a lump sum subsidy on automobile purchases. Thus, the effects of the efficiency standard, given optimizing behavior by the manufacturer, can be directly related to the effects of a gasoline tax plus a lump sum subsidy.

Consider a tax of ET imposed upon sales of gasoline. This tax increases the discounted operating costs, OC_i, facing the purchaser of model i automobile by

$$\Delta OC_i = ET \frac{\sum_t vm(t)\left(\frac{1}{1+r}\right)^t}{mpg_i} \triangleq \frac{ET \cdot TVM}{mpg_i}, \tag{18}$$

where vm(t) is the vehicle miles driven at automobile age t, r is the discount rate, and TVM is the discounted total vehicle miles driven over the auto lifetime.

Consider a situation in which a subsidy of $(-S^1)$ per car is offered to manufacturers and simultaneously a gasoline tax of ET is imposed. Assuming that consumers consider purchase price plus operating cost in selecting new cars, the demand prices will be translated by $-\Delta OC_i$ in response to the gasoline tax. Thus, if the demand function had the form of equation (5), then the new demand function would have the form:

$$P_i' = f_i(x) - \Delta OC_i = P_i - OC_i \tag{19}$$

The firm's marginal cost function would be decreased by $(-S^1)$. The profit-maximizing firm facing the demand function of equation (19) but not facing an efficiency standard would solve the following set of necessary conditions:

$$\mathrm{MR}'_i = P'_i + \sum_j x_j \frac{\partial P'_j}{\partial x_i} = \frac{\partial C}{\partial x_i} + S^1 \qquad (20)$$

where P'_i satisfies equation (19).

Equation (20) can be combined with equations (18) and (19) to obtain:

$$\mathrm{MR}_i = P_i + \sum_j x_j \frac{\partial P_j}{\partial x_i} = \frac{\partial C}{\partial x_i} + \frac{\mathrm{ET \cdot TVM}}{\mathrm{mpg}_i} + S^1 \qquad (21)$$

Comparing equation (21) to equation (11) [with equations (15) – (17)], shows that the former equation is identical to the latter if S^1 is defined by equation (17) and if

$$\mathrm{ET} = \frac{\lambda(\overline{\mathrm{mpg}})^2}{\mathrm{TVM}}. \qquad (22)$$

Thus, it can be seen that the imposition of (a) a gasoline tax (defined by equation (22)], plus (b) a lump sum subsidy [defined by equation (17)], will give identical results to those obtained under the current efficiency standard, if $\overline{\mathrm{mpg}} <$ mst, and if consumers consider the present value of operating costs when purchasing a car.

An equivalent gasoline tax can also be defined for the alternative penalty structure. Using equations (18), (21), and (14), an equivalent gasoline tax, ET′, and subsidy, $S^{1\prime}$, can be defined for the alternative penalty structure:

$$\mathrm{ET}' = \frac{\lambda(\mathrm{mst})^2}{\mathrm{TVM}} \qquad (23)$$

$$S^{1\prime} = \lambda\mathrm{mst} \qquad (24)$$

It can be seen from equation (22) that the equivalent gasoline tax under the current penalty structure increases sharply as the manufacturer's average efficiency increases. Under the alternative penalty structure the effective tax would be independent of $\overline{\mathrm{mpg}}$ but would increase sharply as the standard increases.

For the EPCA penalty structure, *the equivalent gasoline tax is independent of industrial structure* once $\overline{\mathrm{mpg}}$ is given. For the alternative penalty structure, the equivalent gasoline tax is *always independent of industrial structure*. Thus, the equivalent gasoline tax for a monopoly is identical to that for a perfectly competitive industry! Therefore, if the market response to a gasoline tax has been observed. it can be used to infer the response to the efficiency standard.

The concept of an equivalent gasoline tax allows the analysis to be reduced to two dimensions. For a given $\overline{\mathrm{mpg}}$, the equivalent gasoline tax, ET, can be obtained by equation (22) [or (23)]. For a given ET, the resulting consumer response determines $\overline{\mathrm{mpg}}$. The market equilibrium is obtained when the two relationships are satisfied simultaneously.

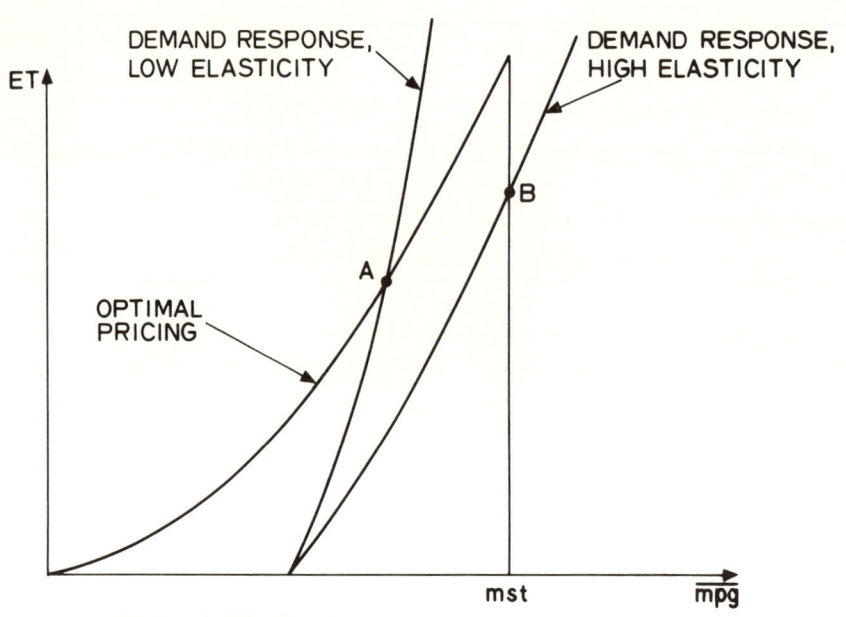

Figure 4. EPCA guided market equilibrium: current penalty

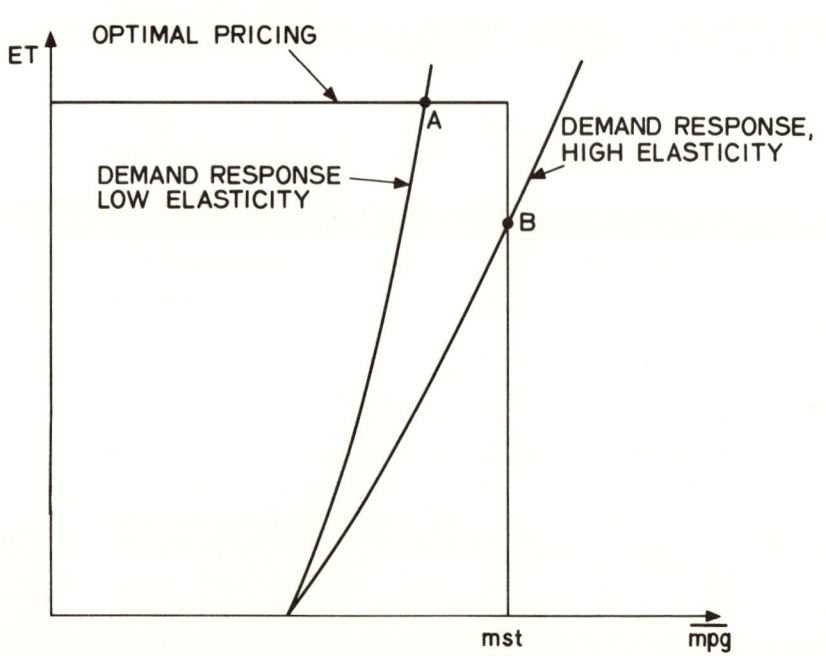

Figure 5. Efficiency standard guided market response: alternative penalty structure

New Car Efficiency Standards

It will be assumed that, to a first-order approximation, the lump sum subsidy will not influence the average efficiency of new cars purchased. There is no available evidence on this point. But microeconomic theory suggests that since the cost differentials among the various cars are not influenced by a lump-sum subsidy, individual decisions on which car to buy would not be influenced by a lump-sum subsidy. Only the total sales of cars would be so influenced.

Figures 4 and 5 illustrate the analysis of market equilibrium. Figure 4 is drawn for the EPCA penalties, and Figure 5 for the alternative penalty structure. In both figures, an "optimal pricing" curve is illustrated, based on equations (22), (23), and (13). Both figures also illustrate two possible demand response curves, illustrating two degrees of consumer responsiveness to price changes. Both demand response curves show $\overline{mpg}$ to be an increasing function of ET.

The equilibrium of the system can be of two types. Point A illustrates the equilibrium obtained with very low demand elasticities. In this case, the full effective tax is imposed, but consumers do not respond sufficiently for the standard to be met. This corresponds to the equilibrium at Point D of Figures 2 and 3. Point B illustrates the equilibrium obtained with a higher elasticity. The standard is met with less than the full effective tax imposed. Just enough of the price differentials are imposed to insure that the standard is met precisely. This corresponds to Point B in Figures 2 and 3. Which type of equilibrium is obtained depends upon the level of the standard (mst) and the responsiveness of consumers to higher prices.

Figures 4 and 5 illustrate market equilibrium but do not clarify the adjustments toward equilibrium. One may ask whether the equilibrium is relevant if the manufacturers do not know the degree of demand responsiveness. Would the market still converge to the equilibrium? The answer will be "yes."

In Figure 6, the equilibrium efficiency is m*, with the equilibrium effective tax at ET*. Assume that a firm (mistakenly) believes that the equilibrium is at m_0, where $m_0 < m^*$. Then the firm will set prices of its automobiles according to equations (11) – (13), giving rise to an equivalent gasoline tax of ET_0. The efficiency obtained will be m_1, where $m_0 < m_1 < m^*$. The obtained efficiency will be above that expected, and will be closer to the equilibrium. The converse occurs for expected efficiencies above the equilibrium level. Each successive choice brings the manufacturer closer to the equilibrium, even if the demand function is not known. Manufacturer errors in estimating the demand functions, and hence in estimating ET*, will be corrected over time as the market responds to the firm's pricing decisions.

Under the alternative penalty structure the convergence process would be more rapid. If the manufacturer believes he will not meet the standard, then the optimal prices will be independent of his perceived $\overline{mpg}$. If in fact

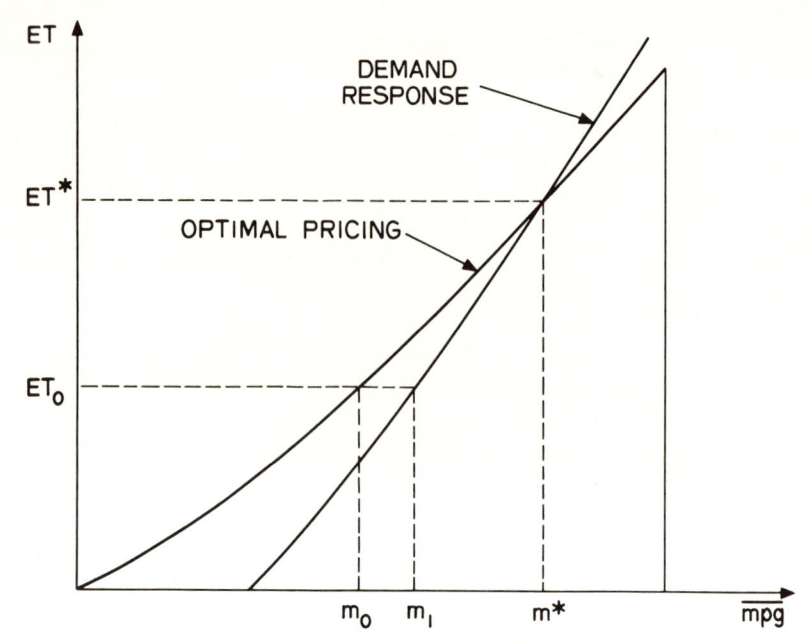

Figure 6. Adjustment processes.

the standards are not met, then the equilibrium will be obtained in a single step.

This section has provided the basic theoretical foundation for examining the response to the EPCA efficiency standard. The next section will provide quantitative evaluations based upon the theory developed here.

IV. INDUSTRY RESPONSE UNDER THE STANDARDS: QUANTITATIVE ESTIMATES

This section presents numerical values of the marginal penalty costs and the associated equivalent taxes. A representation of market demand response is presented in parametric form to show the combinations of technology improvement and demand responsiveness that would imply compliance with the standards. Finally, an econometrically derived estimate of demand responsiveness will be used to argue that the efficiency standards will be met *even if* no technology improvements were to occur.

The marginal penalty costs (T_i) of equation (12) can be evaluated numerically. Table 1 presents values of T_i for several automobile efficiencies, under several alternative assumptions about $\overline{mpg}$, for mst > $\overline{mpg}$. The left column of Table 1 indicates possible efficiencies of automobile models, while entries in the top rows indicate the year and the assumed average efficiency, $\overline{mpg}$,

New Car Efficiency Standards

Table 1. Marginal penalty costs (T$_i$) under EPCA

Year	1980		1985	
$\overline{mpg}$	20	15	20	27.5
mpg$_i$				
5	$6,000	$4,250	$6,750	$12,375
10	2,000	2,000	2,750	4,813
15	667	1,250	1,417	2,292
20	0	875	750	1,031
25	−400	650	350	275
30	−667	500	83	−229
35	−857	392	−107	−589
40	−1,000	312	−250	−859

of autos sold. Entries in the body of the matrix correspond to the T$_i$ for the various model efficiencies.

From Table 1, for a manufacturer almost meeting the 1980 standard ($\overline{mpg} \approx 20$), there is a *negative* marginal penalty cost of $1,000 for automobiles obtaining 40 mpg and a marginal penalty cost of $2,000 for autos obtaining only 10 mpg. In 1985, the maginal penalty cost for an automobile obtaining 10 mpg would be $2,750 if the manufacturer were to sell autos averaging 20 mpg, and $4,813 if the manufacturer approached but did not quite reach the 27.5 mpg standard. Negative marginal penalty costs for efficient cars are far less dramatic, varying between $250 and $859 for 40 mpg automobiles as the average efficiency varies between 20 mpg and 27.5 mpg.[5]

If the alternative penalty structure were substituted for the EPCA structure, then Table 1 would be modified somewhat. The 1980 column and the 27.5 $\overline{mpg}$ column for 1985 would remain unchanged. However, the 15 and 20 $\overline{mpg}$ columns for 1985 would be identical to the 27.5 $\overline{mpg}$ column.

The equivalent tax of equation (22) or (23) can be calculated as a function of $\overline{mpg}$ once vm(t) and r are known. In order to estimate ET, it was assumed that a car would be driven 18,000 miles its first year, 16,000 its second, and so on, declining linearly to an expected value of 8,000 in its sixth year. For years seven through ten the corresponding expected values of mileages driven are 7,000, 6,000, 5,000, and 4,000 miles. After ten years vm(t) is taken to be zero. Under these assumptions, ET was calculated for various values of r and $\overline{mpg}$, for $\overline{mpg} <$ mst. These values are displayed in Table 2 for several interest rates. Values of ET' can be read from Table 2 by substituting mst for $\overline{mpg}$ in the left-hand column. Values displayed in Table 2 determine the "optimal pricing" curve of Figure 4. It should be noted that higher values of the interest rate increase the equivalent gasoline tax. Therefore, in subsequent evaluations, the more conservative 6 percent interest rate will be adopted.

One additional relationship is needed—the "demand response" curve—

Table 2. Current penalty equivalent gas tax (ET)
($\overline{\text{mpg}} < \text{mst}$)

r $\overline{\text{mpg}}$	6%	10%	15%
16	.26	.30	.33
18	.34	.38	.42
20	.42	.46	.52
22	.51	.56	.62
24	.69	.76	.84
26	.71	.77	.87
27	.76	.83	.93
27.5	.79	.88	.97

Units are nominal dollars per gallon

The following formula was used to calculate ET:

$$\text{ET} = \frac{1}{1.14}(\$100)\frac{\overline{\text{mpg}}^2}{\text{TVM}}$$

TVM equals 84,000 for r = 6 percent, 76,000 for r = 10 percent, and 68,000 for r = 15 percent. The factor (1/1.14) was obtained because the law is based upon the EPA-measured efficiency which overstates lifetime average on-the-road performance by about 14 percent.

the relationship between the effective tax and the mean efficiency of automobiles demanded. A simple constant elasticity specification can be chosen to relate mean efficiency of automobiles demanded to technical efficiency and gasoline price. This relationship is as follows:[6]

$$\overline{\text{mpg}} = B\left\{\frac{\text{Pgas}}{\text{EFF}}\right\}^\alpha \cdot \text{EFF}, \qquad (25)$$

where Pgas is the (constant dollar) gasoline price,
  α is the elasticity of $\overline{\text{mpg}}$ with respect to gasoline price,
  EFF is a measure of technical efficiency,
  B is a constant.

The factor EFF captures improvements in the technology of automobiles. Changes such as improved carburetors, more efficient engines, and so forth, can be expected to increase the mean automobile efficiency if the market shares of the various models remain constant. The factor EFF is defined such that if technological changes were to increase mpg_i for each model by 20 percent, then EFF would increase by 20 percent. Therefore, *if market shares are held constant*, then a given percentage change in EFF will lead to that same percentage change in $\overline{\text{mpg}}$. Equation (25) includes a second term: $\{\text{Pgas}/\text{EFF}\}^\alpha$. This term reflects the assumption that changes in gasoline price *or* in technical efficiency may influence the market shares of the various automobiles sold and hence may influence mean efficiency. Its form embodies the notion that consumers select new cars based upon, among other factors, the operating costs of alternative choices. It is assumed that the gasoline price and the technical efficiency influence choice only through their influence on operating costs. Under this assumption, a y percent increase in EFF will have precisely the same impact on operating costs, and hence on market shares, as will a y percent decrease in gasoline prices. The *ratio* of gasoline price to EFF is the relevant variable in operating costs and, hence, in market shares.

In using equation (25), the first approach will be to treat α and EFF as parameters in order to determine whether the standard would be met for various combinations of the parameters. Econometric evidence will be introduced at a later point.

The constant, B, of equation (25) can be calibrated by using 1976 data and normalizing EFF to unity in that year. To obtain the demand response curve, the gasoline price, Pgas, can be replaced by the gasoline price plus the equivalent gasoline tax. Equation (25) then becomes:

$$\overline{mpg} = \overline{mpg}(76)\left\{\frac{Pgas + ET}{Pgas(76)}\right\}^{\alpha} EFF^{1-\alpha}, \qquad (26)$$

where $\overline{mpg}(76)$ and Pgas(76) are values of these variables in 1976.

In equation (26), the 1976 value of $\overline{mpg}$ used is 16.8, the mean efficiency of new domestically produced cars. Gasoline price is $0.60 per gallon in 1976 and is assumed to be $1.09 per gallon in 1985 (nominal dollars). The CPI was 1.727 in 1976 and is assumed to be 2.629 in 1985. These assumptions are consistent with a constant real world price of oil and all U.S. oil selling at the world price in 1985. A higher world oil price will strengthen a conclusion that the efficiency standard will be met.

To evaluate whether the standard will be met in 1985, the value of ET obtained from Table 2 for $\overline{mpg}$ = mst is used in equation (26), and the resulting $\overline{mpg}$ is calculated. If the resulting value of $\overline{mpg}$ is greater than mst,

Table 3. Maximum values of $\overline{mpg}$ — 1985 demand response curve

α \ ΔEFF/EFF	0	20%	40%	60%	80%
0	16.8	20.2	23.5	26.9	30.2
.2	19.4	22.5	25.4	28.3	31.1
.4	22.4	25.0	27.5	29.7	31.9
.6	25.9	27.9	29.7	31.3	32.8
.8	30.0	31.1	32.0	32.9	33.7
1.0	34.6	34.6	34.6	34.6	34.6

Table 4. Combinations of technical efficiency increases and demand elasticities just sufficient for compliance—1985.

Technical efficiency increase ($\Delta EFF/EFF$)	Demand elasticity* (α)	Demand elasticity** (α)
0	.68	.62
10%	.63	.56
20%	.57	.49
30%	.50	.40
40%	.40	.28
50%	.28	.13
60%	.09	0†
70%	0†	0†

*Based upon a 1976 mean efficiency of domestic cars of 16.8 mpg.
**Based upon a 1976 mean efficiency of all cars purchased in the U.S. of 17.6 mpg.
†In these cases the standard would be exceeded.

then the economic incentives are sufficient for compliance, and conversely, if the resulting value is lower. A value of ET of $0.79, based upon a 6 percent interest rate, is used for 1985.

The results are presented in Tables 3 and 4. Table 3 presents the 1985 values of $\overline{mpg}$ obtained through equation (26) for various assumed increases in EFF ($\Delta EFF/EFF$) and values of α. A line has been drawn through the table to separate combinations of EFF and α for which the economic incentives are sufficient for compliance from combinations for which they are not. For low values of α and EFF the incentives are not sufficient, while for higher values they are. Note that for large enough values of α or of ($\Delta EFF/EFF$), the other parameter can be zero and yet the standard would still be met.

These data can be expressed in a different manner. Table 4 presents combinations of technical efficiency improvement and demand elasticities for which the economic incentives are *just* sufficient for compliance. The data are presented for two different calibrations of equation (26). The second and third columns present the demand elasticities that, in combination with the technical efficiency changes of the first column, are just sufficient for compliance. Column two is based upon the 1976 average domestic new car efficiency and corresponds to Table 3, while column three is based upon the mix of all cars (domestic and foreign) purchased.

Tables 3 and 4 show that for either large enough demand elasticity or large enough technology response, the efficiency standard would be met by the optimizing firm. If the demand elasticity exceeds .68, then the standards could be met even with no improvements in technology. Similarly, if technical efficiency increases by 70 percent or more from its 1976 level, then the standards would be met even if demand were perfectly nonresponsive. The greater the technology improvement the less important will be the demand response and, conversely, the greater the demand elasticity, the less will be the required technology improvement.

Equation (25) has been econometrically estimated and the results reported in a separate paper (10). Based upon data for sales of all cars in the U.S. for the time period 1957–1974, the following equation has been developed:[7]

$$\ln(\overline{mpg}) = 3.528 + .721 * \ln\frac{Pgas(-1)}{EFF} + \ln(EFF). \qquad (27)$$

$$\begin{aligned}&(7.9)\\&R^2 = .86\\&DW = 2.1\end{aligned}$$

where $Pgas(-1)$ is the real price of gasoline in the calendar year preceding the model year.[8]

Equation (27) provides empirical evidence to support a conclusion that under currently legislated incentives the efficiency standard will be met.[9] For equation (27) implies a value of α of 0.72. From Table 4, if α exceeds .68, then the efficiency standard will be met *even if there were no improvement* in technology. If a technical efficiency improvement of as little as 30 percent were to occur between 1976 and 1985, then any elasticity above .50 or .40 would imply that the incentives are sufficient for compliance with the standard. Hence, the econometric evidence presented here implies that the standard can be met based upon the currently legislated economic incentives.

In summary, the empirical evidence in conjunction with the theory supports the conclusion that the efficiency standard will be met in 1985. A similar analysis supports the conclusion that the newly promulgated intermediate year standards (20, 22, 24, 26, 27 mpg for 1980, 1981, 1982, 1983, and 1984, respectively) will also be met.

The following section examines the interactions between the efficiency standard and other proposed policy instruments. In particular, a gasoline tax and a "gas-guzzler" tax, as proposed by President Carter, are examined.

V. INTERACTION WITH GASOLINE TAX AND "GAS-GUZZLER" TAX

The analysis can be extended very simply to the situation in which the price of gasoline rises, say through increases in crude oil prices or through a gasoline tax. Since the cause of the price rise is not particularly relevant in this context, the price rise will be referred to as a gasoline tax. It will be assumed that the gasoline tax of GT dollars per gallon causes gasoline price to increase by the amount of the tax.

The effect of a gasoline tax can be seen simply by use of Figures 4 and 5. The gasoline tax of GT shifts the "demand response" curve of these figures downward by the amount of the tax, since the effects of an actual tax and of the equivalent tax were presumed to be equivalent when the "demand response" curve was derived. This is illustrated in Figure 7. If initially the standard were just met with an equivalent tax of ET', and if GT ≤ ET', then the standard would continue to be just met after the tax is imposed. The price differentials between efficient and inefficient cars will now be reduced so as to reduce the equivalent gasoline tax by GT, to ET' − GT. This is illustrated as a move from Point B to Point D in Figure 7. Thus, imposing a moderate gasoline tax when the efficiency standard is just met will not change the average efficiency of new cars ($\overline{mpg}$), but will reduce the equivalent tax by the amount of the gasoline tax. The market penalties and subsidies will be scaled down proportionately.

If the efficiency standard were not met, then the gasoline tax would *increase* the equivalent tax imposed by the manufacturer. The gasoline tax plus the increased equivalent tax combine to increase $\overline{mpg}$. This is represented by the move from Point A to Point C in Figure 7. Thus, if the efficiency standard were not met, then the manufacturer's optimal pricing policy would lead to a multiplied effect of a gasoline tax on efficiency of newly

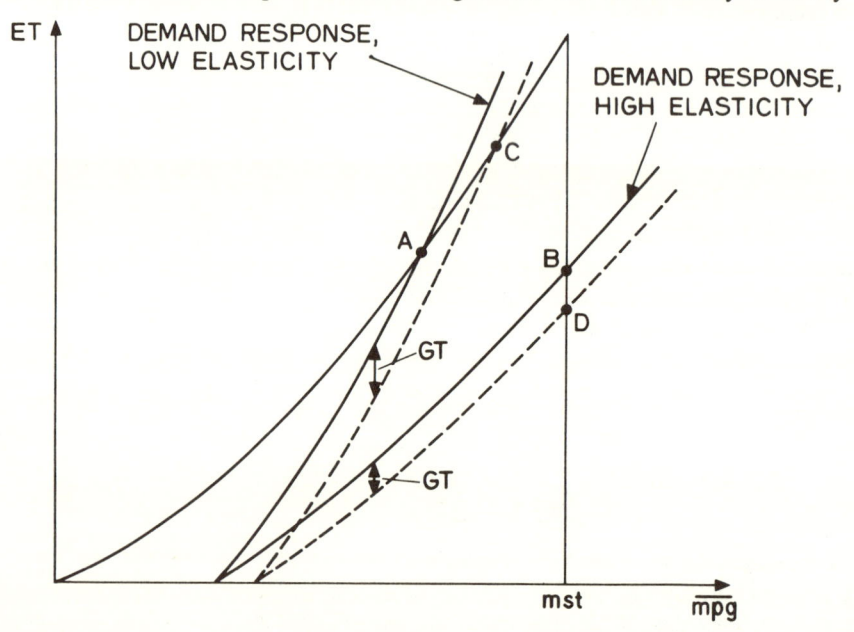

Figure 7. Response to a gasoline tax.

purchased cars. This effect would not occur under the alternative penalty structure, since the equivalent tax is independent of $\overline{\text{mpg}}$ under the alternative.

A third possibility (not illustrated here) is that the gasoline tax would be great enough to increase $\overline{\text{mpg}}$ above mst, even with ET = 0. In this case, ET would be reduced to zero and $\overline{\text{mpg}}$ would be not at all influenced by the existence of the efficiency standard.

A second possible policy instrument to be examined is a set of "gas-guzzler taxes." Under such taxes, a schedule of penalties or subsidies is imposed upon a manufacturer for selling specific automobiles.[10] While such subsidies or penalties would normally depend upon the efficiency of the automobile, they may also depend upon other characteristics, e.g., a station wagon could be treated differently from a sedan.

Let the "gas-guzzler tax" for the ith type of car be denoted by G_i, where $G_i > 0$ represents a penalty and $G_i < 0$ a subsidy. The profit equation expression of equation (6) would be modified by the addition of a term:

$$- \Sigma x_i G_i.$$

Solving for profit maximum still gives equation (11), but now equation (12) is modified:

$$T_i = \lambda \overline{\text{mpg}} \{ (\overline{\text{mpg}}/\text{mpg}_i - 1) + (\text{mst}/\overline{\text{mpg}} - 1) \} + G_i. \tag{28}$$

Expression (13) remains unchanged.

As seen by equation (28), the gas-guzzler taxes may change the T_i in several ways. For constant λ and $\overline{\text{mpg}}$, each T_i changes by G_i. However, if the efficiency standard is just met, λ may change. In particular, if the changing of each T_i by G_i were to increase $\overline{\text{mpg}}$, then λ would decrease. This decrease in λ would decrease the price differentials between inefficient and efficient cars and would compensate for the increases in price differentials caused by the gas-guzzler tax. The net effect would be to leave $\overline{\text{mpg}}$ unchanged, equal to the standard. If the efficiency standard were not met, then λ would remain equal to t. However, the price differentials caused by the gas-guzzler tax would lead to a greater value of $\overline{\text{mpg}}$ and hence to a greater equivalent gasoline tax. This would in turn lead to an even greater value of $\overline{\text{mpg}}$. Thus, if the efficiency standard were not met, then a gas-guzzler tax would have a multiplied effect, in the same manner as would a gasoline tax.

A final possibility could occur. A large enough gas-guzzler tax could shift consumer demand sufficiently for $\overline{\text{mpg}}$ to exceed the standard, even when λ was reduced to zero. In this case, λ would be reduced to zero and the resultant $\overline{\text{mpg}}$ would be in no way influenced by the existence of the efficiency standard.

A special case of gas-guzzler tax can be examined. Let the tax have the following form:[11]

$$G_i = G^0 \left[\frac{\overline{\text{mpg}}}{\text{mpg}_i} - 1 \right]. \tag{29}$$

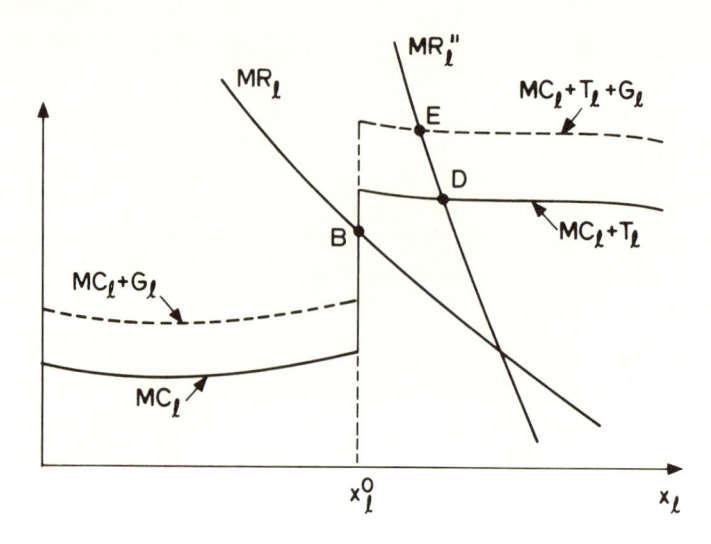

Figure 8. The effect of a gas-guzzler tax on large car sales.

The tax under equation (29) is negative (a subsidy) for automobiles having efficiency greater than the standard and is positive (a penalty) for efficiencies lower than the standard.

To examine the effects of this tax schedule, equation (28) can be evaluated for $\overline{mpg} = mst$, giving:

$$T_i = [\lambda \text{ mst} + G^0]\left[\frac{mst}{mpg_i} - 1\right]. \tag{30}$$

If the standard is met in this special case, as G^0 increases, λ will decrease so as to keep the factor $(\lambda \overline{mpg} + G^0)$ constant. All marginal conditions remain unchanged as G^0 varies. In such a situation, the imposition of the gas-guzzler tax will not change any prices seen by the consumer nor any quantities of automobiles sold. No fine of tax monies will be transferred between the automobile manufacturers and the government.[12] Such a tax would have only one effect on the automobile industry, a change in the prices of imported autos and hence in their market shares.

The effects of the special case given by equation (30) are illustrative in Figures 8 and 9. Using the analysis of Figures 2 and 3, these figures show the firm's response to a gas-guzzler tax. The solid marginal cost curves represent the current situation under the EPCA standard. The dotted lines represent the current situation plus the special case gas-guzzler taxes. Here large cars (l subscript) face a positive G_l and small cars (s subscript) face a negative G_s (a subsidy).

For demand curves that are responsive enough to price changes, the efficiency standard will be met. This situation gives an equilibrium such as Point B in Figures 8 and 9. For demand curves less responsive to prices, the efficiency standard will not be met. Point D in each figure represents this type of solution.

If the efficiency standard were met initially (Point B), then a moderate-sized gas-guzzler tax would have no effect on the numbers of cars of the two types that are sold, nor on the prices of these cars. Point B would remain the equilibrium.

If the efficiency standard were not met initially (Point D), then the gas-guzzler tax would reduce the sales of large cars and would increase the sales of small cars (Point E). These changes would be accomplished by increasing the prices of large cars and decreasing prices of small cars.[13]

The final possibility is not illustrated. If the gas-guzzler tax were large enough, then the broken line in Figure 8 could be raised sufficiently to cross the marginal revenue curve, MR_l, at an x_l lower than x_l^C. Similarly, the broken line in Figure 9 could be lowered enough to cross the curve MR_s above x_s^0. In these cases, T_s and T_l would be reduced to zero. A large enough gas-guzzler tax could cause $\overline{mpg}$ to exceed mst. In this case, the existence of the efficiency standard would be irrelevant to the solution.

Similar analyses could be developed for other policy instruments. One such instrument was promised by President Carter in the *National Energy Plan* (5). The federal government would buy automobiles more efficient on the average than the standard. This action would shift downward the demand curves for inefficient cars and upward the demand curves for efficient cars. If the efficiency standard were initially just met, then the manufacturer

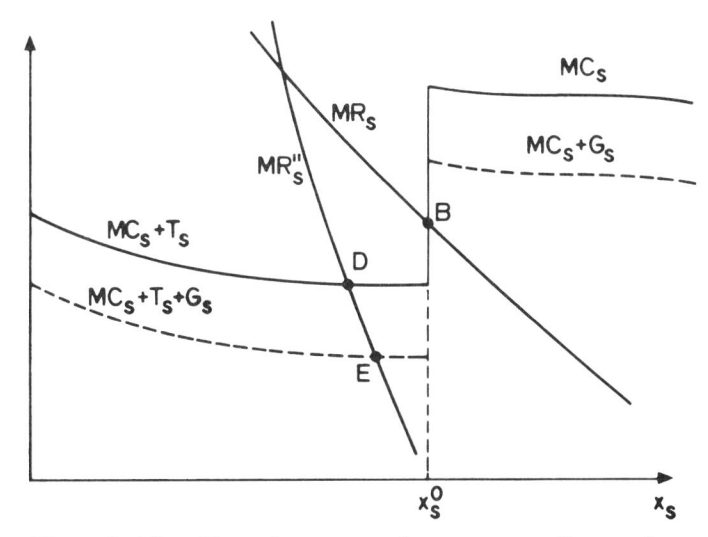

Figure 9. The effect of a gas-guzzler tax on small car sales.

response would be to lower λ, and hence to lower the price differentials between efficient and inefficient cars. The net result would be to keep mean efficiency precisely equal to the standard. The net impact of governmental action would be to increase the purchases of efficient cars by the Federal government and to decrease the purchases of efficient cars by the private sector. The mean efficiency change would be just zero!

This section has examined several policy instruments in the presence of the efficiency standard. It has been shown that if the standard is initially met, then the effect of other policy instruments on mean efficiency is generally reduced or eliminated entirely. The following section examines issues of industrial structure in the presence of the EPCA standard.

VI. INDUSTRIAL STRUCTURE ISSUES

The preceding analysis ignores any shifts in the structure of the automobile industry that could be encouraged by the efficiency standards. This section examines forces in the EPCA efficiency standard that could motivate such structural shifts.

Table 1 illustrates the marginal penalty costs under the EPCA for automobile manufacturers obtaining various efficiencies. These marginal penalty costs will generally be translated into price differences. The greater the mean efficiency (below the standard) of a manufacturer's sales, the greater will be the price penalty on low efficiency cars, and the greater the subsidy on high efficiency cars. For example, a car obtaining 5 mpg would face a marginal penalty cost of $12,000 if made by a manufacturer obtaining a 27 mpg mean efficiency, but only $4,300 if made by a manufacturer obtaining a 15 mpg average. A car obtaining 40 mpg would face a subsidy of $860 if made by a manufacturer averaging 27.5 mpg, but a *penalty* of $300 if made by a manufacturer averaging 15 mpg. A limiting case is provided by the firm selling only one line of automobiles, all of a low efficiency. If in 1985 a manufacturer sold *only* cars obtaining 10 mpg, then the civil penalty would be $1,750 per car.[14] A manufacturer just below standard would face a marginal civil penalty cost of $4,813 (see Table 1).

Under the current penalty structure, if the standards were not met, a manufacturer initially selling a disproportionate number of high efficiency cars would be given a further competitive advantage in selling high efficiency cars, and a manufacturer selling a disproportionate number of low efficiency cars would be provided a competitive advantage in selling inefficient cars. The variation in penalty/subsidy structure as average efficiency changes would be a force toward market segmentation. Initial differences in sales mix could be accentuated in response to the EPCA penalty, as long as mean efficiencies remain below the standard. The EPCA could provide a force toward an industry which includes firms specializing in low-efficiency automobiles rather than offering a mixed line of cars.

A related potential force toward industrial shifts is embedded in the current law. A manufacturer below the efficiency standard could reduce the total tax burden by dividing his firm into two or more separately taxed organizations. This could occur because the current penalty is based upon the harmonic mean efficiency of all cars sold. If a firm were split into two units of differing mean efficiencies, then the total tax paid would be based upon the arithmetic average of the two mean efficiencies. This average of the two mean efficiencies must exceed the mean efficiency of all the cars together.[15] In general, the more units into which the firm could be split, the lower could be the total penalty.

For example, a firm that obtains an 18 mpg mean efficiency in 1985 would face a civil penalty of $475 per car sold. Assuming an annual sales of two million cars, the civil penalty would be $950 million per year. Assume that the manufacturer could segment the firm into two equal-sized components such that one component obtains a mean efficiency of 27.5 mpg, and the other obtains a mean efficiency of 13.4 mpg. Then, the more efficient component would face no penalty, while the less efficient would face a penalty of $705 per car. The total penalty would be $705 million, a net reduction of $245 million per year.

This manufacturer could reduce taxes by further division. Assume that the less efficient half can be divided into two quarters with mean efficiencies of 10.08 mpg and 20 mpg. The least efficient quarter would face a penalty of $871 per car, while the other would face a penalty of $375 per car. The total penalty would be reduced from $705 million to $623 million, for an additional annual penalty savings of $82 million.

The hypothetical division could occur if a firm were to divest itself of one or more divisions. But, less unlikely, the firm could shift some operations to a foreign country. Since the law specifies that the foreign and domestic operations of a firm will be separately penalized, this shift could effect the desired splitting, without requiring divestiture.

While firms are not likely to move part of their operations to foreign countries simply in response to the civil penalty, if the standard were not met the penalty would provide an additional incentive for a firm already considering the shift. Hence, the EPCA could provide some incentive for market segmentation, either geographic segmentation or segmentation by size class of auto.

The alternative penalty structure defined in section II avoids the incentives for structural change discussed above. To see this, equation (4), which defines the alternative penalty structure, can be combined with equation (3), the definition of the harmonic mean, and equation (2). The alternative penalty structure can be expressed as follows:

$$F' = \begin{cases} t(mst)^2 \{\Sigma(x_i/mpg_i) - \Sigma(x_i/mst)\}, & \text{for } \overline{mpg} \leq mst \\ 0 & \text{otherwise} \end{cases} \quad (31)$$

The penalty structure of equation (31) is based upon the average of the factors ($1/mpg_i$). Splitting a firm into two units will not reduce the total penalty paid, since averaging is a linear mathematical operation. The alternative penalty structure would circumvent the potential problems of the current structure discussed above.

The incentives for industrial structural change would be of a different type if manufacturers do meet the standard. Assume two manufacturers face dissimilar demand curves such that manufacturer A initially sells cars with a higher mean efficiency than does manufacturer B. Both would meet the standard under the current penalty structure. However, manufacturer A would need a lower effective tax (a lower value of λ), than would manufacturer B, in order to just meet the standard. The result would be larger penalties and subsidies incorporated into the pricing structure of manufacturer B. Manufacturer B would charge more than A for low-efficiency cars and less than A for high-efficiency cars.

The pricing differences would reduce manufacturer A's market share of efficient cars while increasing his market share of inefficient cars. The net result would be to reduce or eliminate the differences in market mixes sold by the various manufacturers. Segmentation would be reduced.

In summary, if the standard is met by each manufacturer, then the current penalty structure will lead to a greater degree of pricing dispersion among manufacturers, and to a lesser degree of market mix dispersion than would occur without the standards. The net result on total market shares of the various producers is as yet unclear.

VII. SUMMARY AND CONCLUSIONS

This paper has examined the probable market responses to the new car mean efficiency standards mandated by the Energy Policy and Conservation Act. The two types of industry responses—technological responses and pricing responses—have been identified and described briefly. The theory of the latter response has been developed. The theory presented highlighted the interaction between the choice of the firm and the choices of consumers in purchasing new cars and the properties of the resultant equilibrium.

The theory has been merged with quantitative estimates of the effect of the standard. It is shown that only moderate increases in technical efficiency and moderate demand responsiveness are required for compliance with the standard, if manufacturers price in a profit-maximizing manner.

Econometric evidence cited suggests that the demand responsiveness is great enough that the standards would be met even without any changes in the technology of automobiles. Hence, it can be concluded that the standard will be met under current economic incentives.

Other policy instruments—a gasoline tax and a gas-guzzler tax—have been examined in conjunction with the efficiency standard. It is shown that if the efficiency standard is initially met, then for moderate values of the gasoline tax or the gas-guzzler tax, neither policy instrument will change the mean efficiency of cars sold. The standard will be met *precisely* either with or without these additional instruments.

Industrial structure issues associated with the standards have also been examined. Under the current penalty structure, if the standards are not met there is a force toward market segmentation. If the standards are met there is a force toward market mix homogeneity and price dispersion. An alternative penalty formula has been proposed that will eliminate the force toward segmentation.

This paper concludes that the economic incentives of the current penalty structure are sufficient to motivate compliance with the EPCA new car efficiency standards. A small change in the formula for the penalty could eliminate possible anomalous effects. Policy instruments such as moderate gas-guzzler taxes or gasoline tax may have no effect on mean new car efficiency.

FOOTNOTES

*The author is an associate professor of Engineering-Economic Systems at Stanford University. The author would like to thank, without implicating, the following people for helpful comments and criticisms on earlier versions of this paper and on the underlying research: Thomas Cotton, Douglas Finlay, William Hogan, Anjum Mir, J. Michael Power, Mark Rodekohr, Malcolm Shealy, James Stucker, and James Wetzler. Any errors, of course, are the sole responsibility of the author. Partial financial support for the research was provided by the Energy Research and Development Administration, Office of Conservation Planning Policy.

1. The harmonic mean efficiency is equal to the harmonic mean of miles per gallon obtained by each model, with weights corresponding to the fraction of automobiles of the various models sold. The harmonic mean efficiency is simply the inverse of the average of gallons per mile obtained by the various models. The average of gallons per mile corresponds more closely to total gasoline consumption than would the average of miles per gallon. Equation (3) defines harmonic mean efficiency in mathematical terms.

2. Unless otherwise indicated, all summations will be performed over the index i.

3. Recently, an unpublished paper by James P. Stucker (9) has come to my attention. This paper does incorporate both pricing response and technological response. A recently published draft by Allen Jacobs and Lawrence Linden (6) also examines the pricing responses.

4. When $\overline{mpg}$ > mst, the final term, $\partial F / \partial x_i$, equals zero and the normal profit maximization condition is satisfied.

5. The magnitudes of the penalties are greatly influenced by the precise definition of "average efficiency." The EPCA precisely specifies a harmonic mean efficiency. If a conventional averaging of the mpg_i had been specified, then the penalties would have been much smaller. For example, in 1985 penalties would have been $2,250, $1,750, and $750 for autos obtaining 5 mpg, 10 mpg, and 20 mpg, respectively, and subsidies would have been $250 and $1,250 for cars obtaining 30 mpg and 40 mpg, respectively.

6. See Sweeney (10) for a more complete discussion of this relationship.

7. t-statistics are in parentheses.

8. The lagged variable is used primarily because the model year begins well before the calendar year. A similar alternative equation has been developed using a contemporaneous price. Generally the econometric properties of this alternative equation are dominated by those of equation (27). See (10) for further discussion.

9. This conclusion, using somewhat different methods of analysis, is the same as that reached by Stucker, *et al.* (9). Their approach estimated technology response as well as demand response. E. A., Jacobs (6) also concludes that the standards are likely to be met.

10. Quantitative estimates of the effects of President Carter's proposed gas-guzzler taxes and his proposed gasoline tax are presented in another paper (11). The theory used in that paper is identical to that presented here.

11. This form is almost precisely identical to that proposed by President Carter in the *National Energy Plan* (5).

12. This occurs because under equation (30), if the average efficiency standard is just met, then the total gas-guzzler tax paid is precisely zero.

13. The increase in the large car price not only will decrease large car demand, but also will shift small car demand upward. Conversely, the decrease in small car price will shift large car demand downward. These shifts are not illustrated in Figures 8 and 9. The net effect of the demand curve shifts is to reinforce the demand changes illustrated in the two figures.

14. $(27.5 - 10) \times \$100 = \$1,750$.

15. This follows from the mathematical properties of geometric means.

REFERENCES

1. Cato, D., M., Rodekohr, and J. L., Sweeney, "The Capital Stock Adjustment Process and the Demand for Gasoline: A market Share Approach," in *Economic Dimensions of Energy Demand and Supply*, A. B. Askin and J. Kraft (eds.). Lexington Books, Lexington, Mass., 1976.

2. ———, ———, and ———, "Demand for Gasoline: Application of Commodity Hierarchy Theory," *Proceedings of the Business and Economic Statistics Section, American Statistical Association*, 1975.

3. Chamberlain, C., "A Preliminary Model of Auto Choice by Class of Car: Aggregate State Data," Transportation Systems Center, Cambridge, Mass., December 1974.

4. Energy and Environmental Analysis, Inc., *Gasoline Consumption Model*, Arlington, Virginia, July 1975.

5. Executive Office of the President, Energy Policy and Planning, *The National Energy Plan*, 1977.

6. Jacobs., E. A. and L. H. Linden, "Average Fuel Economy Standards and the Automobile Industry," Chapter 3 of MIT Energy Laboratory Report 77-007, *Regulating the Automobile*, Cambridge, Mass., August 1977.

7. Office of the Secretary, U.S. Department of Transportation, *Marketing and Mobility: Report of a Panel of the Interagency Task Force on Motor Vehicle Goals beyond 1980*, Publications Section (TAD-443.1), Washington, D.C., March 1976.

8. Schink, R. R. and C. J., Loxley, *An Analysis of the Automobile Market: Modeling the Long-Run Determinants of the Demand for Automobiles*, 3 volumes, Wharton Econometric Forecasting Associates, Inc., Philadelphia, March 1977.
9. Stucker, J. P., B. K. Burright, and W. E. Mooz, *The Domestic Automobile Industry: Modeling its Response to Incentives for Increased Fuel Economy*, R-2124-NSF, The RAND Corporation (forthcoming).
10. Sweeney, J. L., "The Demand for Gasoline: A Vintage Capital Model," Department of Engineering-Economic Systems, Stanford University, 1977.
11. ———, "The Impact of the President's Gasoline Tax and Gas-Guzzler Tax on Gasoline Consumption," Department of Engineering-Economic Systems, Stanford University, 1977. Also in *DRI Energy Bulletin*, Vol. 4, No. 4, July 1977.

FACTORS LEADING TO STRUCTURAL CHANGE IN THE U.S. OIL-REFINING INDUSTRY IN THE POSTWAR PERIOD

Stephen C. Peck, UNIVERSITY OF CALIFORNIA, BERKELEY, AND ELECTRIC POWER RESEARCH INSTITUTE

Scott Harvey, UNIVERSITY OF CALIFORNIA, BERKELEY

1. INTRODUCTION

In this paper we investigate a number of the factors which led to structural change in the U.S. oil-refining industry in the period following the Second World War. In the first major section of the paper we identify and briefly explore the implications of a number of changes in the technological and institutional environment of the industry. These are the introduction of market demand prorationing by the oil-producing states in the 1930s, of catalytic cracking in the late 1930s, of large-diameter crude and product pipelines in the postwar period, and the well-known Pipeline Consent Decree of 1941. Next, we discuss the operation and effect on refiners of the oil import quota introduced in 1959. We then discuss barriers to entry in the oil-refining industry and give an account of both entry from outside the industry and interregional entry in the postwar period. Finally, we discuss the effects of mergers on industry concentration.

In the second major section of the paper we analyze Gibrat's Law of Proportionate Effect (LPE) with data on the real capacity of surviving firms in the U.S. oil-refining industry for the period 1950–1974. We claim that there are several regional markets in the United States and we study firm growth behavior in the East Coast market and the West Coast market separately. We find that the LPE is rejected in the majority of cases because small surviving firms tended to grow faster than large firms. We also examine the effect on estimated firm growth behavior of incorrectly aggregating the East Coast and West Coast markets. Next, we claim that the population of U.S. refineries should be classified into full-range refineries, on the one hand, and specialty plants producing mainly asphalt and lube oil on the other. Since full-range refineries serve different markets than specialty refiners serve we claim that it is inappropriate to investigate their growth behavior together, and we investigate the effect in our data of excluding known specialty plants. We also investigate the regression error terms.

2. CHANGES IN THE TECHNOLOGICAL AND INSTITUTIONAL ENVIRONMENT OF THE INDUSTRY

In the immediate postwar period, several changes in the technological and institutional environment led to significant changes in the structure of the domestic oil-refining industry. The first change in the environment, the establishment by the major crude oil producing states of an effective system of crude oil production controls, began to effect the industry in the early 1930s; but it was only in the late 1930s that the system became fully effective and the advent of the Second World War delayed the full impact of this change. The introduction of production controls or prorationing was a response to the excessively rapid development of several newly discovered oil fields in the 1930s. The major effect of prorationing on the refining industry was to reduce appreciably the profitability of refineries operating in the major crude producing regions since they no longer were able to take advantage of the enormous crude-product price differentials which had inevitably developed in areas with flush production. A secondary effect of this institutional change was to reduce the quantity of crude oil available to entering firms. Prorationing and its effect on refining is discussed in greater detail in chapter 21 of MacLean and Haigh (8).

The second change which affected the industry technological environment was the spread of catalytic cracking. This development put downward pressure on the profit margin of refineries which did not convert because the process not only allowed the production of a larger volume of high-value products from a barrel of crude oil and permitted greater adaptation of yields to the seasonal variations in product demand but also achieved these gains at a cost which allowed for significantly increased profits at the prevailing price level. The introduction of catalytic cracking affected industry structure because, at least in the early postwar years, it was not possible to construct effective catalytic crackers for refineries of less than 5,000 bbls/day capacity. [For details, see the table on p. 497 of De Chazeau and Kahn (4) and articles by Nelson in the *Oil and Gas Journal* (19).] As a result, many small refineries were shut down as their operating margin deteriorated.

The third change in the industry environment in the early postwar period was the practical introduction and spread of large-diameter pipelines. Cookenboo (2) lists eight crude oil pipelines built between 1944 and 1954 which had diameters of between 16 and 20 inches and another eight built in the same period with diameters of 20 inches or more. This development resulted in a radical fall in the cost of transporting large quantities of crude oil from the producing areas to large market-oriented refineries. Cookenboo (3) calculated that, in this period, the minimum cost per 1,000-barrel miles for transporting crude oil in an 8-inch pipeline (25,000 bbls/day throughput) was about 53 cents, while the cost for a 20-inch pipeline (200,000 bbls/day throughput) was about 13.5 cents. This development eroded the protection available to the small field refinery located at the producing area since its margin was often constrained by the cost of shipping crude oil from the field to a large refinery and shipping product back.

Another important effect of the development of the large-diameter pipeline was the spread of joint-venture pipelines. Since the efficient throughput level of a large-diameter pipeline was greater in most cases than the capacity of a single firm's refineries, only multiple ownership allowed the realization of these scale economies and the preservation of integrated operations. Since 1944, the joint venture pipeline has become increasingly characteristic of the organization of new pipelines transporting both crude oil and various petroleum products.

The fourth change to affect the refining industry was also concerned with pipelines; this was the Consent Decree of 1941. Trunk pipeline transportation of petroleum liquids, because of the large economies of scale, is generally a natural oligopoly and sometimes a natural monopoly. As a result, these pipelines gradually came to be regulated by the ICC as common carriers and were required to provide nondiscreminatory access to all shippers by the time of the Second World War. The Consent Decree of 1941 brought pipeline tariffs under effective regulation by constraining owner shippers to receive a 7 percent return on the value of their pipeline investment rather than the exorbitant returns they had earned previously. The manner in which this was implemented is complex and the reader should refer to Wolbert (21) for a discussion of the details.

These four changes had a number of effects on industry structure. The first three greatly reduced the profitability of the small field refineries which generally belonged to independents and supplied local markets. These left the industry in large numbers between 1935 and the late 1950s. Their exit was not immediate because the operating costs of an existing refinery are a relatively small proportion of total costs and many continued operations for some time after the advent of such unfavorable conditions. Table 1 presents some data indicative of the fate of these small refineries in the north and east Texas, the Los Angeles, and the Houston-Beaumont regions. North and east Texas was primarily a producing region, whereas the latter two were both producing and major market regions.

Probably because of the lack of effective regulation of crude oil pipelines in the prewar period, the majority of independent refiners had been located in areas producing significant quantities of crude oil. Therefore, the changes in the industry which worsened the position of the small crude-oriented refiner also tended to decrease competition and restrict entry in markets where crude production was important. This is indicated by Table 1. However, the falling transport cost due to large-diameter pipelines also tended to increase the size of the geographic market regions and, hence, somewhat offset the rise in concentration in the local markets.

The development of joint-venture pipelines and the Consent Decree of 1941 have tended to improve the position of the independent market-located refinery. Joint ventures in pipelines have sometimes enabled independents to buy interests in large-diameter pipelines and thus achieve competitive shipping costs. The Consent Decree has been effective in reducing the rate of return on pipeline operations below the exorbitant levels of the prewar years and in making crude access substantially freer than before the war, particularly for the relatively large independent.

It is quite doubtful, however, whether these changes in the industry have reduced the monopoly aspects of large-diameter pipelines. Reynolds (11), among others, has shown that an integrated pipeline owner can still reap monopoly profits by restricting the capacity of the pipeline even when rates are regulated. De-integration of pipeline operations has been proposed as a solution of this problem at various times in the postwar period. It seems to us that while this might reduce the ability of integrated pipeline firms to circumvent rate regulation, it does not deal with the fundamental problem that the economies of scale in pipelines dictate a very small number of competitors in pipeline markets and that these firms will have substantial monopoly power. More seriously, this solution would probably worsen the problems associated with the bilateral monopoly which will usually exist at one or both ends of the pipeline.

Table 1.

	Los Angeles Basin refineries						North and East Texas refineries						Houston-Beaumont Region refineries					
	1935		1947		1959		1935		1947		1959		1935		1947		1959	
Size class	op	sd	op	sd	op	sd	op	sd	op	sd	op	sd	op	sd	op	sd	op	sd
0–5,000 bbls/day																		
No of plants	24	3	17	2	5	0	39	44	14	1	5	1	2	0	7	0	1	1
Total capacity	56	7	50	6	19	0	92	84	38	1	9	2	7	0	25	0	3	5
5–15,000 bbls/day																		
No of plants	8	1	7	2	5	2	4	2	9	1	5	0	6	0	1	1	1	0
Total capacity	73	6	61	16	47	24	38	25	81	7	47	0	63	0	7	6	7	0
15–50,000 bbls/day																		
No of plants	5	0	3	0	1	0	0	0	0	0	1	0	6	0	6	2	4	1
Total capacity	155	0	88	0	30	0	0	0	0	0	20	0	178	0	196	38	160	20
50,000 bbls/day																		
No of plants	2	1	4	0	6	0	0	0	0	0	0	0	4	0	7	0	11	0
Total capacity	151	55	301	0	688	0	0	0	0	0	0	0	370	0	903	0	1771	0
Percent of total capacity embodied in largest 8 operating plants	73		81		93		45		61		97		82		84		81	

Notes: Capacity is measured in thousands of barrels per day.

The data used in constructing this table were taken from "Petroleum Refineries Including Cracking Plants in U.S.," Information Circulars, Department of Interior, Bureau of Mines, September 1935, March 1948, January 1959. The table somewhat understates the drop in the number of field refineries since a number of field refineries are unlocatable in 1935.

"op" and "sd" stand for "operating" and "shutdown," respectively.

There can be no question but that the policy of the U.S. government toward oil imports was the major issue of the 1950s and 1960s for the domestic oil industry, especially for areas east of the Rocky Mountains. An examination of oil imports in the postwar period shows that, while the initial impetus to increased imports came from the large international firms and a few established importers, by the end of the 1950s it was the new importers who were endangering the level of the domestic crude price maintained by various state agencies engaged in market demand prorationing. Adelman (1) has argued plausibly that the force which induced the differential behavior between the large international firms and the new importers in the 1952–1959 period was the fear of retaliatory action by the various state regulatory agencies and the Congress. A reading of the trade press during the 1950s, particularly *The Oil and Gas Journal* (19), provides considerable support for this view. Thus, it was small refiners, with little or no domestic crude production and so not intimidated by state agencies, who became increasingly important as crude oil importers in the late 1950s. Since this situation was different from the usual state of affairs in which unintegrated firms had difficulty obtaining crude supplies, the late 1950s saw an increase of entry into the industry and aggressive expansion by independent refiners.

In early 1959 President Eisenhower established a mandatory oil import quota program which put an immediate end to this situation. The import quota eliminated the downward pressure on the price of domestic crude, and, because of its peculiar structure, rewarded existing refiners. The government allocated the right to import foreign crude to domestic refiners on two bases. The first basis was the level of the firm's refinery runs of domestic crude in the previous period (the period varied from three months to a year) with small firms being favored by the use of a sliding scale. The second basis was that quotas were allocated by allowing firms to import a specified percentage of their last allocation under the voluntary import program, if that was higher than their allocation on the basis of refinery runs. Since the allocations under the voluntary program were based on the level of imports in the mid-1950s, the latter provision benefited only the established importers. Because of the large difference between the price of foreign and domestic crude, the quota system subsidized existing refiners. Shaffer (13) contains a good discussion of the quota system as it evolved until about 1968. Generalizing over the period of the 1960s, we believe that the quota system greatly subsidized the operation of small, inefficient plants because of the sliding scale, and that it reduced the profitability of foreign exploration for domestic refiner-producers. In addition, the quota system reduced the ease of entry for efficiently sized new firms by restricting their access to foreign crude. The restriction was due to the provisions which disallowed the purchase of foreign crude, only permitting it to be swapped for domestic crude and the computation of a firm's import quota on the basis of previous runs of domestic crude.

We next discuss entry. Previous students of the industry have identified four important barriers to entry. The first is that owing to economies of scale; the combination of scale economies and quite inelastic demand and supply curves have produced a situation in which supernormal profits could be earned, yet the entry of one efficiently sized refinery of capacity between 60 and 150,000 bbls/day would have driven price substantially below long-run average cost. A second barrier has been difficulty of access to crude oil; vertical integration of existing firms, prorationing and import quotas have in the past provided the potential for substantially higher crude costs for unintegrated entrants. A third barrier has been the difficulty of obtaining access to product markets; vertical integration and long-term contracts for product sales have frequently created a situation in which an entrant had to develop marketing outlets retailing purchased products substantially before the construction of a new refinery if he were to obtain the market price for his output. This barrier has been significant because a 30,000 bbls/day refinery, running at capacity with a 40 percent gasoline yield, produces an output sufficient for 150 high-volume gas stations. The final barrier has been due to absolute capital cost. The high cost of a large, new refinery, particularly if it is necessary also to develop crude production and marketing, has contributed toward substantially reducing the pool of potential entrants. A figure of between $700 and $1,000 per bbl/day of capacity for the late 1950s is a reasonable estimate of capital cost, according to various articles by W. L. Nelson in *The Oil and Gas Journal* (19). Since 1968, entry into the industry has become somewhat easier because of the increasing level of imports, sales of royalty oil from offshore Federal leases, and the Federal oil policy of the 1970s which discriminated in favour of small firms. [See "Small Refiners Due U.S. Offshore Royalty Oil," in *The Oil and Gas Journal* (19), January 24, 1972, p. 33.]

In the postwar period firms have rather frequently entered new regions or new product lines by constructing refiners. But, in view of the barriers mentioned above, it is not surprising that the vast bulk of entrants have constructed extremely small plants, as is shown in Table 2. The table also indicates the dearth of entry during the early years of the oil import program. We examined the fifteen entrants in Table 2 which constructed plants larger than 10,000 bbls/day. It appeared that a necessary condition to enter by building a refinery in this size range was that the firm should have prior access to marketing or crude oil. Six of the entrants were existing refiners expanding into different regional markets where they were already producing or marketing. Four were refineries built by significant marketers which were integrating backward. One was built by a consortium of crude producing firms inte-

Table 2. Entrants into U.S. regional refining markets, 1947–1976.

Size class	1947–1959 Total no. of entrants	1947–1959 No. of entrants w/crack'g	1947–1959 No. of entrants which are asphalt plants	1947–1959 Total initial size	1959–1967 Total no. of entrants	1959–1967 No. of entrants w/crack'g	1959–1967 No. of entrants which are asphalt plants	1959–1967 Total initial size	1967–1976 Total no. of entrants	1967–1976 No. of entrants w/crack'g	1967–1976 No. of entrants which are asphalt plants	1967–1976 Total initial size
0–4,000 bbls/day	37	1	8	48	14	2	2	21	17	0	3	31
4–10,000 bbls/day	10	3	4	56	0	0	0	0	12	1	1	70
10–30,000 bbls/day	4	4	0	61	0	0	0	0	4	1	0	50
30,000+ bbls/day	4	4	0	152	0	0	0	0	3	1	0	146

Notes: Sources of table are *Petroleum Refineries in the United States*, published annually by the U.S. Bureau of Mines, and, in addition, *The Oil and Gas Journal*.
All capacity is measured in thousands of bbls/calendar day.
Total initial size is the capacity of all entering refineries after one full year of operation; we measured capacity in this way because all processing units do not typically come on stream immediately in a new refinery. The table includes both interregional entrants and firms not previously engaged in refining. To construct this table, the United States was divided into five regional markets: the West Coast, Rocky Mountains, midcontinent, East and Gulf Coast, and New Mexico–West Texas.

grating forward. One was built by a firm with limited previous involvement in the industry, and three were recent entrants concerning which there is little documentation.

A second important form of entry into a new product line or region has been by acquisition of an existing refiner and has been fairly common in the postwar period. This form of entry is not subject to many of the barriers associated with the construction of a new refinery. Entry via merger has been the predominant form of entry for firms new to the refining industry. Expecially important in this type of entry have been gas and chemical companies, but a wide assortment of firms have entered in this fashion; occasionally such entry has led to rapid and substantial expansion of the existing plant.

While only one major, Gulf, has used merger to enter a new regional market, a number of large integrated oil firms have done so since 1946. Phillips Petroleum used merger to enter the Rockies in 1947 and the West Coast in 1966. Continental entered the West Coast market in 1961. Atlantic entered the Rockies in 1969, the mid-continent in 1969, and the West Coast in 1966. Union Oil entered the East and mid-continent markets in 1965 by merging, and Sohio also used merger to enter the East Coast Market in 1969. Numerous smaller firms, such as Coastal States Gas, Toscopetro Corp., Signal Oil and Gas, Marathon Oil, Kerr McGee and Murphy used merger to diversify into additional markets. Interregional mergers, however, seemed only rarely to accelerate substantially the expansion of the acquired firm. It is interesting to note that if interregional merger is legally barred, entry may take place by the construction of a new refinery which presumably has a more salutory effect on competition. An example of this is provided by the attempted Exxon acquisition of the Tidewater West Coast refining and marketing properties in late 1963 which was blocked because of Justice Department opposition. In 1969 Exxon entered the West Coast refining market by building a 70,000 bbls/day refinery at Benicia, near San Francisco.

Some systematic information on mergers in the oil-refining industry has been compiled by Weiss (20) for the period 1948–1958. He computed that 66.3 percent of all capacity acquired was smaller than 30,000 bbls/day which he had identified tentatively as the minimum optimal scale. The majority of these mergers was probably prompted by the changes in the institutional and technological environment of the industry identified at the beginning of this section. One hundred percent and 47.1 percent of the capacity acquired by the four and eight majors, respectively, was smaller than 30,000 bbls/day. Partly as a result of this, mergers by the majors caused the four and eight firm concentration ratios to rise by only 0.34 and 0.72 of a percent over the decade. Weiss also showed that during this time the majors did not use interregional acquisitions as a form of entry.

We have computed the following merger data for the period 1959–1976. Of the 20 firms with more than 100,000 bbls/day of capacity in 1959, four disappeared in mergers by 1976 and two more sold significant portions of their refining capacity to other refiners. Of the six firms with between 50 and 100,000 bbls/day of capacity on January 1, 1959, five disappeared in mergers by 1976. Of the 71 firms with more than 10,000 bbls/day of capacity in 1959, 21 were completely absorbed by other refiners by January 1, 1976. Eleven of these firms disappeared in pure interregional mergers, which were discussed above. In contrast, only eight of the 53 firms with more than 10,000 bbls/day capacity on January 1, 1947 had vanished by merger by January 1, 1959, and none of the 17 with greater than 100,000 bbls/day capacity were acquired.

3. AN INVESTIGATION OF FIRM GROWTH BEHAVIOR IN THE U.S. OIL REFINING INDUSTRY FOR 1950–1974.

Economists have long been interested in stochastic model of firm growth. Simon and Bonini (17) pointed out that if the probability distribution of firm growth rate was independent of firm size, then the resulting steady-state probability distribution of firm sizes would have the Yule form if the model allowed for the birth of firms or the lognormal form if the model did not allow for firm birth. They remarked that the actual distribution of firm sizes seemed to approximate these theoretically derived distributions. Hymer and Pashigian (6) tested for the largest firms of nine two-digit industries whether the mean and standard deviation of growth rates were independent of firm size. They found that the mean growth rates appeared to be so, but that there was a strong tendency for the standard deviation of growth rates to decline with increasing firm size. Mansfield (9) investigated for all the firms in three industries—steel, petroleum refining, and tires—whether the mean and standard deviation of firm growth rate were independent of firm size; he found that, on the whole, the mean and standard deviations of the growth rates of surviving firms tended to decline with increases in firm size. Sherman (14) argued that a firm's growth rate should be inversely proportional to its market share in a high-barrier but not a low-barrier industry. He carried out some empirical work which, he claimed, supported this position.

There are two ways in which these models of firm growth may be viewed. First, the models may be viewed as referring to the growth behavior of the whole firm in all its lines of business and all its geographical markets. Second, the models may be viewed as referring to the growth behavior of firms within a particular market. We believe that the actual empirical studies of Simon and Bonini (17), Hymer and Pashigian (6), Mansfield (9) and Sherman

(14) are of the first type although the theoretical parts of some of the papers frequently sound as if they refer to a study of the second type. In this paper we report on what we believe to be the first empirical study of the second type insofar as we analyze firm growth within well-defined markets.

We studied the relationship between firm growth rate and firm size in the U.S. oil-refinery industry in the period 1950–1974. The underlying model was taken to be

$$k_{ij}(t+\Delta) = e^{\alpha j}(k_{ij}(t))^{\beta_j} e^{u_{ij}(t,\Delta)}, \tag{1}$$

where $k_{ij}(t+\Delta)$ is the real capacity of firm i in market j at time $t+\Delta$, α_j and β_j are parameters of the model for market j and $u_{ij}(t,\Delta)$ is an independently distributed random error term with a zero mean. If $\beta_j = 1$ and the variance of the error term is constant, the model collapses to Gibrat's Law of Proportionate Effect, henceforth referred to as LPE.

We believe that the most satisfactory way to interpret equation (1) is to consider it as having been derived from an equation of form (1'):

$$\frac{k_{ij}(t+\Delta)}{k_{ij}(t)} = e^{\gamma j} k_j(t)^{v_j} k_{ij}(t)^{\beta_j - 1} e^{u_{ij}(t,\Delta)}, \tag{1'}$$

where $k_j(t)$ is the size of market j at time t. Equation (1') implies that firm i's proportional growth rate in market j depends on the size of market j and firm i's initial size in that market. Note that equation (1) can be derived from equation. (1') by multiplying both sides by $k_{ij}(t)$ and setting $e^{\gamma j} k_j(t)^{v_j}$ equal to $e^{\alpha j}$. We believe that a persuasive mechanism underlying model (1') is that a firm would be unwilling to increase its capacity excessively during the period t to $t+\Delta$ because too great an increase would depress market price too much or generate too much excess capacity for the firm. Furthermore, the effect of a 5 percent increase in firm capacity would have a greater effect on market price for a large than for a small firm. Thus we would expect β_j to be less than unity, implying that a firm's growth rate is inversely related to its size. In addition, we would expect a firm to feel less constrained the larger is the market; hence we would expect v_j to be positive. A fuller discussion of analytical models underlying firm growth behavior is provided in another paper, Peck (10).

In this paper we analyze the growth behavior of firms in the U.S. oil refinery industry. Our study differs from Mansfield's (9) in three important respects. First, Mansfield's test was made with respect to all refineries of a firm anywhere in the world; our test is made with respect to refinery market regions in the U.S. Furthermore, we investigate the effect of estimating model (1) with data from geographical markets which are too broadly defined. Second, Mansfield's study used all refineries listed in the various surveys, whereas our test is based, insofar as is possible, only on full-range refineries. We also investigated the effect on the estimation of model (1) of introducing specialty refineries into the sample. Third, Mansfield's study treated mergers as growth; we do not.[2]

We feel that the first change is necessary since the refinery products market is not world-wide in extent and the U.S. market is not even national. It is our position that in the United States there are at least four major regional markets and possibly one minor regional market. These regions may be described as the West Coast, Rocky Mountains, midcontinent, East and Gulf Coasts, and New Mexico–West Texas markets. We believe that estimating model (1) with data from markets which are too broadly defined may result in estimates of the slope coefficient which are closer to unity than is justified by the true β_j's in the regional markets.

To illustrate this point, we assume that there are two regional markets, 1 and 2. In each market the model of firm growth is given by an equation such as (1). In market 1 there are three firms of initial capacity 50,100, and 150,000 bbls. per day, respectively; likewise in market 2. The growth behavior of the firms in market 1 is given by equation (2) and that of the firms in market 2 by equation (3). The parameters of these equations have approximately the same magnitudes as those which we estimated; the error terms have been dropped for purposes of simple exposition.

$$\log k_{i1}(t + \Delta) = .30 + .95 \log k_{i1}(t), \qquad (2)$$

$$\log k_{i2}(t + \Delta) = .40 + .95 \log k_{i2}(t). \qquad (3)$$

The data generated by models (2) and (3) are displayed in Table 3.

Now it is obvious that a regression of $\log k_{ij}(t + \Delta)$ on $\log k_{ij}(t)$ for the three observations of market 1 will yield a slope of .95 and an intercept of .30. Likewise such a regression for the three observations of market 2 will yield a slope of .95 and an intercept of .40. Also a regression on the combined six observations of markets 1 and 2 will have a slope of .95 and an intercept of .35. If we introduced the error terms $u_{ij}(t,\Delta)$, it would be possible to claim that the estimates of the slope coefficients in all these three regressions were unbiased. But now suppose that the largest firm in market 1 is identical with the largest firm in market 2; in other words, one of the firms is a multi-region firm and has capacity of 150 in each of the markets. We may now

Table 3

	Market 1			Market 2	
$k_{i1}(t)$	$\log k_{i1}(t)$	$\log k_{i1}(t + \Delta)$	$k_{i2}(t)$	$\log k_{i2}(t)$	$\log k_{i2}(t + \Delta)$
50	3.912	4.016	50	3.912	4.116
100	4.605	4.675	100	4.605	4.775
150	5.011	5.060	150	5.011	5.160

Structural Change in U.S. Oil-Refining Industry 147

carry out a pooled regression on the five observations from markets 1 and 2. These five observations are composed of the first two firms of markets 1 and 2, respectively; the fifth observation is constructed from the largest firm in the two markets. Its size at time t is 300; and its size at time $(t + \Delta)$ is $\exp(5.060) + \exp(5.160)$. In this case the regression coefficient for the slope may be computed to be .969. If the error term $u_{ij}(t,\Delta)$ were introduced, it would be possible to claim that the estimator of the slope coefficient in the pooled regression was biased toward 1.[3] Furthermore, in this particular example chosen with realistic coefficients, the extent of the bias is considerable. The coefficient is shifted 38 percent toward a value of 1, $((.969 - .95) \div (1.00 - .95))$. For ease of future reference we call this source of bias "pooling bias."

We now identify a second source of bias which we call "combination bias." Combination bias is caused by the existence of different intercept terms for the firm growth model in different markets as in equations (2) and (3). It should be evident from our discussion of equation (1') that the intercept term might well be different in different markets. We now provide an example of combination bias. Suppose that the firms in markets 1 and 2 are separate and that the three firms in market 1 are of sizes 50, 50, 100, respectively,

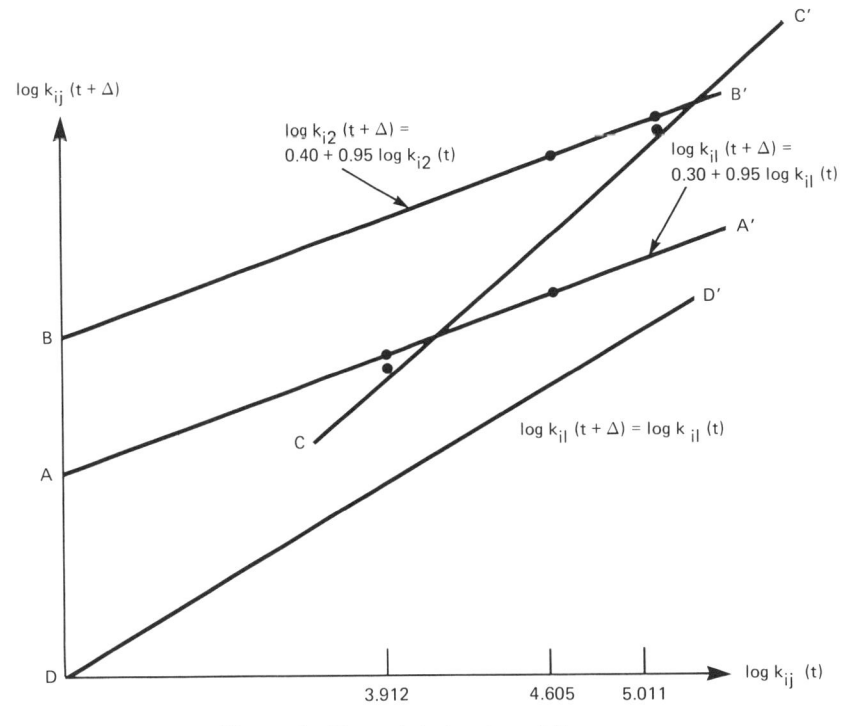

Figure 1. Growth behavior of firms.

and the three firms in market 2 are of sizes 100,150, 150, respectively. Now we claim that even the combined regression will have a slope which is biased upwards. This is evident from inspection of Figure 1.

The three observations generated for firms in market 1 lie on the line AA' given by equation (2); the three observations generated for firms in market 2 lie on the line BB' given by equation (3). The regression line CC' obviously has a steeper slope than that of AA' or BB' because the firms in market 1 are typically smaller than those in market 2. In fact, the regression line has a slope of 1.039. The extent of the bias in this case is very large. The slope coefficient is shifted 178 percent toward a value of unity $((1.039 - .95) \div (1.00 - .95))$. It should be noted at this point that if there is inappropriate regional aggregation, the combination bias can go either way. In the constructed example the slope of the regression line is biased up because the firms in market 2 were growing more rapidly and were typically larger than those in market 1. Pooling bias, on the other hand, is more likely to cause the regression slope to be biased toward unity, because multiregion firms will typically be large in both markets.

Thus we have provided two examples in which the LPE is not true for meaningfully defined markets; yet when a regression is run with data from markets which are too broadly defined, the existence of pooling bias, combination bias and sampling error causes it to be more likely that we will accept the null hypothesis that LPE is valid. Furthermore, in the examples the magnitudes of the biases were considerable. In the regressions which follow we evaluate the effects of pooling bias and combination bias. Our test is made with data from two regional markets in the United States. These markets are the West Coast market and the East and Gulf Coast markets. The West Coast market consists of California, Oregon, western Washington, Alaska, and Hawaii. The East and Gulf Coast market consists of New England, the coastal refineries in New York, New Jersey, Pennsylvania, Delaware, and Maryland, all refineries in the Southeast and those on the Gulf Coast. These market definitions are somewhat arbitrary and represent only our best guess as to the appropriate groupings. In addition to the problem of initially grouping refineries, there is the problem of choosing groupings which persist over time. However, we expect our market definitions to be substantial improvements over world-wide or national market definitions and hence a worthwhile change.

The second change in our study relative to Mansfield's is that we distinguished, insofar as was possible, between full-range refineries and specialty refineries. We believe this change to be necessary because the plants listed in the refinery surveys actually span several industries. First, there are the plants of interest, full-range refineries producing primarily gasoline, residual and distillates; second, there are lube oil plants of various types; third, there are asphalt plants; fourth, there are coking plants; and fifth, plants producing for military bases (jet fuel and special fuel oils). Conceptually, it is clear that we should separate these industries because there is no particular reason to believe that the growth rate of demand is equal across them, and, more importantly, because we believe that the minimum optimum scale, especially for asphalt and lube oil plants, is much smaller than for full-range refineries. Minimum scale seems to be so much smaller that plants tend to be built at or close to efficient scale with less, if any, subsequent expansion than in the case of full-range refineries.

Figure 1 shows how the inclusion of specialty plants can lead the estimated regression slope to be biased toward unity and hence biased toward acceptance of LPE. The argument is presented for market 1 and is initially conditioned on the assumption that all firms are single plant. Neglecting the existence of the error term for ease of exposition, the observations for the full-range refineries in market 1 will lie on the true relationship AA'. The specialty plants are small and by assumption are built close to minimum optimum scale; hence, once installed they tend not to grow. Therefore, the observations for the specialty plants will lie on the line DD' close to the origin, where DD' is the line defined by $\log k_{il}(t + \Delta) = \log k_{il}(t)$. A regression fitted to data for market 1 for both full-range refineries and specialty plants will have a slope intermediate between the true slope of .95 and the unit slope of the line DD'. Once the error terms are introduced we may say that the regression fitted to both full-range refineries and specialty plants has a slope which is biased toward 1. If we now relax the assumption that all firms are single-plant, the argument for the bias becomes less clear. Some firms may have several specialty plants and may grow by building another one. Other firms may have both full-range refineries and specialty plants. Nevertheless, since there is a large number of single specialty-plant firms, we expect the bias to remain. In the regressions which follow, we evaluate the effect of including specialty plants by comparing the estimated slope coefficients from two regressions, one with and one without specialty plants.

Our criterion for deciding the classification of a refinery was that if it was listed as having lube oil and asphalt production equal to 30 percent or more of crude capacity, it was classified as a specialty plant. This is somewhat arbitrary but fits our conceptions of the type of refinery represented by numbers of this sort. The group of other refineries consists of full-range refineries for the most part; however, some are undoubtedly asphalt or lube plants which are not so listed in the survey, others are coking plants, and still others are jet fuel and residual plants near U.S. air bases which sell their production to the government under the Small Business Set Aside Provision established by Congress in 1955.

The third modification we made relative to previous studies was in our treatment of mergers. Hymer and Pashigian (6), in their study, computed firm growth rate as the percentage change in assets over the period 1946 to

1955, hence implicitly treating mergers as growth. Mansfield also viewed as equivalent growth by merger and growth by capacity expansion (9, p. 1047). When companies merge during a period over which we are testing, we treated them as if they had merged prior to the beginning of the period. The only exception is for companies which merge or sell off refineries at the end of the period; they are treated as if the merger did not occur during the period. We believe that our treatment is appropriate because, as was explained above, we understand equation (1) to mean that a firm's growth in any period is restrained by the fact that too much added capacity will upset market equilibrium. When a firm merges with another firm, no new capacity is added to the market and hence we do not view growth by merger as being constrained in the same way as growth by capacity expansion.

RESULTS

Six-year growth rates were computed for the firms in the sample. For single-market firms, the growth rate was just the growth rate in that market; for two market firms, the growth rates in each market were sometimes computed, and the growth rates for all the firm's capacity in the two markets were sometimes computed. Growth rates were computed for the periods 1950–1956, 1956–1962, 1962–1968, 1968–1974. Due to the relative paucity of observations in any time period, two time periods were combined in each regression. Thus one set of regressions was for the periods 1950–1956, 1968–1974, and one set of regressions was for the periods 1956–1962, 1962–1968. The set of regressions for 1950–1956, 1968–1974 was run first to investigate whether we had made any major misspecifications and hence we viewed it as advantageous that it spanned the whole period.[4] Various regressions were run on each set of data. The first two were

$$\log k_{ij}(t + \Delta) = \alpha_j + \beta_j \log k_{ij}(t) + u_{ij}(t,\Delta), \tag{4}$$

$$\log k_{ij}(t + \Delta) = \alpha_j + \delta_j x_{ij}(t) + \beta_j^d \log k_{ij}(t) + u_{ij}(t,\Delta), \tag{5}$$

where $k_{ij}(t)$ is capacity at the beginning of period t and $x_{ij}(t)$ is a dummy variable which takes a value of 1 if the observation is from 50–56 in the 50–56, 68–74 regression and if the observation is from 56–62 in the 56–62, 62–68 regression. Thus in equation (4) both the constant and the slope of equation (1) are taken to be equal across the 1950s and 1960s, whereas in equation (5) only the slope is taken to be equal. The estimated slope coefficient from Equation (4) is denoted $\hat{\beta}_j$ and from equation (5) is denoted $\hat{\beta}_j^d$. They are both reported in Table 4. It was frequently the case that the error terms of equation (4) were heteroscediastic and for the 50–56, 68–74 sample, equations of type (6) were estimated using as data the estimated residuals $\hat{u}_{ij}(t,\Delta)$:

$$\log|\hat{u}_{ij}(t,\Delta)| = \theta_j + \mu_j \log k_{ij}(t) + \varepsilon_{ij}(t,\Delta). \tag{6}$$

The estimated slope coefficient is denoted $\hat{\mu}_j$ and is reported in Table 4. Approximately best linear unbiased estimates of the slope β_j in equation (4) for the 50–56, 68–74 sample were derived by dividing every term in equation (4) by $(k_{ij}(t))^{\mu_j}$, and then carrying out an ordinary leat squares regression on the transformed data. The estimated slope coefficient was denoted $\hat{\beta}_j^h$ and is reported in Table 4. For the 1956–1962, 1962–1968 sample the heteroscedasticity was investigated by means of regression equation (7). This specification was preferable in that it insured that a residual $\hat{u}_{ij}(t,\Delta)$ which was very close to zero would not produce a large negative outlier as it would in equation (6).

$$|\hat{u}_{ij}(t,\Delta)| = \theta_j + \mu_j \log k_{ij}(t) + \varepsilon_{ij}(t,\Delta). \tag{7}$$

The estimated slope coefficient is denoted $\hat{\mu}_j$ and is reported in Table 4. Approximately best linear unbiased estimates of the slope β_j in equation (4) were derived for the 1956–1962, 1962–1968 sample by dividing every term in equation (4) by $(\hat{\theta}_j + \hat{\mu}_j \log k_{ij}(t))$ and carrying out an ordinary least squares regression on the transformed data. The estimated slope coefficient is denoted $\hat{\beta}_j^h$ and is reported in Table 4.[6/]

There are five important results appearing in Table 4. First, for the single-region regressions for West Coast data and for East Coast data, the estimated slope coefficient is significantly less than unity in three out of four cases (regressions X, XI, XIV, and XV, where the t coefficients for a test of the null hypothesis that $\beta_j = 1$ are .6, – 2.0, – 2.0, and – 2.9, respectively). Thus the LPE is disconfirmed in three out of four cases and the point estimates imply that small firms grow faster on average than large firms. The same is true for the regressions which exclude known specialty plants (XII, XIII, XVI, and XVII).

Second, the table enables us to make an evaluation of the effect of pooling bias. Previously, the effect of pooling bias was shown using a simple example in which the slopes of the regression lines in the two markets were identical. In these data, however, certainly the estimated and possibly the true slopes are different from each other. Thus we cannot compare the slope of the pooled regression with the common slope of the East Coast and West Coast regressions. We claim, however, that the extent of pooling bias can be evaluated by comparing the estimated slopes of the pooled regression and the combined regression. Thus, for example, regressions II and IV were run using the same data; the only difference between them was that in regressions II, a multiregional firm contributed only one observation per time period, whereas in regressions IV, a multiregional firm contributed two observations per time period.

By comparing regressions I and III, we see that $\hat{\beta}_j$ is greater for the pooled

Table 4. Regression results.

		N	n	$\hat{\beta}_j$	Firms $\hat{\beta}_j^d$	$\hat{\mu}_j$	$\hat{\beta}_j^h$	N	n	Refineries $\hat{\beta}_j$	$\hat{\mu}_j$
Pooled E. Coast and W. Coast	50–56, 68–74	I	115	.9885	.9876	−.313 (−5.3)	.9936 (−.41)				
	56–62, 62–68	II	118	.9657	.9662	−.040 (−4.3)	.9654 (−3.0)				
Comb. E. Coast and W. Coast	50–56, 68–79,	III	128	.9845	.9841	−.266 (−5.3)	.9786	XVIII	196	.9745	−.185* (−3.7)
	56–62, 62–68	IV	133	.9635		−.041 (−4.6)	.9555 (−3.7)	XIX	197	.9579	−.21** (−5.1)
Pooled E. Coast and W. Coast	56–62, 62–68	V	50	.9610	.9614	−.056 (−3.9)					
Comb. E. Coast and W. Coast	56–62, 62–68	VI	65	.9521							
Pooled E. Coast and W. Coast excl. known speclty	50–56, 68–74	VII	93	.9657	.9665	−.271 (−4.3)	.9810 (−1.0)				
	56–62, 62–68	VIII	89	.9583	.9598	−.052 (−5.1)	.9636 (−2.6)				

Comb. E. Coast W. Coast excl. known spec'ty	50–56, 68–74 56–62, 62–68	IX	106	.9531		−.052 (−5.3)	.9504 (−3.6)	XX	151	.9606	−.234 (−3.6)
W. Coast	50–56, 68–74 56–62, 62–68	X XI	53 50	1.0152 .9711	1.0037 .9706	−.267 (−3.2) −.033 (−2.2)	1.0120 (.6) .9565 (−2.0)	XXI	76	1.0002	−.161* (−1.30)
W. Coast excl. known spec'ty	50–56, 68–74 56–62, 62–68	XII XIII	39 36	1.0071 .9359	1.0030 .9357	−.276 (−3.2) −.032 (−1.8)	1.0136 (.6) .9345 (−2.5)	XXII	57	.9864	−.198 (−1.74)
E. Coast	50–56, 68–74 56–62, 62–68	XIV XV	75 83	.9599 .9611	.9624 .9615	−.261 (−3.9) −.045 (−4.0)	.9517 (−2.0) .9559 (−2.9)	XXIII	120	.9539	−.214 (−3.4)
E. Coast excl. known spec'ty	50–56, 68–74 56–62, 62–68	XVI XVII	65 70	.9346 .9590	.9391 .9603	−.304 (−3.9) −.058 (−4.9)	.9427 (−2.04) .9538 (−2.8)	XXIV	94	.9379	−.208 (−2.5)

Notes: N is the number which identifies a regression; n is the number of observations in a regression. In the columns headed $\hat{\mu}_j$, a number in parentheses is a t-statistic for a test of the null hypothesis that $\mu_j = 0$. In the column headed $\hat{\beta}_j^h$ a number in parentheses is a t-statistic for a test of the null hypothesis that $\beta_j = 1$. The data on refinery sizes and firm sizes in 1950, 56, 62, 68, and 74 are available from the authors on request. * represents the behavior of the residuals from equation (5). ** is $\hat{\mu}_j$ estimated by equation (6).

sample[7] (.9885) than for the combined sample (.9845). Likewise, comparing regressions II and IV, we see that $\hat{\beta}_j$ for the pooled sample (.9657) is greater than for the combined sample (.9635). Hence these point estimates suggest that the bias due to inappropriate pooling may be an important phenomenon. However, it is obvious that the magnitudes of the differences between the point estimates are small. For instance, the shift of the pooled regression coefficient toward 1 in regressions II and IV is only 6.0 percent ((.9657 − .9635) ÷ (1 − .9635)). On reflection it seemed that this was due to the fact that there were only 15 multiregional firm-period observations in a sample of 115. In order to increase the importance of the multiregional firms in the sample, we constructed a new sample for the time period 56–62, 62–68 consisting of all the multiregional firm-period observations and one out of every three of the single firm-period observations. The latter were chosen by picking every third firm from a list of single-region firms ranked by size in 1956–1962 and every third firm from a list of single-region firms ranked by size in 1962–1968. For this sample the shift upward of the pooled coefficient was more pronounced. Thus in the combined regressions VI, the point estimate of the slope was .9521, whereas in the pooled regressions V, the point estimate of the slope was .9610. This represented an 18.6 percent shift toward a slope of 1.

A further investigation was made with a slightly modified version of this smaller sample. It was argued above that inappropriate pooling caused the regression coefficient in a pooled regression to be biased up relative to the regression coefficient in a combined regression. But bias is a property of a sampling distribution, not of an individual drawing from a sample. Accordingly, we used simulation methods to investigate the sampling distribution of the pooled and combined coefficients. The sample used included all fifteen multiregion firms and was composed of 27 West Coast observations and 38 East Coast observations. For these samples the dependence of the standard deviations of the error terms on firm size were estimated as in equation (6) and the approximately best linear unbiased regression lines were computed by dividing both sides of equation (4) by $(k_{ij}(t))^{\mu_j}$ and carrying out an ordinary least squares regression on the transformed data. The results of these computations were:

For the West Coast (n = 27)

$$\log k_{ij}(t + \Delta) = .271842 + .973466 \log k_{ij}(t) + u_{ij}(t, \Delta), \qquad (8)$$

$$\log |\hat{u}_{ij}(t,\Delta)| = -1.502879 - .0942475 \log k_{ij}(t); \qquad (9)$$

For the East Coast (n = 38)

$$\log k_{ij}(t + \Delta) = .570026 + .920119 \log k_{ij}(t) + v_{ij}(t, \Delta), \qquad (10)$$

$$\log |\hat{v}_{ij}(t,\Delta)| = -.777686 - .35564 \log k_{ij}(t). \qquad (11)$$

For the 27 West Coast and 38 East Coast observations, data were generated as if equations (8) and (10) were the true models. The error terms $u_{ij}(t,\Delta)$ and $v_{ij}(t,\Delta)$ were constructed by means of a normally distributed random number generator with a mean of zero. The standard deviations of the error terms, σ_u and σ_v, were constructed by replacing $|\hat{u}_{ij}(t,\Delta)|$ in equation (9) by σ_u and by replacing $|\hat{v}_{ij}(t,\Delta)|$ in Equation (11) by σ_v. Thus it was assumed that the standard deviation of the error term $u_{ij}(t,\Delta)$ was related to log $k_{ij}(t)$ in the same way that the absolute value of $u_{ij}(t,\Delta)$ was related to log $k_{ij}(t)$ and similarly for $v_{ij}(t)$. Now, data were constructed for a combined regression by combining the 27 West Coast observations with the 38 East Coast observations to form a sample of 65 observations. Next, data were constructed for a pooled regression by combining the twelve single-region West Coast firms, the 23 single-region East Coast firms, and the fifteen multiregion firms to form a sample of fifty observations. Finally, ordinary least squares coefficients were computed as in equation (4) for the combined sample ($\hat{\beta}_c$) and the pooled sample ($\hat{\beta}_p$). This was done 20 times.

The result was that the average slope coefficient for the pooled sample was .941255 and the average slope coefficient for the combined sample was .936614. Thus the simulation results suggest that pooling does cause some bias of the slope coefficient toward 1. To summarize the simulation, we prepared a histogram of the percentage shift of the pooled coefficient toward 1; $((\hat{\beta}_p - \hat{\beta}_c) \div (1 - \hat{\beta}_c)) \times 100$. Except for one outlier the shifts lay in the range of 0 to 15 percent with the mode lying between 6 and 9 percent. The outlier was a shift of 34 percent. This came from a sample in which both the pooled and the combined coefficients were very close to 1.

The results in Table 4 also enable us to discuss the effects of combination bias. It was shown above that if the true model of firm size had the same slope in the two markets and if the intercept terms were different, then the regression line for the combined sample might be biased either up or down, depending on the distribution of firm sizes in the two markets. That proposition is difficult to test in this sample because the estimated regression lines for the East Coast and West Coast have different slopes. Thus, for the period 1956–1962, 1962–1968 the West Coast regression XI has a slope of .9711 and the East Coast regression XV has a slope of .9611. The combined regression IV has a slope of .9635, which lies between the slopes of the East Coast and West Coast. A similar result is true for the period 1950–1956, 1968–1974.

In order to investigate the effect of combination bias, we used again the small sample composed of 27 West Coast and 38 East Coast firms in the period 1956–1962, 1962–1968. The estimated growth behavior of these firms was given by equations (8) and (10). It was assumed that the estimated parameters of these equations were the true parameters and that there was no error term. The assumed true regression lines are displayed in Figure 2. WW' depicts equation (8) for the West Coast and EE' depicts equation (10)

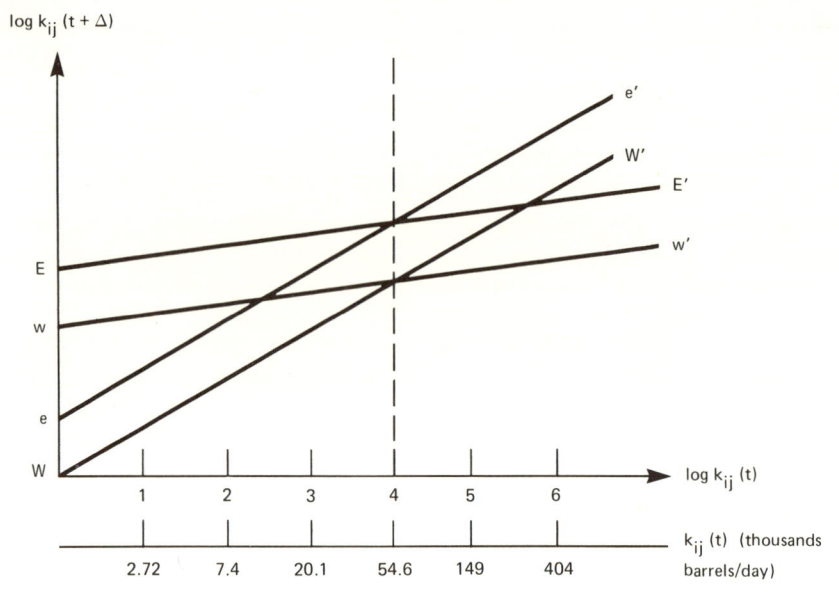

Figure 2. Growth behavior for East Coast and West Coast firms.

for the East Coast. The lines intersect at a value of log $k_{ij}(t)$ equal to 5.584 which corresponds to $k_{ij}(t)$ equal to approximately 266,000 bbls./day. The majority of firms in the sample are smaller than this size, implying that East Coast firms generally grew more rapidly than West Coast firms. Now the medians of the distributions of firm sizes for the West Coast and for the East Coast in this sample are approximately 50,000 bbls./day. Equations (8) and (10) may be employed to show that if an East Coast firm and a West Coast firm were of initial capacity 54,600 bbls./day (log 54.6 = 4), then at the end of a six-year period, the difference between the log of East Coast firm size and the log of West Coast firm size would be .0846. Using this information we constructed two examples in which the effect of combination bias could be investigated. In the first example the behavior of West Coast firms was given by equation (8′) and that of East Coast firms by equation (10), Equation (10) represents the true behavior of East Coast firms. Equation (8′) is represented by ww′ and equation (10) by EE′ in Figure 2. The slopes of equations (8′) and (10) are equal and their intercepts differ from each other by .0846. In the second example the behavior of West Coast firms (line WW′) was given by equation (8) and that of East Coast firms (line ee′) by equation (10′). Equation (8) represents the true behavior of West Coast firms.

Example 1

$$\log k_{ij}(t + \Delta) = .4854 + .9201 \log k_{ij}(t), \tag{8′}$$

Structural Change in U.S. Oil-Refining Industry 157

$$\log k_{ij}(t + \Delta) = .5700 + .9201 \log k_{ij}(t); \qquad (10)$$

Example 2

$$\log k_{ij}(t + \Delta) = .2718 + .9735 \log k_{ij}(t), \qquad (8\,)$$

$$\log k_{ij}(t + \Delta) = .3564 + .9735 \log k_{ij}(t). \qquad (10')$$

Thus, in each example, two growth equations were constructed which had the same slope and yet represented roughly the average growth behavior in the two markets. The histograms of West Coast firm sizes and East Coast firm sizes revealed the West Coast firms were typically smaller than East Coast firms. Hence we expected the regression to be biased up. To evaluate the effect of combination bias in Example 1, we generated data for the 27 West Coast firms using equation (8′) and for the 38 East Coast firms using equation (10). Then we combined the East Coast and West Coast data and ran a regression on the sample of 65 observations. We then did the same in Example 2. These ordinary least squares regression lines had slopes of .9211 and .9745, respectively. Although the direction of the biases were as we had predicted, their magnitudes were quite small. In Example 1, the bias toward unity was 1.2 percent $((.9211 - .9201) \div (1 - .9201))$. In Example 2, the bias toward unity was 3.8 percent $((.9745 - .9735) \div (1 - .9735))$.

The third important result in Table 4 is that exclusion from the sample of lube plants and asphalt plants does result in lower point estimates of the slope. It was argued above that the inclusion of such specialty plants would be likely to bias the slope coefficient toward 1. The point estimates in Table 2 are consistent with such a bias. For instance, for the West Coast, exclusion of specialty plants causes $\hat{\beta}_j$ to fall for both time periods and causes $\hat{\beta}_j^h$ to rise for one and fall for the other (regressions X, XI, XII, XIII). For the East Coast, exclusion of specialty plants causes $\hat{\beta}_j$ to fall for both time periods and causes $\hat{\beta}_j^h$ to fall for both time periods (regressions XIV, XV, XVI, XVII). Furthermore, the effect of the exclusion on the point estimates is quite large in some cases. For instance, for the West Coast in 1956–1962, 1962–1968, $\hat{\beta}_j$ is .9711 for the entire sample (regressions XI) and .9359 for the entire sample excluding known asphalt plants and lube plants (regressions XIII). This is a 55 percent movement away from a slope value of 1; $((.9711 - .9359) \div (1.000 - .9359))$.

The fourth important result in Table 4 concerns the standard deviation of the error term $u_{ij}(t, \Delta)$. The column headed $\hat{\mu}_j$ shows that the absolute value of the residual terms is inversely related to initial firm size $k_{ij}(t)$ for every set of regressions. Furthermore, the null hypothesis that $\mu_j = 0$ can be rejected at the 5 percent significance level for virtually every set of regressions for which $\hat{\mu}_j$ was computed. For instance, for the pooled East Coast and West Coast regressions for 1950–1956, 1968–1974 the point estimate of μ_j is $-.313$ and the t-statistic for a test of the null hypothesis that μ_j equals zero is -5.3. A point estimate of $-.313$ means roughly that as firm size rises by 10 percent, the absolute value of the error term falls by 3 percent. Also for the pooled East Coast and West Coast regressions for 1956–1962, 1962–1968 the point estimates of μ_j is $-.040$ and the point estimate of θ_j is .35. This implies that at a value of log $k_{ij}(t)$ equal to 4 (the approximate median for the sample) as firm size rises by 10 percent, the absolute value of the error term falls by approximately 2 percent. Such a fall in standard deviation was observed in the work of Hymer and Pashigian (6) and Mansfield (9). Mansfield explains the fall by treating the growth rate of a large firm as a weighted sum of the growth rates of its smaller components (e.g., plants). He assumed implicitly that the growth rates of different sized plants have equal standard deviations. Then, unless the growth rates of different plants are perfectly correlated, it follows that the standard deviation of the weighted sum is less than the standard deviation of each component. This view is shared also by Simon (15).

This brings us to the fifth important result in Table 4. A number of regressions were carried out on refineries rather than on firms. Hence $k_{ij}(t)$ and $k_{ij}(t+\Delta)$ were the sizes of refineries at times t and $t+\Delta$ in equations (4), (5), and (6). In all regressions XVIII to XXIV the point estimates $\hat{\mu}_j$ were negative, and in every case but one (regression XXI) it was possible to reject the null hypothesis that μ_j equaled zero at the 5 percent level of significance. Thus the conventional view as to why the standard deviation of firm growth rates declines with firm size is shown to be refuted by this body of data since the same behavior of the standard deviation of growth rates is displayed for refinery data. One reason why the standard deviation of refinery growth rates declines with size may be that a large refinery may serve a number of "markets"—hence the growth rate of the refinery may be viewed as a weighted sum of the growth rates of the "markets" and the same arguments as previously may be used to show that large refineries should have smaller standard deviations. Another reason why the standard deviation may decline with refinery size is that those refineries which invest during the six-year period may conform to equation (4) with $\beta_j < 1$ but some refineries may have invested late in the previous six-year period and be unready to invest again. As shown in detail in another paper, Peck (10), this situation would give the appearance of declining standard deviation.

CONCLUSION

In this paper we gave a sketch of important postwar developments in the U.S. oil-refinery industry and made a study of the Law of Proportionate Effect using data on the real capacity of surviving firms during 1950–1974. We identified various sources of bias and evaluated the extent of some of these for our data. We discussed two types of bias which were due to the incorrect choice of market region. These were pooling bias and combination bias. We found that pooling bias caused the estimated regression coefficient to be biased toward 1 but only by about 10 percent for our sample; we also found that combination bias caused the regression coefficient to be biased towards 1, but the effect was very small, being somewhere between 1 percent and 4 percent. We also identified a source of bias due to the inclusion of lube plants and asphalt plants in the sample of full-range refineries and we found that excluding such plants had a considerable effect on the coefficients. We also identified a further source of bias to which many previous studies had been subject, namely the treatment of firm mergers as growth.

Our results show that for three out of four region time period combinations the small firms typically grew faster than the large firms, owing to a combination of the hypothesized unwillingness of large firms to upset market equilibrium, of the set of government policies in effect during the postwar period, and the various technical and institutional changes in the industry environment. Neglecting birth, death, merger, and heteroscedasticity and assuming that government policies and industry technical changes in the future have the same effect as in the past, the steady state probability distribution of firm sizes would be lognormal with a constant mean and variance.[8] Thus there would not be a tendency for continually increasing concentration.

We feel that our results are of interest for all studies of the relationship between firm growth rate and firm size. Thus, although the concepts of pooling bias and combination bias were introduced in a geographical context, they apply also to diversified firms operating in a number of product markets. The bias due to the inclusion of specialty plants can be viewed as a special case of combination bias and clearly applies to many product markets. And the bias due to the treatment of mergers as growth is clearly not special to the oil-refinery industry.

FOOTNOTES

1. We are indebted to Cheng Hsiao, Darius Gaskins, and Ted Keeler for helpful comments and to the Institute for Business and Economic Research and the Sloan Foundation for financial support. We take responsibility for all errors.

2. The data we used was real crude refinery capacity as of January 1 of a given year. The data were taken from the annual survey of U.S. refineries conducted by *The Oil and Gas Journal*. Various cross-checks were made with the use of a similar survey conducted by the U.S. Bureau of Mines.

3. Pooling bias exists for the following reason. Suppose firm i conforms to the following behavior in both markets 1 and 2:

$$\log k_{ij}(t + \Delta) = \alpha + \beta \log k_{ij}(t). \tag{i}$$

We claim that if firm i has equal size in the two markets at time t, then

$$\log(k_{i1}(t + \Delta) + k_{i2}(t + \Delta)) > \alpha + \beta \log(k_{i1}(t) + k_{i2}(t)). \tag{ii}$$

The proof follows. Since $k_{i1}(t) = k_{i2}(t) = k_i(t)$ by assumption, it follows from (i) that

$k_{i1}(t + \Delta) = k_{i2}(t + \Delta) = k_i(t + \Delta)$, so using wellknown properties of logarithms, expression (ii) becomes

$$\log k(t + \Delta) + \log 2 > \alpha + \beta \log k(t) + \beta \log 2.$$

But, from (i) this inequality reduces to

$$\log 2 > \beta \log 2,$$

which we know to be true for $\beta < 1$.

4. When we carried out tests as to whether it was appropriate to pool data from 1950–1956 and data from 1968–1974, the differences between periods were generally statistically insignificant. The same was true for 1956–1962, 1962–1968.

5. We do not believe that this occurred in the 1950–1956, 1968–1974 sample because all the estimates $\hat{\mu}_j$ reported for that period in Table 4 are quite similar in magnitude.

6. The heteroscedasticity of the error term of equation (5) was also investigated by means of the same techniques and approximately best linear unbiased estimates of β_j^d were derived. In order to save space, these results are not reported. They were not markedly different from the results on the heteroscedasticity of the error term of equation (4). Usually the dummy coefficient $\hat{\delta}_j$ was not significantly different from zero.

7. This pooled sample included one observation which the combined sample did not include, a refinery which Exxon started up on the West Coast in 1968–1974. The pooled regressions, excluding this observation, had coefficients $\hat{\beta} = .9877$ and $\hat{\beta}_j^d = .9868$.

8. In equation 1, if $\beta_j < 1$, $u_{ij}(t,\Delta)$ is normal, independently and identically distributed with zero mean and variance σ_j^2, then the steady state distribution of $\log k_{ij}(t + \Delta)$ is normal with finite mean $\alpha_j/(1 - \beta_j)$ and variance $\sigma_j^2/(1 - \beta_j^2)$. We have not been able to derive the distribution of $\log k_{ij}(t + \Delta)$ if the error term is heteroscedastic but out intuition is that it possesses a steady state.

REFERENCES

1. Adelman, M. A., *The World Petroleum Market*. Johns Hopkins University Press, Baltimore, 1972.
2. Cookenboo, Leslie, J., *Crude Oil Pipelines and Competition in the Oil Industry*. Harvard University Press, Cambridge, Mass., 1955.
3. ———, *Costs of Operating Crude Oil Pipelines*. Rice Institute Pamphlet, Houston, 1954.
4. DeChazeau, Melvin E., and Alfred E. Kahn, *Integration and Competition in the Petroleum Industry*. Yale University Press, New Haven, 1959.
5. Hart, P. E., and S. J. Prais, "The Analysis of Business Concentration: A Statistical Approach," *Journal of the Royal Statistical Society*, Series A, vol. 19 (1956), part 2, 150–181.
6. Hymer, S., and P. Pashigian, "Firm size and rate of growth," *Journal of Political Economy* (December 1962), 556–569.
7. Jacquemin, A. P., and M. Cardon de Lichtbuer, "Size structure, stability, and performance of the largest British and EEC firms," *European Economic Review*, vol. 4 (1973), 393–408.
8. MacLean, John H., and Robert W. Haigh, *The Growth of Integrated Oil Companies*. Graduate School of Business Administration, Harvard University, Boston, 1954.
9. Mansfield, E., "Entry, exit, and the growth of firms," *American Economic Review*, vol. 52 (1962), 1023–1051.
10. Peck, S. C., "Econometric Aspects of Firm Growth Behavior," University of California, Berkeley, Working Paper No. 81, July 1976.

11. Reynolds, Robert J., "Generalizing the Equivalency Result for Oil Pipelines," unpublished paper, January 14, 1976.
12. Scherer, F. M., *Industrial Market Structure and Economic Performance*. Rand McNally, Chicago, 1973.
13. Shaffer, E. H., *The Oil Import Program of the United States*. Praeger, New York, 1968.
14. Sherman, R., "Entry barriers and the growth of firms," *Southern Economic Journal* (October 1971), 238–247.
15. Simon, H. A., "Comment: firm size and rate of growth," *Journal of Political Economy* (February 1964), 81–82.
16. ———, "On a class of skew distribution functions," *Biometrika*, vol. 24 (December 1955), 425–440.
17. ———, and C. Bonini, "The size distribution of business firms," *American Economic Review*, vol. 48 (September 1958), 607–617.
18. Singh, A., and G. Whittington, "The size and growth of firms," *Review of Economic Studies* (January 1975), pp. 15–26.
19. *The Oil and Gas Journal*, The Petroleum Publishing Company, Tulsa, Okla.
20. Weiss, L. W., "An Evaluation of Mergers in Six Industries," *Review of Economics and Statistics*, vol. 47 (1965), 172–181.
21. Wolbert, George S. *American Pipe Lines*. University of Oklahoma Press, Norman, 1952.

INTEGRATION AND INNOVATION IN THE ENERGY MARKETS

David J. Teece, STANFORD UNIVERSITY[*]

I. INTRODUCTION

The exercise of monopoly power in world energy markets by the OPEC cartel has produced considerable economic dislocation. One effect in the United States has been to focus attention on the organization and performance of the firms supplying the energy requirements of the U.S. economy. Some observers have claimed that the organization of the U.S. petroleum industry — in particular its horizontally and vertically integrated structure — has been designed to protect the OPEC cartel and to foster monopolistic behavior among firms operating in the domestic energy markets.

The purpose of this chapter is to elucidate the economic rationale for the organization of the U.S. energy industries and the changes which are currently in progress. An appreciation of the efficiency and competitive properties of various alternative organizational forms seems to be lacking, and this chapter is designed to help remedy this deficiency. Unless the economic rationale for various organizational forms are understood, public policy changes designed to improve performance will surely be confounded. In focusing on organizational considerations and the relative efficiency properties of various kinds of economic transactions, the approach here departs somewhat from traditional analysis, which tends to ignore the internal complexities of the firm and the efficiency properties of various alternative modes of organizing economic activity. In addition to market structure, the manner in which firms span different markets and the nature of their internal organization are recognized here as important determinants of economic performance. The approach adopted is microanalytic and recognizes that it is only by examining the nature of economic transactions that the rationale for a particular mode of economic organization, and the appropriate boundaries of a firm or industry, can be specified. Clearly, this approach is at variance with traditional analysis and its proclivity to invoke monopolistic or regulatory explanations to account for almost all facets of industry structure. As Coase has remarked:

> The situation is such that if we ever achieved a system of limited government and the economic system were clearly seen to be competitive, we would have no explanation at all for the way in which the activities performed in the economic system are divided between firms. We would be unable to explain why General Motors was not a dominant factor in the coal industry, or why A&P did not manufacture airplanes.[1]

While not denying that monopoly or regulatory factors are often important in explaining the evolution of industry structure and industry performance, I feel it is entirely too delimiting to restrict attention to such a narrow set of variables.

In examining integration and innovation in the energy industries, I want to focus attention on the "petroleum" companies. Although many different industries, such as the electrical and chemical industries, are engaged in the energy business, the petroleum companies—defined as those companies with more than half of their sales in oil and gas or refined products—play an especially significant role, and have been the focus of public policy inquiry. Furthermore, the purpose is not to rest once the structure and organization of the petroleum industry has been described. Rather, I will try to explain the rationale for what is observed, and to draw links, albeit partial links, between organization and performance, especially technological performance.[2] The technological issues are of interest not just from the point of view of industrial organization, but also from the perspective of energy policy. This is because it is widely recognized that technological improvements which lower the relative costs of non-oil sources of energy will be important in fostering U.S. energy independence and the weakening of the OPEC cartel. Hence, one purpose of the chapter is to provide a framework within which sensible public policy decisions with respect to industry structure and energy research can be formulated.

II. "HORIZONTAL" INTEGRATION

In the last decade important structural changes have occurred in the activities pursued by oil companies in the U.S. economy. Table 1 displays the fact that these firms are now engaged in many other energy-related activities besides the exploration and production, refining, and marketing of crude oil and natural gas. In fact, firms that have traditionally been referred to as "oil companies" can more properly be specified as energy companies.[3] In many cases, the extent of involvement outside of oil and gas is beyond toehold proportions. For instance, in 1977 Continental Oil derived 64 percent of its income from petroleum, 24 percent from coal, and 12 percent from chemicals. In the same year Kerr-McGee derived about 64 percent of its income from petroleum, 20 percent from chemicals and plant food, and 15 percent from the nuclear business.[4] While these two companies are proportionally less involved in petroleum than most of the larger firms in the oil and gas business, they are prototypes of a new kind of energy company that has been developing in recent years. They could perhaps be labeled as "energy conglomerates" to the extent that the various fuels and products produced are sold in separate markets. Typically, however, these diversification moves are referred to as "horizontal" integration.

Recently, policy debate has questioned whether these developments are in the public interest. It has been suggested that by acquiring significant alternative energy resources, the producers of oil and gas have come to monopolize not just oil and gas but competing fuels as well.[5] One alleged consequence is that oil and gas companies will restrict the output of alternative energy resources, such as the coal, uranium, shale oil, and geothermal energy under their control in order to attenuate interfuel competition and maintain higher prices for oil and gas, thereby enhancing the value of the firms' oil and gas reserves. These arguments have encouraged the drafting and submission of divestiture bills which would require oil and gas companies to divest their assets in other energy fields. Given this policy concern about the current structure and trends in the energy markets, it seems appropriate to analyze the resource allocation and competitive effects of "horizontal" integration. In particular, it is important to address the "withholding of

Table 1. Participation of crude oil producers in other energy industries, U.S.A., 1975.

Company* (Ranked by net crude oil, condensate, and ngl production, 1976)	Coal Reserves	Coal R&D	Coal Production	Solar R&D	Uranium exploration and/or reserves	Uranium mining and milling	Conversion to uranium hexafluoride (uF$_6$)	Uranium enrichment	Conversion into uranium dioxide pellets (uO$_2$)	Fuel fabrication	Fuel reprocessing	Oil shale Reserves	Oil shale R&D	Geothermal Exploration and/or reserves	Geothermal R&D	Geothermal Production	Tar sands Exploration and/or reserves	Tar sands R&D	Tar sands Production**
1 Exxon	X	X	X	X	X	X	O	O	X	O	O	X	O	O	O	O	X	X	O
2 Texaco	X	X	O	O	X	O	O	O	O	O	O	X	X	O	O	O	X	X	O
3 Shell	X	X	O	X	X	O	O	O	O	O	O	X	X	X	O	O	X	O	O
4 Std. Oil of Indiana	O	X	X	O	O	X	O	O	X	O	O	X	X	O	X	O	O	O	O
5 Gulf	X	X	O	X	X	X	X	O	X	O	O	X	X	X	X	O	X	O	X
6 Std. Oil of Calif.	O	O	O	O	X	O	X	O	O	O	X	X	X	X	O	O	X	O	O
7 Atlantic Richfield	X	X	O	X	X	X	O	O	X	O	O	X	O	O	O	O	X	O	O
8 Mobil	X	O	X	O	X	X	O	O	O	O	O	X	X	X	X	X	X	O	O
9 Getty	O	X	O	X	X	O	O	X	O	O	O	X	O	O	O	O	O	X	O
10 Sun	X	X	O	O	X	O	O	O	O	O	O	X	X	X	X	X	X	X	X
11 Union	O	X	O	O	X	O	O	O	O	O	O	X	X	X	X	X	X	O	O

Phillips	12	X	X	O	O	X	O	O	O	O	O	X	X	X	O	O	X	O	O
Continental Oil	13	X	X	X	O	X	X	O	O	O	O	X	X	O	O	O	X	O	O
Cities Service	14	O	O	O	O	X	O	O	O	O	O	X	X	X	O	O	X	O	X
Marathon	15	X	X	O	O	X	O	O	O	O	O	O	X	X	O	O	O	O	O
Amerada Hess	16	O	O	O	O	X	O	O	O	O	O	X	O	O	O	O	X	O	O
Tenneco	17	O	O	O	O	X	O	O	O	O	O	O	O	O	O	O	X	O	O
Louisiana Land	18	O	O	O	O	X	O	O	O	O	O	X	O	O	O	O	O	O	O
Pennzoil	19	O	O	O	O	X	O	O	O	O	O	O	O	O	O	O	O	O	O
Superior	20	X	X	O	O	O	O	O	O	O	O	X	X	O	O	O	O	O	O
Union Pacific	21	X	O	O	O	X	O	O	O	O	O	O	O	O	O	O	O	O	O
Santa Fe Industries	22	X	O	O	O	O	O	O	O	O	O	O	O	O	O	O	O	O	O
R. J. Reynolds	23	O	O	O	O	O	O	O	O	O	O	O	O	X	O	O	O	O	O
International Paper	24	O	O	O	O	O	O	O	O	O	O	O	O	O	O	O	O	O	O
Kerr-McGee	25	X	X	O	O	X	O	O	X	X	X	O	O	O	O	O	O	O	O
Std. Oil of Ohio	26	X	X	X	O	X	O	O	O	O	O	X	X	O	O	O	X	O	O
General American Oil of Texas	27	O	O	O	O	O	O	O	O	O	O	O	O	O	O	O	O	O	O
Ashland	28	X	X	X	O	O	O	O	O	O	O	X	O	O	O	O	O	O	O
American Petrofina	29	O	O	O	O	O	O	O	O	O	O	O	X	O	O	O	O	O	O
Diamond Shamrock	30	O	O	O	O	O	O	O	O	O	O	O	O	O	O	O	O	O	O

*Companies ranked by 1975 crude oil and ngl production. Assignments do not include joint venture activities (except in research) unless the specified firm has more than 50 per cent of the equity in the joint venture.

**Includes Canada.

X Indicates current involvement.

O Indicates no current involvement.

Source: Annual reports, questionnaire data, and interviews with corporate executives.

production" thesis which is used to provide the theoretical underpinnings for some of the industrial reorganization proposals.

In an imaginary world of frictionless markets, complex forms of business organization—such as horizontal and vertical integration—could well be devoid of a compelling efficiency rationale. Frictionless markets with complete information and zero transactions costs could handle every conceivable kind of transaction. However, the nonexistence of many markets and the high transactions costs of using others provide opportunities for the displacement of markets by hierarchies, of which modern corporation is a particular example. Coase made this point explicit in his well-known article in 1937.[6] Because markets and hierarchies can perform similar functions, it is important that their relative efficiency properties be appreciated. The integrated energy companies can be examined in this context.

The analysis to follow suggests that transaction cost considerations, together with certain institutional features of the U.S. economy, and the changing natural resource base, explain in large measure the incentives for "horizontal" integration as it is often referred to in the context of the energy industries. The market failures occur in the market for capital and technological know-how. Clearly, the purpose here is not to present a blanket indictment of market processes for transferring technology and for allocating capital; nor is it to present a blanket endorsement of conglomerate business organization, as some conglomerates cause genuine public policy concern. However, the evidence suggests that the energy conglomerates do not fall into this category.

In order for large integrated firms to realize important efficiency properties, they must be "appropriately" organized. By this is meant the following: first, responsibility for operating decisions must be assigned to operating divisions or quasi firms; second, an elite staff must be attached to headquarters to perform both advisory and auditing functions; third, headquarters, not the divisions, must be responsible for strategic decision making, planning, appraisal, and control, including allocation of capital between the divisions; fourth, the research establishment must be centralized or there must be close formal ties between separate laboratories. The resulting structure can display both rationality and synergy. Following Williamson, firms organized in this fashion are denoted as "m-form" firms.[7] Because of informational processing properties, enterprises organized as m-forms have the potential to improve the functioning of the capital market by more assuredly assigning cash flows to high-yield uses. The reasons why this is possible is that integrated m-form enterprise can offer a wide spectrum of investment opportunities, and the corporate headquarters typically has more detailed information on some potential investments than has the external capital market. (The firm's managers excel with respect to possessing depth of information whereas the external capital market excels with respect to breadth of information.) Management can make detailed evaluations and audits of each of the firm's operating parts, and can make adjustments to the operating parts in response to performance failure. This is particularly important when we realize that the differential tax treatment of dividends tends to create a strong reinvestment bias.

Of course, for this reassignment capacity to be beneficial, cash flows must be subject to an internal competition, and investment proposals from the various divisions must be solicited and evaluated by general management. In this way, integrated m-form enterprises can act as miniature capital markets. Grabowski and Mueller's empirical work on rates of return to plowback suggests that reassignment is particularly important for firms with a maturing product portfolio.[8] Such firms tend to generate a low return on plowback because external capital market discipline tends to weaken. On the assumption that reinvestment proclivities cannot readily by changed, efficiency considerations dictate the establishment of a competitive internal capital market, and this in turn indicates the desirability of including new products and new ventures within a maturing firm's investment portfolio. Hence, the enterprise, appropriately organized, might be viewed as capitalism's creative response to the evident limits which the capital market experiences in relation to the firm.

The hypothesis is extended here to include transactional problems in the market for technology. While synergy in an enterprise need not depend on technological considerations, as the above discussion indicates, technology transfer considerations can breed additional sources of synergy. Integration can facilitate the technology transfer process by improving the coupling between user and supplier, and by overcoming contractual problems involved in the buying and selling of technological know-how. The information asymmetry which necessarily exists between the buyer and the seller of technology means that the sale of technology must take place under conditions which do not satisfy the assumptions of the competitive model. For this and other reasons, the market for technology is often faulted. Under such conditions, internal technology transfer, by checking opportunistic proclivities, can be a superior mode for technology transfer.

The above are essentially affirmative statements that can be made on behalf of appropriately organized diversified enterprises. They must be balanced against potential anticompetitive effects, such as reciprocity, predatory cross-subsidization, and interdependence. This last factor implies that competition is restrained out of a mutually recognized interdependence, and could result in less aggressive competition in markets where interfaces exist, or in a reduction in potential competition in markets where entry might otherwise occur. In the context of the energy industries, the first aspect has been emphasized, and is examined later.

The theory of business organization outlined above suggests the possible superiority of appropriately organized diversfied enterprises over specialized firms. The relevance of the theory to the energy companies depends on the occurrence of a number of factors: first, a maturing product portfolio within firms which are generating cash flow beyond reinvestment needs[9] in traditional markets; second, attractive investment opportunities in allied industries; third, technology transfer opportunities from established to allied industries; and fourth, on "m-form" corporate structure. These factors are sequentially examined below in the context of the U.S. energy industries. It becomes apparent that the new endeavors embraced by the oil companies appear to be quite consistent with the competitive theory of corporate development that has been advanced.

Consider, first, the nation's changing natural resource base. Reserves in the lower forty-eight states have been declining since about 1966, and the Prudhoe Bay discoveries, which have added almost 10 billion barrels, amount to only three extra years' supply at current rates of production. Future discoveries will most probably involve more steeply increasing costs than some alternative fuels, such as coal. Hence, it is to be expected that even aside from the effect of anticipated government policy changes designed to reduce dependence on oil, the shares of alternative fuels in U.S. energy consumption will increase as the price of oil increases. This implies that resources must flow into alternative fuels if risk-corrected rates of return to investment are to be equalized across fuels. It is predictable that the oil companies will be among the first to respond to these new investment opportunities, assuming that the managerial and technological synergies are greater for the oil companies than they are for firms with no experience in the energy business. Hence horizontal integration can be viewed as a vehicle to assist in the resource allocation process by permitting a quick response to new investment opportunities on the part of firms that already possess the requisite capabilities. The FEA estimates that between 1975 and 1984 an additional $44 billion of investment will be needed in coal, synthetic fuels, and the nuclear fuel cycle.[10] The oil companies, because of their satisfactory cash flow positions and low debt-equity ratios, are well placed to respond. By investing in the coal industry, for instance, the oil companies can maintain competitive profits, help moderate price increases, augment production, and in the long run assist in limiting the imports of OPEC oil into the United States.

The oil companies can also bring technological know-how and research and development (R&D) capability to the alternative fuels activities. The exploration and drilling for geothermal resources are not altogether unlike the processes utilized in exploration and drilling for oil. Pipeline technology from the oil industry has likewise been important in bringing about the coal-slurry pipeline. Discoveries of minerals such as uranium are facilitated by knowledge of sedimentary basins. The oil companies have the

Integration and Innovation in the Energy Markets 171

relevant knowledge because of their exploratory activities in oil and gas. Similarly, coal liquefaction technology under development by the oil companies is being based on catalytic processes similar to those developed for refining petroleum. Retorting shale likewise involves processes used in refining. Of course, once oil is produced from coal or shale, the storage and transportation problems are just the same as those encountered with conventional crude.

The importance of the management skills which can also be committed by the oil companies should not be underestimated. The oil companies—like the chemical companies and the steel companies—have had experience managing and coordinating huge, long-gestation capital-intensive investments. These skills will become increasingly critical to the coal and synthetic fuels industries. For instance, it is estimated that plants to produce oil from shale could well cost over $1 billion. It is hard to identify firms currently in the alternative fuels industries which possess the relevant resources.

Consider, finally, the organizational structure issue. A prerequisite of the theory is that energy companies display a multidivisional structure of the variety described earlier. R&D must also be centralized in some fashion. It is into these divisionalized structures that the new ventures are absorbed, eventually as separate divisions. A life-cycle process may be involved if entry is via internal growth rather than acquisition, since the new ventures may be located first within existing divisions and become separate divisions only after these operations exceed threshold proportions. All of the major companies on which data are available are organized in this fashion.[11] Furthermore, all of the major oil companies have some centralized R&D with the exception of Atlantic Richfield, which is decentralized but has strong linkages among its various laboratories.

Thus the oil company participation in other sections of the energy industries appears to be based on competitive considerations, and to be driven by market forces. However, it is sometimes argued that a diversfied energy company will suffer opportunity costs if production of alternative fuels reduces potential profits from oil production. Energy companies internalize costs that in a competitive economy would be external to a specialized producer of a substitute energy source.[12] Or to quote Walter Adams: "Can we really expect these giant firms to undermine their stake in depletable oil and gas resources... by investing the huge sums required to promote the rapid development of economically viable substitutes?"[13] Adams seems to suggest that horizontal integration results in the production of substitutes being withheld below levels that would be generated with an economy of specialized rather than integrated firms. The logic of this argument needs to be examined.

Consider the determination of the optimal private rate of resource extraction. A rational resource owner will compare the expected profits of selling a unit of the resource today with the expected profit, appropriately discounted, of selling the same unit at some future date. Thus if a resource owner expects the difference between the price and the cost of production to increase at an annual rate which exceeds the resource owner's rate of discount, there is an incentive to reduce current production and keep the resources in the ground as inventory. The seminal question is how the state of competition and the degree of horizontal integration influence the firm's optimal rate of resource extraction. While the state of competition affects the resource extraction decision, it would seem that the level of integration has essentially a neutral effect in a competitive market. Consider, to begin with, a situation where there is no horizontal integration. In competitive markets all firms are, by assumption, price takers, and so resource owners have absolutely no influence on the price of their own resource or its substitutes. On the other hand, if monopoly power is imputed to the resource owners, then by changing the level of production, the current prices, can, by assumption, be manipulated. Davidson[14] has claimed that even without monopoly power, the withholding of production could take place, arguing that "it does not require covert collusion. What is required is that they all view the future the same." Two points should be noted about this. First, it is not an indictment of horizontal integration since there is no reason to believe that independent companies will view the future any differently from conglomerates, as both presumably have the same information. Second, it is not clear that the withholding so generated is socially undesirable.[15] Nevertheless it is apparent that, in order to argue that horizontal integration affects the rate of resource extraction, both interfuel substitution possibilities and monopoly power must be assumed, or the source of differing expectations between specialized and integrated companies must be specified. These conditions must hold before the argument is empirically relevant to the U.S. energy situation.

For the withholding theory to have any empirical validity, the above analysis suggests that the following conditions must hold: (1) There must exist strong interfuel substitution, and (2) there must be monopoly power in the energy market exercised by the U.S. oil companies. (The requirement of interfuel substitution implies that the relevant market is the energy market and not the market for individual fuels. Note that concentration statistics show that concentration declines significantly as the market is broadened to include alternative fuels.)[16] If this power does not exist, then it is not possible for the integrated firms to affect the value of their reserves of oil by manipulating the production of alternative fuels. The validity of these assumptions must be established before the withholding theory can provide a viable explanation of production behavior. The second assumption is examined elsewhere[17] and shown to be incorrect. The OPEC cartel, not the oil companies, is the source of market power. The first assumption is likewise questionable since on the demand side interfuel substitution

Table 2. Output of coal companies before and after acquisition by oil companies. (comparison of 5-year averages before and after dates of acquisition)

	Output (000 tons, 5-year average)		Company Percentage increase	U.S. Percentage increase*
Consolidation	43,858	(1962–66)	35.0	16.6
(Conoco—9/15/66)	59,218	(1967–71)		
Island Creek	22,514	(1963–67)	16.8**	12.2
(Occidental—1(29/68)	26,293	(1968–72)		
Old Ben	8,287	(1964–68)	37.2	10.3
(Sohio—8/30/68)	11,372	(1969–73)		
Pittsburgh & Midway	4,869	(1959–63)	73.9	24.6
(Gulf—late 1963)	8,465	(1964–68)		

*In each case the U.S. percentage increase is measured over the same time period as the oil company affiliate. The U.S. percentage increase also refers to a comparison of averages over five-year periods.
**If Island Creek's publicly reported output from 1959–1972 is reduced by subtracting the production of its Maust coal properties acquired in 1969, this figure falls to 2.8 percent.

possibilities are essentially limited to the electric utility sector.[17a]

By laying out the assumptions of the withholding theory in this fashion, its contrived nature is made apparent. The assumptions are not relevant to the situation currently prevailing in the U.S. energy markets. The relevance of the theory is further brought into question when the performance of the oil companies in alternative fuels is examined. Consider the coal industry. The witholding theory would predict that after acquisition by oil companies, the output of coal companies would be "withheld." By contrast, the alternative theory of integration advanced in this chapter would predict that after the completion of a merger, investment—and hence production—will increase in the acquired company over the level that would have occurred had the new subsidiary remained independent. This prediction is difficult to verify, as the investments and production levels which would have taken place without the merger are not observable. One way to approach the problem is to assume that investment and output in the independent companies would have followed the national trend. On this assumption, increases in production and investment greater than the national average would indicate support for the theory. The relevant production data is available for the coal industry. Table 2 presents production data for the four largest coal firms acquired by oil companies: Pittsburgh & Midway (Gulf), Old Ben (Sohio), Consolidation (Conoco), and Island Creek (Occidental). The production statistics indicates that in each case the five-year increase after acquisition was greater than the overall U.S. increase.[18] This does not square with the prediction of the withholding theory, but it is consistent with the alternative theory advanced in this chapter.

Similarly, with respect to capital investment it is hard to argue that the effect of acquisitions has been to curtail investment, at least in coal. The absolute level of investment has increased for each of the major acquisitions. The percentage increase in investment for the five-year post-acquisition period as compared with the five previous years was 267 percent for Pittsburgh & Midway, 139 percent for Old Ben, 325 percent for Consolidation, and 460 percent for Island Creek.[19] These sizable increases in investment are also inconsistent with the allegation that the oil parents attempt to withhold production. Rather, the data support the capital reallocation argument that was outlined above.

With respect to research and development, the theory I have advanced predicts that oil firms integrating into alternative fuels will engage in R&D projects related to the further development of those fuels. (By contrast, the withholding theory would imply that the integrating firms would not engage in any R&D activity in alternative fuels, since their interest is allegedly in restraining production, not enhancing it.) The top four oil firms (ranked by their coal reserves) spent an average of $6,119,800 on coal R&D in 1975; the next spent $2,318,800 on average; and the remaining five spent an average of $755,800.[20] R&D expenditure per ton of coal reserves were almost constant for the reserve classes identified. Since the independent coal companies are spending practically nothing on coal R&D, it is difficult to entertain the notion that the oil companies are retarding the development of coal.

Horizontal integration—a relatively recent and important trend in the energy industries—therefore appears to represent a competitive response to changed circumstances in the energy markets. It is not, however, a unique development. The dimensions of competition in the U.S. economy have expanded, encompassing intra-industry, interindustry competition, international competition, and augmented potential competition. In addition, organizational emphasis is increasingly on missions and capabilities. In a world of continuous change, management must relate to some mission defined in terms of customer needs, wants, or problems to be solved. In addition to products and mission, another important dimension of the concept of industries is a range of capabilities. These include technologies, embracing all processes from basic research, product design and development, and applications engineering through interrelated manufacturing methods and obtaining feedback from consumers. The capabilities concept encompasses important management technologies including planning, information sciences, computerization of information flows, formal decision models, problem-solving methodologies, and behavioral sciences.

Changing product requirements and changing product-market opportunities require new technologies and new combinations of technologies. To illustrate, the aircraft industry moved through stages in which the critical competence shifted from structures to engine and other propulsion methods, to guidance, and finally, to the interaction of structures, propulsion, and guidance as reflected in the concept of aerospace systems.[21] Similarly, in the energy industries, the oil companies are entering a stage where the critical competence will move away from ability to discover and process oil to the ability to supply a customer's energy requirements from a variety of fuels, depending on the customer's needs, and the relative costs of different fuels. Thus, it is important to realize that industry boundaries defined by products become less meaningful than industries defined by the ability to perform the critical functions for meeting the customer's needs. Horizontal integration by the oil companies does not appear, therefore, to offer an avenue of public policy concern at this time; to the contrary, forestalling or reversing these integration trends could have deleterious consequences.

III. VERTICAL INTEGRATION

If a production process can be divided into a series of technologically separate stages, yet these are all performed by one firm, then the firm is said to be vertically integrated. In the oil industry, still the mainstay of the nation's energy production base, a number of separable stages are typically identifed: crude oil exploration and production, crude oil refining, the transportation of crude and refined products, and the marketing of refined products. Practically all of the refiners in the United States are vertically integrated in some fashion into crude production and/or marketing. In fact, in 1973 only about 4 percent of the U.S. distillation capacity was accounted for by refiners without marketing, and about 3 percent was accounted for by refiners with marketing but no production.[22] The pervasiveness of vertical integration, by both large and small refiners, is implied in these statistics. Of course, the possession of some production or marketing capacity by a refiner does not imply complete integration. Typically, while some portion of downstream requirements are supplied from the firm's own upstream capacity, a substantial portion is typically supplied through market exchange with other firms, both integrated and nonintegrated.[23] Table 3 presents self-sufficiency ratios which display the partial nature of backward integration by refiners into production. Similarly, Table 4 shows that forward integration into marketing is likewise only partial. In 1974, for example, 15.51 percent of gasoline sales by refiners were of nonbranded products sold to independent marketers.

The purpose of this section is to explain the economic rationale for vertical integration in the petroleum industry. This will require a microanalytic view typically absent from most studies of industrial structure. It will become

Table 3. Domestic and Worldwide Crude Oil Self-Sufficiency Ratios,*
27 U.S. Companies, 1972 & 1974.

	Domestic "self-sufficiency" ratio (Total domestic production as a % of total domestic refinery runs)				World-wide "self-sufficiency" (Domestic plus foreign production as a % of domestic plus foreign refinery runs)			
	1974		1972		1974		1972	
Company	Ratio	Ranking	Ratio	Ranking	Ratio	Ranking	Ratio	Ranking
Amerada Hess	18.6	20	21.4	21	29.6	22	52	18
American Petrofina	13.7	23	20.1	22	11.4	26	14	21
Apco Oil	16.9	22	62.2	12	74.3	14	62	17
Ashland Oil	7.0	25	6.1	24	17.2	25	13	22
Atlantic Richfield	58.6	10	61.3	13	85.1	11	87	10
Cities Service	91.6	3	83.0	6	96.4	8	84	12
Clark Oil	2.7	26	2.9	25	2.3	27	2	23
Continental Oil	67.7	7	64.8	11	86.6	10	115	7
Diamond Shamrock	38.9	18	39.4	19	38.9	20	39	20
Exxon	79.3	6	94.3	4	69.5	15	97	9
Getty Oil	140.0	1	162.9	1	171.7	3	188	1
Gulf Oil	58.6	10	73.0	9	138.4	4	165	2
Kerr-McGee	24.3	19	104.0	3	28.6	23	111	8
Marathon	65.8	8	78.5	7	118.1	5	159	3
Mobil	51.0	14	46.0	18	115.8	6	86	11
Murphy Oil	17.0	21	23.6	20	35.6	21	40	19
Pasco	40.1	17	NA		40.1	19	NA	
Philips	48.9	15	49.1	17	62.3	17	60	18
Shell Oil	58.3	11	65.0	10	58.3	18	65	16
Skelly	98.3	2	126.0	2	108.0	7	132	6
Standard Oil of Ca.	47.6	16	61.0	14	207.3	2	154	4
Standard Oil (Ind.)	57.6	12	50.9	16	80.7	13	79	14
Standard Oil (Ohio)	9.2	24	7.4	23	15.9	24	13	22
Sun Oil	54.2	13	58.0	15	65.6	16	80	13
Tenneco	83.5	5	NA		93.2	9	NA	
Texaco	85.4	4	90.5	5	147.0	1	136	5
Union Oil	61.1	9	78.4	8	81.6	12	77	15

Source: "National Petroleum News Factbook," 1971 and 1975, *National Petroleum News*, New York.

*Since the production figures cited include natural gas liquids, these 'self sufficiency" ratios are overstated since most natural gas liquids are not processed in refineries.

Table 4. Total motor gasoline: summary of marketing categories, 1974 only.

Category	Total Direct sales %	Total branded independent marketer %	Nonbranded product sold to independent marketers %	Total national sales %
Large integrated	15.96	75.83	8.21	74.96
Large independent	24.94	40.20	34.85	8.35
Small independent	21.28	40.09	38.63	16.69
All refiners	17.60	66.89	15.51	100% (101,410,634 thousand gals.)

Source: Federal Energy Administration, Market Shares Monitoring System, Refiner/Importer Survey. (Office of Statistical Analysis, Federal Energy Administration, Washington, D. C., 1975.)

apparent that the fundamentals of the technology and the market environment are such that vertical integration implies efficiency advantages which cannot be replicated by market exchange.

Integration Between Refining and Crude Oil Production

An examination of the characteristics of oil-refining operations and crude oil production will reveal that the fundamental technology is such that the backward integration by refiners into crude production yields rather compelling efficiency advantages. The very large capital cost of refineries and the long-life nature of the investment, together with the specialized character of the typical refinery[24] (they cannot be easily converted to alternative uses), means that an uninterrupted throughput throughout the life of the equipment contributes importantly to the profitable operation of the facility. Furthermore, a refinery can make only very limited use of crude oil inventories to guard against short-run shortages in supply. This is because the cost of carrying sizable inventories is enormous, given the small margins available in refining operations. The cost of crude oil constitutes a very high percentage of the value of the products sold by a refiner. Therefore, the cost of crude oil is an extremely important factor in determining the refiners' competitive position. All of these considerations point to the critical importance, to the refiner, of crude oil supply dependability at a competitive price. Standard Oil of Ohio, for example, has had a relatively low self-sufficiency ratio and is well aware of its vulnerable position. It has continuously made efforts to improve its competitive stance. "In a sense, the history of Standard Oil of Ohio since 1911 has been a history of trying to overcome the deficiencies of no crude oil reserves."[25] However, some economists have suggested that the necessity for vertical integration results simply from the existing structure of the industry. F. M. Scherer, for instance, asserts that "if crude markets were made competitive, if they were made workably competitive, that compulsion would be minimized."[26] This argument ignores the technological considerations prevailing in the industry and the problems associated with small numbers bargaining relations. A market which is competitive or workably competitive by all objective standards may still provide an incentive for vertical integration. Large-numbers bargaining relationships can easily degenerate to a small numbers situation. This could occur irrespective of the degree to which a market was currently pre-empted by other vertically integrated firms. This point, and the motives for integration between refining and crude production, are explored below.

A salient feature of refining is that the typical refinery can draw crude only from those areas to which it has access by pipeline or deep water. Although the pipeline system allows a degree of flexibility, the bargaining relationship between refiner and crude oil supplier can sometimes be one of small numbers.[27] It may therefore be difficult for the refiner to secure a dependable source of supply at competitive prices via market mediated transactions. Where these small numbers supply conditions exist, they open possibilities for opportunistic behavior by both parties. Contracts can be broken and promises forgotten. Normal market contracting is likely to be defective on this account. Consider, for example, the possibilities for a once-and-for-all contingent-claims contract, or an incomplete long-term contract, or a series of short-term contracts between crude suppliers and refiners. Under conditions of uncertainty, bounded rationality[28] makes it impossible, or prohibitively costly, to attempt to write a comprehensive contract in which contingent crude supply relations are exhaustively stipulated. Unfortunately, incomplete long-term contracts are not a solution, since they pose obvious trading risks. There are incentives for both crude suppliers and refiners to bargain opportunistically when contractual ambiguities develop. Presumably, however, short-term contracts would permit terms to be redrawn at the contract renewal interval. New information could be appropriately taken into account as events unwind. While short-term contracts offer advantages in these respects, they may still prove unsatisfactory if, for example, only one field is linked by pipeline to the refinery. Accordingly, and even if the initial bargaining situation was one of large numbers, the bargaining relationship could be readily transformed into one of small numbers, since the pipeline connection would limit potential suppliers by the limited extent of its geographical reach. An additional problem is that short-term contracts also permit the refiner to be without supply during periods of shortage, especially if prices are being regulated below the market clearing level, or if no extra supply is available in the short run because of various other contractual commitments. Under these circumstances, backward integration by refiners into crude production is likely to be indicated.

Integration Into Pipelines

Since transportaion costs are an extremely important element in the final delivered cost of petroleum products, pipelines play an important role in the structure of competition in the petroleum industry. The very first great crude oil trunk and product pipelines systems were allied with producing interests,[29] and the great bulk of today's crude oil gathering, crude oil trunk, and product pipelines mileage is owned by companies engaged in refining or some combination of refining, producing, and marketing activities. The purpose of this section is to come to an understanding and assessment of the reasons why pipelines are generally vertically integrated into the petroleum industry. An examination of some of the competitive and technical dimensions of pipelines construction and operation will provide the basis for an understanding of why pipelines are very often owned by the shippers of crude oil and petroleum products.

The first and perhaps the most important consideration, and one that is frequently overlooked, is that many pipelines face competition from other pipelines, as well as from other transportation modes such as ocean tankers, ocean and river barges, and to a somewhat lesser extent, railroad tank cars. The Colonial Pipeline, for instance, faces competition not only from the Plantation Pipeline, but also from ocean tankers. Furthermore, any given pipeline also competes—indirectly but powerfully—with refineries served by other pipelines and other modes. Accordingly, unless throughput guarantees are secured, the number of customers wishing to use a given pipeline rather than alternative arrangements is subject to variability induced by changes in the prices of competing modes, or changes in the underlying transportation economics. For crude oil pipelines there is sometimes an additional degree of variability in the production of crude which can be induced by the uncertain nature of government price regulations and allocation programs, the uncertain size of existing reserves, the uncertain nature of new discoveries,[30] and the vagaries of the international political arena.[31]

A second consideration is that pipelines involve the utilization of specialized long-life equipment. The pipeline is fixed with respect to geographic location and is entirely dependent for its existence on the shipment of crude oil or refined products. A third consideration is that supply to and from some pipelines is often characterized by small-numbers relationships; in other words, the number of customers from which a pipeline must draw its main volume of business may be very small.

Because of these various factors—variability in the demand for pipeline services, specialized long-life equipment, and small-numbers bargaining relationships—vertical integration (in other words, ownership of the pipelines by producing, refining, or marketing companies) may be desirable since market forces may not draw forth sufficient pipeline capacity in a timely fashion, thereby exposing the industry to higher transportation costs than are really necessary. The disabilities that are associated with the market stem from problems in the sharing of risks and the rewards for risk-taking. Given variability in the demand for pipeline services, the viability of a pipeline very often rests on the throughput guarantees of the shippers. If sufficient throughput guarantees from potential shippers are forthcoming, the viability of the project is assured and the requisite capital can be raised in the market. However, in offering such guarantees, the shipper is exposing himself to a degree of risk, since unanticipated economic changes quite conceivably could render the throughput guarantees burdensome. Since the risk in the project is being transferred to the grantor of the throughput guarantee, the shipper is in a position to bargain for a return for the risk inherent in providing the throughput guarantee. Vertical integration into pipeline ownership is an effective means of capturing a return for the risk that is being carried. However, it is necessary to explain the advantages of integration over a contract in which the shipper would provide a throughput guarantee to an independent pipeline in return for some kind of profit-sharing arrangement. The problems associated with the latter would seem to center around the costly haggling that it would entail, since there does not seem to be an objective way of determining the amount of compensation that is warranted for the risk that the throughput grantors incur. Unfortunately, small-numbers bargaining may prevent the competitive level from being easily discovered.

A further incentive for vertical integration can be found in an information-impactedness condition which could well be important in many circumstances. Supply and demand variability for crude and refined products could mean that opportunities for new pipeline investments arise rather suddenly. Producers, refiners, or marketers may sometimes be in positions where they cannot afford to wait for an outside firm to discover and exploit the pipeline opportunity which certain firms have been able to identify. These firms may have sufficient information to convince themselves that the investment is profitable, but they may not be able to effectively and quickly convey this information to outsiders. An integrated company with investment in the producing and refining facilities has the greatest incentive to get the crude or refined product moving. Information impactedness coupled with opportunism (the outsider may not know the reliability of the firm's pronouncements about volumes to be shipped) may supply the incentive for the shipper to embark on the pipeline project.

The rationale for the shippers' owing a crude or product pipeline seems to be well founded and affirmative. A related issue of concern to the FTC and the Congress is the reason for the proliferation of joint ventures in pipeline ownership. As viewed by the FTC, this kind of cooperative behavior is anticompetitive and it recommends that "to reduce concentration and to minimize anticompetitive contracts among respondents, a limit on their joint ventures should be imposed."[32] The FTC comes to this conclusion without first considering the affirmative characteristics of joint ventures. If it can be shown that joint venture activity in pipelines has compelling efficiency advantages which would not otherwise be captured, than the FTC's concern would seem to be misplaced.

It can be argued that an important technical consideration provides the incentive for joint ventures to be established. Unit costs for pipeline transportation decline approximately with the square of the diameter of the pipe. Because of these scale economies, it is inefficient to have several small lines running parallel to each other. To insure efficiency over many routes, a greater number of shippers than pipelines is required. However, it was argued that integration into pipeline ownership by shippers is necessary before the shippers have an incentive to provide the throughput guarantees. The only way that this condition can be satisfied and the scale economies of pipelines simultaneously realized, is by a joint venture arrangement among the shippers, who in turn provide the throughput guarantees.

It is important to note that this rationale for joint ventures does not depend on risk-pooling arguments. This seems valid since in some cases these are not very compelling, given the great size of many integrated oil companies. The $36 million equity required for the construction of the Colonial Line would not seem beyond the capital market capabilities of any one of its joint venture partners. The $7 billion required for Trans-Alaska Pipeline is clearly a different matter.

Integration Between Refining and Marketing

The rationale for integration can be explained by reference to the technical and competitive conditions surrounding the marketing of gasoline. Historically, the development of integration between refinery and marketing has resulted primarily from forward integration by refiners. Backward integration by marketers was only of secondary importance. Still, there are various degrees of integration. Refiners can integrate forward into various levels of wholesaling, leaving retailing in the hands of others; or they can integrate through to service stations, either by complete ownership or through franchise arrangements with lessees.

The rapid growth in demand for gasoline in the early twentieth century, and the economies of scale associated with distribution through specialized outlets, led to the emergence of the service station separated from the general store. The first service stations were often owned and operated by dealers, but the refiners became dissatisfied with the service that was being provided. This dissatisfaction, coupled with a belief that company-owned stations would enable the firm to use its superior control machinery to maintain high standards, was apparently one of the main reasons why the Atlantic Refinery declined in 1913 to experiment with owning its own outlets.[33] Since it would be competing against its own dealers, it appeared to the company that this strategy would also help improve standards at other outlets. Furthermore, dealers were often poor credit risks, and their opportunistic behavior in these respects was also a motivation to look for other methods of distribution. This kind of behavior on the part of refiners seems to have been quite general, so the structure that had emerged by the mid-1920s involved the coexistence of both independent dealer-owned outlets and outlets owned and operated by refiners.

Historically, the nonconvergence of expectations also seems to have supplied a motivation for integration. From 1926 to 1935 the forward integration into marketing by refiners was motivated by a desire to dispose efficiently of more product in the face of increased crude supplies.[34] Ideally, the refiners' drive for additional outlets should induce an increase in the supply of appropriate outlets by independent dealers. However, such a coordinated response is difficult to achieve. The marketers sometimes do not know the number of additional outlets needed or their locations. Furthermore, they will be reluctant to make investments without knowledge or assurances that the refiner will not open additional stations within close proximity. It is difficult to bring the expectations of the refiners and independent markets into congruence on this issue. Presumably a refiner could issue contracts stating the number of stations it wanted constructed, their locations, and the terms offered. However, this is strategic information which a competitor might use in deciding to buy those locations.[35] Hence, when information-impactedness conditions prevail, and expectations between refiners and potential marketers to not converge exactly, there is an incentive for the refiner to integrate forward.

The development of the product pipelines also precipitated a considerable amount of forward integration into both wholesaling and retailing activities by refining companies.[36] Integration into wholesaling often occurred at the time a line was built since it was necessary to erect new distributing facilities (terminals) in order that products might be drawn off the line. Presumably, the pipeline owners were in a favored position to perform these activities since they were suitably placed to anticipate the required investments. Under circumstances where it is difficult to achieve a coordinated response between pipeline owners and independent distributors, and an adaptive sequential decision process was called for, forward integration was indicated, given the limitations of contracting.

Integration into retailing often followed the construction of pipelines and integration into wholesaling. Construction of new pipelines, to the extent that they yielded the anticipated transportation cost savings, would increase many a new refiner's marketing potential in a given area, thus providing the basis for an expansion of market share. As indicated above, the wholly-owned and dealer-operated service station is often the best available device to secure market penetration. Accordingly, the construction of product pipelines commonly led to forward integration into both wholesaling and retailing.

Backward integration by marketers into refining was an additional source of integration. It was generally stimulated by abnormally tight supply situations, such as prevailed under price controls during World War II and immediately thereafter. Supply dependability was the predominant motivation. Clearly, problems with contractual incompleteness under uncertainty, and the deficiencies associated with incomplete long-term contracts or a series of short-term contracts, provided the stimulus for backward integration as a method of securing supply dependability.

The thrust of the above argument is that vertical integration into marketing overcomes several problems associated with relying exclusively on the intermediate product market. Basically, the argument centers around the importance of harmonizing expectations, plans, and interests. A nonintegrated marketer is not well placed to cope with changes in the refiners' production scheduling. Conversely, the nonintegrated refiner is not well placed to handle changing market circumstances. There is a tremendous volumetric interdependence in the industry, all the way from the crude oil liftings through the crude pipelines, into the refineries, terminals, and bulk stations, and ultimately into consumer service stations. The elements of flexibility are limited to the tankage and the size and location of the pipelines. These units are small relative to total throughput. This means that production and disposal have to be scheduled. The expectations and plans of the refiners and marketers must be coordinated and harmonized. The refiner needs to be confident that the marketer will draw out of bulk inventories when the refiner wants to augment them. Tankage at service stations, bulk terminals, and refineries needs to be viewed as part of a unified system if its utilization is to be optimized. The market could conceivably perform this function if all the relevant information moved accurately and speedily, and if the objectives of marketing, refining, and transportation were perfectly harmonized. It is, however, difficult to achieve such perfect harmonization across a market interface. In some industries, close approximation to these conditions would suffice and an intermediate product market would be adequate. However, given the great volumetric interdependence in the industry, the huge throughput relative to inventory capacity, and the high costs of inventories relative to refining margins, there is clearly an incentive to devise a method of economic organization which can provide the highest degree of resolution to these problems. By facilitating information flows and harmonizing interests, vertical integration provides a suitable organizational structure for the petroleum industry.

Besides facilitating these continuous scheduling problems, vertical integration facilitates convergence of investment expectations. This was critical during periods of rapid expansion, as was outlined above. More recent instances can be cited. The introduction of nonleaded gasoline is one such example. The president of General Motors said on January 14, 1970, that the new generation of automobiles would require a nonleaded gasoline for the advanced emission control standards. "Within six weeks, Shell's president announced that Shell would offer a nonleaded fuel to the public in time for the fall introduction of the new 1971 model cars. Most of the integrated companies were able to follow with low lead or nonleaded gasoline."[37] Delivering on this promise involved changes in refinery process and in transportation and distribution plans, as well as new investments in tanks, pumps, and lines in the service stations. Once again, it is doubtful that a nonintegrated concern could have responded as quickly. Indeed, many of the nonintegrated marketers did not provide nonleaded or low lead gasoline facilities for some months after the large integrated refiners were able to do so.

While much of this argument has stressed the advantages to the refiner of forward integration into marketing, there are also incentives for the marketer to be integrated backward into refining. As Allvine indirectly points out, "in order to compete successfully with the majors, private brand marketers must have an assured source of product at reasonable prices and must be able to market their product at a price below that set by the major brand marketers. The most essential element to successful operation is a ready and reliable source of supply."[38] An astute strategy to secure access to supply would seem to be either long-term contracts, or where these faulted, vertical integration. Vertical integration helps remove the marketer from the vagaries of the spot market.[39] Of course, competitive market considerations would suggest that this strategy would reduce returns since risk and return can be expected to be positively correlated under realistic assumptions about how competitive markets operate.[40] The spot market can be competitive by objective criteria, yet small-numbers supply relationships—a function perhaps of pipeline locations or transportation costs—can render reliance on it risky.

Other Efficiency Attributes of Vertical Integration

Although vertical integration in the petroleum industry has commonly been undertaken to overcome specific disabilities associated with market contracting, the vertically integrated structure created was often discovered to yield manifold and sometimes unexpected managerial and operating advantages which facilitated an adaptive decision-making process. Indeed, the existence of these economies provides a further incentive to integrate. Accordingly, even though changing circumstances might seem to modify or nullify the original motivation for vertical integration, the superiority of the integrated structure for facilitating information exchange and control often held the pressures for vertical disintegration in abeyance. Some of the important planning and managerial advantages to the industry which follow from vertical integration and efficient information exchange are now summarized.

A significant managerial benefit resulting from vertical integration in the petroleum industry is the opportunity to plan capital investments in the various stages of the industry on a coordinated basis. For the efficient utilization of capital resources, investment in oil exploration and development, pipelines, refineries, and marketing properties needs to take place in a coordinated manner with respect to both timing and physical complementarity. An adaptive, sequential decision process is called for. This is possible if the relevant transactions are internalized within a vertically integrated structure. The reason is that each department usually has full access to the plans and programs of other departments. Accordingly, an investment decision can be made with more complete information than would be available to a nonintegrated firm. Nonintegrated companies operating in different phases of the business are generally not able to exchange information freely among themselves on their current and future investment plans or their current and future production plans and input requirements. Furthermore, the nonintegrated firm may not be in a position to secure commitments from firms engaged in upstream and downstream operations. Since contingencies cannot be predicted perfectly in advance, comprehensive contingent claims contracts cannot be written. Even if short-term contracts are not defective either on account of investment disincentives or first-mover advantages, such contracts can be invalidated by the costs of negotiations and the time required to bring the system into adjustment. Exclusive reliance on market signals is apt to involve larger costs than administrative processes under vertical integration.

Consider the integrated refiner. The integrated refiner can base his expansion and modification investment decisions on more complete information regarding his crude supplies (both volume and crude type) and has more complete data on the expected demand for his products. This permits the integrated refiner to move with a greater degree of assurance on investment decisions,[44] since the continued availability of crude supplies and product outlets are required to assure amortization of the large capital investment required in refining. Vertical integration can effectively attenuate uncertainty and thus assure the amortization of long-life equipment. Thus a stable crude supply reduces the risk for refining. Conversely, an assured outlet for crude facilities exploration and production. Furthermore, marketing expansions can be more attractive if there are assurances of a growing product supply.

Unfortunately, the gains that integrated companies have been able to make are difficult to quantify objectively. However, they can be expected to become manifested in superior overall performance and a strengthening of the competitive position of the vertically integrated firms.

Vertically integrated oil companies also have advantages over nonintegrated companies in the handling of the logistical problems associated with the producing, refining, and distribution processes. Again, this is because information flows more freely within the firm than across markets. Refining operations, for instance, are highly complex and the short-run coordination problems are rather formidable. A major company with several refineries will typically operate a great number of processes, utilize an even larger number of discrete processing units, and manufacture hundreds of grades of different petroleum products. Confident access to crude, and ready access to product demand data from the marketing department, allows the refiner to more efficiently schedule his operations. One important saving is that inventory and tankage reductions are made possible. Refining activities are given protection by knowledge of the production or supply departments inventories in the field. The refinery's inventory and the flexibility of refining operations to make more products in turn provide protection to marketing. Consider how the nonintegrated refiner might decide on the optimal level of seasonal inventory. The building of seasonal inventories necessarily requires accurate estimates of future market demand. Ordinarily, the integrated refiner will have better access to service station sales and inventory data than a nonintegrated refiner. Although the nonintegrated refiner can draw upon his customers for estimates of stock positions and future needs, he will face greater difficulties in collecting accurate information quickly and systematically. There is an obvious asymmetry in the distribution of information between refiner and retailer. The achievement of information parity is likely to involve a high cost. This is the information-impactedness condition, and the vertically integrated firm, with its relatively reliable and efficient information channels, is a device well-suited to reduce or eliminate the information-impactedness problem.

Hence the pervasive vertical integration found in the oil industry appears to be based on efficiency considerations. There are, of course, potential anticompetitive effects which can result from vertical integration. However, the horizontal market power necessary for vertical integration to be anticompetitive is absent, and so vertical integration can have at worst only an innocuous effect on competition.[42] Rather, by fostering production and distribution efficiencies, vertical integration coupled with competition enables consumers to enjoy lower prices than would otherwise be possible. In addition, vertical integration is revealed in the next section to have a positive impact on technological innovation in the industry and is thereby a source of further social benefit.

IV. RESEARCH AND INNOVATION IN THE ENERGY INDUSTRIES*

United States industry spent $1.2 billion for energy R&D in 1974[43] and was expected to spend $1.27 billion in 1975.[44] Federal funds accounted for 40 percent of the total in 1974.[45] In the same year 50 percent of the total energy R&D spending and 93 percent of Federal spending was directed towards nuclear energy R&D, mostly nuclear fission. Table 5 indicates that almost exactly one half, or $359 million of total company funds of $718 million spent on energy R&D was accounted for by the petroleum industry. It is this portion of the total private R&D funds spent on energy which is examined in this chapter. In addition to describing the pattern of R&D spending in the petroleum industry some critical determinants of innovational performance will be discussed. The interrelationship between market structure, internal structure, and innovational performance are analyzed with a view to understanding the possible implications of industrial reorganization on technological performance.

The Structure of Petroleum Company Research Expenditures

Since the ultimate objective of R & D programs is to produce innovations, not to spend dollars, research expenditures per se are of little intrinsic interest as a measure of innovative performance. However, since innovation is very difficult to quantify, R&D expenditures can be viewed as a useful proxy. Tables 6-11 summarize major facets of research expenditures by the petroleum industry.

Table 6 shows that in 1976[46] about $625 million were allocated to R & D by firms in the "petroleum refining and extraction" category.[47] The relative unimportance of Federal funds is also indicated: Federal funds typically account for only about 3 or 4 percent of total R&D in this industry. Table 7 shows that in 1974, 38.6 percent of industry funds were spent in R&D programs larger than $100 million dollars, and that 92.4 percent of the total was spent in programs larger than $10 million per year. Clearly, most of the industry's R&D is not dispersed in numerous small programs. Rather, most of it is conducted in very large R & D programs. Table 8 shows that the top eight companies (by sales) accounted for 76.8 percent of the industry's R & D in 1974. R & D companies (by sales) other than the 20 largest accounted for only 2.6 percent of industry R & D. Table 9 shows that

Table 5. Expenditures for energy research and development, by selected industry and source of funds: 1974–1975.
($ millions)

Industry	Sic Code	1974 Total	1974 Federal	1974 Company	1975 (NSF est.) Total
Total	789,807,891	$1,197	$479	$718	$1,266
Chemicals and allied products	28	84	(1)	(1)	92
Industrial chemicals	281–82	82	(1)	(1)	90
Petroleum refining and extraction	29,13	372	(1)	359*	416**
Primary metals	33	22	(1)	(1)	28
Machinery	35	13	(1)	(1)	14
Electrical equipment and communications	36,48	374	292	82	400
Aircrafts and missiles	372,19	129	(1)	(1)	105
Professional and scientific instruments	38	14	(1)	(1)	15
Other manufacturing industries	07–12,14–17	139	(1)	(1)	139
Nonmanufacturing industries	41–47,49–67,	50	7	43	57

[1]Not separately available but included in total.
*This figure is not provided by the NSF but is estimated by the author as follows. It is assumed that the percentage of company R&D in energy is the same as the percentage of Company R&D in total R&D, which is 96.65 percent (from Table 1 96.65 percent of $372 million is $359.54 million. The lower bound on this number must be 352 since total federal funds in the industry amounted to no more than $20 million in 1974). (See Table 1).
**The author's survey indicates that this figure is about $420 million.
Source: *Research & Development in Industry, 1975, op. cit.,* p. 59.

Table 6. Petroleum refining and extraction* R&D expenditures 1956–58, 1963–75
($ millions)

	1956	1957	1958	1963	1964	1965	1966	1967	1968	1969	1970	1971	1972	1973	1974	1975**
Total this industry	182	211	246	317	393	397	371	371	437	467	515	505	468	498	598	—
Federal funds		11	12	21	61	48	18	16	34	10	22	17	15	14	20	—
Company funds		200	234	296	332	349	353	355	403	457	493	488	454	485	578	625
Total company funds all industries			3,396	3,630	5,360	5,792	6,445	7,216	8,020	8,869	9,857	10,283	10,645	11,326	12,696	14,038	—

*This industry classification is based on the 1967 Standard Industrial Classification (SIC) Manual.
**Estimate based on company survey.
Source: Research and Development in Industry, 1975, op. cit., p. 26, 28, and 31.

Table 7. Funds for research and development, 1974; by selected R&D program size groups, petroleum refining and extraction
($ millions)

Size of R&D Program:	< $.2	$.2–.999	$1–9.999	$10.000–99.999	$100.000 or more	Total
Expenditures:	$1	$2	$42	$322	$231	$598

Source: *Research and Development in Industry, 1974*, p. 27.

the top four companies, ranked by assets, accounted for 44.7 percent of the industry total, and the next four accounted for another 30.2 percent, making 74.9 percent for the top eight (by assets). It is also noteworthy that the top four account for $24.7 million or 73.6 percent of the industry's basic research. It is also apparent that firms below number 22 in asset ranking do not perform R & D.

The structure of R & D in the industry is thus made clear by these tables. Firms other than the top 22 do not perform any R & D. Within the class of firms that perform R & D, the top ten account for proportionally more of the industry R & D than do firms somewhat smaller.[48] The giants, as a group, also account for almost all of the basic research. Hence, there are differences both as to the amount and type of R&D performed by firms in different size classes. This view is reinforced when we examine the structure of the industry's expenditures on energy R & D, which is displayed in Table 10. Firms ranked 9–12 spend a larger proportion on coal (21 percent) than any other group. Firms ranked 13–16 spend a larger proportion of their funds on oil shale (26 percent) than any other group. The largest four firms spend less than 1 percent of their budgets on this activity. On the other hand, the top four spend proportionally more of their R & D funds on solar and nuclear, while firms 5–8 spend proportionally more of their funds (23 percent)

Table 8. R&D funds, and R&D funds as percentage of net sales, top eight, and next twelve petroleum refining and extraction companies ranked by size of net sales, 1974.

	Company R&D funds	Net sales	R&D as a % of sales	Percent of total company funds
Top 8	444	89,634	.5	76.8
Next 12	119	34,974	.3	20.6
Remainder*	15	—	—	2.6

Source: *Research and Development in Industry, 1975* op. cit., p. 57, 58.
*Derived from total company R&D of $578 million.

Table 9. Expenditures on basic Research, applied research and development, 1975*

Asset ranking	Company	Basic Amount ($ millions)	Applied Amount ($ millions)	Development Amount ($ millions)	Total Amount ($ millions)	Percent of industry
1 2 3 4	Exxon Texaco** Mobil Std. of California	24.706	138.677	114.854	278.238	44.7
5 6 7 8	Gulf Std. of Indiana Arco Shell	3.586	79.602	104.406	187.594	30.2
9 10 11 12	Continental Phillips Sun Std. of Ohio	4.345	30.538	42.296	77.323	12.4
13 14 15 16	Union Occidental Getty Cities Services	.614	12.687	42.924	56.225	9.0
17 18 19 20 21 22	Marathon Ashland Kerr-McGee Superior Offshore Damson	.293	11.112	9.783	22.188	3.6
	Totals	33.544	272.616	314.263	621.568	100

*Basic Research—Includes the cost of research projects which represent original investigation for the advancement of scientific knowledge and which do not have specific commercial objectives, although they may be in the fields of present or potential interest to the reporting company. Applied Research—Includes the cost of research projects which represent investigation directed to discovery of new scientific knowledge and which have specific commercial objectives with respect to either products or processes. Note that this definition of applied research differs from the definition of basic research chiefly in terms of the objectives of the reporting company. Development—Includes the cost of projects which represent technical activity concerned with nonroutine problems which are encountered in translating research findings or other general scientific knowledge into products or processes. Does not include routine technical services to customers or other items excluded from definition of research development above. (See *Research and Development in Industry, 1975, op. cit.*, p. 81.)

**Data on the breakdown of Texaco's R&D expenditures into the specified categories were not available. Accordingly, it was assumed that the structure of Texaco's expenditures was the mean of the firm lying immediately above and the firm lying immediately below it in ranking by total R&D expenditures.

Source: Questionnaire circulated by author. Although these same data are supplied separately to the NSF by the respondents on form RD-1, they are not published in this form by the NSF.

Table 10. Expenditures for energy R & D by categories of companies and by primary energy source, 1975*

Asset Ranking (1975): Company Names Primary energy source	1–4 Exxon Texaco Mobil Std. of CA	5–8 Gulf Std. of Ind. Arco Shell	9–12 Continental Phillips Sun Std. of Ohio	13–16 Union Occidental Getty** Cities Service	17–22 Marathon Ashland Kerr McGee Superior Offshore Damson	
Oil & Gas						
Amount (millions of $)	126.646	75.858	25.044	15.96	11.959	255.467
Percentage	58.70	64.07	71.72	48.33	68.82	
Coal						
Amount (millions of $)	23.413	7.498	7.436	1.78	.350	40.477
Percentage	10.85	6.33	21.29	.54	14.88	
Shale						
Amount (millions of $)	1.401	3.797	.914	8.53	2.586	17.228
Percentage	.65	3.21	2.62	25.83	14.881	
Other Fossil Fuels						
Amount (millions of $)	.293	2.192	.233	0	0	2.718
Percentage	.14	1.85	.67	0	0	
Geothermal						
Amount (millions of $)	.068	.115	.315	.202	0	.698
Percentage	.03	.10	.90	.59	0	
Solar						
Amount (millions of $)	3.336	1.09	.007	0	0	4.343
Percentage	1.55	.92	.02	0	0	

Nuclear					
Amount (millions of $)	13.652	.583	.215	0	.412	15.053
Percentage	6.32	.49	.62	0	2.37	
Other Energy					
Amount (millions of $)	3.399	0	0	2.500	0	5.899
Percentage	1.58	0	0	7.29	0	
Conservation and Pollution Abatement					
Amount (millions of $)	43.561	27.261	7.827	4.050	2.07	84.769
Percentage	20.19	23.03	2.18	12.26	11.91	
Amount (millions of $)	215.749	118.392	42.202	33.022	17.377	426.742
% of Industry Energy R & D	51.45	18.12	8.33	7.87	4.14	

*Data are not presented on an individual firm basis in order to honor the confidentiality agreement arranged with the companies who supplied the data.

**Although Getty's total energy R&D expenditures were available, expenditures disaggregation by all of the energy sources was not available. For these categories (oil and gas, shale, coal and energy conservation and pollution abatement) it was assumed that Getty spent the same proportion of its R&D in these categories as Union, Occidental, and Cities Services spent on average.

Source: Data were obtained by a questionnaire circulated to all firms in the industry. These same data are reported to the National Science Foundation on form RD-1 but are not published in this form by the NSF. We are confident that our data are complete in that no significant R & D spending has been omitted. Our total R & D figure of $420.73 million corresponds very well with the NSF estimate that total energy R & D spending for the petroleum refining and extraction industry was $416 million. (See Table 2.)

193

Table 11. Regression coefficients, t-statistics, and F-tests in regression equations to explain development research expenditures using pooled time series–cross section.

Observations: 1954–1975 (211 observations)

Independent variable	Equation 1	Equation 2
C	−0.247938 (−0.484)	−0.118956 (−0.227)
VI	0.292991 (0.973)	0.120926 (0.428)
DIVO	−0.109494 (−0.752)	−0.109320 (−0.796)
SIZE	0.191229×10^{-2} (5.172)	0.251794×10^{-2} (5.013)
SIZE^2	-0.226045×10^{-7} (−1.587)	-0.112308×10^{-6} (−2.163)
SIZE^3	—	0.220392×10^{-11} (1.776)
CASH$_{t-1}$	0.2054×10^{-2} (2.093)	0.2120×10^{-2} (2.146)
CASH$_{t-2}$	0.2739×10^{-2} (2.093)	0.2827×10^{-2} (2.146)
CASH$_{t-3}$	0.2054×10^{-2} (2.093)	0.2120×10^{-2} (2.146)
R^2	0.428	0.432
$\bar{R}^2$	0.414	0.416
F	30.689	25.902
D-W	1.722	1.720

on energy conservation and pollution abatement. The considerable differences in emphasis within R & D programs is thus made apparent from the data in Table 10. This suggests that firms in the industry have different R & D strategies with respect to energy development. It is by no means apparent that they are pursuing a common course of development. Given the government programs have, at least historically, tended to emphasize one course (such as nuclear) to the virtual exclusion of others, this mix of approaches is especially valuable since it reduces the risk associated with failure to successfully develop and commercialize any one technology.[49]

In this section, an attempt is made to analyze petroleum company R & D investment behavior. It is distinctive from most treatments of the topic in that linkages are explored between integration (both vertical and horizontal) and innovative performance, as proxied by the firms' R & D expenditures.

Consider, to begin with, how vertical integration might enhance the productivity of R & D by permitting innovations to be "shared" amongst stages and by facilitating the more astute formulations of research objectives.

The existence of technologically similar production activities in various stages of an industry would seem to create opportunities for the sharing of relevant technological innovations and refinements thereof. The existence of technological synergies in turn increases the returns from technological endeavors, thereby inducing greater investment in R & D than might otherwise be justified. The argument, of course, implicitly assumes the existence of "failures" in the market for technological information or know-how. Otherwise, it would be possible for a firm in one stage of an industry to sell know-how to firms in another stage, thereby capturing returns equivalent to those which could be achieved through internal transfer. That contractual problems may occasion market "failure" can be seen from the following example. Consider an industry with technological similarities between stages of production which result in opportunities for technology transfer amongst the various stages. If this technology is to be sold via arms-length transactions in the marketplace, then a number of difficulties can be anticipated. They arise from difficulties associated with contrasting for the exchange of a commodity like technical information, the characteristics of which do not become apparent until the transaction has been completed. The kind of complete disclosure necessary for accurate evaluation of the technical knowledge by a potential buyer might well render the transaction superfluous, since exposure of the technical knowledge during the negotiation process could result in its acquisition by the transferee without the transferee incurring a reciprocal financial obligation. Of course, since the seller is likely to be aware of the opportunistic proclivities of potential buyers, the seller will most likely exercise caution and attempt to display the relevant performance characteristics of the technology while omitting the display of other critical dimension of the know-how. Hence, full disclosure will be avoided, and transactions will need to take place under conditions of informational asymmetry between buyer and seller. Under various assumptions about the risk preferences of the potential buyer and the seller, the price that technological knowledge commands in the market could well be below the value it would command were the condition of information asymmetry to be relieved. A departure from pareto optimality will result if the *ex ante* valuation of the technology differs from the *ex post* valuation. Vertical integration in the presence of technological similarities in various stages of the production process can be expected to resolve the transactional dilemma by relieving the condition of information asymmetry; opportunism is attentuated by the inability of vertically integrated units to appropriate gains at the expense of the total corporation.

Consider, now, the formulation of research objectives. One of the primary ingredients of successful R & D is that it be well directed in terms of objectives. Very often, where production processes are interdependent, familiarity by the R & D department with technology in the separate stages of an industry can assist in the setting of optimal R & D goals, particularly in the realization (in both the planning and subsequent activity phases) of synergistic research projects. The selection of the appropriate goals and the transfer of technology typically require a dialogue among individuals from many different parts of an industry. The R & D organization must be familiar with the problems and needs of the various functional areas. Conversely, the functional areas need to have awareness of the capabilities of the R & D establishment. The mutual understanding necessary for an intelligent dialogue is promoted if personnel move freely between R & D and other functional areas in the industry. Vertical integration clearly facilitates this process. The transactions costs associated with buying and selling engineering and scientific manpower is reduced when personnel can move from R & D to one of several stages of production. Furthermore, a common coding system, or language, can develop within the vertically integrated enterprise which facilitates the transfer of technical information. As Thomas Allen of M.I.T. has pointed out, every organization, like every individual, develops a coding system with which to order its world. This coding scheme, in turn, enhances the efficiency of communication among those who hold it in common. It can, however, detract from the efficiency of communicating with the holders of a different coding system, such as individuals in a different corporation. Besides facilitating technology transfer, the existence of a common coding system and the attendant dialogue between departments or divisions facilitates the formulation of appropriate research objectives. Consider, for instance, a situation where the performance of a product can be enhanced by some mix of product and process improvement. The R & D organization, if it has intimate knowledge of problems in both the production and marketing functions, is better able to select the optimal allocation of R & D funds into product and process improvement. Vertical integration facilitates the acquisition of the necessary information. The R & D group in a vertically integrated firm will typically have easy access to individuals in both production and marketing. Indeed, ongoing committees can be established to maintain a continuous dialogue between the various stages of manufacturing and the R & D department. In addition, personnel can be readily transferred from department to department (or division to division). As a result, the research activity is likely to be better directed and hence more productive.

The petroleum industry can be used to exemplify the notion of shared technologies and the product/process innovation trade-off. Consider the tertiary recovery techniques that are presently being developed to increase the crude production yield from oil fields. These techniques rely to a considerable extent on the chemical science common to contemporary refining process research. While the relevant information could conceivably be sold to a production company by a refining company, it is likely that this exchange could be confounded by the factors discussed above. Common ownership, that is, vertical integration, could, on the other hand, facilitate the exchange, for the reasons enunciated earlier. To illustrate the problems of formulating an appropriate research objective, consider the industry responses to the EPA emissions standards. A new gasoline was required for the engines that Detroit developed (and is developing) to meet the EPA standards ("drive-ability" problems such as stalling having arisen with the new engines). The gasoline could conceivably be developed either through a refining process modification, a product additive modification, or some combination of the two. Because an integrated firm participates in both the refining and marketing stages of the industry it is more likely than a non-integrated firm to possess the information required to decide upon the optimal product and process modification mix. Hence, we would expect that, *ceteris paribus*, R & D productivity, and hence R & D spending, to be positively correlated with vertical integration. As mentioned earlier, the internal coupling interaction mechanism is further aided by the interchange personnel between R & D and the other functional divisions of the corporation. For instance, between 1965 and 1975, 48 professionals were transferred out of Union Oil Research Department into other parts of Union Oil. During this same period, 20 were transferred back in. Of these 20, eight were former Research employees returning to the Research Department. These data, although merely illustrative, suggest that human capital is mobile within vertically integrated firms; the importance of this kind of mobility to the success of technology transfer is well recognized in the literature.[50]

The hypothesis that vertical integration may induce superior innovative performance in situations of overlapping stage technologies suggests that the productivity of a given R & D dollar is higher for vertically integrated firms than for less integrated ones. That is, while at the margin the productivity (or rate of return) associated with R & D expenditures can be expected to be the same for integrated and nonintegrated firms (assuming similar discount rates and risk preferences) the total productivity of the expenditures will be greater for the integrated firms, provided the above hypothesis is correct. This suggests that an appropriate dependent variable for testing the hypothesis would be the value of innovations produced by the R & D program, normalized by the level of R & D expenditures. Needless to say, the numerator of such a ratio is nearly impossible to generate empirically. However, expenditure data can be viewed as a useful proxy for innovative performance in that it reveals the intensity of innovative activity. Furthermore, if the discount rate facing nonintegrated firms is similar to that facing integrated firms, and if similar risk preferences exist across the management of these firms, the higher productivity per dollar of research expenditure posited in vertically integrated firms implies that, other things being equal, such firms will devote more resources to the R&D function.

A final comment with respect to research expenditures, the proposed dependent variable, is in order. The possibility of synergistic spillover results (which, combined with market failure conditions, result in higher expected payoffs) seems to be much more likely when the research activity is more general in nature (as in basic and applied research) than when it is directed at solving a very specific problem. This is not to say that what is learned in one development project may not be at all relevant to research activity in another stage of the production process (which is the key to the shared technologies argument) but rather that the likelihood of this is lower for development projects than for basic and applied research projects. The implication is that one should expect the effect that vertical integration has on development activities to be less than the corresponding effect on basic and applied research.

In order to test this "shared technology" hypothesis empirically, other determinants of the firm's R&D spending must be identified, lest the proposed model be misspecified. It is clear that understanding R&D activity with an industry involves different considerations from those likely to prevail across industries. For one thing, technological opportunity—which is to a large extent determined by the state of science in the relevant field—is relatively constant for firms within a given industry, whereas it is likely to be very different for firms in different industries.[51] This is because all members of an industry will draw from essentially the same stock of basic scientific knowledge whereas firms in different industries pursuing different objectives will be drawing from different fields of science and hence from different stocks of knowledge. Also, within an industry, the objectives and tasks of R&D are likely to bear closer similarities than they do across industries. Hence, opportunities and tasks are relatively similar for the different firms in an industry.

Given this assumption, differences in R&D commitment and performance between firms within an industry can be attributed mainly to firm specific attributes. In particular, it is hypothesized that a firm's R&D expenditures in the petroleum industry are a function of its size, its liquidity or cash flow, and its organization as reflected in its degree of vertical integration. Firm size has long been thought to be an important determinant of research and development expenditures.[52] It is often suggested that large firms may possess scale economies with respect to plant size and/or the marketing function thereby rendering the results of research activity more profitable for large firms, either because of scale economies in production and marketing, or because of faster market penetration (and hence a greater discounted present value of the expected returns).[53] It has also been maintained that larger firms tend to have more stable cash flow characteristics and are hence able to more easily absorb the relatively high riskiness associated with investments in R&D projects.[54] Furthermore, large firms are more capable of simultaneously conducting a large number of R&D projects than are smaller firms, the total risk of the R&D program being reduced through portfolio diversification effects.[55] Finally, it has been proposed that in the case of process innovations, the larger the firm the larger will be the absolute cost savings resulting from the adoption of an innovation, and hence, given the existence of market failure conditions, the more incentive there is for a large firm to engage in R&D.[56]

Cash flow is also hypothesized to influence R&D expenditures (or any other investment decision) because the internal cost of capital is often less than the external cost of capital. This is because of both the tax and transaction cost considerations discussed in section II. Given the validity of this proposition, one would expect cash flow to have approximately the same effect on each of the components of R&D (basic research, applied research, and development).

A firm's technological diversity can also be hypothesized to influence its R&D investment. Nelson has argued that with respect to basic research, which is inherently risky, and unclear in terms of the domain of its commercial applicability, a firm with a broad technological base stands a better chance of capturing the returns to its R&D activity. According to Nelson,[57] a firm with a narrow technological base is likely to find research profitable only at the applied end of the spectrum, where research can be directed toward solution of problems facing the firm, and where the research results can be quickly and easily translated into patentable products and processes. Such a firm is likely to be able to capture only a small share of the social benefits created by a basic research program it sponsors. On the other hand, a firm producing a wide range of products resting on a broad technological base may well find it profitable to support research toward the basic-science end of the spectrum. Hence, a broad technological base insures that, whatever direction the path of research may take, the results are likely to be of value to the sponsoring firm. It is for this reason that firms which support research toward the basic-science end of the spectrum are firms that have their fingers in many pies. It is not just the size of the companies that makes it worthwhile for them to engage in basic research. Rather, it is their broad underlying technological base, the wide range of products they produce or are willing to produce if their research efforts open possibilities. This argument of course implies some kind of failure in the market for technological know-how, otherwise the firm could always capture the return from its R&D activities by selling the research results to others.

The functional form of the proposed model is thus: R&D = f(size, cash flow, vertical integration, diversity (other than that represented by vertical integration). In its most general form, the model can be written as:

$$RD_{it} = \beta_0 + \beta_1 \text{size}_{it} + \beta_2 \text{size}_{it}^2 + \beta_3 \text{size}_{it}^3 + \beta_4 VI_{it} + \beta_5 DIVO_{it}$$
$$+ \beta_6 \text{cash}_{i,t-1} + \beta_7 \text{cash}_{i,t-2} + \beta_8 \text{cash}_{i,t-3} + e_{it}$$

where

RD_{it} = the ith firm's expenditure on basic applied, and development research in period t

size_{it} = the size of the ith firm in period t as measured by the level of end of year total book assets.[58]

VI_{it} = the number of petroleum industry production process stages (i.e., crude production, refining, transportation, and marketing) in which the ith firm participated in the ith period

$DIVO_{it}$ = $DIV_{it} - VI_{it}$, where DIV_{it} is the number of technological areas in which the ith firm is involved in period t

$\text{cash}_{i,t-s}$ = the level of cash flow associated with firm i in period $t - s$[59]

e_{it} = a random disturbance term.

If the "Shared Technology" hypothesis advanced above is correct we should expect β_4 to be greater than zero. In addition, we might expect that β_4 will be larger in regressions run on basic and applied research data than in regressions run on development expenditure data. β_6, β_7, β_8, and β_1 are also expected to be positive. The signs of β_2 and β_3 will depend upon the presence and relative importance of any economies or diseconomies of scale. The data and the econometric techniques used in estimating the above equations are discussed in the Appendix.

The results of the investigations into industry R & D and the determinants of the effect that vertical integration may have on basic and applied research expenditures and on development activity appear in Tables 11, 12, and 13. The results with respect to the vertical integration variables are especially interesting and particularly robust. Vertical integration significantly influences (at the 95 percent level) basic and applied research expenditures. The regression results indicate that participation in an additional stage of the petroleum industry production process (holding other variables constant) increases basic research spending by approximately $700,000 annually and applied research spending by about $500,000 annually. As hypothesized, vertical integration does not appear to affect development activities nearly

Table 12. Regression coefficients, t-statistics, and F-tests in regression equations to explain applied research expenditures using pooled time series–cross section.

Observations: 1954–1975 (206 observations)

Independent variable	Equation 1	Equation 2
C	−0.511503 (−1.810)	−0.39034 (−1.140)
VI	0.538906 (2.915)	0.402629 (1.942)
DIVO	−0.281363 (−2.615)	−0.344009 (−2.058)
SIZE	0.131026×10^{-2} (5.081)	0.190079×10^{-2} (5.350)
SIZE^2	-0.334771×10^{-8} (−0.324)	-0.876374×10^{-7} (−2.498)
SIZE^3	—	0.213951×10^{-11} (2.503)
CASH$_{t-1}$	0.2382×10^{-2} (3.590)	0.2503×10^{-2} (3.897)
CASH$_{t-2}$	0.3176×10^{-2} (3.590)	0.3337×10^{-2} (3.879)
CASH	0.2382×10^{-2} (3.590)	0.2503×10^{-2} (3.879)
R^2	0.671	0.705
R̄^{2}	0.663	0.696
F	81.505	79.190
D-W	1.726	1.720

as much as it influences basic and applied research. The coefficients in the development regressions are both smaller in absolute size and in statistical significance. Although the regression results associated with the residual diversity variable (DIVO) are expected in the basic and development analyses, in the applied research regression statistically significant and negative coefficients resulted. The reasons for this unexpected result are not apparent.

The estimated coefficients of the cash flow variables are positive, as hypothesized, significant, and indicating maximum influence in the second lagged period. A pattern of first less than proportional increases in research expenditures with increases in firm size and then more than proportional increases is exhibited in the applied research results and, to a lesser extent, in the development investigation.[60] Apparently there exists some threshold above which scale economies are realized and below which diseconomies with respect to firm size occur.[61]

The empirical results reported in this section suggest the existence of a definite relationship between internal organization and innovative performance. In addition, firm size and cash flow were found to be very significant determinants of the components of the R&D budget, the latter having approximately the same effect on each component, the former having quite different effects. The behavior of cash flow was consistent with the prior expectation (based on transactional and tax-related arguments) that the internal cost of capital is less than the corresponding external cost. With

Table 13. Regression coefficients, t-statistics, and F-tests in regression equations to explain basic research expenditures using pooled time series–cross section.

Observations: 1954–1975 (199 observations)

Independent variable	Equation 1	Equation 2
C	−1.71813 (−0.787)	−1.94407 (−0.218)
VI	0.728575 (1.802)	0.686676 (1.953)
DIVO	0.28265×10^{-1} (0.699)	0.174028×10^{-1} (0.437)
SIZE	-0.228683×10^{-3} (−2.341)	0.356340×10^{-8} (0.218)
SIZE^2	0.134812×10^{-7} (4.709)	-0.985987×10^{-2} (−0.786)
SIZE^3	—	0.5033×10^{-12} (1.895)
CASH$_{t-1}$	0.5742×10^{-3} (2.616)	0.4672×10^{-3} (2.065)
CASH$_{t-2}$	0.7656×10^{-3} (2.616)	0.6229×10^{-3} (2.065)
CASH$_{t-3}$	0.5742×10^{-3} (2.616)	0.4672×10^{-3} (2.065)
R^2	0.285	0.291
$\bar{R}^2$	0.267	0.269
F	15.410	13.152
D-W	1.703	1.723

respect to firm size, there appear to be increasing returns to scale for basic research activities throughout the sample range of firm sizes and first declining then increasing returns for applied and development research endeavors.

V. CONCLUSION

The U.S. energy industries, like many others in the U.S. economy, are characterized by considerable vertical and growing horizontal integration. While vertical integration has been long established, horizontal integration is much more recent and is a competitive response to the changed circumstances prevailing in the energy markets. Both forms of integration appear to have desirable effects. In particular, it was possible to show that vertical integration has a positive and statistically significant effect on R&D performance.

The oil companies remain the centerpiece of the U.S. energy supply situation. A good deal of oil industry technology and expertise is relevant to alternative sources of energy, such as coal, geothermal, and shale. This is one reason why the boundaries of many oil companies are changing, and many of the larger ones are becoming "energy" companies. The R&D activities of the oil companies are changing as well. The structure of energy markets will undoubtedly be somewhat different ten years from now. If public policy does not confound these socially beneficial organizational changes and the allocative properties of markets then the long-run U.S. energy picture must be one of considerable optimism.

APPENDIX: ECONOMETRIC PROCEDURES

The data base consisted of pooled time-series and cross-sectional observations. The general econometric approach and specific procedures used in the empirical investigations were as follows.[62] Every equation was first estimated using ordinary least squares procedures (OLS) with raw data. The familiar Durbin-Watson test for autocorrelation was then applied to the generated residuals.[63] Throughout the investigation it was assumed that the autoregressive scheme characterizing the residuals was the same across cross-sectional units (firms). The relatively few number of time-series observations for each firm motivated this assumption. The particular form of the Durbin-Watson statistic that is appropriate for pooled cross-section/time-series models (and hence the one that was utilized in the investigation) is:

$$d = \frac{\sum_{i=1}^{N} \sum_{t=2}^{T} (e_{it} - e_{i,t-1})^2}{\sum_{i=1}^{N} \sum_{t=1}^{T} (e_{it})^2}$$

where e_{it} = the residual corresponding to the tth observation for the ith firm.[64]

If significant autocorrelation was suggested by the Durbin-Watson statistic, the following first order autoregressive scheme was assumed.

$$e_{it} = \rho e_{i,t-1} + u_{it}$$

where e_{it} is defined as above and

$$U_{it} \sim N(0, \sigma_{u_i}^2)$$
$$E(e_{i,t-1} U_{jt}) = 0 \quad \text{for all i,j}$$

The autoregressive parameter ρ can be consistently estimated[65] by

$$\hat{\rho} = \frac{\sum_{i=1}^{N} \sum_{t=2}^{T} e_{it} e_{i,t-1}}{\sum_{i=1}^{N} \sum_{t=2}^{T} (e_{i,t-1})^2}$$

Once ρ was estimated, the raw data were then transformed using a procedure developed by Kadiyala in order to produce asymptotically more efficient estimates of the coefficients in the original model.[66] The first period observation for each firm was transformed by multiplying the observation by $\sqrt{1-\hat{\rho}^2}$. All other period observations were transformed by multiplying the observation in the previous period by $\hat{\rho}$ and subtracting the result from the current period observation (i.e., $Y_{i,t} = Y_{i,t} - \hat{\rho} Y_{i,t-1}$ and $X_{i,t} = X_{i,t} - \hat{\rho} X_{i,t-1}$, $i=1,\ldots,N$; $t=2,\ldots,T$). The resulting transformed data were subsequently used to re-estimate the original equation. If the transformation is not made and significant autocorrelation is present, the coefficient estimates will be unbiased though inefficient. That is, they will not possess the minimum variance properties of all linear unbiased estimators.

In addition to investigating the possible violation of the ordinary least squares (OLS) assumption of non-autocorrelated error terms, the appropriateness of the homoscedasticity assumption (constant variance across disturbance terms) was also examined.[67] It was postulated that if heteroscedastic error terms were present, the structure of the variance of the error term was:

$$\sigma_{u_i}^2 = \sigma_u^2 X_i^\delta e^{v_i} \tag{1}$$

where X_i = firm size in terms of total assets and e = the number e. The variance of the disturbance term was thus assumed to be a function of firm size. Equation (1) can be equivalently written as:

$$\ln(\sigma_{u_i}^2) = \ln(\sigma_u^2) + \delta \ln(X_i) + v_i \tag{2}$$

where v_i is assumed to be a well behaved disturbance term.

Using the residuals $\hat{u}_i$ from the OLS equation corrected for autocorrelation, an estimate of δ in equation (2) was obtained by regressing $\ln(\hat{\sigma}_u^2)$ on $\ln(X_i)$. In order to test for significant heteroscedasticity one simply tests whether $\hat{\delta} \neq 0$, using a conventional t-test.[68] If the null hypothesis of homoscedasticity, $\delta = 0$, was rejected the data was again transformed, this time by dividing all variables by $X_i^{\delta/2}$, the resulting error term in the equation having homoscedastic properties. OLS was then applied to this transformed data. Asymptotically more efficient estimates of the coefficients in the original model are thereby obtained, provided that the true autoregressive scheme and the true structure of the variance of the error term are as postulated.

A comment involving goodness of fit statistics is extremely important. Buse points out[69] that when generalized least squares (OLS) estimation procedures are used in empirical investigations (or equivalently, when OLS is applied to transformed data) the conventional goodness of fit measure

$$R^2 = 1 - \frac{e'e}{y'y}$$

where: e = the vector of residuals; and
y = the dependent variable vector (expressed in mean deviations)

is no longer appropriate. The goodness of fit measure specified below can be used for such circumstances. The measure has a range of zero to one, is zero when all the estimated coefficients except the constant are zero, and is monotonically related to the F-statistic used in testing the null hypothesis that all coefficients except the constant are zero—that is, it has the characteristics of the conventional goodness of fit measure in the absence of autocorrelation and/or heteroscedasticity.

$$R_*^2 = 1 - \frac{e'\hat{\Omega}^{-1}e}{(Y - \bar{Y}_* f)'\hat{\Omega}^{-1}(Y - \bar{Y}_* f)}$$

where: e = the vector of residuals;
Y = the dependent variable vector (expressed in absolute terms not in mean deviations);
f = a column vector of ones (included for comformity purposes);
$\hat{\Omega}$ = the estimated variance/covariance matrix of the disturbance term; and
$\bar{Y}_* = (f'\hat{\Omega}^{-1}Y)/(f'\hat{\Omega}^{-1}f)$.

Note that if $\hat{\Omega}$ is a diagonal matrix with a constant value along the diagonal, R_*^2 (the Buse R^2) reduces to the conventional R^2.

In terms of a model of transformed data, the statistic can be defined as:

$$R^2_* = 1 - \frac{e^{*'}e^*}{(Y^* - \bar{Y}^*_* f^*)'(Y^* - \bar{Y}^*_* f^*)}$$

where e^* = the vector of residuals from the transformed equations;
Y^* = the transformed dependent variable vector (expressed in absolute terms not in mean deviations);
f^* = the transformed constant vector; and
$\bar{Y}^*_* = (f^{*'}Y^*)/(f^{*'}f^*)$

All of the R^2's reported in this study have been calculated using this algorithm. Readers are cautioned against carelessly comparing these R^2's with those reported in studies in which heteroscedastic and/or autocorrelation transformations have been made and where misleading conventional R^2's are reported. Though the divergence of the conventional R^2 and the Buse R^2 can be in either direction, the Buse R^2 were characteristically below the conventional R^2's in this study.

A nontrivial econometric problem was encountered in attempting to estimate the cash flow coefficients in the innovative performance investigation. Because the cash flow variables were highly collinear, the standard errors associated with their estimated coefficients were considerably inflated. As a result, reliable estimates of the significance of the variables became difficult to obtain. In order to overcome this problem it was assumed that the lag structure corresponding to the cash flow variables follows a polynomial of a given degree.[70] That is, the equation could be expressed as:

$$Y_{it} = \alpha_0 + \sum_{j=1}^{n} \alpha_j X_{jit} + \gamma(W_0 CASH_{i,t} + W_1 CASH_{i,t-1} + W_2 CASH_{i,t-2} + W_3 CASH_{i,t-3}) + e_{it}.$$

where Y_{it} = the dependent variable observation associated with the ith firm in the tth period;
X_{jit} = the observation on the X_j independent variable (e.g., DIV) associated with the ith firm in the tth period;
$CASH_{i,t-s}$ = the cash flow associated with the ith firm in the $(t-s)^{th}$ period; and
e_{it} = a random disturbance term.

A polynomial of a given degree was then fitted to the weights W_0, W_1, W_2, and W_3. As an example, suppose a third degree polynomial was selected to fit. To make each of the weights (W_0, W_1, W_2, and W_3) lie along a third degree polynomial curve, one specifies:

$$W_i = \lambda_0 + \lambda_1 i + \lambda_2 i^2 + \lambda_3 i^3, \quad (i = 0, 1, 2, 3)$$

The polynomial distributed lag (PDL) model then becomes:

$$Y_{it} = \alpha_0 + \sum_{j=1}^{n} \alpha_j X_{jit} + \gamma[\lambda_0 CASH_{it} + (\lambda_0 + \lambda_1 + \lambda_2 + \lambda_3)CASH_{i,t-1}$$
$$+ (\lambda_0 + 2\lambda_1 + 4\lambda_2 + 6\lambda_3)CASH_{i,t2} + (\lambda_0 + 3\lambda_1 + 9\lambda_2 + 27\lambda_3)$$
$$CASH_{i,t-3}] + e_{it}$$

By appropriate collection of terms one can proceed to estimate the α's and λ's using ordinary least squares procedures.[71] Note that the parameter γ is not identified; it is common to all of the cash flow terms so the convention of taking its value to be unity was followed. By adopting this polynomial distributed lag procedure the multicollinearity[72] problem was alleviated and thereby more reliable estimates of the influence of cash flow on R&D expenditures (or components thereof) were obtained.[73]

FOOTNOTES

*Assistant Professor, Graduate School of Business, Stanford University. I gratefully acknowledge the comments and assistance of Henry Ogden Armour in preparing this chapter. I also owe a considerable intellectual debt to Oliver Williamson whose work on markets and hierarchies has influenced my thinking considerably. I also wish to thank those firms which supplied the proprietary data on R & D expenditures utilized in Section IV.

1. Ronald Coase, "Industrial Organization: A Proposal for Research," in Victor Fuchs (ed), *Policy Issues and Research Opportunities in Industrial Organization* (New York: National Bureau of Economic Research, 1972).

2. Readers desiring a more descriptive treatment are referred to "The Petroleum Industry," by Thomas G. Moore, in Walter Adams (ed.), *The Structure of American Industry* (London, Macmillan, 1971).

3. Indeed, several oil companies have changed their names to reflect this transformation. For example, the Sun Oil Company is now the Sun Company, and the Kerr-McGee Oil Company is the Kerr-McGee Corporation.

4. *See Continental Oil Company Annual Report 1975* and *Kerr-McGee Corporation 1975 Annual Report.*

5. See, for example, Walter Adams, "Horizontal Divestiture in the Petroleum Industry: An Affirmative case," in W. S. Moore (ed.), *Horizontal Divestiture* (Washington, D.C., American Enterprise Institute, 1977).

6. Ronald Coase, "The Nature of the Firm," *Economica,* November 1937.

7. Oliver Williamson, *Markets and Hierarchies* (New York: Free Press, 1975).

8. Henry Grabowski and Dennis Mueller, "Life Cycle Effects of Corporate Returns on Retentions," *Review of Economics and Statistics,* November 1975; and Dennis Mueller, "A Life Cycle Theory of the Firm," *Journal of Industrial Economics,* July 1972.

9. "Needs" here simply refers to opportunities for profitable plowback.

10. Federal Energy Administration, *National Energy Outlook,* 1975.

11. See David Teece, "Horizontal Integration in the Energy Industries: A Markets and Hierarchies Analysis," Research Paper n. 352, Graduate School of Business, Stanford University, 1977.

12. Paul Davidson, *et al.,* "Oil: Its Time Allocation and Project Independence," *Brookings Papers on Economic Activity,* 2, 1974.

13. Walter, Adams, "Horizontal Divestiture in the Petroleum Industry: An Affirmative Case," in W.S. Moore (ed.), *Horizontal Divestiture* (Washington, D.C., American Enterprise Institute, 1977).

14. Davidson, *op. cit.*, 1974.

15. How is it different from a wheat farmer who withholds this year's harvest in storage in anticipation of a future shortage?

16. See Jesse, Markham, "Market Structure and Horizontal Divestiture of the Energy Companies," in W.S. Moore (ed.), *Horizontal Divestiture* (Washington, D.C., American Enterprise Institute, 1977).

17. See David Teece, Research Paper No. 352, *op. cit.*

17a. *Ibid.*

18. With the possible exception of Island Creek, as noted in Table 2.

19. See David Teece, Research Paper No. 352, *op. cit.*

20. *Ibid.*

21. See J. Fred Weston, "Changing Environments and New Concepts of Firms and Markets," in *New Technologies, Competition, and Antitrust* (transcript of National Industrial Conference Board Ninth Conference on Antitrust Issues in Today's Economy, March 5, 1970.

22. National Petroleum Refiners Association, Annual Refining Capacity Report, 1972.

23. For an explanation of the partial nature of vertical integration, and the survival of nonintegrated firms, see David Teece, *Vertical Integration and Vertical Divestiture in the U.S. Oil Industry* (Stanford: Stanford University Institute for Energy Studies, 1976), pp. 57–68.

24. The design of any given refinery will depend, among other things, upon the specific characteristics of the crude oil and other raw materials to be processed, and the product mix that is desired from the refinery. There are many different grades of crude oil, and there will be differences in the yield of products which will be obtained from them. "Sour" crude contains significant amounts of sulfur, and refineries have to be designed to remove the sulfur compounds. A light crude will yield a high percentage of useful products by distillation, whereas a heavy crude will produce significant amounts of crude oil material which must be sold as heavy fuel oil or processed further. Accordingly, it is quite difficult to switch a refinery to alternative crude streams, at least in the short run. Switching from oil refining to some other function is quite impossible as a practical matter.

25. Statement of Mr. Whitehouse, Standard Oil Company of Ohio, before Antitrust and Monopoly Subcommittee, Committee on the Judiciary, *U.S. Senate, Hearings 1970–1972*, p. 584 (University of Pennsylvania Library Shelf Title).

26. F.M. Scherer, Director, Bureau of Economics, Federal Trade Commission, Hearings, January 30, 1976: in *Vertical Divestiture in the Petroleum Industry*. (Majority Staff Report, Senate Antitrust and Monopoly Subcommittee, January 1976, reproduced from typescript).

27. This need not mean that the market is monopolistic according to commonly used measures of market power.

28. Bounded rationality refers to the limited capacity of the human mind to formulate and solve complex problems. For instance, when the future is uncertain, it is very costly, if not impossible, to identify all future contingencies and to specify all the appropriate adaptations ahead of time. The problem is that for even moderately complex problems, the entire decision tree needed for a complex contract cannot be generated. There are several reasons why this is so. One is the size of the tree. The number of alternatives in complex decision problems is very large. A second reason is that in most decision situations, unlike chess, neither the alternative paths nor a rule for generating them is

available. A third reason is the problem of estimating consequences. For many business problems, the consequences of alternative situations is difficult, if not impossible, to estimate. Accordingly, a comprehensive decision model is not feasible for most real world decision problems.

29. The reference here is to the Empire Transportation Company which developed a large crude-gathering and trunk-line system, and to the United States Pipeline Company, an independent concern which developed, closely allied with producing interests, one of the first products pipelines. See J.G., McLean, and R.W., Haigh, *The Growth of Integrated Oil Companies* (Boston, Division of Research, Graduate School of Business, Harvard University, 1954), p. 181.

30. See McLean and Haigh, *ibid.*, p. 190, for an indication of the historical importance of this consideration. More recently, the Four Corners Pipeline from Aneth, Utah, to the refineries near Los Angeles has not done as well as expected since in the final analysis the reserves were not as abundant as had been thought. In the future, Alaska North Slope oil, if brought into the northern tier states, could adversely affect the Explorer Pipeline.

31. For example, as a direct result of the Arab oil embargo and its ramifications, the Explorer Pipeline found its throughout halved between November 1973 and January 1974. This has not been a short-term effect since throughput did not increase sufficiently to produce a profit in 1975. According to Vernon Jones, President and Chief Executive Officer of the Explorer Pipeline Company, between October 1971 and year end 1975 Explorer made calls for cash advances totaling $25 million against its stockholders, and under the terms of its throughput and deficiency agreement, Jones claims that "without this access to additional funds, Explorer could be in receivership right now." See testimony of Vernon T. Jones before the Subcommittee on Antitrust and Monopoly, Senate Committee on the Judiciary, January 29, 1975.

32. FTC Report to the Senate Committee on Interior and Insular Affairs, 1973, p. 28; and the Prediscovery Statement filed with the Administrative Law Judge, p. 141.

33. See McLean and Haigh, *Growth of Integrated Oil Companies, op. cit.*, p. 169.

34. *Ibid.*, p. 270.

35. Since markets are never frictionless, there is no reason to assume that the competitor following such a strategy is necessarily going to secure a higher return from locations acquired in this manner. Hence, it is difficult to argue that this result is necessarily socially preferred.

36. See McLean and Haigh, *op. cit.*, p. 272.

37. Statement of Frank Staub, Shell Oil Company, before Antitrust and Monopoly Subcommittee, Committee on the Judiciary, *U.S. Senate, Hearings, 1970–1972* (University of Pennsylvania Library Shelf Title), p. 680.

38. See Fred Allvine, testimony before the Antitrust and Monopoly Subcommittee. Committee on the Judiciary, U.S. Senate, July 15, 1970, p. 100.

39. There are many examples of the risks associated with relying on the spot market. For instance, Farmland Industries recently announced that it cut off shipments of refined products to 17 large customers to assure its member cooperatives of adequate supplies. See "Farmland Halts Shipments of Some Petroleum Products," *Wall Street Journal*, September 29, 1975, p. 17.

40. This would help explain why nonintegrated marketers would, in some periods, have a cost advantage over integrated firms. However, by deliberately embracing a high-risk strategy, the cognizant nonintegrated marketer is aware that supply may be jeopardized at various times by normal market circumstances. Government intervention in recent years has served to attenuate these risks at the expense of the integrated marketers.

41. The lead time for a large refinery is about four to seven years.

42. See David Teece, *Vertical Integration, op. cit.*, chapter 4.

43. The most recent year for which National Science Foundation data were available at time of writing.

44. There was a 10 percent increase in R&D spending on energy between 1973 and 1974, although the expected increase between 1974 and 1975 was 6 percent. See *Research and Development in industry, 1974* (National Science Foundation, Washington D.C., 1975), p. 8.

45. The electrical equipment industry received $292 million or 61 percent of Federal energy R&D funds, principally for nuclear energy projects.

46. Using Securities and Exchange Commission (SEC) data, the 1976 figure is about $753 million. Since 1974 the accounting definition of R&D expenditures used by the SEC closely matches the definition used by the National Science Foundation.

47. This category corresponds with SIC codes 29 and 13. Of the many hundreds of firms in this category, data made available to the author indicate that only the following firms perform R & D: Exxon, Texaco, Mobil, Standard of California, Gulf, Standard of Indiana, Arco, Shell, Continental, Philips, Sun, Standard of Ohio, Union, Occidental, Getty, Cities Services, Marathon, Ashland, Kerr-McGee. Superior, Offshore, Damson, American Petrofina, Amerada Hess, and Penzoil.

48. Specifically, if one takes the sample and divides it into the top ten, and the next twelve (ranked by assets), then:

$$\sum_{i=1}^{10} \frac{R\&D}{assets}/10 = .46317 \text{ and}$$

$$\sum_{i=11}^{22} \frac{R\&D}{assets}/12 = .2981$$

Hence the average ratio of R & D/assets of the top ten is larger than the average R & D/assets of the next twelve firms *who perform R & D*. If one were to rank *all* of the firms in the industry then the role of the largest firms in the industry would come through more clearly, Since some quite large firms and most small firms do not allocate any resources to R & D.

49. To give a specific example, consider solar energy development. In the direct conversion of sunlight to electricity, the Energy Research and Development Administration (ERDA) is concentrating almost exclusively on the development of silicon solar cells through its Low Cost Silicon Array program. Yet there is another technology, cadmium sulfide, which is being developed in a serious way with Shell Oil funds. Shell looked at production problems from the point of view of chemical engineering rather than semi-conductor technology and chose to back an alternative route. It is too early to tell who will turn out to be right, but given the uncertainties involved in both approaches it is desirable to have several projects under parallel development until the best alternative becomes apparent. Parallel development is an accepted principle of R&D management.

50. Rosenberg, for instance, is impressed by the extent to which the transfer of technological skills is dependent on the transfer of skilled personnel. See N. Rosenberg, "Economic Development and the Transfer of Technology: Some Historical Perspectives," *Technology and Culture*, October 1970. Corroborating views can be found in W. Gruber & D. Marquis (eds.), *Factors in the Transfer of Technology* (Cambridge, Mass.: MIT Press, 1969).

51. See F. M. Scherer, *Industrial Market Structure and Economic Performance*, and M. I. Kamien and N. L. Schwartz, "Market Structure and Innovation: A Survey," in *Journal of Economic Literature*, March 1975. For more detailed discussions of the relationship between technological opportunity and innovative performance.

52. J. A. Schumpeter, *Capitalism, Socialism, and Democracy* (New York: Harper, 1942); F. M. Scherer, "Size of Firm, Oligopoly, and Research: A Comment," *Canadian Journal of Economics and Political Science*, May 1965, pp. 256–266; D. Hamberg, "Size of Enterprise and Technical Change," *Antitrust Law and Economics*, July/August 1967, pp. 43–51; W. S. Comanor, "Market Structure, Product Differentiation, and Industrial Research"; E. Mansfield, *Industrial Research and Technological Innovation: An Econometric Analysis* (New York: W. W. Norton, 1968); Mueller, "A Life Cycle Theory of the Firm, *op. cit.*; J. W. Markham, "Market Structure, Business Conduct, and Innovation," *American Economic Review*, Part II Supplement, May 1965, pp. 323–332; and David J. Teece and Henry Ogden Armour, "Innovation and Divestiture in the U.S. Oil Industry," in David Teece (ed.) *Research and Development in Energy: Implications of Petroleum Industry Reorganization* (Stanford University Institute for Energy Studies, 1977).

53. F. M. Scherer, *Industrial Market Structure and Economic Performance*, *op. cit.*, p. 353; A. R. Bright, Jr., *The Electric Lamp Industry* (New York: Macmillan, 1949), p. 346; and P. S. Johnson, *The Economics of Invention and Innovation* (London: Martin Robertson & Co., 1975), p. 58.

54. Kamien and Schwartz, "Market Structure and Innovation," *op. cit.*; Scherer, *Industrial Market Structure and Economic Performance*, *op. cit.*, p. 353; and P. S. Johnson, *op. cit.*, p. 58.

55. P. S. Johnson, *The Economics of Invention*, *op. cit.*, p. 58.

56. David J. Teece and Henry Ogden Armour, *op. cit.*; and Scherer, *Industrial Market Structure and Economic Performance*, *op. cit.*, p. 354.

57. Richard Nelson, "The Simple Economics of Basic Scientific Research," in *Journal of Political Economy*, June 1959.

58. It is felt that total assets is superior to the value of the firm's sales as a firm size measure since the latter is partly a function, in this industry, of OPEC pricing decisions. For instance, the OPEC price increases raised the sales of the U.S. oil companies without significantly changing the size of their operations. However, whether one uses assets, sales, or employment statistics as the measure of firm size actually makes very little statistical difference, since all of these measures are highly correlated. The size-squared and size-cubed variables are included in the model to allow for economies and/or diseconomies of scale effects posited in section IV.

59. Cash flow is defined as (operating income before depreciation, income taxes and interests) less (interest payments) less (income taxes). This definition is quite similar to (net income) plus (depreciation). It was selected over the latter definition because less ambiguity from alternative accounting procedures arise. It was assumed that the impact of cash flow in several previous periods influences R&D expenditures in the current period. The movitating assumption is that the capital budgeting process is one whereby funds allocated to R&D vary according to the firm's cash position (assuming that the internal cost of capital is below the external cost of capital.) Hence investment decisions which could be justified only on the basis of the lower internal cost of funds will be postponed or abandoned when the firm's cash position is less liquid. A lag effect over several years was assumed because the capital budgeting decision takes time and because sustained changes in the firm's cash positions have more effect than one year fluctuations. However, the investigation of the cash flow influence was restricted to a three-year maximum lag. The rationale for this restriction was that although a five-year planning horizon is used in some companies, funds for any particular project are rarely committed more than three years in advance.

60. The points of inflexion (assuming $\frac{\partial \text{cash}_{i,t}}{\partial \text{size}_{i,t}} = 0$ for $s = 1, 2$ and 3) are approximately \$12,700 million (basic and applied) and \$17,000 million of sales (development).

61. While it is unclear why this first less than proportional and then more than proportional response of applied research and development expenditures to increases in firm size occurs, one possible explanation is that the characteristics of the most cost effective research facility (including human as well as physical equipment) vary across the range of firm sizes. That is, it may be the case that below a certain firm size it is most efficient to utilize multipurpose/multitask equipment and scientists and engineers with broad technical training. However, as the firm increases in size and undertakes a larger number of research projects (with a likely increase in the diversity of projects) diseconomies of scale are encountered with respect to the general research facility. Then once a certain size is reached (say, because of the increased number and variety of research projects), it may be more cost effective to possess a research department with sophisticated special purpose equipment and more specialized researchers, economies of scale being realized for some time (though certainly not indefinitely) as the firm increases further in size. That basic research does not appear to be characterized by such a phenomenon probably results from the fact that such research requires a specialized research environment to begin with.

62. For an excellent discussion of models involving pooled cross-section time-series data see Jan Kmenta, *Elements of Econometrics* (New York: Macmillan, 1971), pp. 508–517.

63. J. Durbin and G. S. Watson, "Testing for Serial Correlation in Least-Squares Regression," *Biometrika*, Vol. 37, 1950, pp. 409–428, and Vol. 38, 1951, pp. 159–178.

64. James N. Rosse, "Estimation and Prediction with Complex Heteroscedasticity," *Studies in Industry Economics*, No. 75 (Department of Economics, Stanford University, 1977), p. 20.

65. Kmenta, op cit., p. 510.

66. K. R. Kadiyala, "A Transformation Used to Circumvent the Problem of Autocorrelation," *Econometrica*, Vol. 36, 1968, pp. 93–96. See Also J. Johnston, *Econometric Methods*, (New York: McGraw-Hill, 1972), 2nd ed., pp. 259–261.

67. The methodology developed by R. E. Park, "Estimation with Heteroscedastic Error Terms," *Econometrica*, Vol. 34, 1966, p. 888, was utilized.

68. If $\delta = 0, \sigma_{u_i}^2 = \sigma^2 X_i^0 e^{\gamma_i}$, which implies homoscedasticity.

69. A. Buse, "Goodness of Fit in Generalized Least Squares," *The American Statistician*, Vol. 27, 1973, pp. 106–108.

70. Both second and third degree polynomials were investigated (zero, one, and two turning points thus being allowed) with a variety of zero restrictions (e.g., the front end of the polynomial ($CASH_{it}$) tied to zero, neither, and both ends tied). In most cases varying the zero restrictions did not significantly change the shape of the fitted polynomials. In the results reported in section IV, both ends of a second-degree polynomial have been tied to zero. This implies that current period cash flow does not effect (by imposition of the zero restriction) current R&D expenditures, nor does the cash flow in any period before the third previous year.

71. As mentioned in the previous footnote, the restriction $W_0 = 0$ was imposed.

72. In order to attenuate the multicollinearity problem a relationship has, however, been imposed between the cash flow variables in the form of the specified PDL. That significant changes did not occur when the degree of the PDL and the zero restrictions were varied suggests that the approach was not excessively restrictive.

73. For a discussion of polynomial distributed lags and appropriate estimation techniques see Shirley Almon, "The Distributed Lag Between Capital Appropriations and Expenditures," *Econometrica*, Vol. 33 (January 1965), pp. 178–196); Kmenta, *op. cit.*, pp. 494–495; and Johnston, *The Economics of Invention, op. cit.*, pp. 294–297.

THE ECONOMICS OF THE THROWAWAY NUCLEAR FUEL CYCLE

John B. Gordon, UNIVERSITY OF TEXAS AT AUSTIN

Martin L. Baughman, UNIVERSITY OF TEXAS AT AUSTIN

Nuclear power has been the subject of intense debate covering such topics as safety, economics, the size of the Federal research and development (R&D) budget, disposition of spent fuel, and provision of permanent waste storage. The long-term health of the nuclear industry has long been predicated on the notion that the fuel cycle would be closed, permitting the extraction, refabrication, and reintroduction into the reactor of fissionable material generated during reactor operation. This reprocessing and use of fissionable material in spent fuel has been held desirable for economic reasons for the light water reactor industry and indeed is indispensable to the breeder concepts where more fuel would be produced than consumed during reactor operation.

Historically the electric utility industry has counted on a closed nuclear fuel cycle in which the uranium and plutonium in the spent fuel would be reprocessed. Reprocessing the spent fuel could effectively increase the resource base for Light Water Reactor (LWR) nuclear plants by 25 percent. The LWR program has always been considered as a temporary (at most forty to fifty years) nuclear energy program in the transition to long-term nuclear energy sources such as the Liquid Metal Fast Breeder Reactor (LMFBR), the Gas-Cooled Fast Breeder Reactor (GCBR), and the Light Water Breeder Reactor (LWBR).

To supply an increasing percentage of the nation's energy needs many planners—including the Federal Energy Administration (FEA), the Energy Research and Development Administration (ERDA), the electric utility industry, and the engineering community associated with energy production—have counted on additional nuclear power plants being constructed. They project that an increasing number of nuclear power plants are needed (along with coal plants) to reduce the amount of oil and gas used to generate electricity and meet future growth in consumption. These same planners at various times in the past five years have estimated that the capacity of nuclear power plants operating by the year 2000 would range from 500 to 1000 gigawatts electric (Gw(e)).

During the period 1972 through mid-1974 those projections appeared to be realistic. In 1972 and 1973 the electric utility industry contracted for over 60 Gw(e) of additional nuclear power plant capacity. The momentum of ordering spilled over into the first half of 1974 as the cumulative level of electric utility commitments (firm and tentative orders) approached 230 Gw(e). However, by late 1974 the electric utility industry moved into a period of severe difficulty. The industry experienced the first hiatus in demand growth in over a quarter century and was beset with serious cash-flow problems resulting in the outright cancellation of several nuclear plants including Quanticasee 1 and 2, Vogtle 3 and 4, Sterling 2, Arnold 2, Allens Creek 2, Florida Power Corporation 2 and 3, South River 1 through 3, Fulton 1 and 2, Summit 1 and 2, St. Rosalie 1 and 2, and other unannounced units. Other nuclear plants were delayed so far into the future that the contract wording was modified to constitute little more than an agreement to do business with a particular nuclear vendor if the occasion arose. Since this time the industry has experienced a series of factors impeding the implementation of a closed nuclear fuel cycle. As a result, since early 1975 the total commitment to nuclear power plants by the electric utility industry has remained around the 200 Gw(e) level.

However, the light water reactor industry need not consider its near term future dependent upon a series of favorable Federal actions and technological developments at the back end of the fuel cycle. Another way of stating the same thing is that electric utilities need not await decisions on the back end of the fuel cycle to proceed with light water reactor installations. An economically viable and institutionally attractive alternative is the "throwaway" fuel cycle.

Going to a throwaway nuclear fuel cycle does not change the nature of the LWR nuclear technology, a short-term energy source; however, the use of a throwaway nuclear fuel cycle for LWR nuclear plants will slow down the development of the long-term sources since reprocessing of spent fuel is essential to the operation of breeder nuclear plants. Significant operational reprocessing experience could be gained prior to the introduction of breeder reactors if a closed fuel cycle were developed. The throwaway nuclear fuel cycle will not provide that experience, but it will allow a significant portion of the overall nuclear fission program to proceed, thus providing valuable operational experience and maintaining a viable industry base.

The purpose of this paper is to portray the economic, environmental, and institutional benefits of a "throwaway" fuel cycle when compared to the traditional fuel recycle concept. The principal findings are:

> The most significant factors preventing the electric utility industry from expanding its commitment to LWR nuclear plants involve the nuclear fuel cycle.

> The complexity and number of problems involving the nuclear fuel cycle can be reduced if the electric utility industry bases its analyses and plans on the "throwaway" nuclear fuel cycle.

> The proven and probable domestic reserves of uranium available at $30 per pound (forward costs) or less are sufficient to supply the thirty-year lifetime demand of 300 Gw(e) of LWR nuclear plants using a "throwaway" nuclear fuel cycle and operating at a 66 percent lifetime capacity factor average with enrichment based on a 0.2 percent tails assay.

> The average price of uranium in 1990 should be between $18 and $34.5 (constant 1975 dollars) and in 2000 should be between $28.5 and $67.5 based upon today's proved and probable reserves using today's mining technology.

> Nuclear fuel cycle average costs for the "throwaway" fuel cycle will remain below 10 mills per kilowatt-hour in constant 1975 dollars through the year 2000.

> In the long term, the nuclear fuel cost for the throwaway cycle is basically insensitive to major changes in the price of waste disposal, transportation, and spent fuel storage.

FACTORS AFFECTING THE NUCLEAR OPTION

The process of fissioning uranium and plutonium to release energy to generate electricity was demonstrated on a commercial basis in the early 1960s. Today there exist in the world many varieties of nuclear fission power plants such as the Canadian Heavy Water Reactor (CANDU); the British and French gas-cooled, graphite-moderated reactors; the British Steam-Generating Heavy Water Reactor (SGHWR); the High Temperature Gas Reactor (HTGR); and the British Advanced Gas Reactor (AGR); but the nuclear system used predominantly in the United States is the Light Water Reactor (LWR). In 1976 almost 10 percent of U.S. electricity was generated by 58 nuclear plants, with 56 of those plants being LWR nuclear plants (22). These LWR nuclear plants within the U.S. consist of two types of commercial designs; the Boiling Water Reactor (BWR) and the Pressurized Water Reactor (PWR).

Implementing the nuclear option requires the purchase, construction and operation of LWR nuclear plants by electric utilities. No matter how desirable today's operating LWR nuclear plants are in producing energy, electric utility management must be confident of their future if they are to choose the nuclear option for additional energy. But many factors pose substantial short- and long-run risk to the operational viability of the conventional light water reactor technology. With a slight amount of oversimplification, the major factors can be broken down into three main areas: institutional and regulatory factors, plant technical and economic factors, and nuclear fuel cycle factors.

Institutional and Regulatory Factors

State Moratorium: Electric utilities in many areas of the country have been forced to agressively defend their decisions in the political area. To date seven state referenda to severely restrict the nuclear option have been voted on (all failed to pass) (26).

State Licensing: California, Wisconsin, Vermont, and several other states have established regulations requiring siting and other type permits before a utility can begin construction (32). This licensing procedure is in addition to the Nuclear Regulatory Commission (NRC) licensing procedures.

Load Growth: Because of the long lead time involved in ordering, licensing, and constructing an LWR plant, actual load demand at the time of initial operation could vary considerably from first projections. One of the major factors in the recent delay of many nuclear plants under order was the abnormally low load growth of 1974 and 1975 due to the nation's severe recession.

Backfitting and Redesign: The NRC may order future LWR nuclear plants to have a second separate shutdown system to protect against Anticipated Transients Without Scram (ATWS) and to have fire suppression systems designed under "design basis" seismic conditions. The NRC may also order electric utilities to update safety systems to more recent standards for their LWR nuclear plants already operating.

Plant Technical and Economic Factors

Capacity Factor: Not counting those nuclear plants starting up this past year, the industry-wide capacity factor for LWR nuclear plants for 1976 will average only about 60 percent (22). The large new units such as Browns Ferry 1 through 3, Zion 1 and 2, Indian Point 2 and 3, Peach Bottom 2 and 3, D. C. Cook 1, and Trojan as a group have had capacity factors below the average.

Plant Costs: The past five years have seen high inflation rates driving nuclear plant costs skyward. Plant changes ordered in the early 1970s by the Atomic Energy Commission, forerunner of the NRC, have increased real plant costs significantly. Delays, strikes and other difficulties have pushed the future costs of many LWR nuclear plants under construction above $1,000 per installed kilowatt (10).

Financing: The rapid rise in costs and fuel prices has placed severe financial strains on many of the nation's investor owned electric utilities (37). Because of the long time period required for licensing and constructing a nuclear plant, financing of "work in progress" has proved to be a real challenge.

Nuclear Fuel Cycle Factors

Uranium Supply: The announcement by Westinghouse that it would be unable to supply over 50 million pounds of uranium oxide has brought into focus the difficult problem of timely and adequate uranium supply (38). Government decisions to delay reprocessing and increase the enrichment tails assay will require that utilities in the short term use more uranium than they had planned.

Uranium Price: Since 1972 the price for newly contracted uranium has jumped from $6 per pound of uranium oxide (U_3O_8) to $40 per pound (27). An international uranium cartel has been operating since 1972 with the approval of the governments of Australia, Canada, and South Africa (4).

Enrichment Capacity: Since 1974 ERDA has maintained a moratorium on further sales of enrichment (separative work units) due to an anticipated shortage of future capacity (1). In three years of effort, the Nixon-Ford administration was unable to get Congress to pass legislation to enable private industry to build additional enrichment facilities (29).

Reprocessing: The only commercial reprocessing plant at West Valley, New York, has been abandoned by its former owner because of uneconomic operation (20). The General Electric reprocessing plant at Morris, Illinois, was not completed because of technological defects in its processes. The Barnwell, South Carolina, reprocessing plant lies nearly completed waiting for finalization of Federal regulations governing operation.

Reprocessing Costs: The cost of reprocessing at the West Valley, New York, reprocessing plant after modification was projected to be $1,000 per kilogram of heavy metal (kghm) (20). Estimates of costs are difficult to make as long as final Federal regulations governing operation are not established.

Plutonium Recycle: Recycle of plutonium cannot begin until reprocessing plants are on line and mixed oxide fabrication facilities are operational. Further, in all likelihood Congress will make the final determination on whether plutonium will be used or not.

Mixed Oxide Fabrication: Mixed oxide fabrication plants will not be constructed until reprocessing plants are assured of operating. Mixed oxide fabrication plant designs are yet to be approved by the NRC.

High-Level Waste Disposal: ERDA has yet to identify its future high-level waste burial sites. Cost of service has yet to be accurately determined.

Long-Term Fuel Cycle Costs: With all the above uncertainties in the technology and cost of components of the nuclear fuel cycle, an assessment of long-range nuclear fuel costs is very difficult.

The above factors are not meant to be inclusive of all problems, but the discussion does highlight many uncertainties influencing the nuclear energy industry. The problems presented by the institutional, regulatory, and plant technical factors will require management attention, significant amounts of time and resources, and could result in substantial delays. Yet, with the exception of state moratoriums, the first two areas will not likely completely stop the implementation of the nuclear option.

However, the third area—nuclear fuel cycle factors—presents a more formidable problem. Many of the factors in this area are completely outside the control of electric utility management (summarized on Table 1).

No one electric utility nor the entire utility industry and its suppliers has the ability to solve the group of problems associated with the nuclear fuel cycle. Many of the factors are international in nature and will require political decisions associated with a clear national energy policy.

Electric utility management has two distinct routes to follow in dealing with the nuclear fuel cycle. They could continue to pursue a totally closed fuel cycle including recycle of spent fuel, or they could discount the possibility of recycle and make their analysis based on a "throwaway" fuel cycle. If this latter option were chosen, then the factors of reprocessing and its costs, plutonium recycle, and mixed oxide fabrication are no longer applicable. The major factors which would be left to be considered by management would be the uranium supply factor—which utilities can influence; uranium price factor—which utilities can influence; enrichment capacity factor— which Congress has taken action to remedy; high-level waste storage

Economics of the Throwaway Nuclear Fuel Cycle

Table 1. Factors affecting the nuclear option and the entities with significant control over those factors

Item	Electric utilities	State and local	Nuclear Regulatory Commission	ERDA	EPA	Congress	State courts	Federal courts	Nuclear vendors	International community
Institutional and System Factors										
States moratoriums	X	X					X	X		
State licensing	X	X					X	X		
Load growth	X	X								
Backfitting and redesign	X		X		X			X	X	
Nuclear Plant Factors										
Capacity factor	X		X						X	
Plant cost	X		X		X				X	
Financing	X	X								
Nuclear Fuel Cycle Factors										
Uranium supply	X			X				X	X	X
Uranium price	X							X	X	X
Enrichment capacity					X		X		X	X
Reprocessing			X	X	X	X		X		X
Reprocessing costs			X	X	X	X				
Plutonium recycle			X	X	X	X		X		X
Mixed oxide fabrication			X		X	X		X	X	
High-level waste disposal		X	X	X	X	X	X	X		X
Long-term fuel cycle costs	X		X	X	X	X				

factor—which must be solved anyway to dispose of massive amounts of military waste which are a full order of magnitude greater than electric utility nuclear wastes; and the nuclear fuel cycle cost factor—which is reduced in complexity when spent fuel is not recycled.

The benefit of the throwaway cycle is that a significant portion of the overall nuclear fission program can continue to proceed, thus providing valuable operational experience and maintaining a viable industry base. The spent fuel can be stored in retrievable long-term storage for several decades while awaiting the political, social, and technical solution of the reprocessing problems. Even if the final decision in the future is made against reprocessing and the breeder reactor, the country will still have benefited from the short-term LWR program. Thus the throwaway process allows the short-term LWR nuclear program to proceed by decoupling it from the problems of the longer-term technology.

THE THROWAWAY FUEL CYCLE

The term "throwaway" describes literally the mode of operation of the open nuclear fuel cycle. Each fresh nuclear fuel assembly is limited by material properties of the cladding and by fission product buildup to a maximum total thermal output. A throwaway fuel cycle is defined here to mean that once a nuclear fuel assembly has released this designed quantity of thermal energy, it is discarded irrespective of the potential fuel remaining which might later be reused.

The required processing steps of a throwaway nuclear fuel cycle are fairly straightforward, consisting of:

a. Mining, and milling uranium-bearing ores into "yellowcake"— U_3O_8.
b. Converting U_3O_8 into high purity UF_6 in preparation for introduction into the enrichment plant.
c. Raising the level of U-235 from 0.7 percent to around 3.0 percent (depending on the reactor/fuel core physics) at a government enrichment plant to provide sufficient reactivity in the nuclear fuel to insure that the fission chain reaction can be maintained over the useful life of the fuel assembly.
d. Fabricating the enriched uranium into uranium oxide fuel pellets and inserting them in metal-clad fuel assemblies.
e. "Consuming" the useful part of the nuclear fuel assembly over a period of from 36 to 60 months.
f. Storing the spent fuel in swimming-pool-type containments for up to ten years to allow a majority of the radioactive fission products a chance to decay, thus reducing the residual decay and subsequent heat output of the spent fuel.
g. Transporting spent fuel to the Federal repository.
h. Storing the spent fuel on a semipermanent basis.

The throwaway nuclear fuel cycle exhibits a straight line or open series of events as visually displayed in Figure 1. After power production there is a minimum amount of activity remaining to complete the open type nuclear fuel cycle; therefore, the potential for disruption in the smooth functioning of the throwaway fuel cycle at the back end is small compared to other nuclear fuel cycle schemes.

The term "other nuclear fuel cycle schemes" for an LWR refers primarily to those cycles which reprocess the spent nuclear fuel assembly to recover the uranium and plutonium remaining in the fuel assembly. There are many variations on the timing and mode of operation of a nuclear fuel cycle utilizing reprocessing. One scheme which has been proposed would separate

Economics of the Throwaway Nuclear Fuel Cycle 221

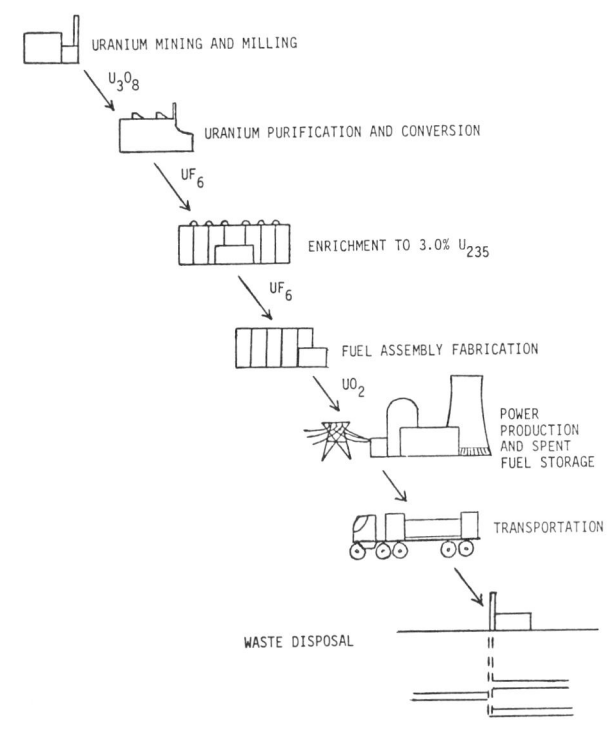

Figure 1. Throwaway nuclear fuel cycle.

the uranium from the plutonium, with the plutonium then being held at a Federal depository. A second scheme would produce a stream of uranium enriched with plutonium and a stream of uranium only. But for purposes of comparison, a fully (closed) cycle with separate plutonium and uranium output streams will be assumed as depicted in Figure 2. The additional components of this closed nuclear fuel cycle are as follows:

i. Reprocessing the spent fuel where the fuel assemblies are chopped up, the contained materials are dissolved, uranium is separated out in the form of UF_6, plutonium is separated out as PuO_2, low-level radioactive processing and waste material are separated out and buried either on site or at a low-level waste disposal site, and a high-level radioactive liquid waste stream is produced.

j. Fabricating the plutonium oxide into mixed oxide PuO_2—UO_2 fuel pellets and inserting them in the fabricated metal-clad fuel assemblies with the mixed oxide fuel assemblies being

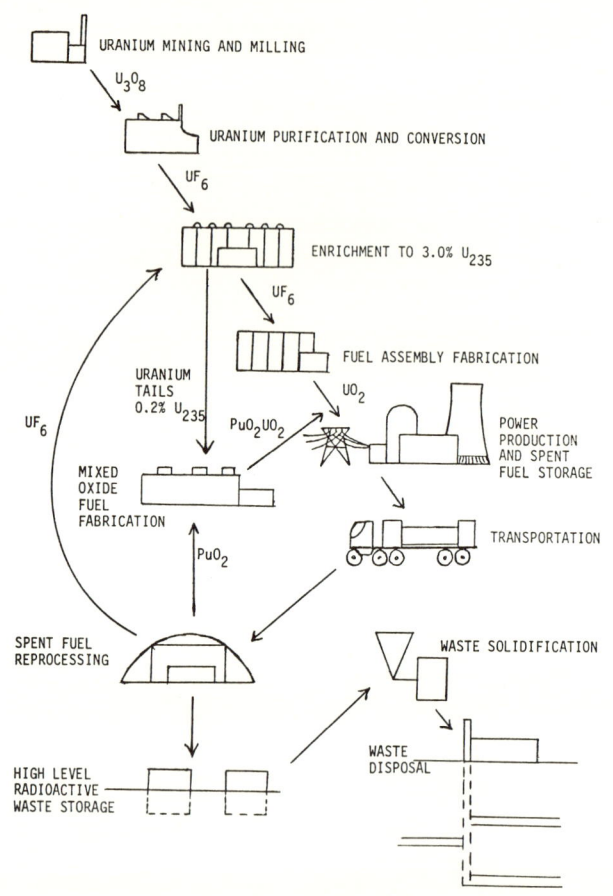

Figure 2. Closed nuclear fuel cycle.

inserted into the LWR along with the conventional slightly enriched uranium oxide fuel assemblies.

k. Adding a second type of storage scheme where the fuel assemblies are stored in the swimming-pool-type facilities for only two years prior to reprocessing but the high-level liquid waste stream is stored for eight more years in specially designed tanks prior to solidification and vitrification.

l. Solidifying the high-level radioactive waste in a calcined form and vitrification of the calcined waste in glass.

Note: Although transportation is shown as one step in both Figure 1 and 2, in actuality, the step represents several activities. Included in the transportation activities is the shipment of yellowcake U_3O_8, uranium hexafluoride UF_6, enriched uranium, fresh uranium fuel assemblies, fresh mixed oxide fuel assemblies, spent fuel assemblies, plutonium oxide, and high-level wastes. Only the cost of shipping spent fuel, wastes, and plutonium are significant; thus the transportation activity depicted in Figures 1 and 2 is positioned only at the back end of the nuclear fuel cycle.

Without analyzing in great detail the specific environmental effects, a fair generalization can be made about the differences between the two cycles. The throwaway nuclear fuel cycle will involve considerably less processing of the radioactive spent fuel and will minimize the processing and transportation of plutonium. The throwaway nuclear fuel cycle will, on the other hand, increase the rate at which a mineral resource, uranium, is depleted and will discharge a greater quantity of long-lived radiation material to the long-term waste disposal system. One might wish to decide which route is most environmentally acceptable; however, a comparison of the two fuel cycles is most appropriate in an economic setting where the cost of lowering individual environmental effects to insignificant levels is fully reflected in the price of each step of the fuel cycle.

As pointed out previously, the closed nuclear fuel cycle presents a formidable task in implementing the back-end steps. The areas of reprocessing and use of plutonium have become the battleground for segments of society diametrically opposed on the issue of long-term dependence on nuclear fission as a source of energy for society. Furthermore, in a society where legal and political delay of energy projects is commonplace, a complex process involving separate yet interdependent facilities is extremely vulnerable. In order that the overall closed cycle process can be implemented, each back-end component must be accepted simultaneously. The throwaway fuel cycle does not suffer from this vulnerability due to its straightforward simpleness.

The Economics of the Throwaway Fuel Cycle

The principal economic differences between the throwaway fuel cycle and a closed fuel cycle are (a) the amount of uranium required, (b) the amount of enrichment required, and (c) the disposition of the spent fuel. In this section we compare the needs and costs of uranium, enrichment, and waste disposal of the throwaway fuel cycle with the reprocessing and plutonium recycle option.

Uranium Resources

The nation's endowment of uranium resources is the topic of the ongoing National Uranium Resource Evaluation (NURE) (19), a program initiated by the U.S. Atomic Energy Commission (AEC) in 1974 and being continued by the U.S. Energy Research and Development Administration. It is a

Table 2. Summary of U.S. uranium resources

$/lb U_3O_8 Cost Category	Reserves	Probable	Possible	Speculative
A. U.S. uranium resources as of January 1, 1976				
$10	270,000	440,000	420,000	145,000
$10–15	160,000	215,000	255,000	145,000
$15–30	210,000	405,000	595,000	300,000
By-products Production	140,000	—	—	—
TOTAL	780,000	1,060,000	1,270,000	590,000
B. U.S. resources as of January 1, 1977				
$10	250,000	275,000	115,000	100,000
$10–15	160,000	310,000	375,000	90,000
$15–30	270,000	505,000	630,000	290,000
$30–50	160,000	280,000	300,000	60,000
By-products Production	140,000	—	—	—
TOTAL	980,000	1,370,000	1,420,000	540,000

(Columns are Tons U_3O_8; Potential Resources comprises Probable, Possible, Speculative.)

comprehensive nationwide program to evaluate uranium resources and to identify areas favorable for uranium exploration. However, a comprehensive reporting of the results of the program is not due until 1981. A preliminary report, the latest published in June 1977 (15), presents resource estimates little different from those that existed in January 1976. These recent estimates are reproduced on Table 2. The primary differences in the two estimates is a shift in some resources between cost categories due to the inflationary increase in production costs. The January 1, 1977, table also includes resources in the $30–50 cost bracket; however, the total of reserves, probable resources, and possible resources under $30 has remained virtually the same (2,970,000 tons for 1976; 2,890,000 for 1977).

Before a utility planner can make a choice of fuels for future use on his system, he must be satisfied of the likelihood that the fuel will be available. Along this line of inquiry, a knowledge of the meaning of the different categories of resources is helpful. The NURE program defines the resource categories as follows: (19).

> Uranium *reserves* are estimates of the quantity of uranium in ore that satisfy certain criteria, including minimum grade and thickness.

Reserves are the most reliable class of resources with respect to location, size, grade, and economic availability, being based on direct measurements from drilling and sampling of the deposits.
Probable potential resources are those estimated to occur in known productive uranium districts as extensions of known deposits or in undiscovered deposits within known geologic trends or areas of mineralization.
Possible potential resources are those estimated to occur in undiscovered or partly defined deposits in formations or geologic settings productive elsewhere within the same geological province.
Speculative potential resources are those estimated to occur in undiscovered or partly defined deposits in formations or geological settings not previously productive or within a geological province not previously productive.

From the definitions above, it is clear that the level of certainty of the actual quantities or uranium resources available decreases as one moves from reserves to speculative potential resources. In fact, a utility planner would have a difficult time justifying to a public utility commission the choice of a fuel if the long-range use of the fuel required the future availability of possible and speculative potential resources.

A 1,000 Mw(e) LWR nuclear power plant requires approximately 5,650 tons of U_3O_8 over a thirty-year lifetime based on operation at an average capacity factor of 66 percent with an enrichment tails assay of 0.2 percent utilizing the throwaway fuel cycle. Based on reserves and probable potential resources of U_3O_8 at a production cost of $30/lb or less, the domestic resource base is sufficient to fuel a little over 300 Gw(e) (a Gw(e) equals a moderately large nuclear system) of LWR nuclear plants. This rough analysis assumes that foreign sources will supply to U.S. utilities about as much yellowcake (U_3O_8) as will be purchased from domestic sources by foreign utilities. Before addressing the prospects that these reserves can be delivered to the market on a time scale commensurate with the demand, let us briefly review the derived demand for uranium.

The Derived Demand for Uranium

The maximum level of LWR nuclear plant additions between now and the end of 1985 is fixed because of the minimum thirty-month licensing period, the long lead time for ordering reactor vessels and other major components, minimum sixty-month construction and testing period, and so forth. From the January 1, 1976, level of about 40 Gw(e), LWR nuclear plant capacity could achieve an expansion of 100 Gw(e) by January 1, 1985. There is very little likelihood that the additional 60 Gw(e) on order for

Table 3. Maximum probable installed LWR
nuclear plant capacity
(as of January 1 in GW(e))

Year	Capacity	Additions
1976	40.0	7.6
1977	47.6	5.7
1978	53.3	10.2
1979	63.5	8.3
1980	71.8	12.9
1981	84.7	12.0
1982	96.7	12.0
1983	108.7	14.0
1984	122.7	17.3
1985	140.0	20.0
1986	160.0	20.0
1987	180.0	20.0
1988	200.0	20.0
1989	220.0	20.0
1990	240.0	20.0
1991	260.0	20.0
1992	280.0	10.0
1993	290.0	5.0
1994	295.0	5.0
1995 and beyond	300.0	

initial operation in 1985 and beyond could be brought on line earlier, since nuclear equipment manufacturing slots are tightly scheduled, large quantities of material such as steel might not be available in time, and construction forces would be disrupted if second units were constructed simultaneously with first units at a site.

Beyond 1985, LWR nuclear plant capacity would reach 300 Gw(e) as a projected 20 Gw(e) of LWR nuclear plants per year were added in 1985 and beyond. The primary reason that yearly expansion would be limited to 20 Gw(e) per year is that this appears to be the present nuclear manufacturing capacity. Further the nuclear vendors would be unwilling to put in more manufacturing capability because of the limited long-term LWR market. Table 3 lists the maximum probable installed LWR nuclear plant capacity as of January 1 of each year up to the 300 GW(e) limit.

Once the installed capacity of LWR nuclear plants is projected, the primary influences on uranium needs are the annual average capacity factor and the enrichment tails assay. Table 4 lists the annual capacity factor of LWR plants used to calculate the demand for U_3O_8. Should the industry wide average not reach a 66 percent capacity factor level, the demand for U_3O_8 would be somewhat less. Table 4 also lists the enrichment plant tails assay. The assay level is assumed to be 0.25 percent from now through 1980. This is

Table 4. Annual capacity factors and enrichment plant tails assay

Year	Capacity Factor	Tails Assay
1975 (actual)	0.54	0.20%
1976	0.60	0.20%
1977	0.63	0.25%
1978	0.66	0.25%
1979	0.66	0.25%
1980	0.66	0.25%
1981 and beyond	0.66	0.20%

consistent with ERDA intentions. However, as the Cascade Uprating Program and Cascade Improvement Program increase the total capacity of ERDA's enrichment plants, the tails assay is assumed to be lowered back to 0.20 percent. Should the tails assay be held at 0.25 percent, U_3O_8 demand would increase by about 9 percent yearly.

Table 5 lists the yearly and cumulative demand for uranium using the above assumptions. The table is based on delivery of U_3O_8 for the initial fuel loading two years in advance of initial operation and delivery of U_3O_8 for refueling one year in advance of refueling. It is assumed that the utilities will operate their LWR nuclear plants on an annual fuel cycle basis and that the amount of reload is based on the capacity factor of the previous year. The resulting estimate could be sizably altered by a deviation from the above assumptions. At present, the completion and ordering rate of LWR would indicate at least a 10 percent decrease in operating plants by 1990 which would reduce demand by roughly an equal amount. The Federal government, on the other hand, has indicated that it will expand its stockpile

Table 5. Maximum uranium demand for the throwaway cycle

Year	LWR plants (Gw(e)) Initial	LWR plants (Gw(e)) Reload	U_3O_8 (tons) Initial[a]	U_3O_8 (tons) Reload[b]	Yearly total	Cumulative (Tons in thousands)
1976	10.2	47.6	5,480	8,500	13,980	14
1977	8.3	53.3	4,840	10,870	15,710	30
1978	12.9	63.5	7,520	13,600	21,120	59
1979	12.0	71.8	7,000	15,370	22,370	73
1980	12.0	84.7	7,000	18,130	25,130	98
1981	14.0	96.7	7,520	19,050	26,570	125
1982	17.3	108.7	9,290	21,420	30,710	156
1983	20.0	122.7	10,740	24,170	34,910	190
1984	20.0	140.0	10,740	27,580	38,320	229
1985	20.0	160.0	10,740	31,520	42,260	271
1986	20.0	180.0	10,740	35,460	46,200	317

Table 5. (Contd.)

Year	LWR plants (Gw(e)) Initial	LWR plants (Gw(e)) Reload	U_3O_8 (tons) Initial[a]	U_3O_8 (tons) Reload[b]	Yearly total	Cumulative (Tons in thousands)
1987	20.0	200.0	10,740	39,400	50,140	367
1988	20.0	220.0	10,740	43,340	54,080	422
1989	20.0	240.0	10,740	47,280	58,020	480
1990	10.0	260.0	5,370	51,220	56,590	536
1991	5.0	280.0	2,690	55,160	57,850	594
1992	5.0	290.0	2,690	57,130	59,820	654
1993	—	295.0	—	58,120	58,120	712
1994	—	300.0	—	59,100	59,100	771
1995	—	300.0	—	59,100	59,100	830
1996	—	300.0	—	59,100	59,100	889
1997	—	300.0	—	59,100	59,100	948
1998	—	300.0	—	59,100	59,100	1,007
1999	—	300.0	—	59,100	59,100	1,067
2000	—	300.0	—	59,100	59,100	1,126
2001	—	292.0	—	57,530	57,530	1,183
2002	—	284.0	—	55,950	55,950	1,239
2003	—	276.0	—	54,370	54,370	1,293
2004	—	268.0	—	52,800	52,800	1,346
2005	—	260.0	—	51,220	51,220	1,397
2006	—	252.0	—	49,650	49,650	1,447
2007	—	244.0	—	48,070	48,070	1,495
2008	—	234.0	—	46,100	46,100	1,541
2009	—	222.0	—	43,740	43,740	1,585
2010	—	210.0	—	41,370	41,370	1,626
2011	—	195.0	—	38,420	38,420	1,665
2012	—	180.0	—	35,460	35,460	1,700
2013	—	160.0	—	31,520	31,520	1,732
2014	—	140.0	—	27,580	27,580	1,759
2015	—	120.0	—	23,640	23,640	1,783
2016	—	100.0	—	19,700	19,700	1,803
2017	—	80.0	—	15,760	15,760	1,818
2018	—	60.0	—	11,820	11,820	1,830
2019	—	40.0	—	7,880	7,880	1,838
2020	—	20.0	—	3,940	3,940	1,842

[a] Initial U_3O_8 = (110%) × ((2.6 − tails assay)/(.711 − tails assay)) × (80,000 Kg U/Gw(e)) × (ton/2000 lb) × (2.5988 U_3O_8/Kg U) × (Gw(e) initial)

[b] Reload U_3O_8 = (110%) × ((3.0 − tails assay)/(.711 − tails assay)) × (Gw(t)/.32 Gw(e)) × (tonne U/30 Gw(t) − days) × (365 days) × (capacity factor) × (2598.8 lbs U_3O_8/tonne U) × (ton/2000 lbs) × (reload Gw(e))

Table 6. Reprocessing impact on uranium demand

Year	Reprocessing capacity (tonnes)	Equivalent U_3O_8 saved (in tons) Uranium recycle[a]	Plutonium recycle[b]	Reduced U_3O_8 requirements cumulative
1980	750	880	1,000	1,880
1981	750	880	1,000	3,760
1982	1,500	1,760	2,000	7,520
1983	1,500	1,760	2,000	11,280
1084	2,250	2,630	3,000	16,910
1985	2,250	2,630	3,000	22,540
1986	3,000	3,510	4,000	30,050
1987	3,000	3,510	4,000	37,560
1988	3,750	4,380	5,000	46,940
1989	3,750	4,380	5,000	56,320
1990	3,750	4,380	5,000	65,700
1991	3,750	4,380	5,000	75,080
1992	3,750	4,380	5,000	84,460
1993	3,750	4,380	5,000	93,840
1994	3,750	4,380	5,000	103,220
1995	3,750	4,380	5,000	112,600
1996	3,750	4,380	5,000	121,980
1997	3,750	4,380	5,000	131,360
1998	3,750	4,380	5,000	140,740
1999	3,750	4,380	5,000	150,120
2000	3,750	4,380	5,000	159,500

[a]Uranium recycle = (reprocessed tonnes fuel) × (90% U recovered) ×(1.2994 tons/tonne)
[b]Plutonium recycle = (reprocessed tonnes fuel) × (8 Kg Pu/tonne fuel) × (.1667 tons U_3O_8/Kg Pu)

of enriched uranium as a protection against unforeseen events at its operating and planned enrichment plants. The cumulative demand, when cast against domestic uranium resources, ignores the effects of foreign purchases of U_3O_8 and shipment of domestic U_3O_8 to foreign customers (actually a balance between export and import was assumed). The demand for U_3O_8 includes a 10 percent factor which reflects losses during processing and the need by utilities to increase their inventory of U_3O_8. Furthermore, an increase in tails assay to 0.3 percent could increase uranium demand by about 15 percent. With the above in mind, Table 5 represents a reasonable assessment of uranium demand for a healthy, growing LWR program. Table 6 represents the possible effect of reprocessing on uranium demand based on 3,750 tonnes* of reprocessing (an amount equal to the AGNS

---

*One tonne (or metric ton) is equivalent to 1.1 tons.

reprocessing plant plus a 2,250-tonne EXXON reprocessing plant) capacity being developed in increments of 750 tonnes every two years, starting in 1980. Even with this limited buildup of reprocessing capacity, cumulative demand for uranium through the year 2000 would be reduced by about 14 percent.

What are the prospects that this uranium can be delivered? A recent survey of the uranium industry indicated that production would rise to 24,300 tons U_3O_8 by 1980 (14). The estimate was "entirely based on ore bodies known today and mainly keyed to existing reserves and is subject to revision as exploration effort proceeds." However, supplying 300 Gw(e) of LWR nuclear plants by the mid-1990s will require (from Table 5) the production of about 60,000 tons U_3O_8 per year.

Can the domestic uranium industry expand its production capacity to a level as high as 60,000 tons per year in a short period of time from the 1975 level of 14,500 tons per year (14)? Historically, uranium production in the United States increased from 800 tons U_3O_8 in 1952 to its maximum output of 17,640 tons in 1960 (33). In a broader sense, many mineral industries have sustained high growth rates over several decades. The net growth over the twenty-year maximum growth period (domestic) for crude petroleum, molybdenum, copper, and coal was 202, 291, 336, and 168 percent, respectively (33). The needed growth from today's level to 1995's 60,000-ton capacity (about 300 percent net growth) to support 300 Gw(e) of LWR nuclear plants appears to be difficult but not beyond historical precedent.

For the commitment to LWR nuclear plants to grow, additional proven reserves must be brought in sufficient to produce a net increase in proven reserves after the year's production of U_3O_8 has been delivered. The level of exploratory drilling is the most critical aspect in increasing domestic proven reserves. In the early 1970s exploration drilling has hovered around 20 million feet per year with a discovery rate between one and two pounds of U_3O_8 per foot drilling. To determine the level of exploration required, one must look at the maximum rate of production from proven reserves and at the projected needs from Table 5. If during a given year production is assumed to be equal to a maximum 1/20 of proven reserves, then present domestic reserves could support up to 40,000 tons of production. A minimum proven reserve of 1,200,000 tons would be required by 1990 to support 60,000 tons U_3O_8/year demand of 300 Gw(e) of LWR nuclear plants. Therefore, to provide for an increase to 300 Gw(e) based on domestic reserves, exploration must prove up reserves to replace the cumulative consumption between now and 1990 (approximately 500,000 tons U_3O_8 from Table 5) and prove up 400,000 tons of additional reserves to expand the total proven reserves to 1,200,000 tons. The total reserves needed to be found amount to approximately 900,000 tons over the next fifteen years, or an average of about 60,000 tons per year.

Unfortunately, the past level of exploration is insufficient to support expansion beyond the present 200 Gw(e) level of LWR nuclear plant commitments; however, technological changes in the method of exploring for uranium (such as sniffing for helium) could drastically change the level of discovery. The level of conventional exploration has been increased substantially in 1976 and 1977, but whether the increase is sufficient and sustainable is not yet clear.

Foreign Uranium

In addition to the domestic sources, imports primarily from Canada have supplied a small but significant portion of the overall demand. Present uranium import commitments by domestic buyers average 3,000 tons U_3O_8 per year to 1990 (35). The present foreign supply commitments amount to over 10 percent of uranium contracted for domestic utilities.

With the present tight supply situation domestically, what is the availability of foreign supplied uranium? The present U_3O_8 resources in Australia recoverable at costs of up to $15.00 per pound, are estimated at about 331,000 tons (3). Of this amount less than 10,000 tons is committed. The six major potential Australian uranium producers have the capability of increasing production to 15,000 to 20,000 tons U_3O_8 per year by the early to mid 1980s (3). However, the present Australian production capacity of several thousand tons per year has been restricted by government policy.

Canada has already committed 110,000 tons U_3O_8 for export and has reserved 81,000 tons to cover the thirty-year fueling requirements for the 14,700 Mw(e) of nuclear capacity expected to be operating in Canada by 1986 (21). Canada's presently measured, indicated, and inferred resources, recoverable at costs less than $40 per pound, amount to 562,400 tons U_3O_8 (21). In addition, "prognosticated" resources in and adjacent to mineable deposits based on extrapolated geological information amount to 450,000 tons (21).

Thus sizable amounts of uncommitted reserves are available in Canada and Australia. Domestic utilities might be able to contract for some additional uranium from these two countries by the mid 1980s even with foreign utilities bidding for supplies. Additional exploration activities throughout the world could bring in significant quantities of U_3O_8 from areas with high potential, such as the Moroccan Sahara.

In sum, the above analysis indicates that the prospects are good that there will be sufficient potential to supply 300 Gw(e) of LWR nuclear plants for their 30-year lifetime. The uranium mining industry should be able to meet peak U_3O_8 demands provided exploratory drilling is stepped up. However, to put the availability of uranium supply in perspective, consider that the present domestic proven reserves of U_3O_8 are sufficient to provide at least 75 percent of the maximum probable needs of an *expanded number of nuclear plants* in 1985. In contrast, today's domestic reserves of natural gas will not be able to supply 40 percent of gas demand in 1985, while today's proven domestic reserves of crude oil will not be able to supply 33 percent of oil demand in 1985.

Uranium Price

While the cost of production of U_3O_8 can be accurately established, electric utilities are more concerned with the price of uranium. Unfortunately, the market price for uranium has been buffeted high and low by unusual circumstances. The circumstances can be broken down into three main areas.

Normal pricing has been disrupted on account of the *historical development* of the uranium industry. The original uranium mining industry's development was tied exclusively to the nation's nuclear weapons program. The industry's output grew to 18,000 tons of U_3O_8 per year by 1960 but then the U.S. government phased out its buying program. Thus, there existed an entire mature industry without a significant market for its product. Prices for uranium delivered and contracted in the late 1960s and early 1970s plummeted to the producer's short-run incremental cost of mining their highest-grade ores. Since most of the industry's facilities had been amortized under the weapons buying program there were no capital charges included in the price (14). Since uranium demand was low, little exploration was undertaken, thus adding no incentive component to the low uranium price hovering around $6 to $8 (14). Then during 1973–1975, as future demand for uranium started to come in balance with supply, i.e., the needs of an expanding commercial nuclear power program started approaching the maximum output of the "old" uranium industry, the price for the major competing fuels, oil and coal exploded upward, placing additional upward pressure on uranium prices.

A second disruption to the market was the *uncertainty in the level of supply*. In the early 1970s the U.S. government had a stockpile of 50,000 tons of U_3O_8 which could meet about four years of demand by the utility industry. Foreign suppliers had an excess production capacity of 50 percent in the early 1970s as worldwide demand for uranium for nuclear weapons dropped. Canada and Australia had large supplies of uranium which were uncommitted. Domestic producers were uncertain as to whether they should expand their production capacity or prepare for a glut of additional uranium in the market. By 1975, the U.S. government had decided to use its uranium stockpile to build up a reserve of enriched uranium and had decided to restrict the use of foreign uranium until the late 1970s. In addition, the

Australian and Canadian governments placed a temporary moratorium on uranium sales.

The third disruption to the market was and continues to be the *uncertainty of demand*. The early nuclear program (1960s) was supposed to take off exponentially but didn't; however, in 1972, 1973, and early 1974, reactor orders surged upward. Then the financial crisis of 1974–1975 and lack of load growth caused nuclear plant delays and cancellations. The effect has been to disrupt the uranium producer's ability to plan for future demand, estimates of which have swung by as much as 50 percent. Lack of action by the U.S. government on enrichment capacity expansion and spent fuel recycle has led to another 40 percent uncertainty in demand. The threat of spreading state moratoria have made producers wary of long-term investments to expand production capacity because of the risk that it might not be recovered. Finally a major "middleman"—Westinghouse—sold short on uranium and was not able to cover its commitments. The 25,000-plus tons U_3O_8 shortage produced an immediate 50-100 percent increase in demand in the market through 1980.

These factors have produced the rapid rise in short-term price from $6 per pound U_3O_8 in January 1973 to $40 per pound U_3O_8 in March 1976. There has been a dramatic increase in the amount of exploration and mining development in response to the price increase. Yet projecting uranium prices is extremely difficult. A measure of the difficulty can be found in many of the recently negotiated uranium supply contracts. Pricing provisions in some of the long-term supply contracts now provide flexibility over a considerable price range with the actual price to be determined by market conditions at the time of delivery (35). Much of the frustration in attempting to determine future prices lies in our inability to completely understand recent short-term behavior.

In a free market situation a decrease in the long-term demand function should result in a decrease in the long-term price. In 1973 yearly demand for uranium was projected to increase by a factor of 12 by 1990, due to a rapid expansion of LWR nuclear plant capacity (33). Today the projected maximum yearly demand by 1990 (Table 3) is only 50 percent of the 1973 projection; however, the long-term price trend for U_3O_8 still appears to be increasing in constant dollars. On a short-term basis (1975–1980), the Westinghouse announced shortage of greater than 25,000 tons U_3O_8 would be expected to drive short-term prices higher. On the other hand, since mid-1974, LWR nuclear plant delays have compensated to yield a net reduction in the short-term demand (35); yet short-term prices have increased to four times production cost.

Are the three major factors above totally responsible for the domestic uranium market behavior? Has there been explicit manipulation of the market by suppliers? How much control over the price of uranium do the mining companies exert? These questions are all germane to the understanding of the uranium market and future uranium prices; however, a complete analysis of these questions is beyond the scope of this paper.

For the purpose of comparing the economics of the throwaway and closed fuel cycle option, uranium prices will be assumed to be related to the cost of production as follows. For a uranium mining company cost of production includes labor, materials, ore transport, power, royalties, taxes directly applicable to operation, mine development, mill and related facilities, profit, property aquisition, exploration, and severance taxes. The production costs listed in Table 2 do not include profit, property aquisition, exploration, and severance taxes (35). Severance taxes alone could add a 10 percent increase or more to the price of uranium (36). A recent analysis of uranium prices for U_3O_8 produced from reserves equivalent to ERDA's $10 or less production cost category predicted that the actual price ranged from $16 to $25 per pound U_3O_8 (14). Due to the uncertainties in the uranium market as described above, the U_3O_8 price will be estimated at 1.5, 2.0, and 3.0 times the production cost schedule of Table 2.

Proceeding on the basis that in the future the uranium market will be orderly, projected prices for two sets of conditions will be determined: a projected price for the yearly average delivered price and a projected price for the incremental amount of uranium for one additional nuclear unit starting up in a given year. The projected average delivered uranium price through 1980 will be somewhat depressed due to the contracts signed in the late 1960s and early 1970s under the previously discussed depressed price conditions (35). The projected incremental price between 1975 and 1985 will be above the expected level due to the previously discussed market disruptions.

Table 7. Uranium reserves (tons U_3O_8).

Production cost 1975 $/lbs U_3O_8	1977	1980	1985	1990
Total under 10	250,000	340,000	430,000	525,000
10–15	160,000	260,000	365,000	470,000
Total under 15	410,000	600,000	795,000	995,000
15–30	270,000	435,000	605,000	775,000
Total under 30	680,000	1,035,000	1,400,000	1,770,000
30–50	160,000	250,000	345,000	440,000
Total under 50	840,000	1,285,000	1,745,000	2,210,000
By Product Production	140,000			

Economics of the Throwaway Nuclear Fuel Cycle

Of great importance is the speed at which potential resources are converted into reserves through an aggressive exploration program. The rate of conversion is important since uranium production in general would come from the ore bodies which tend to have the lowest production costs. As stated earlier, about 900,000 tons of additional U_3O_8 must be proved as reserves by 1990 if the utilities are to prudently expand their commitment to LWR technology to 300 Gw(e). For purposes of this analysis, 33 percent of the probable potential resource category of January 1, 1977 (Table 2), will be assumed to be converted to reserves by 1980, 1985, and 1990. The reserve base without regard to cumulative production is shown in Table 7.

Table 8 lists the projected average and incremental uranium price to the

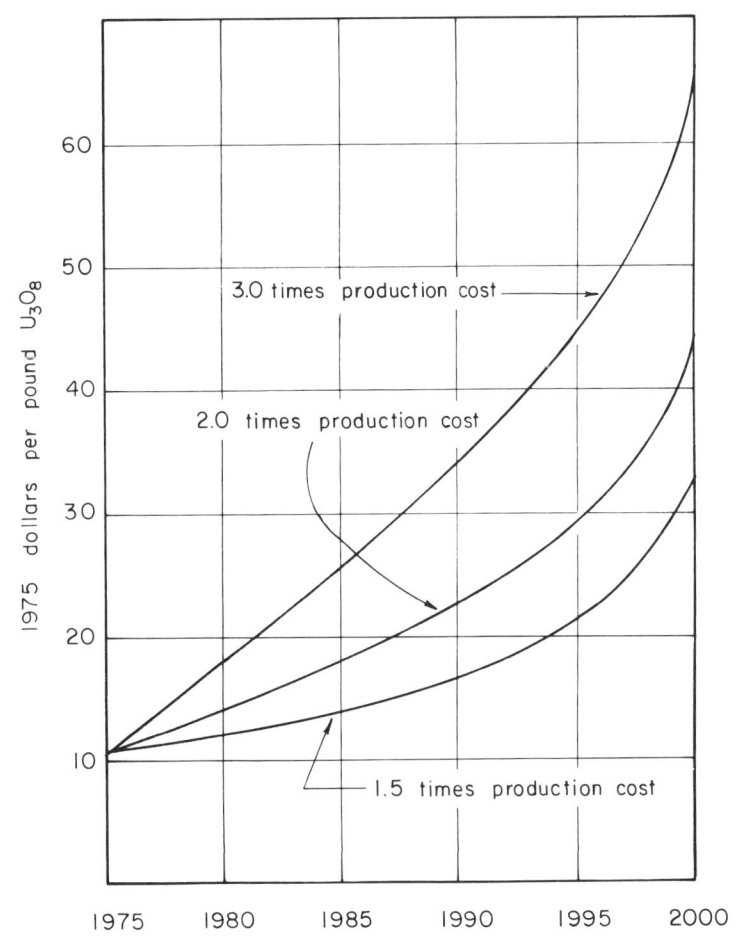

Figure 3. Projected average price of uranium.

Table 8. Projected uranium prices
(dollars per pound U_3O_8 in 1975 dollars)

	1976	1980	1985	1990	1995	2000
Nuclear plants Operational (GW(e), Table 3)	47.6	84.7	160	260	300	300
Projected average price						
Cumulative deliveries (tons U_3O_8)	14,000	98,000	271,000	536,000	830,000	1,126,000
Production cost category (Table 7)	<10	<10	10	10	15	15–30
Price at 1.5 times cost	<15	<15	15	15	22.5	22.5–45
Price at 2 times cost	<20	<20	20	20	30	30–60
Price at 3 times cost	<30	<30	30	30	45	45–90
Projected incremental price						
Committed production (tons U_3O_8)[b]	154,000	348,000	691,000	1,101,000	1,420,000	
Production cost category (Table 7)	<10	10–15	15	15–30	30	—[a]
Price 1.5 times cost	<20	15–22.5	22.5	22.5–45	45	—[a]
Price 2 times cost	<30	20–30	30	30–60	60	—[a]
Price 3 times cost	<40	30–45	45	45–90	90	—[a]

[a] Resource base totally committed.
[b] Committed production equals cumulative deliveries plus 10 years production at the current rate. This level provides some measure of the situation where operating nuclear units have long term production contracts in force with reserves committed prior to the addition of another nuclear unit.

Economics of the Throwaway Nuclear Fuel Cycle

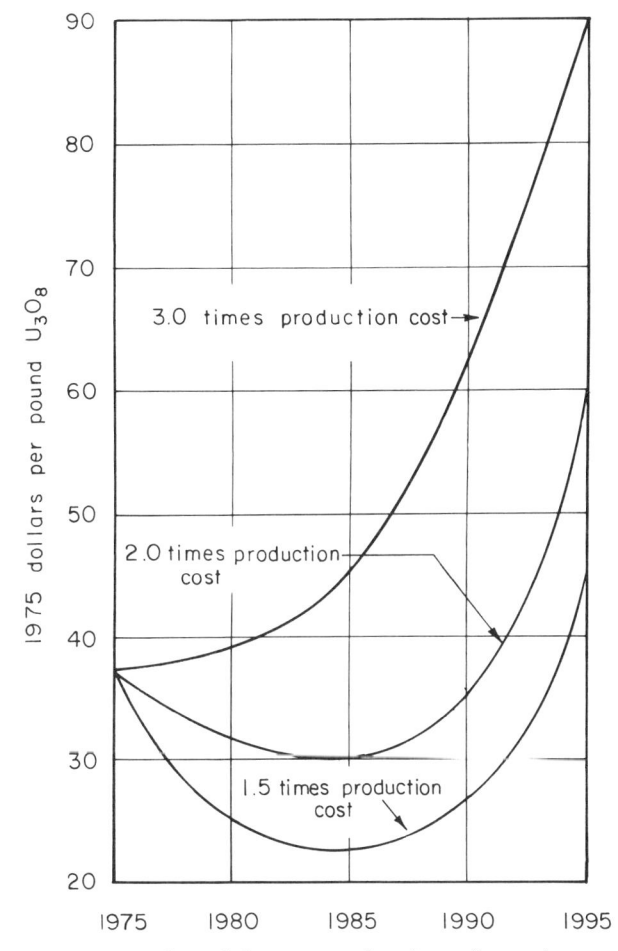

Figure 4. Projected incremental price of uranium.

year 2000 based on the production cost categories of Table 7. The delivered or committed uranium will be assumed to have come from the lowest available production cost category. Where the majority of uranium available in a certain production cost category is already considered delivered (average price) or committed (incremental price), U_3O_8 will be assumed to come from the next higher cost category since in reality many mines would be working from lower grade, higher cost formations even with some high-grade ore still available.

Figures 3 and 4 show the projected price trends, especially the movement to higher cost production of the lower-grade ores. The solid line on each figure will be used to indicate the price in any given year up to 2000. The incremental price has little meaning after 1995 (once the 300 nuclear power plants are in operation) since the reserves and probable potential resource base as defined today will be almost totally committed. The incremental price has meaning only for the time frame between 1975 and 1995; this is the price utility management would use to compare the costs of new nuclear plants with other options—coal, oil, solar, etc.

The curves of Figure 4 suggest that the incremental (spot market) price for uranium may have overshot its equilibrium price level in response to the disruptions to the marketplace of the late 1960s and early 1970s. The Nuexco spot market prices since April of 1976 have shown a slight decline in constant 1975 dollars. Further, several experts around the world have suggested that the price of uranium might fall below $30 per pound once again. Projections of declines in the spot market price are generally based on the assumption that Canada and Australia will allow timely development of their uranium resources. Unfortunately, the pace of governmental approval in those two countries has been slow. One other disruption which may drastically affect short-term uranium prices in a totally unpredictable way is the legal proceedings between uranium producers and uranium-supplying nations, Westinghouse, utilities, and the U.S. Justice Department. Barring unforeseen disruptions to the uranium market in the future, and assuming the official estimates of reserves and potential resources are at worst conservative and at least accurate, it is entirely possible the spot market price of uranium could decline in the future when measured in constant dollars.

ENRICHMENT CAPACITY AND PRICE

Light Water Reactor (LWR) nuclear plants require uranium which contains from 2 to 4 percent uranium isotope 235. Natural uranium contains only 0.711 percent uranium 235, with uranium 238 making up the other 99 percent (ignoring traces of uranium 234); therefore, before naturally occurring uranium can be used as fuel, it must be enriched with uranium 235. Before analyzing the demand and supply of enrichment, a discussion of "tails assay," "SWU," "burnup," and "product enrichment" is necessary.

Tails Assay

In the enrichment processes used today, natural uranium "feed" is processed in a diffusion plant which concentrates the uranium 235 isotope in the "product" and produces a "tails" stream of uranium which has been depleted of some of the uranium 235 during the separation process. The product and tails are usually defined in terms of the contained percentage of uranium 235, i.e., 3.0 percent product and 0.3 percent tails.

The relationship between feed, product, and tails is defined in kilograms of uranium (kgU) where:

X_f = enrichment of feed = 0.00711 U-235
X_p = enrichment of product
X_t = enrichment of tails
P = kgU of product needed
T = kgU of tails = $P \times (X_p - X_f)/(X_f - X_t)$
F = kgU of feed = $P + T$

Listed below is the amount of feed (natural uranium) required to supply 1 kgU of product as the enrichment tails assay is varied.

Xp	P(kgU)	Xt	T(kgU)	Xf	F(kgU)
0.03	1.0	0.00300	5.5693	0.00711	6.5693
0.03	1.0	0.00275	5.2500	0.00711	6.2500
0.03	1.0	0.00250	4.9653	0.00711	5.9653
0.03	1.0	0.00225	4.7099	0.00711	5.7099
0.03	1.0	0.00200	4.4795	0.00711	5.4795
0.03	1.0	0.00175	4.2705	0.00711	5.2705
0.03	1.0	0.00150	4.0802	0.00711	5.0802

To obtain one kgU of 3 percent enriched product, 6.5693 kgU of natural uranium would be required as feed if the enrichment tails assay were 0.3 percent; however, only 5.0802 kgU of natural uranium would be required as feed if the tails assay were lowered to 0.15 percent. This lowering of tails assay would produce a savings of 22.7 percent in the yearly amount of natural uranium required as feed.

Separative Work Units (SWU)

Enriching uranium requires separative work to be performed at the diffusion plant. The amount of "separative work units" (SWU) required is defined in kg as follows (6):

$$SWU = P \times [(2X_p - 1) \times \ln(X_p/(1 - X_p)) \\ + ((X_p - X_f)/(X_f - X_t)) \times (2X_t - 1) \times \ln(X_t/(1 - X_t)) \\ - ((X_p - X_t)/(X_f - X_t)) \times (2X_f - 1) \times \ln(X_f/(1 - X_f))]$$

Listed below is the amount of SWU required to produce 1 kgU of 3.0 percent product as the enrichment tails assay is varied from 0.3 percent to 0.15 percent.

SWU(kg)	P(kgU)	Xp	Xt	Xf
3.4241	1.0	.03	.00300	.00711
3.6071	1.0	.03	.00275	.00711
3.8115	1.0	.03	.00250	.00711
4.0424	1.0	.03	.00225	.00711
4.3064	1.0	.03	.00200	.00711
4.6134	1.0	.03	.00175	.00711
4.9775	1.0	.03	.00150	.00711

To obtain one kgU of 3 percent enriched product, 3.4241 kg of SWU would be required with a tails assay of 0.3 percent; however, 4.9775 kg of SWU would be required if the tails assay were lowered to 0.15 percent. This lowering of tails assay would produce an increase in required SWU of 45.4 percent. Thus lowering the tails assay lowers the amount of natural uranium required as feed but increases the amount of SWU required to produce a given quantity of product.

Burnup

The level of enrichment of the product necessary for use in a LWR nuclear plant depends upon the amount of energy which will be drawn from the fuel. While reactor core loadings are very complex issues requiring highly sophisticated computer programs to determine fuel loading plans, the fuel in general must maintain at least an average 2 percent level of fissionable content (U-235, Pu-239, Pu-251) to maintain the chain reaction. Therefore, every year a certain amount of fuel which has had its fissionable material depleted will be replaced with fresh fuel.

To determine the core fraction to be replaced by a reload "region" of fuel requires the following computation:

cf = core fraction to be replaced
CF = capacity factor of the past years operation
0.32 = thermal efficiency of the model LWR
BU = the average burnup of the core fraction removed from the reactor (megawatt days per metric ton uranium—MWd/tonne U).
80 tonnes U = 80 metric tons of uranium in model LWR

cf = (100 MWe × 365 days × CF)/(BU × 0.32 × 80 tonnes U)

Under steady state operation of a LWR nuclear plant, i.e. after the first two years of operation, the average core burnup at the end of core life which occurs just prior to refueling can be determined by the following equation (17):

ACB = average core burnup at end of life (MWd/tonne U)
RL = reload lifetime = 1/cf
ACB = BU × (RL + 1)/(2 × RL)

Product Enrichment

The steady state enrichment for each reload is calculated based on the average core burnup at end of core life as follows (17):

Xp = 0.032 − [0.001 × (22,000 MWd/tonne U − ACB)/(900 MWd/tonne U)]

Listed below is the level of enrichment required in reload fuel as the capacity factor—thus average core burnup—is varied.

Xp	CF	BU (MWd/tonne U)	cf	ACB (MWd/tonne U)
.02898	.60	30,000	.2852	19,278
.02921	.63	30,000	.2994	19,491
.02937	.65	30,000	.3089	19,634
.02945	.66	30,000	.3137	19,706

The fuel in the PWR nuclear plants of Westinghouse (13), Combustion Engineering, and Babcock and Wilcox design are generally designed for reload burnup levels of 33,000 MWd/tonne U. The fuel in the Boiling Water Reactor (BWR) nuclear plants of General Electric design (16) are designed for reload burnup levels of 28,000 MWd/tonne U. With a future 70/30 percent reactor-type mix (PWR/BWR) and with an achieved burnup of 32,000/25,000 MWd/tonne U, a burnup level of 30,000 MWd/tonne U will be used in this analysis. Further Xp will be assumed to be 0.0300 to reflect some slight excess reactivity remaining in the core at reload time.

The actual burnup of the initial fuel placed into PWR nuclear plants is about 15,000 MWd/tonne U for the fuel unloaded at the end of the first year and about 25,000 MWd/tonne U for the fuel unloaded at the end of the second year of operation (28). (Note: If the LWR nuclear plant has low capacity factors during the first several years during the "breaking in" of the plant, the electric utility may choose to stretch the interval between reloadings to eighteen months in order to achieve design burnups.) Because the actual burnups of the original core are lower than the burnups of the reload fuel, the initial average enrichment of the core is 2.6 percent (Xp of 0.026) (30). For an enrichment tails assay of 0.3 and 0.2 percent the amount of SWU required is 2.7135 and 3.4416 kg SWU respectively for one kgU of 2.6 percent enriched product.

Table 9 lists the projected maximum SWU requirements for domestic utilities through the year 2000 based on Table 3, the above information, and the same capacity factors and enriched tails assay used to calculate

Table 9. Projected maximum enrichment demand (throwaway cycle)

Year	LWR plants (Gw(e)) Initial fuel	Reload fuel	Kg Swu (in thousands) Initial[a]	Reload[b]	Cumulative
1976	10.2	47.6	2,810	4,680	7,490
1977	8.3	53.3	2,020	4,860	14,370
1978	12.9	64.5	3,130	6,180	23,680
1979	12.0	71.8	2,920	6,800	33,400
1980	12.0	84.7	2,920	8,110	44,430
1981	14.0	96.7	3,860	10,460	58,750
1982	17.3	108.7	4,770	11,760	75,280
1983	20.0	122.7	5,510	13,280	94,070
1984	20.0	140.0	5,510	15,150	114,730
1985	20.0	160.0	5,510	17,310	137,550
1986	20.0	180.0	5,510	19,480	162,540
1987	20.0	200.0	5,510	21,640	189,690
1988	20.0	220.0	5,510	23,800	219,000
1989	20.0	240.0	5,510	25,970	250,480
1990	10.0	260.0	2,760	28,130	281,370
1991	5.0	280.0	1,380	30,290	313,040
1992	5.0	290.0	1,380	31,370	345,790
1993	—	295.0	—	31,920	377,710
1994	—	300.0	—	32,460	410,170
1995	—	300.0	—	32,460	442,630
1996	—	300.0	—	32,460	475,090
1997	—	300.0	—	32,460	507,550
1998	—	300.0	—	32,460	540,010
1999	—	300.0	—	32,460	572,470
2000	—	300.0	—	32,460	604,930

[a]Initial kg SWU = (80 tonnes fuel/Gw(e)) × (Initial Gw(e)) × (Kg SWU in thousands/tonne fuel)
where 1976 = 3.4416 kg SWU in thousands/tonne fuel
1977–1980 = 3.0332 kg SWU in thousands/tonne fuel
1981–2000 = 3.4416 kg SWU in thousands/tonne fuel.
[b]Reload kg SWU = (80 tonnes fuel (Gw(e)) × (Reload Gw(e)) × (core fraction) × (kg SWU in thousands/tonne fuel)
where 1976 = 4.3064 kg SWU in thousands/tonne fuel
1977–1980 = 3.8115 kg SWU in thousands/tonne fuel
1981–2000 = 4.3064 kg SWU in thousands/tonne fuel
and "core fraction" was defined earlier in the text.

Table 5. The initial loading of fuel is assumed to be enriched two years in advance of startup while reload fuel is assumed to be enriched one year in advance.

To supply enrichment demand, the United States has successfully used for over twenty-five years the gaseous diffusion technology. Table 10 lists the best estimate of enrichment capacity including the add-on centrifuge plant at Portsmouth, Ohio, recently approved by Congress (5, 8). The actual enrichment demand on U.S. enrichment plants is difficult to estimate since both domestic and foreign electric utilities contract for SWU. At present, contracts to supply enrichment services to foreign electric utilities will require somewhere between 5 and 10 million SWU per year by 1985. With this level of SWU provided to foreign sources, the U.S. enrichment capacity appears to be marginally sufficient to supply SWU at a future tails assay of 0.2 percent through 1987.

However, to provide adequate backup protection to existing enrichment plants, to allow for lowering of the tails assay to conserve the uranium resource base, and to provide for some increase in the SWU supply to foreign sources, domestic enrichment capacity needs to be expanded significantly. Adequate backup capacity should be at least 10 percent of necessary capacity to allow both enriched uranium to be stockpiled and to replace forced capacity outages. The domestic demand of 30 million SWU in 1990 plus 10 million SWU for foreign sources at 0.2 percent tails assay would require at least 44 million SWU of installed capacity. Therefore at least another 8 million SWU of enrichment capacity beyond the 8.75 million SWU "add on" plant should be built as the electric utility industry expands its commitment to the nuclear option to the 300 Gw(e) level. In the short run to 1990, though, adequate enrichment capacity appears available to supply the enriched uranium requirements of an expanding LWR industry (18).

What are the options for expanding the enrichment capacity? There are two types of enrichment plants which could be built in the future: diffusion

Table 10. Projected enrichment capacity
(thousand SWU)

Year	Base Plants	CIP	CUP	Add On	Total
1976	15,100	300	—	—	15,400
1977	16,100	1,300	500	—	18,000
1978	16,400	2,500	1,500	—	20,400
1979	17,200	3,800	2,700	—	23,700
1980	17,200	4,900	3,600	—	25,700
1981	17,200	5,800	4,500	—	27,500
1982	17,200	6,000	4,800	—	28,000
1983	17,200	6,000	4,800	—	28,000
1984	17,200	6,000	4,800	—	28,000
1985	17,200	6,000	4,800	1,500	29,500
1986	17,200	6,000	4,800	4,500	32,500
1987	17,200	6,000	4,800	8,750	36,750
1988	17,200	6,000	4,800	8,750	36,750

CIP—Cascade Improvement Program-ERDA
CUP—Cascade Uprating Program-ERDA

and centrifuge (12). Laser enrichment technology has not been developed sufficiently to be considered, whereas nozzle enrichment is not under consideration in the United States. The diffusion technology has been used for over twenty-five years, whereas the centrifuge technology is in the first stages of commercial demonstration in the Unites States (31). With the decision to build the next enrichment plant as a centrifuge type plant, the Federal government or private industry will most likely construct centrifuge enrichment plants with Exxon, Garrett Nuclear, and ENI as the ones interested at present (9).

Centrifuge enrichment plants are economically built in increments of 2 to 3 million SWU. Table 11 provides a summary of economic information on the centrifuge enrichment plants (12, 34). The cost of a kg SWU of enrichment from a privately operated enrichment plant is estimated to be about $80. One advantage of an operating centrifuge plant over a diffusion plant is that a higher percentage of the cost of its enrichment is fixed, thereby reducing the effects of inflation on its future SWU charges.

Unfortunately, predicting an SWU price charged to new customers is made difficult by the government's pricing policies. In 1976 the charge for a fixed amount of enrichment was $61 per SWU (7). The government has expressed interest in raising the price to a level which would be more on a par with private rates (31). The government in the past has used a "rolled in" charge which was the same for old and new customers. However, enrichment

Table 11. Economic information for future enrichment plants (1975 dollars)

		3.0 Million SWU[d] Centrifuge Plant
Plant costs		$1,000,000,000
Power costs @ 2.4 mills/kwh	var.	17,000,000/yr
Tax revenues (local)[a]	fix	15,000,000/yr
Operations payroll	var.	19,000,000/yr
Capital recovery[b]	fix	100,000,000/yr
Maintenance & general costs	var.	22,000,000/yr
Royalties to U.S. government	fix	20,000,000/yr
Return on equity (est.)[c]	fix	22,500,000/yr
Federal income tax (est.)	fix	22,500,000/yr
		$238,000,000/yr
SWU price		$79/kg SWU

[a] $1\frac{1}{2}$ percent local and state tax rate.
[b] 11.7 percent for private enterprise, on 85 percent of total capitalization with plant amortized over a 20-year period.
[c] Equity is 15 percent of total; return on equity is 15 percent after taxes.
[d] Private investor owned plant.

charges by private industry would probably not be rolled in but would remain separate. The following assumptions are made to estimate future enrichment (SWU) charges.

a. The government will charge $75 per SWU in constant 1975 dollars to generate funds for its expansion program through 1990.
b. The government will match the private industry charges after 1990 at an average price of $75 per SWU in constant 1975 dollars.

OTHER COMPONENTS OF THE NUCLEAR FUEL CYCLE

Purification/Conversion

Once the natural uranium has been mined and milled, it is sold to an electric utility in the uranium oxide (U_3O_8) "yellowcake" form. This uranium is not suitable for use at the enrichment plant and must be further purified and converted to uranium hexafluoride (UF_6). Purification/conversion is a well-established process. The price charged for purification/conversion will be assumed to be $1.5 per pound uranium oxide (lb/U_3O_8) in 1975 dollars (11, 25).

Uranium Fuel Fabrication

After the enrichment plant has produced the required amount of enriched uranium in the form of UF_6, the enriched product is shipped to a fuel-fabrication facility. At the fuel-fabrication facility the UF_6 is converted to UO_2 which is then powder milled, pelletized, sintered, and ground. The pellets are then loaded into Zircaloy fuel tubes which are sealed (and pressurized with helium in some instances). The fuel-fabrication processes are fairly well established with over fifteen years of experience in the industry. The Boiling Water Reactor (BWR) fuel-fabrication process is somewhat less expensive than the fuel-fabrication process for Pressurized Water Reactor (PWR) fuel since BWR fuel rods are larger in diameter. However, the achieved burnup per metric ton of uranium is higher for PWR nuclear plants than for BWR nuclear plants. As a result, both the PWR and BWR require about the same dollar amounts of fuel fabrication for the same output of energy. Estimates of fabrication costs range from $70 to $150 per kgU (11, 17). The price charged for fabrication will be assumed to be $110 per kgU in 1975 dollars.

Spent Fuel Storage—Throwaway Cycle

After the nuclear fuel has been "burned" in the reactor over a period of three or four years, it is removed from the reactor and kept in pools for from five to fifteen years. A primary reason for pool storage of a spent fuel assembly is to allow the decay heat over a period of time to decrease. A lower level of decay heat will allow a higher density distribution of waste containers to be maintained in the Federal repository (salt mine). For this analysis it will be assumed that the spent fuel is stored at the LWR nuclear plant spent fuel pool for ten years. Normally about two years pool storage is considered necessary for operations and contingencies of an LWR nuclear plant. This pool storage at the plant is considered part of the plant capital cost; therefore, no charge is involved for the first two years of storage. The cost to provide the additional eight years of storage will be assumed to be $60 per kilogram of spent fuel (11).

Transportation—Throwaway Cycle

After ten years of storage in the LWR nuclear plant pool, the spent fuel is shipped to the Federal repository for final disposal. The price for transportation by special trains of spent fuel ranges from $10 to $20 per kilogram of spent fuel (11, 24). Since most of the nuclear plants operating are along the Atlantic coast, Great Lakes, and deep South, the distances traveled in most cases by the special trains will be greater than 1,000 miles; therefore, $20 per kilogram of spent fuel will be used as the price for transportation.

Waste Disposal—Throwaway Cycle

After the spent fuel has cooled for approximately ten years, its decay heat is sufficiently low to allow final disposition. The major costs for spent fuel disposal are packaging charges and Federal repository charges. The sum of these costs ranges from $50 to $150 per kg of spent fuel (11, 24). For this analysis the price of waste disposal of spent fuel will be assumed to be $100 per kilogram of spent fuel in constant 1975 dollars. Since the Federal government has announced that it intends to start up a commercial waste depository by 1985, additional pool storage of spent fuel beyond ten years is assumed unnecessary.

Spent Fuel Storage—Closed Cycle

Under a reprocessing scheme, the spent fuel is stored in pools for a shorter period of time. A two-year storage period will be assumed to occur at the LWR plant. There will be no charge for this storage (as previously discussed).

Transportation—Closed Cycle

Under a closed cycle mode of operation, transportation of radioactive materials increases. Not only is transportation of the spent fuel to a reprocessing plant necessary, but also transportation of high-level radioactive waste and plutonium is required. For this analysis transportation costs per kgU for the closed cycle will be assumed to be 50 percent greater than for the throwaway cycle.

Reprocessing/Waste Disposal—Closed Cycle

This particular category consists of a large amount of activities including the physical and chemical processing of spent fuel, the storage of fission products for up to eight years, the burial of process material and low-level radioactive wastes, the solidification of high-level radioactive wastes, the vitrification of high-level radioactive wastes, and the disposal of the high-level radioactive wastes (2, 11). The total costs of these operations is at best an educated guess with ours being $300 per kilogram of spent fuel (11, 24).

Recovered Uranium and Plutonium—Closed Cycle

One of the positive benefits of utilizing a closed cycle is the recovery of useful fuel from the spent fuel assembly. For this analysis it is assumed that 90 percent of the uranium originally contained in the nuclear fuel assembly is recovered. The other 10 percent is either consumed—thus included as fission products, transmuted into plutonium, or lost during processing. After a 30,000-megawatt days per tonne burnup, the recovered uranium is considered to have an enriched level comparable to natural uranium (17, 30). Based on the above assumptions each kilogram of spent fuel which is reprocessed will yield uranium equivalent to 2.339 lbs of natural

Table 12. Values for reprocessed uranium and plutonium
(1975 dollars per kilogram of spent fuel)

Fuel cycle year	Future value of U_3O_8 ($/lb)[a]	Value of U in spent fuel[b]	Value of Pu in spent fuel[c]
1980	18	42	109
1985	23	54	125
1990	31	73	152
1995	50 (*est.*)	117	214
2000	60 (*est.*)	140	247

[a] Future value of U_3O_8 in constant 1975 dollars. Values are determined from the two times cost category of Figure 3 from the date plus six years, i.e., for 1980 fuel cycle calculations, the value would be for 1986 from Figure 3.
[b] Value of U = (value of U_3O_8) × (2.339)
[c] Value of Pu = [(value of U_3O_8) × (3.3)] + [(conversion cost) × (3.3)] + [(SWU cost) × (0.9)] − [(Δ fabrication cost) × (0.21)]

The value of $247 per kilogram of spent fuel is equivalent to about $30,000 per kilogram of plutonium.

U_3O_8. The value of the recovered uranium will be assumed to be that of natural uranium in the year of spent fuel reprocessing.

A 30,000-megawatt day per tonne U burnup will result in the buildup of about 8 kilograms of plutonium (Pu 239, 240, 241, 242) per tonne of spent fuel (17, 30). The core physics is extremely complex as to the relative buildup of plutonium isotopes, especially with respect to whether the nuclear fuel was fabricated from UO_2 pellets or from recycled PuO_2-UO_2 pellets. For this analysis, a kilogram of plutonium recovered will be assumed to have the same reactivity as 0.75 kilograms of U-235. Based on the above assumptions, a kilogram of spent fuel will produce plutonium equivalent to about 0.21 kg of fresh fuel manufactured from 3.300 lbs of natural U_3O_8 including allowance for processing losses. This amount of natural uranium will require about 0.9 kg SWU to enrich the equivalent uranium. Assuming further that mixed oxide fuel fabrication ($PuO_2 UO_2$) costs twice as much as uranium fuel fabrication, the following values for reprocessed plutonium per kilogram of spent fuel are derived in Table 12.

NUCLEAR FUEL COSTS

Nuclear fuel costs encompass many separate charges spread out over a significant period of time. The electric utility normally pays for mining, purification and conversion, enriching, and fabrication to separate business concerns. The nuclear fuel is then "burned" over a period of thirty-six to forty-eight months, during which time the utility incurs carrying charges. Finally, after the nuclear fuel has been consumed, there are significant delayed charges for transporting and disposing of the fuel assemblies.

The time frame of the "throwaway" cycle has two critical points in calculating fuel costs. The first is the date of fresh fuel assembly loading. The second is the midpoint of the average core lifetime. The first date signifies the cutoff point where interest during manufacture of a fuel assembly is stopped with the fuel assembly being "capitalized" over its in-core life. The fuel assemblies loaded each year will not all be removed at the same time. Some of the assemblies will remain in the reactor for three years while others will remain for four years. The average lifetime of the assemblies would be equal to R.L. = 1/cf as explained earlier. Those fuel assemblies which remain only three years are usually placed in core positions with higher flux densities and higher power densities. As an example, a reactor with 200 assemblies and a core fraction of 30 percent removed each year would have 60 assemblies removed which had an average lifetime of three and a third years. Out of the 200 fuel assemblies 120 would be on a three-year lifetime with 40 being replaced each year while 80 assemblies would be cycled on a four-year lifetime with 20 being replaced each year. For LWR operating at 66 percent capacity factor, the core fraction removed each year is 0.314 with

Table 13. Nuclear fuel cycle payment and activity timing.

Activity	Months	
	Throwaway	Closed
Purchase U$_3$O$_8$	< 12 >	< 12 >
Conversion to UF$_6$	< 12 >	< 12 >
Enrichment	< 9 >	< 9 >
Fabrication	< 3 >	< 3 >
Completed nuclear fuel assembly loading	0	0
Power production (average lifetime)	0–38	0–38
Midpoint (average lifetime)	19	19
Pool storage	38–158	38–62
Shipment	150	64
Waste disposal	163	—
Reprocessing/waste disposal	—	67
Uranium credit	—	72
Plutonium credit	—	72

an average reload lifetime of 3.18 years or thirty-eight months. The midpoint of average reload lifetime is nineteen months after refueling. Table 13 lists the payment timing of activities of both the throwaway and closed fuel cycle.

Since different parts of the fuel cycle are paid for in different years and accrue differing interest charges, this analysis cannot deal totally in constant 1975 dollars. This analysis therefore assumes a 10 percent cost of money and a 7 percent inflation rate. With these two rates in effect, goods or services bought in advance will increase in constant dollar value at the rate of about 3 percent per year (a historical relationship between interest and inflation) while funds for future charges can be discounted at 3 percent year. In addition, while the nuclear fuel is in the reactor it accrues a carrying charge of 10 percent for interest and 6 percent for Federal, state, and local taxes for an average nineteen months (RL/2) (25). The total fuel cycle cost will be paid for by the net generation of:

$(.32) \times (.314) \times (80 \text{ tonnes U}) \times (30{,}000 \text{ MWd/tonne U}) \times (24 \text{ hr/day}) = 5.79 \times 10^9$ kilowatt hours

where .32 is the thermal efficiency, .314 is the core reload fraction, 80 tonnes U is the amount of uranium in the LWR, and 30,000 MWd/tonne U is the burnup.

The paper analyzes the steady state (reactor operating for at least three years) nuclear fuel costs for the throwaway cycle and the closed cycle based on the conditions listed below. These two cases analyzed represent the most likely situation; however, there are numerous other combinations which could be analyzed.

Case A
(Throwaway cycle)
Capacity factor—66 percent
Reload lifetime—thirty-eight months
Burnup—30,000 MWd/tonne U
Enrichment tails assay—0.2 percent
Product enrichment—3 percent
Uranium price – two times production cost (Figure 3)

Case B
Same as Case A except with a closed cycle.

Table 14. Calculated nuclear fuel costs

CASE A	Base price	B.C.	C.C.	N.F.C.C.	T.C.
1980					
Purchase	$13.5/lb U_3O_8	5.32	0.16	1.45	6.93
Conversion	1.5/lb U_3O_8	0.59	0.02	0.16	0.77
Enrichment	75/kg SWU	8.25	0.18	2.23	10.66
Fabrication	110/kg U	2.76	0.02	0.74	3.52
Storage	60/kg SF	1.51	—	—	1.51
Transportation	20/kg SF	0.50	< 0.15 >	—	0.35
Waste disposal	100/kg SF	2.51	< 0.75 >	—	1.76
				Total cost	25.50
	Average price—4.4/mills/kwh				
1985					
Purchase	$17.5/lb U_3O_8	6.90	0.21	1.88	8.99
				Total cost	27.56
	Average price—4.8 mills/kwh				
1990					
Purchase	22.5/lb U_3O_8	8.87	0.27	2.42	11.56
				Total cost	30.13
	Average price—5.2 mills/kwh				
1995					
Purchase	28.5/lb U_3O_8	11.23	0.34	3.06	14.63
				Total cost	33.20
	Average price—5.7 mills/kwh				
2000					
Purchase	42.0/lb U_3O_8	16.55	0.50	4.52	21.57
				Total cost	40.14
	Average price—6.9 mills/kwh				

Economics of the Throwaway Nuclear Fuel Cycle

CASE B	Base price	B.C.	C.C.	N.F.C.C.	T.C.
1980					
Purchase	$13.5/lb U$_3O_8$	5.32	0.16	1.45	6.93
Conversion	1.5/lb U$_3$O$_8$	0.59	0.02	0.16	0.77
Enrichment	75/kg SWU	8.25	0.18	2.23	10.66
Fabrication	110/kg U	2.76	0.02	0.74	3.52
Storage	—	—	—	—	—
Transportation	30/kg SF	0.75	<0.08>	—	0.67
Reprocessing waste disposal	300/kg SF	7.54	<0.84>	—	6.70
U credit	42/kg SF	<1.06>	.13	—	<.93>
Pu credit	109/kg SF	<2.78>	.34	—	<2.44>
				Total cost	25.88
	Average price—4.5 mills/kwh				
1985					
Purchase	17.5/lb U$_3$O$_8$	6.90	0.21	1.88	8.99
U credit	54/kg SF	<1.36>	.17	—	<1.19>
Pu credit	125/kg SF	<3.14>	.38	—	<2.76>
				Total cost	27.36
	Average price—4.7 mills/kwh				
1990					
Purchase	22.5/lb U$_3$O$_8$	8.87	0.27	2.42	11.56
U credit	73/kg SF	<1.83>	.22	—	<1.61>
Pu credit	152/kg SF	<3.82>	.47	—	<3.35>
				Total cost	28.92
	Average price—5.0 mills/kwh				
1995					
Purchase	28/lb U$_3$O$_8$	11.23	0.34	3.06	14.63
U credit	117/kg SF	<2.94>	0.36	—	<2.58>
Pu credit	214/kg SF	<5.38>	0.66	—	<4.72>
				Total cost	29.65
	Average price—5.1 mills/kwh				
2000					
Purchase	42.0/lb U$_3$O$_8$	16.55	0.50	4.52	21.57
U credit	140/kg SF	<3.52>	0.43	—	<3.09>
Pu credit	247/kg SF	<6.20>	0.76	—	<5.44>
				Total cost	35.36
	<Average price—6.1 mills/kwh				

B.C.—Base charge = (quantity) × (base price)
C.C.—Carrying charge = (1.03 exp (time) − 1) × (b.c.)
N.F.C.C.—Nuclear fuel carrying charge = [(1.16 exp (R.L./24)) − 1][b.c. + c.c.]
T.C.—Total charges = b.c. + c.c. + n.f.c.c.
time = either (months prior to reload)/12 or (months after reload − R.L./2)/12

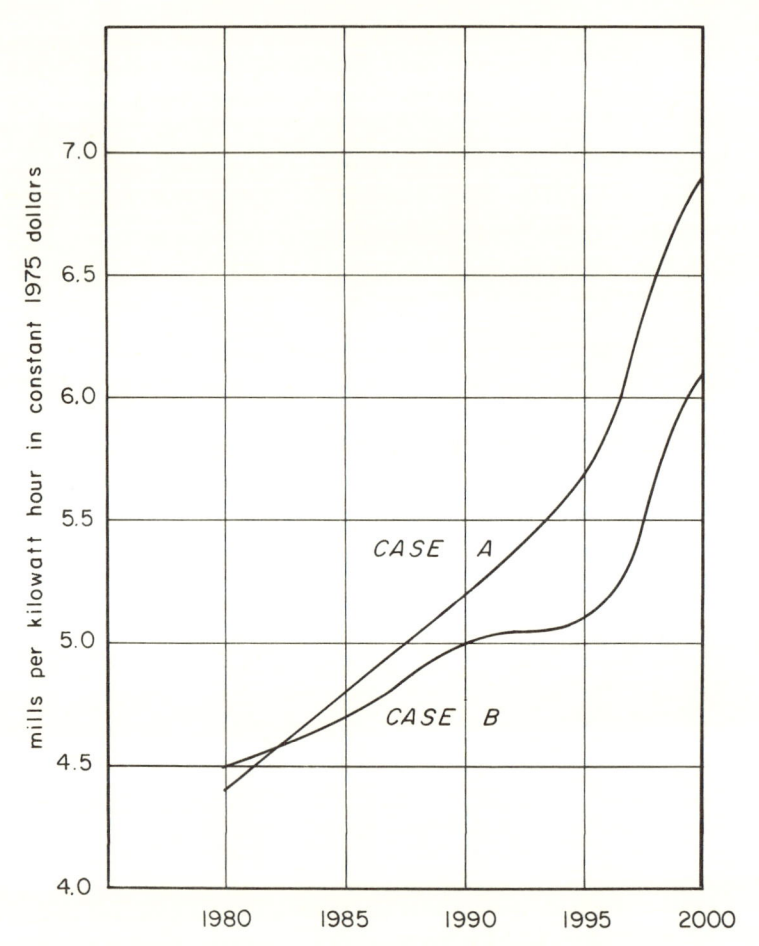

Figure 5. Case A — Throwaway nuclear fuel cycle average cost
Case B — closed nuclear fuel cycle average cost

The quantities of material per 1000 Mw(e) LWR in the same units as the price are as follows:

Uranium	394,000 lbs of U_3O_8
Enrichment	110,000 Kg SWU
Fuel	25,120 Kg U
Spent Fuel	25,120 Kg spent fuel

Table 14 lists the calculations and Figure 5 displays the results for nuclear fuel costs for Cases A and B. The throwaway cycle is initially the cheaper of the two alternatives, thus reflecting an abundant reserve of low-cost uranium. However, as the mining of uranium ore proceeds into the more marginal (higher production cost) areas, the benefits of recycling uranium and plutonium become more pronounced. This benefit does not include the effect on uranium prices due to the decreased demand caused by recycle; therefore, the projected benefits of a closed nuclear fuel cycle by 2000 may be understated considerably. In both cases, though, the fuel charge remains substantially below 10 mills per kilowatt hour in constant 1975 dollars through the year 2000.

Table 15 lists the percentage of the nuclear fuel cost by component. From table 15 one can readily see that U_3O_8, enrichment, and fabrication are the major items in the throwaway nuclear fuel cycle cost, and beyond 1985, U_3O_8 and enrichment charges make up 70 percent of the nuclear fuel cost. Although there may be large uncertainties in the cost of storage, shipment, and waste disposal, a doubling of any of their prices would affect the nuclear fuel cost less than 10 percent. For the closed nuclear fuel cycle, U_3O_8, enrichment, fabrication, reprocessing/waste disposal, and plutonium credit are the major components. Beyond 1985 U_3O_8 and enrichment charges account for at least 70 percent of the total cost for the open cycle also; however, reprocessing/waste disposal and plutonium credit are sufficiently large that the increases in cost and decreased value of each respectively could affect total cost by at least 25 percent. The certainty of nuclear fuel cost using the throwaway cycle is higher than that of the closed cycle.

Table 15. Percentage of nuclear fuel cost by component

Component	1980	1985	1990	1995	2000
CASE A					
U_3O_8	27.2	32.6	38.4	44.1	53.7
Conversion	3.0	2.8	2.6	2.3	1.9
Enrichment	41.8	38.7	35.4	32.1	26.6
Fabrication	13.8	12.8	11.7	10.6	8.8
Storage	5.9	5.5	5.0	4.5	3.8
Transportation	1.4	1.3	1.2	1.1	0.9
Waste disposal	6.9	6.4	5.8	5.3	4.4
CASE B					
U_3O_8	26.8	32.9	40.0	49.3	61.0
Conversion	3.0	2.8	2.7	2.6	2.2
Enrichment	41.2	39.0	36.9	36.0	30.1
Fabrication	13.6	12.9	12.2	11.9	10.0
Storage	—	—	—	—	—
Transportation	2.6	2.4	2.3	2.3	1.9
Reprocessing/ waste disposal	25.9	24.5	23.2	22.6	18.9
U credit	<3.6>	<4.3>	<5.6>	<8.7>	<8.7>
Pu credit	<9.4>	<10.1>	<11.6>	<15.9>	<15.4>

CONCLUSIONS

The national posture on nuclear energy as an alternative for production of electricity is unsettled. The major uncertainties surrounding the viability of the light water reactor as a technology for electricity production are related to fuel availability, fuel processing, and spent fuel disposition.

In this paper it has been shown that a "throwaway" fuel cycle, even when using a conservative "bookkeeper's approach" to cataloging uranium resources, offers a possible, indeed in some ways more attractive, fuel cycle concept to support a continuing nuclear industry. The "throwaway" fuel cycle will result in total fuel costs less than the conventional closed fuel cycle prior to 1985, will result in fuel costs no more than 12–15 percent higher than a closed fuel cycle up to the year 2000, and will allow the lifetime operation of around 300,000 Mw(e) of electricity production capacity.

Given the urgent short-term need for non-petroleum energy resources, and given that the "throwaway" fuel cycle offers an institutionally simpler alternative than the closed fuel cycle, it appears that development of a closed fuel cycle is not essential to the conventional light water reactor industry. This is not to say that a closed fuel cycle is not essential; indeed it is for most all advanced reactor concepts. However, one need not delay the transition to nuclear energy, at least until around 300,000 Mw(e) of nuclear capacity have been installed, due to political and regulatory inability to resolve the status of reprocessing and plutonium recycle.

REFERENCES

1. "AEC Temporarily Suspends Uranium Enrichment Contracting," press release, U.S. Atomic Energy Commission, July 2, 1974.
2. *Alternatives for Managing Wastes from Reactors and Post-Fission Operations in the LWR Fuel Cycle*, ERDA 76–43, U.S. Energy Research and Development Administration, May 1976.
3. *Australia's Uranium Resources*, Australian Uranium Producer's Forum, May 1976.
4. "Canada Bars Compliance with U.S. Subpoenas on Alleged Price Fixing," *Energy Users Report*, no. 164, The Bureau of National Affairs, Inc., September 30, 1976.
5. "Committee Okays Portsmouth Site, Limits Centrifuge Contractors," *Nucleonics Week*, McGraw-Hill, June 30, 1977.
6. "Economics of Nuclear Power," course material, Massachusetts Institute of Technology.
7. "ERDA Announces New Charges for Uranium Enrichment," *Information from ERDA*, U.S. Energy Research and Development Administration, July 30, 1976.
8. *ERDA Quarterly Report on Capacity Expansion of the Gaseous Diffusion Plant—Oak Ridge Operation*, U.S. Energy Research and Development Administration, August 1976.
9. "Exxon Nuclear Denies Report That It is Pulling Out of Uranium Enrichment," *Nucleonics Week*, McGraw-Hill, December 2, 1976.

10. "Falling Out of Dow and Consumers Exposed as Midland Licensing Explodes," *Nucleonics Week*, McGraw-Hill, December 9, 1976.
11. *Final Generic Environmental Statement on the Use of Recycle Plutonium in Mixed Oxide Fuel in Light Water Cooled Reactors*, NUREG-0002, U.S. Nuclear Regulatory Commission, August 1976.
12. *Final Environmental Impact Statement: Expansion of U.S. Uranium Capacity*, ERDA-1543, U.S. Energy Research and Development Administration, April 1976.
13. Henderson, R. R., "The Design of PWR Fuel to Meet Utility Requirements and Its Operational Demonstration," Westinghouse Electric Corporation, Nuclex 75, Brussels, Belgium, 1975.
14. Hogerton, et al., (S. M. Stoller Corporation), "Report on Uranium Supply—Task III," *Nuclear Fuels Supply*, Edison Electric Institute, December 5, 1975.
15. *Information from ERDA*, #77–105, U.S. Energy Research and Development Administration, June 22, 1977.
16. Information provided by Babcock and Wilcox personnel, August 1976.
17. Information provided by Westinghouse Electric Corporation personnel, Water Reactor Division Marketing Division, August 1976.
18. Jacoby, Henry D., "Uranium Dependence and the Proliferation Problem," *Technology Review*, Massachusetts Institute of Technology, June, 1977.
19. *National Uranium Resource Evaluation Preliminary Report*, GJO-111(76), U.S. Energy Research and Development Administration, June 1976.
20. "NFS Quits Reprocessing, but Waste Solidification Problem Remains," *Nucleonics Week*, McGraw-Hill, September 23, 1976.
21. *1975 Assessment of Canada's Uranium Supply and Demand*, Canadian Department of Energy, Mines, and Resources, May 1976.
22. "Nuclear Electricity Generation for November," *Nucleonics Week*, McGraw-Hill, December 23, 1976.
24. *Nuclear Fuel Cycle Closure Alternatives*, Allied-General Nuclear Services, April 1976.
25. *Nuclear Fuel Economics*, Westinghouse Electric Corporation, 1973.
26. "Nuclear Power Sweeps Six States; But Help for Missouri Utilities Fails," *The Energy Daily*, November 4, 1976.
27. *NUEXCO Monthly Report to the Nuclear Industry*, no. 100, Nuclear Exchange Corporation, November 30, 1976.
28. *Preliminary Safety Analysis Report, Bellefonte Nuclear Plant*, Tennessee Valley Authority, January 11, 1974.
29. "President Ford's Enrichment Bill Dies in the Senate," *The Energy Daily*, October 1, 1976.
30. *Reference Safety Analysis Report (RESAR 41)*, Westinghouse Electric Corporation, 1973.
31. *S.2035 and H. R. 8401: Nuclear Fuel Assurance Act of 1975*, Hearings before the Joint Committee on Atomic Energy, Congress of the United States, 1975 and 1976.
32. "State Legislatures Tighten Regulation of Nuclear Fuel Cycle," *Energy Users Report*, no. 168, The Bureau of National Affairs, Inc., October 28, 1976.
33. Statement of George F. Quinn, Atomic Energy Commission, "Future Structure of the Uranium Enrichment Industry," Hearings before the Joint Committee on Atomic Energy, Congress of the United States, July 31, 1973.
34. Statement of Jerome W. Komes, *S.2035 and H. R. 8401: Nuclear Fuel Assurance Act*, Hearings before the Joint Committee on Atomic Energy, Congress of the United States, April 6, 1975.
35. *Survey of United States Uranium Marketing Activity*, ERDA 76–46, U.S. Energy Research and Development Administration, April 1976.

36. "Uranium Btu Tax Could Help N. M. Producers," *Nuclear Fuel*, McGraw-Hill, December 27, 1976.
37. *Wall Street Journal*, numerous articles during 1975.
38. "Westinghouse Trial Halted Until Jan. 3; Gulf Will Submit Papers," *Nucleonics Week*, McGraw-Hill, November 11, 1976.

PROSPECTS FOR NUCLEAR POWER IN THE DEVELOPING COUNTRIES

Alan M. Strout, MASSACHUSETTS INSTITUTE OF TECHNOLOGY*

This paper deals with two questions: How important will nuclear power be to developing countries over the next twenty-five years? And how many developing countries are likely to have constructed nuclear power plants by the year 2000?

Each of these questions raises a number of subsidiary questions and issues. These are discussed in turn below. A final section covers the conclusions to be drawn from the discussion.

I. THE IMPORTANCE OF ENERGY TO DEVELOPMENT

When the entire spectrum of rich and poor countries is included on a chart showing per capita energy consumption plotted against per capita income, there is a close relationship between energy use and income. This is usually interpreted as indicating how energy use increases as per capita incomes increase.

The implied cross-country statistical relationship is valid, but its use to describe future developments can be wrong for at least four reasons. First, per capita income is almost inevitably measured using official exchange rates to convert national currency into common units, usually U.S. dollars. This exaggerates purchasing power differences among countries by as much as two or three times for the lower-income countries [Kravis, et al. (10), Chapter 1].

Income growth is usually expressed in constant prices, and this in turn is roughly comparable to constant purchasing power. The relationship between per capita energy use and per capita income measures in equivalent purchasing power would have a much steeper slope than when incomes are based upon official exchange rates. Using the official exchange rate relationship for projecting future energy use when income growth is projected at constant prices thus produces estimates that are too low.

The second cause for bias in the usual chart relating energy use to per capita income is that energy prices in the past have been low or declining. In a future of high energy prices, would these relationships continue to be valid? Some projection models for the United States, where much energy use is of a "luxury" nature and hence presumably more readily influenced by relative price changes, suggest that future GDP growth might be accomplished with far less use of fuel and power than would be suggested by past relationships. This may be less true, however, for developing countries.[1]

The third reason for possible bias is that cross-country relationships reflect the distribution of industry among countries at a particular point in time. Relationships based on time series account for past changes experienced by a particular country or group of countries. Neither situation may adequately reflect future changes in industrial structure.

Although a country's industrial structure has many different dimensions, the dimension most clearly related to energy use is the production of a rather small group of basic materials whose manufacture requires large amounts of energy both directly and indirectly. The production of these materials may account for one-fourth of all energy used in the United States and over one-half of energy use in countries with a higher concentration of national product derived from steel, other basic metals, paper, pulp, fertilizer, cement, etc. [Strout (20), pp. 135–141].[2] When the production of a sample of these commodities is combined using energy weights, the resulting aggregate measure of "energy-intensive material" (EIM) is highly correlated with energy and electricity use at all levels of development.[3]

The developing countries, with few exceptions, are historically low producers of energy-intensive materials. (See Figure 1.)[4] In this respect the developing countries have evolved more in the direction of such developed countries as Denmark, New Zealand, and Switzerland. The major producers of energy-intensive materials with respect to GDP are Belgium-Luxembourg, Austria, Norway, Sweden, Canada, and Japan. Japan is by far the most important quantitatively of this group and supplies much of the import requirements for deficit countries. Most other developed countries, including those of the socialist bloc, are in an intermediate position with regard to the production of energy-intensive materials. The dashed line in Figure 1 shows the production needed to satisfy domestic consumption requirements. The larger European countries lie relatively close to the self-sufficiency line. The Unites States lies below. Quantitatively, the United States is the world's largest net importer of the particular commodities included in the EIM measure. Transitional developed countries such as Portugal and Greece lie closer to the historical LDC relationship between energy-intensive materials production and per capita income, while Spain, South Africa, and Yugoslavia are closer to the self-sufficiency line.

The self-sufficiency and LDC-production lines from Figure 1 are reproduced in Figure 2. The lines, derived from cross-country relationships observed in 1969–1971, are juxtaposed with *time-trends* for three groups of non-OPEC developing countries.[5] Each group shows a fairly linear growth over time (in relationship to per capita GDP). The slopes all appear to be steeper than the long-run production curve for the same countries (taken from cross-country results for 1969–1971) but less steep than the "self-sufficiency" long-run relationships for all countries. No subgroup of developing countries, including the "higher income" group containing Taiwan and Chile, shows production increasing at anywhere near the rate which in the past must have characterized countries such as Austria, Japan, South Africa, or Australia.

It may be assumed that some developing countries in the future, particularly those endowed with relatively plentiful energy resources, will attempt to follow the heavy industry development strategy of South Africa, Spain, and many of the socialist bloc countries. It is significant, however, that during the 1960–1973 period of relatively inexpensive energy prices the non-OPEC developing countries as a whole made little progress in this direction. If anything, the gap between normal consumption and actual production of energy intensive materials has appeared to widen. It is possible that in the future the developing countries as a group may have even less

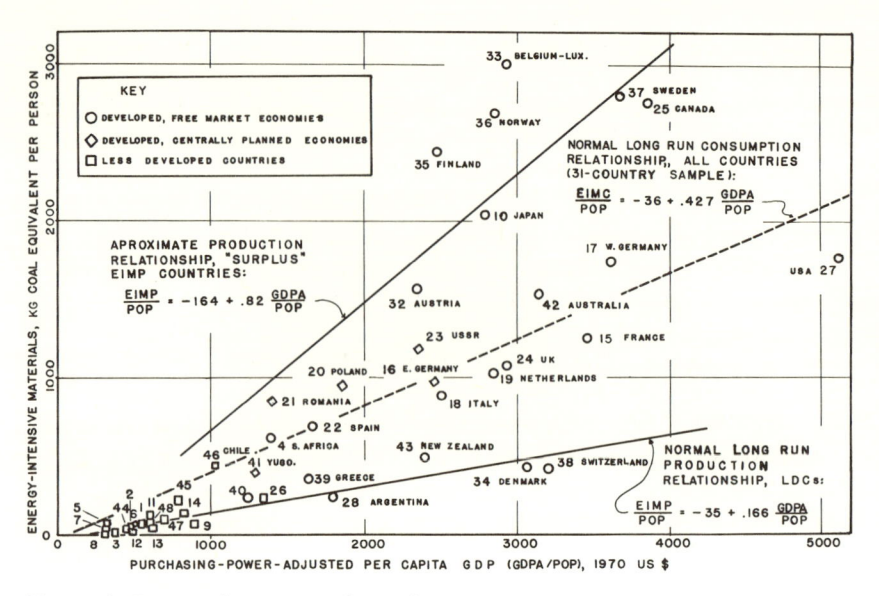

Figure 1. Per capita energy-intensive materials production (EIMP/POP) vs. purchasing-power-adjusted per capita GDP (GDPA/POP), 48 countries, mean values 1969/71.

Countries included in Figure 1

Less Developed Countries

1 Egypt	9 Iran	29 Brazil
2 Morocco	11 Republic of Korea	30 Colombia
3 Nigeria	12 Pakistan + Bangladesh	31 Venezuela
5 Zaire	13 Philippines	44 Thailand
6 China	14 Turkey	45 Taiwan
7 India	26 Mexico	46 Chile
8 Indonesia	28 Argentina	47 Peru
		48 W. Malaysia

Developed, Centrally Planned Economies

16 Germany, D.R.	21 Rumania	41 Yugoslavia
20 Poland	23 U.S.S.R.	

Developed, Free Market Economies

4 South Africa, Rep.	24 United Kingdom	36 Norway
10 Japan	25 Canada	37 Sweden
15 France	27 U.S.A.	38 Switzerland
17 Germany, F. R.	32 Austria	39 Greece
18 Italy	33 Belgium/Luxembourg	40 Portugal
19 Netherlands	34 Denmark	42 Australia
22 Spain	35 Finland	43 New Zealand

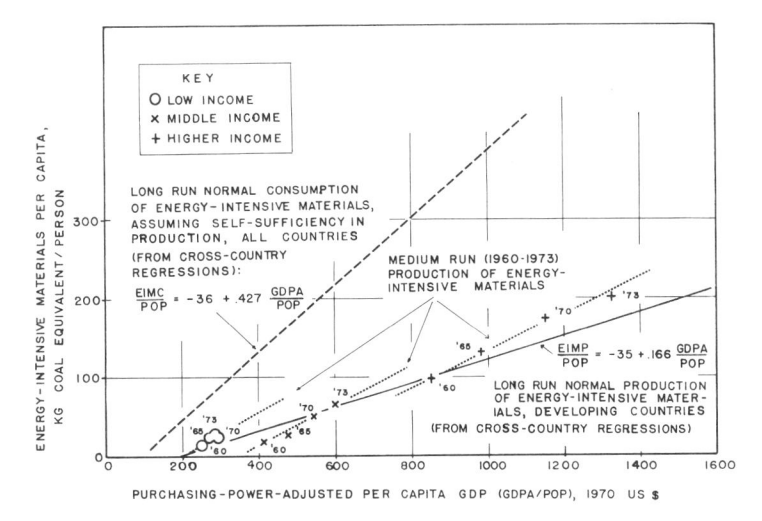

Figure 2. Per capita production of energy-intensive materials vs. purchasing-power-adjusted per capita GDP, non-OPEC developing countries, 1960, 1965, 1970, and 1973.

success in overcoming the historical advantage of today's industrialized net exporters of energy-intensive materials.

Total commercial energy (and electricity) consumption is strongly influenced by the production of energy-intensive materials. It thus appears likely that the non-energy-rich developing countries will *not* experience income elasticities of demand for energy in the future that are as high as those recorded by today's more industrialized countries. There is even some question as to whether the energy/GDP relationship for these countries may not in the future fall below the historical trend for the developing countries themselves.

Finally, the fourth reason for possible bias in the historical relationship between per capita energy consumption and per capita income lies in the fact that in the past not all fuels have been burned with equal efficiency in use. Coal-fired equipment, for example, has generally been less efficient than that using oil or natural gas. When fuel consumption in a country is added up to produce an energy total, no allowance is made for differing efficiencies in actual use. Some investigators have attempted to arrive at such estimates of country-wide average efficiencies, and statistically it appears that a country's total per capita energy use is positively related to the portion of the total consumed in the form of coal. That is, when all other factors are equal, the higher proportion of total fuel consumption in the form of coal (usually burned at lower efficiencies than oil or natural gas), the greater is a country's total consumption of fuel and power.

II. FUTURE ENERGY AND ELECTRICITY REQUIREMENTS OF THE DEVELOPING COUNTRIES

The intent of the previous section was to confirm the oft-cited strong association between economic growth and energy consumption, but to raise doubts about the exact nature of the relationship. Cross-country statistical relationships are suspect unless country incomes are made comparable in terms of purchasing power. Future price changes will have some effect upon demand, but the magnitude of the effect is very difficult to assess and may be relatively minor. Aside from the general growth rates in per capita income, the largest future effect on energy use will probably come from any changes which may occur in the production of energy-intensive materials. In the recent past for three groups of non-OPEC developing countries, the per capita production of energy-intensive materials has borne a roughly linear relationship to the growth of purchasing-power-adjusted per capita GDP. (See Figure 2.) In the future this past relationship is likely to continue even though it will imply a widening gap between aggregate production and "normal" consumption of energy intensive materials.

The linear relationship between per capita GDP and energy-intensive materials production is paralleled for these same three groups of developing countries by approximately linear relationships between per capita income and energy use. These are shown in the top portion of Figure 3. "Commercial" energy in this case follows the definition of the United Nations in excluding fuelwood, dung, and all vegetal wastes. The production of primary electrical energy (hydro, geothermal, nuclear) as well as net electricity imports or exports are included at the direct calorific equivalent of electricity rather than at the amount of fossil fuels saved through not having to generate this amount of electricity in conventional thermal power plants.[6]

The bottom half of Figure 3 shows the 1960–1973 relationships between per capita electricity consumption and per capita GDP. The relationships again appear to be roughly linear.

It is suggested that the relationships shown in Figure 3 may prove acceptable guides to future energy use in these three groups of non-OPEC countries, assuming the continuation of past trends in energy-intensive materials production for each country group. The effect of higher current energy price levels than existed over most of the historical period would be to depress the lines. This would also be the effect of any failure to maintain past rates of energy-intensive materials production. (Some countries, of course, will always differ from the averages shown, and the Figure 3 curves can represent no more than a central tendency for each subgroup of countries.)

For projection purposes assumptions are needed about future growth

Nuclear Power in Developing Countries

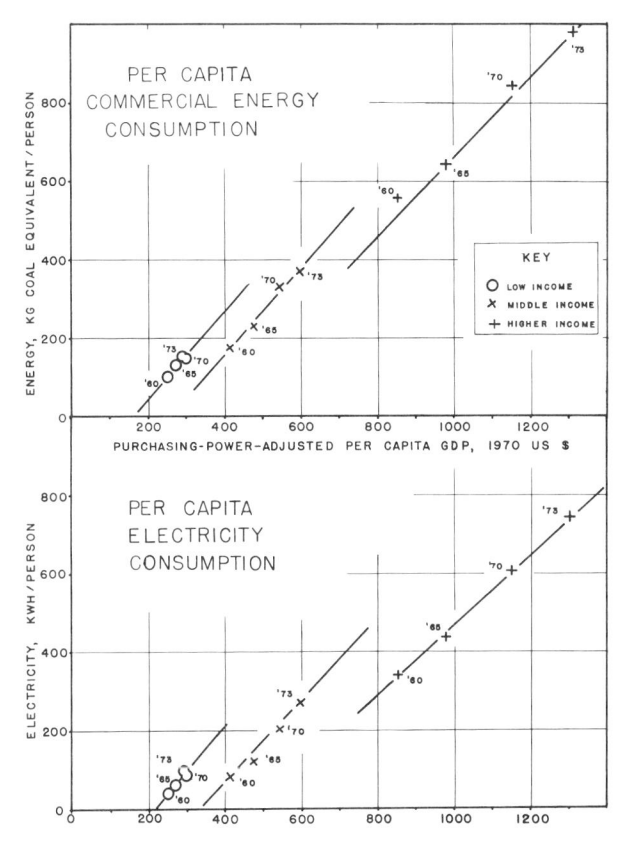

Figure 3. Per capita energy consumption vs. purchasing-power-adjusted per capita GDP, non-OPEC developing countries, 1960, 1965, 1970, and 1973.

rates of population and real income. These are given for each country subgroup in Table 1, along with historical rates during 1965–1973. Population growth rates for each subgroup have been assumed to decrease slightly over the next twenty five years with somewhat greater decreases occurring in the higher income groups. The 1973–1980 real (purchasing-power adjusted) GDP growth rates are those used in a recent World Bank study and are more conservative than recent growth rate targets for many of these same countries [Lambertini (11), p. 2, n. 1]. The 4.5 percent per year assumption for the low-income group is the only case where future growth is at a higher rate than that of the recent past. (For this group of countries the 1960–1970 average was 4.0 percent per year, and this rate fell to 1.8 percent annually between 1970 and 1974.)

For the middle- and higher-income countries GDP growth during 1980–

Table 1. Growth rate assumptions for energy consumption projections, 1973–2000, non-OPEC developing countries.

Country Subgroup	Variable	1965–73 Actual	1973–1980 Assumed	1980–2000 Assumed
Low Income	Population	2.51	2.40	2.25
	Real GDP	3.41	4.5	5.0
Middle income	Population	2.75	2.65	2.50
	Real GDP	5.62	5.5	5.5
Higher income	Population	2.76	2.60	2.40
	Real GDP	6.52	5.5	5.5

Source: 1965–1973 population growth based on U.N. country estimates, *Monthly Bulletin of Statistics*, Jan. 1975, supplemented in a few cases by World Bank *Atlas*, 1975. 1965–1973 GDP growth rates from World Bank Staff Working Paper No. 229, Lambertini, Table 2. For discussion of assumptions, see text.

2000 has been projected at the 1973–1980 rate of 5.5 percent per year. That for the lower-income group is assumed to increase slightly to 5.0 percent per year.

Energy and electricity projections based upon the Table 1 assumptions and the Figure 3 graphical relationships are shown in Table 2. They have been plotted against time in Figures 4, 5, and 6. Several observations may be made about these results.

Table 2. Projections of population, gross domestic product, commercial energy and electricity consumption, Non-OPEC developing countries, 1973–2000.

Variable	Units	Actual 1973	Projected[a] 1980	1990	2000
Low income countries					
Population	10^6	996.0	1176	1466	1835
GDP, 1970 US$	10^9	98.32			
GDP adjusted to common purchasing power, 1970 US$[b] (GDP-Adj.)	10^9	298.8	406.6	662.4	1078.9
GDP per capita	1970 US$	101.4[c]			
GDP-adj. per capita	1970 US$	300	346	452	588
Commercial energy, coal equivalent	MT × 10^6	151.66	239.90	472.05	871.62
Electricity	Kwh × 10^9	96.60	171.70	378.23	778.04
Per capita:					
Commercial energy, coal equivalent	kg	152	204	322	475
Electricity	Kwh	97	146	258	424

Variable	Units	Actual 1973	Projected[a] 1980	1990	2000
Middle income countries					
Population	10^6	244.0	293	375	480
GDP, 1970 US$	10^9	64.25			
GDP-adj.,[b]	10^9	124.4	211.5	361.4	617.2
GDP per capita	1970 US$	263			
GDP-adj. per capita	1970 US$	596	722	964	1286
Comm. energy, coal equivalent	MT × 10^6	90.66	150.60	294.38	549.60
Electricity	Kwh × 10^9	66.07	118.08	246.48	477.60
Per capita:					
Commercial energy, coal equivalent	kg	372	514	785	1145
Electricity	Kwh	271	403	657	995
Higher income countries					
Population	10^6	305.4	366	463	587
GDP, 1970 US$	10^9	199.15			
GDP-adj.,[b] 1970 US$	10^9	399.2	580.6	991.8	1694.2
GDP per capita	1970 US$	652			
GDP-adj. per capita	1970 US$	1307	1586	2142	2886
Commercial energy, coal equivalent	MT × 10^6	299.60	463.36	848.68	1521.50
Electricity	Kwh × 10^9	228.08	365.27	694.04	1272.62
Per capita:					
Commercial energy, coal equivalent	kg	981	1266	1833	2592
Electricity	Kwh	747	998	1499	2168

[a] Using the initial figures shown in the 1973 column, the growth rate assumptions from Table 1, and the following approximate relationships from Figure 3:

	Per Capita Commercial Energy		Per Capita Electricity	
	Intercept	Per Capita GDP-adj. coef.	Intercept	Per Capita GDP-adj. coef.
Low income	−185	1.12	−248	1.15
Middle income	−295	1.12	−355	1.05
Higher income	−352	1.02	−429	.90

[b] See note 4 for the equation used to calculate a purchasing power price index for 1969/1971. Since the 1973–2000 GDP projections were in "real" prices of 1970, this index was then used to adjust the real GDP estimate for each of these latter years.

[c] Actual 1973 GDP per capita was reported at $98.7. This was below the 1970 average of $101.2, and the 1973 figure shown has consequently been adjusted upward to be consistent with actual energy use reported for 1973.

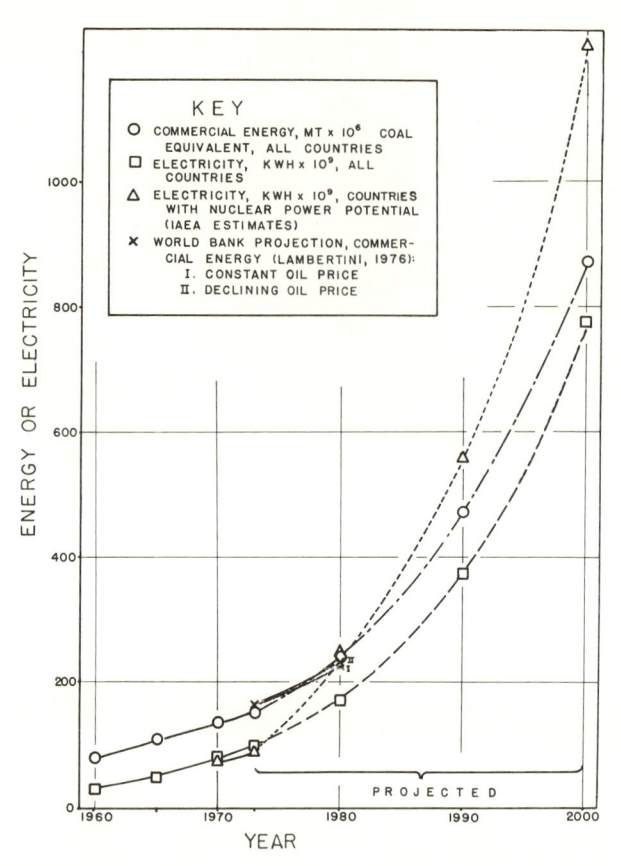

Figure 4. Projected growth of commercial energy and of electricity consumption, 1973–2000, low income developing countries (non-OPEC).

First, the 1973–1980 growth rate projected for total commercial energy is considerably higher than that currently employed by the World Bank. The Bank projections led to the rather sanguine conclusion that "all the non-OPEC developing countries together have enough economically recoverable energy resources to reduce their dependence on energy imports from other groups of countries from about 30 percent in 1974 to between 12 percent and 5 percent in 1980" [Lambertini (11), Abstract, title page]. The probable explanation for the difference between the two sets of results is that the Bank projections gave a greater weight to the early 1970s price changes than would seem justified by the low price elasticities found by the same Bank study.

The second observation is that the electricity projections shown in Table 2 for the low- and higher-income groups are much lower than those made in

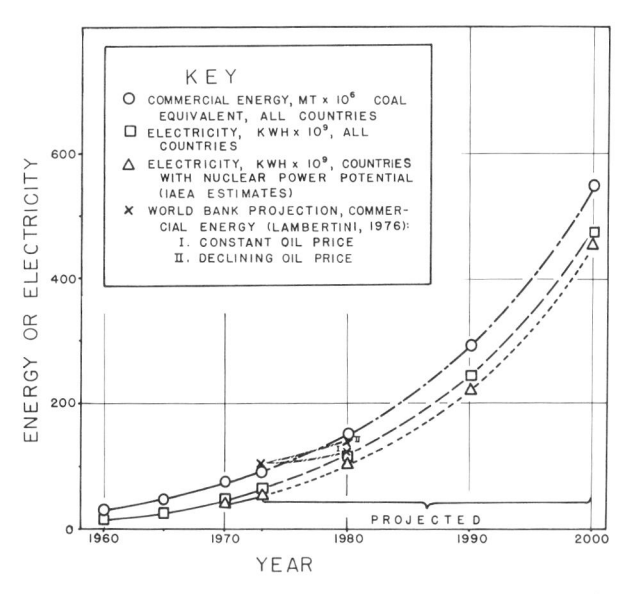

Figure 5. Projected growth of commercial energy and of electricity consumption, 1973–2000, middle income developing countries (non-OPEC).

1974 by the International Atomic Energy (8), Table IX. The IAEA projections are important because they form the basis for that Agency's projections of the future market for nuclear power in the developing countries. The projections are confined to a relatively small group of 35 non-OPEC developing countries identified by the IAEA as being potential producers of nuclear power. (This more limited group nevertheless accounts for almost all electric power consumption in the non-OPEC developing countries.) The two sets of projections are compared in greater detail in Table 3.

The differences for the low-income group are largely accounted for by one country, India. The IAEA projects India's electric power generation to grow at 13.3 percent per year between 1970 and 1980 and by 8.2 percent annually in the following decade. The IAEA does not report the GDP growth rate assumption on which this estimate is based, and the projection is probably too high. According to the "demand path" chart of electricity use which the IAEA presumably used for country projections where special studies had not been made, a 13.3 percent electricity growth rate for India would seem to correspond to a 9.5 percent annual growth of total GDP.[7] This is considerably greater than most observers believe possible for India during the remainder of this decade.

The differences for the higher income group probably arise from two causes: higher GDP growth rate and slightly higher income elasticities of demand assumed for the IAEA projections. The IAEA may have projected

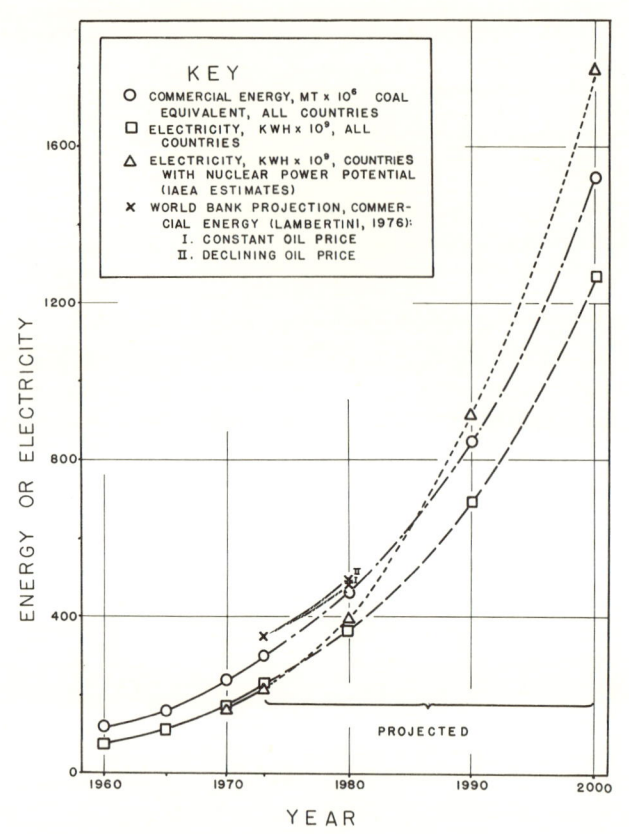

Figure 6. Projected growth of commercial energy and of electricity consumption, 1973–2000, higher income developing countries (non-OPEC).

GDP growth for this group to be as great as 7 percent per year between 1970 and 1980 and perhaps 6.5 percent in the decade thereafter.[8] These rates contrast with the 5.5 percent growth assumed for Tables 2 and 3.

The income elasticity differences arise from a more complicated set of reasons. The electricity demand model underlying the IAEA projections is based essentially on cross-country consumption and income data from the 1960s.[9] It is thus subject to all of the biases described in the earlier section on the relationship between energy use and economic growth. Most importantly the purchasing power bias in GDP conversions will lead to an understatement of electricity needs when projections are based on assumed growth of real income. On the other hand, the worldwide "normal" or "universal" relationship assumes a certain pattern of industrial structure changes (particularly the production of energy-intensive materials) as economic growth proceeds. If, as seems likely, the developing countries are not following the

Table 3. Alternative projections of energy consumption and production, 1970–2000.

	\multicolumn{5}{c}{(kilowatt hours × 10⁹)}			
	Actual		Projected		
	1960	1970	1980	1990	2000
Non-OPEC developing countries					
Low income					
All countries, consumption	27.9	80.8	171.7	378.2	778.0
Five countries with nuclear potential					
Consumption	23.0	70.5			
Generation (IAEA)	—	70.2	245.5	559.6	1214.7
(Of which India)		(60.0)	(210.0)	(462.0)	(1000.0)
Middle Income					
All countries, consumption	13.9	46.3	118.1	246.4	477.6
Ten countries with nuclear potential					
Consumption	11.1	38.8			
Generation (IAEA)	—	35.0	101.2	222.4	451.9
Higher Income					
All countries, consumption	73.9	171.6	365.3	694.0	1272.6
Twenty countries with nuclear potential					
Consumption	70.8	163.1			
Generation (IAEA)	—	153.1	395.9	914.1	1794.9
OPEC Countries					
All 13 countries, consumption	11.1	33.7	na	na	na
Nine countries with nuclear potential					
Consumption	11.0	32.9			
Generation (IAEA)	—	30.2	96.8	233.6	451.2

Source: 1960–1970 consumption from United Nations (22), Table 2.
1980–2000 projected consumption from Table 2.
1970 actual and 1980–2000 projected generation from IAEA (8), Tables VIII, IX.

historical pattern, then electricity consumption will be overestimated.

A further complication has been introduced in the current instance by the decision to use the *linear* relationships of Figure 3 for projection purposes. A logarithmic relationship would have fitted the 1960–1973 time paths equally well and would have led to much higher estimates of future electricity consumption. Logarithmic projection curves were not used, however, since the slopes for the three country groupings differed strongly. This raised serious questions about how the slope should be projected to change during the course of future economic growth. This problem was largely avoided when using nonlogarithmic curves since, as can be seen from Figure 3, the slopes of the three country groupings are quite similar.[10]

The net effect of these various differences for the higher-income countries was to produce slightly higher-income elasticities of demand for electricity, as already noted, and thus to increase the gap between the IAEA projections and those derived in Table 2. For the middle-income countries, however, the various biases about canceled one another out, and the projections summarized in Table 3 are quite consistent with each other.

The third and most important observation about the projections of Table 2 is that, in spite of the relatively conservative assumptions employed, energy and electricity consumption are seen to increase enormously over the remainder of this century. Between 1973 and 2000, population in the non-OPEC developing countries is assumed to not quite double and total Gross Domestic Product to increase by a factor of 4. Commercial energy, however, would increase by a factor of 5.4 and electricity by 6.5.

III. ALTERNATIVE SOURCES OF ENERGY SUPPLY

Where will the non-OPEC developing countries obtain the large amounts of energy needed for the relatively modest economic growth projected in Table 2? And in particular, how important a role might be anticipated for nuclear power?

To put this issue in perspective it should be noted that the energy requirements for the developing countries come to only a fraction of global demand. The developing country share of total world consumption was about 6 percent in 1960 and 9 percent in 1974.[11] By 1980 the share might reach 13 percent, rising to perhaps 23 percent by the year 2000.[12] Secondly, if the large "recoverable" world reserves of coal can be fully used, the world appears to have adequate supplies of conventional, nonrenewable energy resources for at least another fifty years.[13] Thus the choice of a particular fuel, including the nuclear fuels, will be largely determined by economic and perhaps environmental or strategic considerations. Third, unless the historical use of electricity changes far more rapidly than now anticipated or unless the use of nuclear power for industrial process heat is resurrected as a desirable option, nuclear power could at most provide one-third of energy needs in the non-OPEC developing countries in the year 2000. (This assumes that all the electricity shown in Table 2 is nuclear-generated at an average thermal efficiency of about 32 percent.) Thus conventional fuel sources are likely to play an important role in developing countries throughout the foreseeable future.

In the near term, at least, prospects appear good that the non-OPEC countries can, as a group, provide most of their energy needs from indigenous sources. The World Bank study already referred to estimates that this group of countries increased its production of fuel and primary energy at the rate of almost 7 percent per year between 1965 and 1974. The growth rate to 1980 could be accelerated to 9.6 percent annually, according to the same study, at only a relatively minor increase in the share of GNP used for domestic fuel and power investment.[14] Investment in absolute terms might have to increase by a large amount, from an annual average of $4.2 billions (1973 prices) during 1968 to $7.1 billions annually (also in 1973 prices) during 1974–1980. As a percentage of GDP however, the increase would only be from 1.2 percent in the first period to 1.4 percent in the latter. (The relative increase for the group of low-income non-OPEC countries, however, would be greater: from 0.6 percent of GDP in 1968–1973 to 1.3 percent in 1974–1980.)

It appears, furthermore, that economically recoverable, currently known energy resources in the non-OPEC countries would be sufficient to supply this group of countries with their energy needs until almost the end of the century.[15] Since the prospects for additional discoveries of hydrocarbons appear to be very good, this reinforces the conclusion of this section that absolute shortages of energy should not be a general problem in the foreseeable future. There may be some further increases in energy prices (although even that is a debatable point), and individual countries may continue to have difficulties in earning sufficient foreign exchange to pay for imported energy when domestic sources are deficient. Choice of particular fuels by individual countries in the future should continue to be determined by the same factors which have operated in the past: relative costs, ability to earn foreign exchange, and strategic considerations.

IV. ECONOMICS OF ELECTRIC POWER GENERATION AND DISTRIBUTION

The uncertainties about nuclear generating costs and about future fossil fuel prices are as great for developing countries as they are for the rest of the world. These uncertainties translate into a high degree of risk when trying to choose a least-cost solution to an LDC's future power system expansion. The International Atomic Energy Agency has borrowed extensively from the AEC and has developed careful and shophisticated techniques for converting capital costs to LDC conditions and for planning future power system growth.[16] The particular assumptions chosen by the IAEA lead to the clear conclusion that nuclear power plants will provide the least-cost alternative for almost all future additions to LDC generating capacity.[17]

The IAEA assumptions and procedures have in turn been carefully scrutinized in a recent study by Richard J. Barber Associates (hereafter abbreviated as RJBA). The latter study, which includes a detailed and generally excellent review and discussion of the many and various generating cost elements, believes that the IAEA assumptions lead to the "most favorable" scenario for nuclear power expansion. The RJBA study proposes a more conservative, "medium" set of assumptions and a still more conservative scenario designed to be unfavorable to nuclear power. (All three scenarios deal only with economic issues vis-à-vis alternative production of electricity by coal or oil.)

The most important difference among the various assumptions concern the cost and utilization of capital. RJBA believes that initial capital costs will be more expensive in developing countries than in the United States, rather than less expensive. The differences apply about equally to fossil plant costs, however, and do not greatly affect the choice between nuclear and fossil. A more important assumption is that of the discount rate for converting total capital investment to an equivalent annual cost. The 1973 IAEA study assumed an 8 percent discount rate and made "sensitivity" tests of rates ranging from 6 to 10 percent. In the 1974 study the discount sensitivity limit was raised to 12 percent. The IAEA results were not greatly affected by the choice of a discount rate [IAEA (8), Table XVI, p. 28].

The IAEA rates of discount may reflect true capital costs to an individual borrower but probably do not reflect the value to society of alternative uses of the capital. It is this latter rate which should be used if capital scarcities in a country are to be accurately taken into consideration. Use of an 8 percent discount rate plus the generally conservative assumption employed in the "medium" RJBA alternatives would mean that 600 MW nuclear plants become competitive with 600 MW oil-fired plants once delivered fuel oil price (in 1974 dollars) had risen to $6.90. If a 15 percent discount rate were used, the oil price would have to rise to $9.40/barrel, while a 20 percent rate would imply that a 600 MW nuclear plant would not be the preferred choice

Table 4. Delivered electricity costs from 600 MWe generating plant in developing country (1974 prices).

Line	Nuclear[a]		Coal[b]			Oil[c]	
	(A)	(B)	(C)	(D)	(E)	(F)	(G)
I. *Assumptions*							
Fuel price, delivered							
1. Nuclear, $/lb U_3O_8	$20	$20					
2. Coal, $/MT			$15	$45			
3. Fuel oil, $/bbl					$4	$9	$12
4. Capital cost of generating plant, $/KWe	420	712	548	548	420	420	420
5. Discount rate, %	12	20	20	20	20	20	20
6. Capacity factor (CF), %	65	60	60	60	60	60	60

Table 4. (*Contd.*)

Line		Nuclear[a] (A)	(B)	Coal[b] (C)	(D)	(E)	Oil[c] (F)	(G)
7.	Heat rate, Btu/kwh	10,229	10,595	8,805	8,805	8,714	8,714	8,714
8.	Heat content of fuel million Btu/MT			27.8	27.8	6.3	6.3	6.3
II. Cost Elements (expressed in US¢/kwh)								
A. Generating								
9.	Capital	.92	2.72	2.09	2.09	1.60	1.60	1.60
10.	Operating & maintenance	.06	.06	.04	.04	.04	.04	.04
11.	Fuel	.33	.47	.48	1.43	.55	1.24	1.66
12.	Subtotal	1.31	3.25	2.61	3.56	2.19	2.88	3.30
B. Transmission and distribution								
13.	Capital[d]	.57	.92	.92	.92	.92	.92	.92
14.	Losses[e]	.63	1.39	1.18	1.49	1.04	1.27	1.41
15.	Subtotal	1.20	2.31	2.10	2.41	1.96	2.19	2.33
16. C. Total delivered		2.51	5.56	4.71	5.97	4.15	5.07	5.62

Source: Strout (21), Table 4.

[a] Column (A) corresponds to the "IAEA scenario most favorable to nuclear" power, as interpreted by Richard J. Barber Associates (chapter 2). Column (B) represents the RJBA "medium" estimate of nuclear power costs. It is comparable in most of its assumptions to the remaining columns shown for coal and fuel oil.

[b] The $15 figure corresponds to the delivered cost of coal in the U.S. in June 1974 (RJBA, p. 11–19, footnote *). The world foreign trade price in that year was closer to $45/MT or about $1.6 per million Btu.

[c] The $4/bbl ($.63/million Btu) figure is included solely to give an idea of cost elements prior to the early 1970's. Current (1976) delivered prices are closer to $14 in 1976 prices and to $11.50 in 1974 prices. The intermediate price would represent a 25 percent reduction from current costs.

[d] Based on an average cost of transmission and distribution of $240 per kw, from Friedman (5), p. 17. The average ratio of actual to peak demand has been estimated at 60 percent based on the IAEA estimates of future power needs for 14 countries [IAEA (8), p. 7, Table IV]. The annualized value, using calculations analogous to those for line 9, is thus:

$$\frac{1.14155\,(\$240)}{60} \cdot \frac{r}{\left[1 - \left(\frac{1}{1+r}\right)^N\right]}$$

where r = discount rate in %
N = project life in years

[e] Assume 25 percent transmission and distribution losses between the generating plant and the final consumer. Equals (line 12 + line 13) ÷ 3.

below a delivered fuel oil price of $11.40.[18] At 1976 delivered prices for fuel oil of about $11.50 per barrel, this means that even under fairly conservative assumptions, including a 20 percent rate of discount, 600 MW and larger nuclear plants are probably fully competitive with oil plants in many developing countries. If the original 8 percent IAEA discount rate were used with the same assumptions, including the plant cost scale factors adopted by the RJBA report, nuclear plants as small as 250 or 300 MW would not be economical. Thus the "medium" RJBA assumptions *in conjunction with an 8 percent discount rate* would produce nuclear expansion projections, at current petroleum costs, not greatly different from those of the IAEA.[19]

Table 4 has been constructed to show the general structure of electricity costs, except for those arising from different sizes of generating plants. Because of the high capital costs of distribution and transmission and the large line losses which typically occur once the electricity has been generated, it is seen from the table that generating costs may be little more than half of costs paid by the final consumer. Under the low fuel prices which existed prior to the early 1970s (reflected by the assumptions of column E in the table), capital was the major cost factor. The increasing importance of fuel costs in recent years can be seen in line 11, columns E, F, and G.

The cost structure of nuclear power generation does not differ too greatly from that of oil under the low, historical price assumptions (compare columns B and E) although the lower capital costs of oil plants would lend them an economic advantage. As fuel costs increase, the capital advantage of oil decreases until, even at a 20 percent capital discount rate, nuclear plants become more profitable.

The original projections of the IAEA paid little attention to the use of "indigenous" fuels such as coal, lignite, and natural gas, although they did make fairly optimistic assumptions about the growth of hydro generation. The RJBA report correctly criticizes the IAEA on this score, and the column (C) estimates of Table 4 show the cost advantage that coal-fired plants have when indigenous coal supplies are available. If a country could export its coal, however, at prices approaching those of column (D), then nuclear would still be a preferred alternative. The Nuclear Energy Policy Study Group, after careful review of relative costs, concluded that "nuclear power has and will probably continue to have a small economic advantage over coal" both in the United States and elsewhere where coal is locally available [NEPSG (15), pp. 3–4, 11].

Table 4 does not deal with questions of risk and uncertainty which may be more severe for the relatively new nuclear technology. There is distinct possibility, for example, that some nuclear plants (or systems) might have difficulty in operating at a capacity factor as high as 60 percent. Of the world's nuclear powers in 1974, for example, only six (Canada, Netherlands, Belgium,

United Kingdom, Spain, and Switzerland) were able to operate at a system capacity factor of about 60 percent or better. Another five countries (United States, Sweden, West Germany, East Germany, and the USSR) were able to average less than 50 percent of capacity [United Nations (22), Table 18]. For its "unfavorable to nuclear" scenario, the RJBA study assumed a 50 percent capacity factor. This factor alone in conjunction with a 20 percent discount rate and the "medium" assumption of Table 4 would increase minimum nuclear plant size to at least 850 MWe at a delivered oil price of $11.50 per barrel. Adding the assumption of a further 26 percent escalation in plant costs of both nuclear and oil-fired generation would raise the minimum plant size to 1,300 MWe.

It is unlikely, however, that plant costs in *real terms* (that is in relationship to the general level of prices in international trade) are likely to increase as much as assumed under the most conservative RJBA alternative. (Under this alternative the cost of a 1,000 MWe station would be 2.1 times that assumed by the IAEA for nuclear plants and 2.4 times that assumed for oil-fired installations.)[20] It is also to be expected that as time goes by the alternative returns to capital in developing countries will fall, thus reducing the corresponding rate of discount.

Two further points should be made about future costs of power generation. The first is the distinct possibility, examined in the RJBA study (p. III-9) and assumed as an alternative in at least one World Bank document [Lambertini (11), p. 2], that crude oil prices will fall in the future. The present reality is that crude oil prices in real terms have probably fallen slightly from their high point of early 1974 and that this situation is being tolerated by the OPEC countries at least partly out of fear of encountering future energy conservation measures or causing economic slowdowns if oil prices were to be increased further. The "overhang" of surplus OPEC production capacity seems likely to continue for a number of years, contributing to the strains within the cartel. The cartel might even find it advantageous to adopt a two-price system under which LDC's would pay less. This might appeal to the OPEC members' desire to aid development in the world's poorer countries as well as to preserve a petroleum market in those countries which might otherwise be lost to nuclear power.

The second point is that further technological change in conventional power generation is still a possibility. As past changes have tended to conserve capital so future changes may be expected which conserve the new dominant cost element, fuel. The easiest way that this can be done, with no new technological requirements at all, is to combine electrical generation with the provision of process heat for industry. (This is the so-called "cogeneration of electricity" as discussed in NEPSG (15), p. 55.) Energy-use efficiencies by this step, even with relatively small power plants, may immediately be increased from the single-use efficiency of 30–40 percent to two-thirds or better.[21]

A system of small power plants converting two-thirds of their fuel into useful work may have been uneconomical when energy costs were low (because of the higher capital costs of small plants) but may become more than competitive with single-purpose 1,000 MWe plants burning high-cost fuel at one-half the small-plant-system efficiency.

In the case of this option, the innovations needed are institutional rather than technological. The role of industrial (as opposed to public) power generation would have to expand with industries being encouraged to buy peak power from a common grid and sell surplus power to the same grid. This type of arrangement is generally discouraged in countries with utilities organized as they are in the United States and the United Kingdom, and developing countries are prone to regard industrial generators as high-cost indicators of "unsatisfied" public utility demand. Similarly, individual industrial firms cannot afford to generate their own electricity (in competition with a public utility) unless they can buy and sell freely from a common grid and thus avoid high capital costs of peaking and standby capacity. If such an arrangement is permitted by electric grid managers, then industrial self-generating of electricity can be expected to become considerably more widespread.

V. CAN DEVELOPING COUNTRIES AFFORD THE ECONOMIC COST OF NUCLEAR POWER?

This question is sometimes raised because the power needs for economic development are known to increase faster than the rate of gross domestic product and because the capital costs of nuclear power are so much greater than those of fossil generation. The question, however, has little meaning if it is used to raise doubts about a nuclear power choice made using the analytical methods employed by both the IAEA and RJBA. Capital scarcities are explicitly taken into consideration in these analyses through the use of the discount factor. The question posed, given an assumed shortage of capital, is, Which of several systems will be least expensive? If nuclear is the answer, then if a country cannot "afford" nuclear power it will be even less able to afford an alternative source of power. (The controversy between the IAEA and RJBA on this point, it should be noted, revolves not over the use of a capital discount factor but the exact rate chosen. The IAEA rate most closely reflects the private financial cost of capital borrowing while the higher rate proposed by RJBA more nearly reflects the economic worth of capital to the country as a whole.)

Special problems may exist when a country is faced with acute difficulty in earning foreign exchange. This may be handled analytically by assigning a "shadow" value to foreign exchange which is higher than indicated by the current foreign exchange rate and which more nearly reflects longer-run scarcity. This indeed was done in a number of IAEA country analyses [IAEA (7), p. k-2]. The RJBA report also dealt with this point, suggesting that foreign exchange shortages might make the exploitation of indigenous energy sources more attractive. The study also suggested that if a country had to finance power system expansion entirely or largely from its own foreign exchange holding, the larger first cost of nuclear power might argue for choosing fossil fuel instead. The numerical example used in the RJBA report to demonstrate this latter point, however, leads to exactly opposite conclusions if foreign borrowing is possible and if the fossil fuel must be imported. In the case of nuclear and oil-fired units of 600 MWe capacity and assuming a $10 per barrel oil import cost, then the foreign exchange savings in oil import costs would offset the higher initial foreign exchange costs of nuclear construction and nuclear fueling after only 3.4 years of operation [RSBA (19), pp. II-50 to II-51]. In this case a shortage of foreign exchange might thus reinforce the economic advantage of a nuclear over an oil-fired plant.

It is true that electric power consumption and hence power investment in general can be expected to increase at rates faster than GDP. This means only that power investment may account for a larger proportion of total investment and perhaps of foreign exchange borrowings. Even with a complete conversion to nuclear power, the higher investment costs of nuclear plants would lead to only a very small increase in the total share of investment in GDP. Nuclear plants having a 70 percent higher cost than oil plants (see lines 4 in Table 4) might lead to a 50 percent increase in energy sector investment, but this should imply no more than a 3 percent increase in total investment, say from 17 percent of GDP to $17\frac{1}{2}$ percent.[22] This would be an increased cost to the country only in a short-run accounting sense, furthermore, since if nuclear power were truly the most economic choice then the higher capital investment would eventually be offset by lower outlay for fuel.

Thus, there may be some institutional problems in shifting a larger proportion for foreign borrowing into the electric power sector [Friedmann (5), p. 20], but there is no reason why the developing countries, if they can afford electric power at all, cannot afford nuclear power when the economic advantage lies with nuclear power.

What about situations when initial assumptions turn out to have been optimistic, and nuclear power ends up by costing more than a conventional alternative? Or those cases where a country opts for nuclear power on strategic grounds or because it believes that it must gain experience with nuclear power even though it may not yet be economic? What are the economic costs to the country in these situations?

The answer depends partly on the cost difference between nuclear and conventional power and partly on the scale of the nuclear experiment.

Given the most antinuclear assumptions of the RJBA study, including that of a 50 percent plant capacity factor and a 25 percent rate of discount, a country would lose $25 million annually if it were to build a 1,000 MW nuclear plant in place of a 1,000 MW oil-fired plant and if oil were worth $11.50 per barrel [Strout (21), n. 39]. The nuclear plant, nevertheless, might still be financially profitable if the actual cost of borrowing were lower than 25 percent. If the actual interest rate were 12 percent, for example, the nuclear plant might show a "financial" profit of about $11 million per year when compared with the oil-fired alternative. (The economic cost to the country, however, would nevertheless be $25 million per year if the difference in the two investment costs could have been invested elsewhere at a 20 percent rate of return.)

Because the higher capital costs per kilowatt outweigh gains from producing a smaller amount of electricity, a 200 MWe nuclear plant under the above conditions might be more costly than a 1,000 MWe plant. The cost disadvantage of the smaller plant when compared to an oil plant of the same size would amount to $36 million per year. Even with a money cost of only 12 percent the financial losses to the country would be in the order of $14 million annually.

A $14 million annual financial loss would be large in absolute terms but small in relationship to the government budgets of most developing countries. It might be regarded by many countries as a reasonable price to pay for joining the Nuclear Club.

VI. CONCLUSION

The preceding sections have shown that energy use by developing countries can be expected to increase greatly in the future, even under rather conservative assumptions about economic growth rates and the growth of heavy industry. Conventional energy resources remain relatively plentiful and prospects for further increases are good. Energy prices may remain at the high level of the past few years but are unlikely to increase further in real terms, at least for the next decade. There is at least some possibility that crude oil prices may drop in relative terms, and this possibility may be higher for developing countries.

A developing country's choice among competing fuels for power generation can be expected increasingly to favor indigenous sources if only to conserve scarce foreign exchange. Coal-powered plants based on domestic deposits will have a distinct cost advantage over both nuclear and oil. At the current price of oil (assumed to be about $11.50 f.o.b. Persian Gulf in 1976 dollars and about the same price *delivered* in 1974 dollars), nuclear plants in most developing countries would appear to be more economic than oil-fired units when plant size is 600 MWe or greater. Given the known cost factors, the higher degree of uncertainty about nuclear plant costs and operating characteristics as well as the possibility of some further erosion in the price of imported oil, oil-fired plants appear preferable to nuclear in smaller plant sizes. This advantage could be further solidified through future technological or institutional changes which result in improved system-fuel-use efficiencies.

These cautionary remarks, however, should not be interpreted as meaning that the future LDC market for nuclear plants will be unimportant. A large fraction of future LDC power expansion will be most economical using large nuclear installations even under fairly conservative assumptions. To discourage the use of nuclear power in these markets would be to increase significantly the future cost of power generation.

The 1974 International Atomic Energy Agency projections of the LDC nuclear market are summarized in Table 5. Countries in this table are grouped into those whose future systems would mainly employ plants of 600 MWe and larger and countries whose maximum size units would lie below this limit. It can be seen that the size of the nuclear market would remain large, although the number of nuclear-producing countries would be cut by two-thirds, even if all plants of less than 600 MWe should turn out to be uneconomical.

The 1974 IAEA projections were prepared prior to capital cost increases which have made smaller-sized nuclear plants less competitive.[23] They appear to be overly optimistic in other ways as well, and they have been accordingly adjusted downward in Table 6 to reflect (a) lower rates of anticipated electric power growth for certain countries, (b) the increased use of indigenous fuel resources, and (c) the elimination of most nuclear plants below 600 MWe. The result is to lower the nuclear power estimate for 1960 by more than one-half and for the year 2000 by almost half. (Note that the elimination of smaller plants accounts for a relatively small fraction of these decreases.) Of the 244,000 MWe downward adjustment in nuclear power for 2000, 138,000 MWe would be compensated for by a higher use of indigenous fossil fuels. (The increased exploitation of geothermal resources will also undoubtedly occur and should be included in these totals.) Another 106,000 MWe may simply not be needed if the demand assumptions discussed earlier in this paper should turn out to be accurate.

The trend toward increased use of nuclear installations, however, is nevertheless apparent from Table 6, even though the nuclear share does not increase as rapidly as with the IAEA projections. Nuclear power, according to Table 6, might represent 19 percent of total generating capacity in 1990 and 36 percent by the year 2000.[24] Although country detail has not been prepared for the Table 6 projections, it is assumed that the same "large nuclear" countries will be producing nuclear power in the future as under the IAEA projections. In 1990 the list should include India, Pakistan, Taiwan,

Table 5. International Atomic Energy Agency projections of total and nuclear electrical generating capacity, developing countries with nuclear potential, 1990 and 2000.

Country group and nuclear plant size*	No. of Countries	1990 Capacity ('000 MWe) Fossil	1990 Capacity ('000 MWe) Nuclear	1990 Capacity ('000 MWe) Hydro	1990 Capacity ('000 MWe) Total	No. of Countries	2000 Capacity ('000 MWe) Fossil	2000 Capacity ('000 MWe) Nuclear	2000 Capacity ('000 MWe) Hydro	2000 Capacity ('000 MWe) Total
I. Non-OPEC										
Low income										
Large nuclear	2[a]	29.2	36.3	47.8	113.3	3[c]	30.3	145.9	67.3	243.5
Small nuclear	3[b]	1.6	5.2	3.2	10.0	2[c]	3.0	15.3	3.9	22.2
Middle income										
Large nuclear	4[d]	13.2	23.3	8.9	45.4	4	14.2	58.7	11.8	84.7
Small nuclear	6[e]	1.6	1.6	3.7	6.9	6	3.0	6.5	5.9	14.5
Higher income										
Large nuclear	6[f]	32.3	57.4	72.8	162.5	9[h]	44.1	189.6	103.1	336.8
Small nuclear	14[g]	18.3	16.6	10.2	45.1	11[h]	13.9	30.9	6.3	51.1
II. OPEC										
Large nuclear	2[i]	12.8	14.4	11.4	38.6	3[k]	14.0	42.1	22.8	78.9
Small nuclear	8[j]	6.7	5.5	2.9	15.1	7[k]	8.2	12.2	2.3	22.7
III. Other										
Turkey (large)	1	3.4	5.0	10.5	18.9	1	3.5	23.3	13.6	40.4
Cuba (small)	1	2.6	2.1	—	4.7	1	2.6	5.5	—	8.1
IV. All developing countries										
Large nuclear	15	90.9	136.4	151.4	378.7	20	106.1	459.6	218.6	784.3
Small nuclear	32	30.8	31.0	20.0	81.8	27	30.7	70.4	17.5	118.6
TOTAL	47	121.7	167.4	171.4	460.5	47	136.8	530.0	236.1	902.9

Source: International Atomic Energy Agency (8), Tables XIII and XIV, and RJBA (19), pp. II–35c, 35d and 42b.
*"Large nuclear" countries are those with projected nuclear plants in the year shown of 600 MWe or more. "Small nuclear" countries are projected to have no nuclear plants in the year shown which are as large as 600 MWe.
[a] India and Pakistan.
[b] Bangladesh, Vietnam (South), and Uganda.
[c] Bangladesh shifts from the small to the large category.
[d] Egypt, South Korea, Philippines, and Thailand.
[e] Cameroon, Ghana, Morocco, Syria, Bolivia, and El Salvador.
[f] Argentina, Brazil, Colombia, Mexico, Taiwan, and Singapcre.
[g] Peru, Hongkong, Chile, Malaysia, Israel, Uruguay, Jamaica, Lebanon, Costa Rica, Dominican Republic, Panama, Tunisia, Guatemala, and Zambia.
[h] Countries shifting from small to large are: Chile, Peru, and Hong Kong.
[i] Iran and Venezuela.
[j] Indonesia, Kuwait, Iraq, Nigeria, Algeria, Ecuador and Saudi Arabia.
[k] Indonesia shifts from the small to the large category.

Table 6. Proposed adjustments to IAEA projections of nuclear and other generating plant capacity, developing countries with nuclear potential, 1990 and 2000.

	Installed capacity ('000 MWe)			
	Fossil	Nuclear	Hydro	Total
1990				
IAEA Total[a]	121.7	167.4	171.4	460.5
(% by fuel type)	(27%)	(37%)	(37%)	(100%)
Adjustments				
Increased exploitation indigenous fuel:				
Coal (Bangladesh, Indonesia, Turkey)	6.2[b]	−6.2	0	0
Natural gas (Bangladesh)	2.1[c]	−3.8[c]	0	−1.7[c]
Reduced growth rates:				
India[d]	15.0	−22.4	−14.6	−22.0
Higher income, non-OPEC[e]	6.0	−46.7	0	−40.7
Elimination most nuclear plants below 600 MWe	14.4	−14.4[f]	0	0
Subtotal, adjustments	43.7	−93.5	−14.6	−64.4
Adjusted Totals, 1990	165.4	73.9	156.8	396.1
(% by fuel type)	(42%)	(19%)	(39%)	(100%)
2000				
IAEA Total[a]	136.8	530.0	236.1	902.9
(% by fuel type)	(15%)	(59%)	(26%)	(100%)
Adjustments				
Increased exploitation indigenous fuel:				
Coal (Bangladesh, Indonesia, Turkey)	18.7[b]	−18.7	0	0
Natural gas (Bangladesh)	3.6	−3.6	0	0?
Reduced growth rates:				
India[d]	63.0	−94.0	0	−31.0
Higher income, non-OPEC	13.4	−88.4	0	−75.0
Elimination most nuclear plants below 600 MWe	39.5	−39.5	0	0
Subtotal, all adjustments	138.2	−244.2	0	−106.0
Adjusted Totals, Year 2000	275.0	285.8	236.1	796.9
(% by fuel type)	(34%)	(36%)	(30%)	(100%)

[a]International Atomic Energy Agency totals from Table 5.

Table 6 (*Contd.*)

[b]Additional fossil fuel plant capacity, over and above that projected by the IAEA, representing exploitation of indigenous coal reserves such that one-half of coal is consumed by the year 2000:

('000 MWe)

	1974 Thermal capacity (UN, 1976, Table 18)	Estimated coal additions by 2000*	1974 Cap. + coal additions	Year 2000 total thermal capacity Total estimated by IAEA**	Increase†
India	12.0	78.0	90.0	27.0	63.0
Brazil	3.0	13.5	16.5	3.1	13.4
Turkey	2.1	12.5	14.6	3.5	11.1
Indonesia	.8	4.0	4.8	1.1	3.7
Bangladesh	.7	4.3	5.0	1.1	3.9

*Estimates from Richard J. Barber Associates (19), pp. II–40, 43.
**IAEA (8), Table XIII.
†For the year 2000. The 1990 increase is assumed to be one-third of the amounts shown.

[c]Represents increased gas plant capacity and decreased total generating capacity (for 1990). Compare IAEA [(8), Table VI, p. 10] with IAEA (9) p. 131, Table XV-2.

[d]See text for a discussion of the Indian electricity consumption estimates. Changes shown here assume that Indian generating capacity grows as follows:

	1974–1980	1980–1990	1990–2000
Total capacity	8.6% p.a.	9.0% p.a.	9.0% p.a.
Fossil fuels	8.0	8.0	8.0*
Nuclear	IAEA est.**	8.0	14.3
Hydro	residual	residual	IAEA est.**

*Conforms with RJBA estimate of increased coal-burning capacity. See note b.
**IAEA (8).

Table 6. (Contd.)

^eSee text. Assumes that for the countries with nuclear potential in this subgroup, generating capacity increases at the same rate as does electric consumption for the total subgroup. From Table 3 this is seen to be about 7.0% p.a. during 1974–1980 and 6.5% p.a. during 1980–2000. IAEA estimates were used for hydro and fossil capacity except that increased coal capacity was added for Brazil as shown in note b, above. Nuclear capacity was then taken as a residual. The revised growth rates for capacity increases are thus:

	1980–1990	*1990–2000*
Total	6.5% p.a.	6.5% p.a.
(cf. IAEA est.*)	(8.6%)	(6.5%)
of which: Hydro	7.3	2.8
Fossil	2.2	2.6
Nuclear	22.5	16.4
(cf. IAEA est., nuclear*)	(29.2)	(11.5)

*IAEA (8).

^fPlants of under 600 MWe capacity. Equals sum of all "small nuclear" countries from Table 5, except for the higher income, non-OPEC subgroups where the nuclear reductions described in the previous footnote would probably have already eliminated most of the smaller nuclear systems. Also not included are minor amounts of small-plant capacity in Thailand and Singapore (1990) and in Bangladesh, Thailand, and Indonesia (2000).

Republic of Korea, Iran, Turkey, Egypt, the Philippines, and possibly Thailand and Singapore. The Latin American producers would consist of Mexico, Brazil, Argentina, Venezuela, and probably Colombia (although Colombian coal remains a largely unexploited and unexplored alternative). By the year 2000, the LDC nuclear group should have added Hong Kong, Peru and Chile. Active exploitation of indigenous gas and coal resources may raise questions about the nuclear role of Bangladesh. Indonesia is firmly anticipating a nuclear future but may have second thoughts about using its reportedly very large coal reserves whose only presently contemplated use is for exports to Japan.

Whether the nuclear producing group is enlarged beyond the above list of twenty countries depends very much upon the future cost and availability of smaller-size nuclear plants and upon how much individual countries may be willing to pay to join the Nuclear Club. The possibility of a future market for small (especially 300 MWe and under) nuclear plants is dismissed almost unequivocally by the U.S. nuclear industry. [RJBA (19), V-72 ff.] The grounds for dismissal are the probable high cost and the fact that such reactors are not yet available commercially. The IAEA, however, has been actively promoting the idea of a small plant market for a number of years. Two staff members reported in early 1976 that

Three organizations (Technicatome, France; Interatom, F. R. Germany; and UKAEA and/or Fairey Engineering of UK) which have designs for plants in the size range 92–345 MWe have informed the IAEA that they would respond reasonably promptly to a bid invitation. The reactor system (pressurized light water and steam generating heavy water) which these organizations propose are stated to be based on present, proven reactor technology. The light water reactors are essentially land-based versions of French and German ship propulsion reactors while the heavy water reactor design is based upon the SGHWR plant at Winfrith in the United Kingdom. [Polliart and Goodman (18), p. 43].

None of the three firms mentioned are currently major suppliers for the nuclear electric power market, but this may increase their appetite for a small and presently neglected share of that market.

FOOTNOTES

*Lecturer, Department of Urban Studies and Planning, Massachusetts Institute of Technology. The study was undertaken with Ford Foundation support while the author was a Research Affiliate with the MIT Energy Laboratory. An earlier version appeared as MIT Energy Laboratory Working Paper No. MIT-EL 77-006WP (Strout, 1977).

1. Four of the developed country studies are cited in Richard J. Barber Associates (19, pp. I-29 to I-38). At earlier stages of development, higher fuel prices should undoubtedly lead to some savings in energy use, especially in the longer run as more efficient machinery and processes can be introduced. Attempts to measure the relevant "price elasticities" are complicated by lack of data and by the fact that price changes in competing fuels should be looked at simultaneously. It is probable, however, that price elasticities in developing countries are much lower than in richer countries. One World Bank study, for example, found price elasticities for petroleum products in the order of − .06 to − .11 [Lambertini (11), Annex II, pp. 11–12]. Neither elasticity, however, was significantly different from zero. For developed countries, in contrast, other internal Bank studies have assumed an overall energy price elasticity of − .15. (Much of the Bank's conclusions about developed countries are derived from a "Simrich" model described in Gunning, et. al. (6), pp. 41–51).

2. Commodities included in the energy-intensive materials category were those which consume large quantities of energy under 1967 U.S. technological conditions and for which fairly homogeneous production statistics were available in physical units for a large number of countries. The commodity group is considerably more narrow than "heavy industry," as usually defined, in that it does not include materials fabrication. In many countries, however, the production of these energy-intensive materials will be strongly correlated with the broader category, heavy industry.

3. For statistical computations reported in the current study, the energy-intensive materials group includes basic iron and steel, other primary metals (aluminium, copper, lead, zinc, and tin), fertilizer production (measured by NPK content), hydraulic cement, pulp, paper and paperboard.

4. In Figures 1 and 2 a crude effort has been made to show per capita incomes in

comparable purchasing power dollars. This has been done by fitting a regression to the ten GDP price indexes (USA = 100) shown in Kravis, et al. (10) Table 1.5, p. 9. The fitted regression was then used to calculate crude GDP price indexes for all countries, and these price indexes were divided into observed per capita GDP (based on official exchange rates) to give an approximate adjustment for purchasing power comparability. The exact relationship was:

$$\ln \text{YGDP} = .834 + .477 \ln\left(\frac{\text{GDP}}{\text{POP}} + 500\right) - .071 \ln \text{POP}$$
$$(1.85) \quad (7.92) \quad\quad\quad\quad\quad\quad\quad (1.93)$$

$\overline{R}^2 = .871$, standard error of estimate $= .134$
(t-ratios are in parentheses)
where YGDP = GDP purchasing power index (USA = 100) from Kravis, et al., for 1970
GDP = Gross Domestic Product converted into U.S. dollars at official exchange rates, mean 1969/1970, from United Nations, *Monthly Bulletin of Statistics*, January 1975.
POP = mid-year population, 1970 (U.N. data)
ln = natural logarithm

The graphical results shown in Figures 1 and 2 are not greatly sensitive to the particular form chosen for the above regression.

5. The country grouping is the same as that used for World Bank Staff Working Paper No. 229 [Lambertini (11), Annex III]. The low income non-OPEC countries had 1972 per capita incomes below $200, and the higher income group, above $375.

6. For further details of definitions and for source of the data see United Nations 22, p. x–xxiv.

7. J. A. Lane, "Long-Range Forecasting of the Demand for Electrical Energy" [IAEA (9), Appendix D, p. 185]. Lane's demand-path chart is based upon the "Aoki method" of electricity demand forecasting described in the 1973 IAEA nuclear power market survey report [IAEA (7), Appendix F]. To calculate an implicit GDP growth rate for India, 1970 data for India from IAEA sources [IAEA, (8), Table VIII] were used and the assumption was made that 1970–1980 population growth continued at the 1963–1970 rate of 2.1 percent per year.

8. For five of the higher income countries IAEA growth rate assumptions are available in IAEA (7), p. 10. Other GDP growth rates were taken from Felix (4), Part Two. This latter source was referred to by J. A. Lane in the article cited in the previous footnote and seems to have been the basis for IAEA GDP projections when other sources were not available.

9. The model is associated with the name of H. Aoki and is briefly described in H. Aoki. "Long Range Forecasting of the Demand for Electrical Energy" [IAEA (7), Appendix F]. See also H. Aoki (1). A more up-to-date description of the current IAEA procedure is given in J. A. Lane, "Long Range Forecasting ..." [IAEA (9), Appendix D]. While the electricity/GDP relationship is basically that obtained from cross-country analysis for the year 1968, countries whose initial positions lie above or below the "normal" or "universal" curve are assumed to move closer to the norm as time progresses.

10. The logarithmic slopes for the three country groups may be compared with those from Figure 3 as follows:

Medium-run 1960–73	Mean per capita GDP, 1973	Linear slope Fig. 3	Log-linear Slope
Low income	$ 101	1.15	6.75
Middle income	263	1.05	3.68
Higher income	652	.90	1.88
Long-run, cross-country			1.39

11. The United Nations (22), Table 2. "Developing country" as used in the present study conforms to the World Bank definition and differs from that of the U.N. by excluding Turkey, Cuba, Greenland, Puerto Rico, and the Panama Canal Zone and by including Israel.

12. Harry Perry (16). The Perry estimates were derived through rather crude correlations between past GNP growth and energy consumptions but nevertheless indicate the rough orders of magnitude for future demand. Consumption by developing countries is projected to increase at the rate of 6.5. percent annually between 1980 and 2000, a result remarkably close to the 6.4. percent rate projected for the non-OPEC countries in Table 2. (Both studies assumed weighted average LDC growth rates of GDP of about 5.3–5.4 percent per year.) Consumption for the nondeveloping portion of the world, including China, was projected to increase at the rate of only 2.9 percent annually, thus resulting in a further increase of the LDC relative share.

13. Harry Perry (17). "Proved recoverable" nonrenewable energy resources are estimated at 32.8 Btu $\times$ 10^{18} as of 1972. The demand forecasts cited in the previous footnote suggest that these recoverable reserves (of which 73 percent are coal and only 4 percent are uranium) would be just about fully exhausted by 2025 if no use at all were made of renewable energy resources. Renewable energy resources, particularly hydropower, would of course be used, and Perry also estimates that an *additional* 200 Btu $\times$ 10^{18} of energy resources will be discovered in the earth's crust and will be recoverable at prices prevailing in the future. See also Nuclear Energy Policy Study Group (15), p. 3.

14. Lambertini (11), Tables 1 and 5. The consumption estimates in the Lambertini report appear to start from a higher base than would seem indicated by the latest United Nations estimates and to grow at a slower rate than projected in the present study. Total 1980 demand as estimated by Lambertini, however, is only slightly less than that shown in Table 2 of this study. For the non-OPEC developing countries as a whole, assuming no relative change in future oil prices, the difference between 1980 supply and demand as given by Lambertini would be seven percent. The 1980 difference using the Lambertini supply forecast and the demand projections from the present study would be nine percent.

15. Lambertini (11), p. 6, Table 3. The estimates shown are for "medium term" reserves. For oil and natural gas (one-fourth of the total), they are estimates of amounts economically recoverable at current prices and costs, for coal (65 percent of the total) and nuclear power (6 percent) they are the "measured or reasonably assured fraction of resources which should be economically exploited in the coming five years," while for hydro power (2 percent) all estimated reserves have been included. The total of 22,320 million metric tons of oil equivalent or 930 Btu $\times$ 10^{15} compares with 1973–2000 cumulative production of 1056 Btu $\times$ 10^{15} based upon the projections of Table 2.

16. See the series of fourteen country studies summarized in International Atomic

Energy Agency (7). The cost calculating procedures are described in lengthy appendices included with each of the reports and with the General Report.

17. In a follow-up report made after the full impact of the oil price increases had been felt, the IAEA examined a group of fifty countries outside of the Soviet bloc, mostly LDC's but including such transitional countries as Spain, Yugoslavia, Greece, Turkey, and Israel. Between 1980 and 2000 the IAEA estimated that nuclear power would account for 75 percent of all expansions in generating capacity while 20 percent would be hydro. Only 5 percent would consist of fossil fuel plants. (See also Table 5, below.) The fifty-country sample includes almost all electrical generating capacity in the developing world. See IAEA (8), Table XIII. By mid-1976, however, it appears that increases in capital costs were sufficient to modify the IAEA's earlier optimism, and nuclear projections were revised sharply downward. See below, footnote 23.

18. See Table 4. The assumptions upon which these calculations are based differ from the RJBA "medium" assumptions only in the heat content of oil where a 6.3 instead of a 6.0 million Btu/barrel figure has been used for the present study. With nuclear plant costs of $712/KWe and oil of $420/KWe, the "break-even" oil cost (line 11 in Table 4) is found from:

Oil cost (¢/kwh) = .47 + 5.555 CRF

where CRF = Capital Recovery Factor

$$= \frac{r}{1 - \left(\frac{1}{1+r}\right)^N}$$

and r = discount rate (%/100)
N = project life in years (= 30)

19. The IAEA study found that nuclear plants as small as 150 MWe would in some cases be competitive. The 150 – 200 MW nuclear plants, however, accounted for only 5 percent of the estimated 1981–1990 additions to nuclear capacity. [IAEA, (8), Table XIV.] This share of the market is important from the nuclear proliferation standpoint, however. The IAEA study indicates that nineteen developing countries would adopt nuclear power *only* if plants as small as 150 and 200 MW become available.

20. Richard J. Barber Associates (19), p. II–37, Figure II–13. See also IAEA (8), p. 27, Table XV, where the costs are specified as being in January 1, 1974, U.S. dollars. (The RJBA report is rather vague at times about the year in which prices are quoted, but they seem to be generally for 1974.)

21. See Bohm (2). Nuclear-based complexes of industrial and agricultural activity ("nuplexes") were a fond dream of nuclear scientists in the 1960s [Michel and Mrochek (14) and Delyannis (3)]. This idea seems to have been discouraged by the recent concern over reactor safety, but an adaptation of the multipurpose idea to small plants would make good economic sense at today's fuel prices.

22. This calculation assumes that (a) nuclear investment for the same size plant exceeds its conventional alternative by 70 percent, (b) energy investment as a share of GDP is 1.8 percent and under conventional power plant conditions would consist of 70 percent power investment, of which 60 percent would be for generating plants.

23. Based on mid-1976 costs the IAEA has itself reached the conclusion that 600 MWe oil-fired plants could generate electricity about as cheaply as could 600 MWe nuclear plants. The situation may have become even less favorable for nuclear power thereafter [Lane (12)].

24. The Table 6 estimates, prepared in mid-1976, are within the range of IAEA forecasts presented to the May 1977 International Conference on Nuclear Power and Its Cycle (Salzburg, Austria). These forecasts show a 49,000 to 88,000 MWe range for

developing countries outside of Eastern Europe in 1990, as compared to 74,000 MWe from Table 6. For the year 2000, the 1977 IAEA forecast was 209,000 to 317,000 MWe compared to 286,000 MWe from Table 6. For the developing countries plus six Eastern European countries, the share of nuclear was reduced from the 1973–1974 estimate of 50–60 percent of installed capacity to 27–40 percent by the year 2000. [Lane, et al. (13), p. 5 and Table II.]

REFERENCES

1. Aoki, H., *New Method of Long Range or Very Long Range Demand Forecast of Energy, Including Electricity, Viewed from a Worldwide Standpoint*. Electric Power Development Co., Ltd, Tokyo, 1974.
2. Bohn, E., "Nuclear Power Plants for Combined Power and Heat Supply," in *Small and Medium Size Power Reactors*. Proceedings of a Panel, Vienna, June, 24–28, 1968, International Atomic Energy Agency, Vienna, 1969.
3. Delyannis, A. A., *Nuclear Energy Centers and Agro-Industrial Complexes*. Technical Reports Series 140, International Atomic Energy Agency, Vienna, 1972.
4. Felix, Fremont, *World Markets of Tomorrow*. Harper and Row, New York, 1972.
5. Friedmann, Efrain, "Financing of Power Expansion for Developing Countries," in *International Atomic Energy Agency Bulletin*, vol. 17 (December 1975), 13–24.
6. Gunning, J. W., M. Osterrieth, and J. Waelbroech, "The Price of Energy and Potential Growth of Developed Countries, An Attempt at Quantification," in *European Economic Review*, vol. 7 (January 1976), 35–62.
7. International Atomic Energy Agency, *Market Survey for Nuclear Power in Developing Countries: General Report*. International Atomic Energy Agency, Vienna, 1973.
8. ———, *Market Survey for Nuclear Power in Developing Countries*, 1974 edition. International Atomic Energy Agency, Vienna, 1974.
9. ———, *Nuclear Power Planning Study for Bangladesh*. International Atomic Energy Agency, Vienna, 1975.
10. Kravis, Irving B., Zoltan Kenessey, Alan Heston, and Robert Summers, *A System of International Comparisons of Gross Product and Purchasing Power*. Johns Hopkins University Press for the World Bank, Baltimore, 1975.
11. Lambertini, Adrian, "Energy and Petroleum in Non-OPEC Developing Countries, 1974–1980," World Bank Staff Working Paper No. 229, February 1976.
12. Lane, J. A., personal communication, June 3, 1977.
13. ———, A. J. Covarrubias, B. J. Csik, A. Fattah, and G. Woite, "Nuclear Power in Developing Countries," paper no. IAEA-CN-36/500, prepared for International Conference on Nuclear Power and Its Fuel Cycle, Salzburg, Austria, May, 2–13, 1977.
14. Michel, J. W., and J. E. Mrochek, "Recent Developments in the Agro-Industrial Complex Studies at Oak Ridge National Laboratory," in *Nuclear Energy Costs and Economic Development*. Proceedings of a Symposium, Istambul, October 20–24, 1969, International Atomic Energy Agency, Vienna, 1970.
15. Nuclear Energy Policy Study Group (NEPSG), *Nuclear Power Issues and Choices*. Ballinger Publishing Co., Cambridge, Mass., 1977.
16. Perry, Harry, "Energy Demand—World Less the United States," unpublished working paper prepared for Resources for the Future, April 6, 1976.
17. ———, "World Energy Resources and Reserves and Estimated Production Rates," unpublished working paper prepared for Resources for the Future, February 18, 1976.
18. Polliart, Andre-Jacques, and Eli Goodman, "Prospects for Utilization of Nuclear

Power in Africa," *International Atomic Energy Agency Bulletin*, vol. 18 (February 1976), pp. 40–43.
19. Richard J. Barber Associates (RJBA), *LDC Nuclear Power Prospects, 1975–1980: Commercial, Economic and Security Implications*. Report prepared for the Energy Research and Development Administration, ERDA-52, 1975. Distributed by the National Technical Information Service of the U.S. Department of Commerce.
20. Strout, Alan M., "Energy and the Less Developed Countries: Needs for Additional Research," in Ronald G. Ridker, ed., *Changing Resource Problems of the Fourth World*. Resources for the Future, Washington, D. C., February 1976. Distributed by The Johns Hopkins University Press, Baltimore.
21. ———, "The Future of Nuclear Power in the Developing Countries," report prepared for the Nuclear Energy Policy Study Group, MIT Energy Laboratory Working Paper No. MIT-EL 77-006WP, 1977.
22. United Nations, *World Energy Supplies, 1950–1974*. Statistical Papers Series J, no. 19, United Nations, New York, 1976.

FINANCIAL MARKETS AND THE ADJUSTMENT TO HIGHER OIL PRICES

Tamir Agmon, TEL AVIV UNIVERSITY

Donald Lessard, MASSACHUSETTS INSTITUTE OF TECHNOLOGY

James L. Paddock, MASSACHUSETTS INSTITUTE OF TECHNOLOGY*

I. INTRODUCTION

A great deal has been written about the actual and potential effects of the oil price increase on world financial markets, but relatively little emphasis has been placed on the role played by financial markets in the adjustment of the energy markets themselves. This paper explores the linkages between energy and financial markets and points out why these should be taken into account in interpreting energy market adjustments.

The existence of financial markets allows several degrees of freedom which otherwise would not exist. Immediate adjustment to current account balance is not required, as claims on future output of goods and services can be exchanged for oil. Since producer countries can hold claims on future goods as well as oil reserves which they can exchange for goods in the future, they may alter their output and pricing decisions from what they would be in the absence of financial markets. Furthermore, the risk and return characteristics of the claims issued by net consumers of oil need not be the same as those desired by oil producers since these can be altered through financial intermediation. Finally, since the future consumption of the producer countries will depend on returns from their financial portfolios as well as future oil sales, they will have to consider the impact of their output and pricing decisions on financial markets in making these decisions.

Section II of this paper analyzes the role of international financial markets in accommodating the change in oil prices. In particular, it examines the pattern of adjustment over time among importing and exporting countries as they respond to both transitory and permanent changes in relative prices and income. It is shown, by means of a general equilibrium model, that multilateral trade in financial claims (international financial intermediation) facilitates an otherwise unobtainable continuation of physical flows of oil. This accommodation should be reflected in the observed elasticities of demand for oil. Available empirical evidence on accommodation through financial markets is examined.

Section III presents a portfolio approach to the behavior of the oil-exporting countries with respect to their "surplus funds." It focuses on their investment decisions and the possible feedback of these on their pricing and production decisions. Finally, Section IV briefly describes the creation of stress in the international financial system, and the implications of this stress for the behavior of oil-exporting countries.

II. FINANCIAL MARKETS AND ADJUSTMENTS IN ENERGY MARKETS

The radical increase of the price of oil at the end of 1973 brought about a transfer of wealth from the oil-importing countries to the oil-exporting countries and changed desired patterns of consumption and investment for both groups. The resulting exchanges between the two groups were of two types: exchanges of oil for current real consumption and investment goods, and exchanges of oil for financial claims on future real consumption and investment goods.

The major vehicle for the transfer of current consumption from the oil-importing countries to the oil-exporting countries was the trade of goods and services for oil. OPEC imports of goods and services rose sharply in 1974 and have been growing ever since. Table 1 below presents the actual imports of goods and services for the period 1973–1976 and the preliminary figures for 1977.

Financial Markets and Higher Oil Prices

Table 1. OPEC Imports of Goods and Services
(billions of dollars)

	1973	1974	1975	1976	1977ᵖ
Imports of goods, fob	N/A	36	59	70	82
Imports of services	N/A	15	23	30	36
Total imports	20	51	82	100	118

Sources: Morgan Guaranty, *World Financial Markets*, September 1976; *Direction of Trade, Annual* 1969–75.
p = preliminary.

In addition to these current exchanges, substantial exchanges of oil for claims on future consumption took place. The volume of these transfers for the period 1974–1977 is presented in Table 2 below.

The first type of exchange has been referred to as "paying" for oil, while the second type of exchange has been termed "financing" oil.[1] The transfer of claims for future goods, "financing," is also called recycling. A further distinction is drawn between primary and secondary recycling.[2] Primary recycling refers to the direct issue of claims on future goods (financial assets which hereafter are termed "bonds") by an oil-importing country to an oil-exporting country. Secondary recycling refers to multilateral exchanges of bonds among oil-importing countries which eventually result in a net transfer of such claims to oil-exporting countries. This net transfer facilitates the flow of oil from exporters to importers. For example, Italy may borrow from (issue bonds to) the United States and Germany, and these countries in turn may borrow from (issue bonds to) OPEC countries. The recycling process takes place in a world in which there is multilateral trade in goods as well, and hence some secondary recycling may be accommodated by current exchanges of goods among the oil-importing countries.

An increase in the relative price of oil changes the allocation of real income and wealth between oil-importers and oil-exporters. Total spending by the two groups will change in obvious directions. The changes in desired spending will depend on how each group views the long-term redistribution

Table 2. OPEC Current Account Surplus
(billions of dollars)

	1974	1975	1976	1977ᵖ
Four Arabian peninsula countries	37.0	N/A	32.3	33.6
Rest of OPEC	27.7	N/A	5.3	0.5
Total	64.7	32.0	37.6	34.1

Source: Morgan Guaranty, *World Financial Markets*, September 1976 and June 1977.
p = preliminary.

of real income resulting from the change in the relative price of oil. The change in actual spending will further depend on the cost of adjusting the rate of spending over time. The real wealth transfer is the present value of the real income changes for all future periods. This wealth transfer, however, may be considerably smaller than suggested by the immediate change in real income. Both the oil-importing and the oil-exporting countries may view the current transfer of real income as reflecting both permanent and transitory elements.

Transitory elements arise for two reasons. First, it takes time to adjust the consumption patterns of the oil-importing countries to the new distribution of wealth, especially when the increase in the price of oil is not fully anticipated. This adjustment time is even more pronounced given the intermediate nature of oil in the production function of the importing group. Until new real investments are made which reflect the new relative price of oil, existing capital-in-place must be used. Once the productive base is changed, however, the demand for oil will become more elastic and the permanent real income transfer will be smaller. Second, there is uncertainty regarding the stability of the new price. If the monopolistic position of the oil-exporting cartel is eroded, perhaps by new technologies which create competition for oil, or by conflicts over price or quantity within the cartel, the future oil price in real terms may be lower than today's price. This also implies a smaller total transfer of real wealth.

The transitory element in the current transfer of real income from the oil-importing countries to the oil-exporting countries gives rise to both primary and secondary recycling. The oil-importing countries realize that the current decline in real income includes a component of transitory loss, and thus they will borrow in order to transfer income from future periods to the current period to reduce transitory changes in their consumption. Also, while adjusting production processes to the new relative price of oil, they must work with the pre-increase system of production and thus their demand for oil will be relatively inelastic in the short term. All these considerations lead the oil-importing countries to adjust more slowly to the new circumstances. If a current account deficit results, they will borrow on capital account to finance the deficit.

Oil-exporting countries face an analogous situation. They too realize that a portion of the shift in income is transitory and, as a result, increase their current consumption by less than the full increase in real income. They can do this by acquiring real capital goods to be employed in the domestic economy or financial claims on other countries. However, the existing physical infrastructure may limit the absorptive capacity for real investment and, thus, much of the adjustment will take place in financial markets.

The simplest adjustment in the international capital market following a change in the terms of trade is a bilateral exchange of capital assets, or in

Financial Markets and Higher Oil Prices

other words, borrowing and lending. In a two-country world in which one country is a net oil-exporter and one country is a net oil-importer, primary recycling (direct bilateral borrowing and lending) will suffice to accommodate the effect of transitory elements and provide the time needed for change to new permanent output and consumption patterns. However, once more than two countries are introduced primary recycling alone may be suboptimal, and financial intermediation either through private markets or public institutions may be desirable. It is a common belief that the gains from multilateral trade are greater than those of a series of bilateral trade arrangements. The same argument applies to trade in financial assets and will favor a mixture of primary and secondary recycling through intermediaries as the mechanism for adjustment.

The precise nature of multilateral trade, whether in goods or financial assets, can be described in a simple general equilibrium, full-employment paradigm as follows.

Assume a three-country world. One country is a net oil-exporter (country X) and the other two countries, 1 and 2, are net oil-importers. Within each one of the three countries there are three all-inclusive markets. One market is for oil and the other two markets are for other goods and bonds. Without loss of generality, let us assume that the importing countries each specialize in one type of composite good and one type of bond—a contract for the future delivery of the good they produce—respectively, and that the oil-exporting country produces no other goods and no bonds. Assume further that trade in oil, in other goods, and in bonds can take place only on a bilateral basis between the oil-exporting country and each one of the oil-importing countries directly. For now, no trade is allowed between the two oil-importing countries.

In such a world of "pure" primary recycling, the world excess demand for oil can be defined as a function of the relative prices in the two importing countries, i.e.

$$E_{x1} = E_{x1}(P_{x/g1}, P_{x/b1}) \tag{1}$$

and

$$E_{x2} = E_{x2}(P_{x/g2}, P_{x/b2}) \tag{2}$$

where: E_{xj} ≡ excess demand for oil (denoted by subscript x) in importing country j measured in some unit of account

$P_{x/gj}$ ≡ price of oil in terms of other good j, j = 1,2 oil-importing countries

$P_{x/bj}$ ≡ price of oil in terms of bond j, j = 1,2 oil-importing countries

Bonds are claims on future goods and thus share the risk characteristics associated with the future relative price of such goods.

The excess demand for goods and bonds is also a function of the relative prices and can be defined as:

$$E_{gj} \equiv E_{gj}(P_{gj/x}, P_{gj/bj}); \quad j = 1, 2 \text{ oil-importing countries} \tag{3}$$

$$E_{bj} \equiv E_{bj}(P_{bj/x}, P_{bj/gj}); \quad j = 1, 2 \text{ oil-importing countries} \tag{4}$$

where
$E_{gj} \equiv$ excess demand for other goods in country j
$E_{bj} \equiv$ excess demand for bonds in country j

all measured in some unit of account.

Given our assumption of the bilateral nature of the trade in oil (where one country is a net oil-exporter and the other two are net oil-importers) and because the three markets are all inclusive, it follows that:

$$E_{xj} > 0 \quad j = 1, 2 \text{ oil-importing countries}$$
$$E_{gj} \leq 0 \quad j = 1, 2 \text{ oil-importing countries}$$
$$E_{bj} \leq 0 \quad j = 1, 2 \text{ oil-importing countries}$$

and
$$E_{gj} + E_{bj} < 0 \quad j = 1, 2 \text{ oil-importing countries.}$$

For the exporting country (country X) the excess demand for oil is negative (net exporter) and equal in value terms to the sum of the oil-exporter's excess demands for goods and bonds of the two importing countries 1 and 2. In equilibrium the world system maintains:

$$E_{oil} + E_{goods} + E_{bonds} = 0, \quad \text{in value terms.} \tag{5}$$

However, given the assumption of bilateral trade, equation (5) is just the sum of equations (1) to (4). The export of oil by country X, $-E_{xx}$ (measured in physical terms), is equal to the sum of excess demand for oil by the two importers:

$$-E_{xx} = E_{x1} + E_{x2}. \tag{6}$$

Once the assumptions on exporter-importer bilateralism are dropped, and multilateral transactions are allowed there will be trade in goods and bonds between the two oil-importing countries, and the relative prices of goods and bonds in terms of oil may differ from those specified above. Triangular transactions may take place and the equilibrium condition (5) will include terms for the excess demand of country 1 for good 2, or the excess demand of country 2 for bond 1. Country X, the oil-exporting country, may now ship oil to country 1 and acquire good 2 (the good which country 2 produces) in exchange. Multilateral trade will give rise to secondary recycling both in terms of goods and in terms of bonds. The effect of multilateral trade on the flow of oil between exporting and importing countries will depend on the price and income elasticities in the three countries. Thus multilateral trade opportunities may change the process of adjustment to permanent and transitory elements.

The fact that the oil-exporting country has a monopoly position changes the precise conditions under which the physical flow of oil will increase, but not the general nature of the solution. To the extent that multilateral transactions effectively shift outward the demand for oil, and given a zero marginal cost of oil, the physical flow of oil will increase. The only case where a monopolist would not behave in this manner is where a cutback in physical production of oil, and thus a change in the relative price of oil, will affect the relative price of other goods in a favorable way given the monopolist's preference function. That is, if the monopolist can affect the relative prices of consumption goods by cutting back the quantity of oil supplied. Assuming no such changes in relative prices of other goods, the direction of the changes in the flow of oil resulting from allowing multilateral trade will be the same under monopoly or in a competitive market. To illustrate the nature of the process by which triangular trade in financial assets may accommodate a larger flow of oil between the trading partners, consider the following example.

Suppose that country 1 is Germany, country 2 is Italy, and country X is Saudi Arabia. Let their three produced goods be steam shovels, wine, and oil, respectively. Under what we have defined as bilateral trade, Germany trades steam shovels to Saudi Arabia for oil. Prior to the trade each country had an excess demand for the other's good. By assumption, no trade occurs between Germany and Italy. Also, no trade occurs between Italy and Saudi Arabia as the latter has no desire for wine at any price. In the multilateral case, however, Italy trades wine to Germany, which does consume wine, for steam shovels. Then Italy trades some of the newly acquired steam shovels for Saudi oil. As previously discussed, the opportunity for multilateral trade may have an effect on the relative prices of these goods.

The same argument applies for financial assets ("bonds") which are viewed here as claims on future goods. By allowing free movement of assets in international capital markets the trading countries can transact more optimally by acquiring financial assets which are better suited to their desired consumption pattern over time. Since the distribution of such financial assets among the importing countries will not correspond, in general, to the distribution of excess demands for oil, some "secondary recycling" of goods and bonds will occur and may increase the world trade in oil.[3]

In the context of a three-country, three-good general equilibrium model with full employment it can be shown that multilateral trade opportunities in goods and in financial assets may result in a higher volume of trade, depending on the elasticities. Such a model indicates the different components of the total changes in the supply of oil by the oil-exporter. The components include the income and substitution effects on consumption, and the concomitant substitution effects on production in the general equilibrium framework.

The analysis of these components is shown in equation (7) where ΔE_x^x is the total change, in a comparative statics context, in the physical amount of oil supplied by country X after multilateral trade is allowed (between countries 1 and 2).[4] For reasons of exposition country superscripts will replace the country subscripts heretofore used.

$$\Delta E_x^x = (\eta^1 + \pi^1 + \varepsilon^1)(\Delta P_{g1/x}^1)E_x^1 + (\eta^2 + \pi^2 + \varepsilon^2)(\Delta P_{g2/x}^2)E_x^2 \qquad (7)$$

where: $E_x^j \equiv$ excess demand in country j (= 1,2,X) for good x (oil)
 $\eta^j \equiv$ country j price elasticity of oil import demand (with respect to $P_{gj/x}^j$).
 $\pi^j \equiv$ country j marginal propensity to consume of its imported good (oil) with respect to a change in its real income.
 $\varepsilon^j \equiv$ country j price elasticity of export supply (with respect to $P_{gj/x}^j$).
 $P_{gj/x}^j \equiv$ domestic price in country j of good j relative to oil.

Thus η^j captures the country j substitution in consumption effect with respect to a change in the relative price of its exportable, gj. Likewise π^j represents the real income effect on the country j demand for oil. The change in relative prices also implies a substitution in production effect in country j as captured by ε^j.

Equation (7) expresses the change in the supply flow of oil from the oil-exporter in terms of the parameters of the importing countries with whom multilateral trade is now allowed. We need only evaluate the right hand side of (7) to determine the conditions under which $\Delta E_x^x > 0$, i.e., country X increases its supply of oil to world markets under multilateral trade. We have:

 $\eta^j > 0$ by definition and our demand assumption.
 $\pi^j > 0$ by ruling out inferior goods.
 $\varepsilon^j > 0$ by our production assumption, i.e., if the relative price of our exportable increases then we produce more of it.
 $\Delta P_{gj/x}^j > 0$ by our assumption that all goods are gross substitutes.
 $E_x^j > 0$ by assumption (i.e., trade exists).

These conditions imply $\Delta E_x^x > 0$, i.e., accommodating flows (via multilateral trade) of goods and financial assets among importing countries 1 and 2 increase the supply of oil relative to the level under bilateral trade in goods alone. More importantly, they imply that in analyzing the adjustment to higher prices, it is insufficient to focus on the current account balances of single countries in isolation, let alone the "oil component" of these balances. The adjustment of any particular country will reflect its role in accommodating the adjustments of all other countries. For example, a country able to issue financial claims which are attractive to oil exporters may find it desirable to issue these claims and, in turn, acquire either goods or financial claims from other oil-importing countries. This may result in a current account deficit which in no way reflects the strength or basic pattern of adjustment of the country in question.

Payment for and Financing of Oil—Some Empirical Observations

The preceding analysis suggests that by providing adjustment services, both for transitory elements and for a slower rate of change to a new permanent level, international capital markets allow for a higher volume of trade in oil. The adjustment takes place through direct exchanges in capital assets (borrowing and lending) between exporters and importers, as well as by accommodating flows of goods and bonds among importers of oil. The actual magnitude of the accommodating flows in 1974, 1975, and 1976 is estimated here. This is done as an indication of the extent by which the actual trade in oil between OPEC members and the major importing countries was facilitated by these adjustment flows. However, before we proceed to examine the data, two caveats have to be stressed. First, the data represent only three years, and although it is true that most of the adjustment may have taken place during this period, the data undoubtedly contain errors and reflect some indecision on the part of the exporting and the importing countries. Second, the data reflect some adjustments which took place in markets other than the capital or the goods markets. This is true in particular with regard to the labor market as some of the adjustment was carried out by unemployment.

In Table 3 the balance of trade of the six major oil-importing countries with OPEC is presented. As seen in line (3) for each country, all six countries run a trade deficit with OPEC, which means that this amount of "financing" of oil must take place.

The actual "financing" of the flow of oil in Table 3 was accomplished both by "primary recycling" and by "secondary recycling" in terms of goods and financial assets. In the aggregate, the six major importing countries had deficits with OPEC of $51.9, $32.2, and $41.5 billion in 1974, 1975, and 1976, respectively. These deficits were partially offset by $29.9, $41.8, and $21.8 billion trade surpluses with the other, non-OPEC countries (including trade among the six importing countries). The balance of trade of the six importing countries with the non-OPEC countries is presented in Table 4.

The TOTAL row in Table 4 reflects the net trade position of the six major industrialized countries which was accomplished both by intra-six accommodating flows as well as by exchanges with the non-six, non-OPEC group. The distribution of net trade positions among the three groups is presented in Table 5.

Table 3. Flows of trade between OPEC and six major importing countries, 1973–1976.
(billions of current dollars)

	1973	1974	1975	1976
U.S.				
(1) Imports from OPEC	5.0	17.0	18.4	26.6
(2) Exports to OPEC	3.8	7.0	11.2	12.2
(3) Trade deficit with OPEC [(1)–(2)]	1.2	10.0	7.2	14.4
U.K.				
(1) Imports from OPEC	3.7	8.9	7.3	7.4
(2) Exports to OPEC	2.0	2.8	5.0	5.3
(3) Trade deficit with OPEC [(1)–(2)]	1.7	6.1	2.3	2.1
West Germany				
(1) Imports from OPEC	4.0	9.2	8.2	9.6
(2) Exports to OPEC	2.3	3.8	6.9	8.2
(3) Trade deficit with OPEC [(1)–(2)]	1.7	5.4	1.3	1.4
Japan				
(1) Imports from OPEC	7.5	21.6	21.1	22.5
(2) Exports to OPEC	2.8	5.6	8.6	9.2
(3) Trade deficit with OPEC [(1)–(2)]	4.7	16.0	12.5	13.3
France				
(1) Imports from OPEC	3.9	10.3	9.8	11.1
(2) Exports to OPEC	1.9	3.1	5.0	4.7
(3) Trade deficit with OPEC [(1)–(2)]	2.0	7.2	4.8	6.4
Italy				
(1) Imports from OPEC	3.4	9.5	7.9	8.1
(2) Exports to OPEC	1.2	2.3	3.8	4.2
(3) Trade deficit with OPEC [(1)–(2)]	2.2	7.2	4.1	3.9
Total Deficit of Six with OPEC	13.5	51.9	32.2	41.5

Sources: *Direction of Trade* and *International Financial Statistics*.

Of the six major oil-importing countries, West Germany was able to finance all of its OPEC trade deficit by exporting goods to non-OPEC members. Japan, the United States, and France accommodated part of their oil-related deficit by exports to non-OPEC countries. Italy and the United Kingdom have maintained a trade deficit with the other non-OPEC countries in addition to their oil-related deficit. Italy and the United Kingdom have financed their total trade deficit by the sale of financial

Financial Markets and Higher Oil Prices

Table 4. Balance of trade of six major oil-importing countries with other, non-OPEC countries, 1973–1976.
(billions of current dollars)

	1973	1974	1975	1976
U.S.	3.2	7.6	17.9	−0.2
U.K.	−6.7	−9.4	−7.2	−7.6
West Germany	14.4	25.0	16.5	15.2
Japan	3.4	9.4	10.4	15.7
France	1.1	0.8	3.7	−0.8
Italy	−3.4	−3.5	0.5	−2.5
Total	12.0	29.9	41.8	21.8

Sources: *Direction of Trade* and *International Financial Statistics*.

Table 5. Net trade positions of the major groups in the world, 1973–1976.
(billions of current dollars)

With OPEC	1973	1974	1975	1976
OPEC with six	13.5	51.9	32.2	41.5
OPEC with others	8.4	33.5	24.6	23.9
Total OPEC	21.9	85.4	56.8	65.4
Six with other non-OPEC	12.0	29.9	41.8	21.8
Other non-OPEC with OPEC and six	−20.4	−63.4	−66.4	−45.7

Sources: *Direction of Trade* and *International Financial Statistics*.

Table 6. Computed* net capital flows of six major oil-importing countries, 1973–1976.
(billions of current dollars)

	1973	1974	1975	1976
U.S.	−3.2	0.7	−4.1	17.0
U.K.	7.5	15.1	10.9	8.4
West Germany	−22.0	−18.9	−16.6	−10.0
Japan	7.5	5.3	2.8	1.4
France	2.4	6.0	−2.7	4.3
Italy	5.3	10.2	5.7	8.3
Total	−2.5	18.4	−4.0	29.4

Sources: *Direction of Trade* and *International Financial Statistics*.
*Computed as a balance of payments' residual.

assets. The United Kingdom sold capital assets directly to the oil-exporting countries (primary recycling), while Italy sold capital assets mostly to the United States and West Germany (secondary recycling).

In addition to financing their own trade deficits with OPEC, several of the six major countries played a role in financing the overall deficits of the other non-OPEC countries vis-à-vis OPEC and the industrial group. This can be seen in Table 6, which shows the net capital flows for each of the six countries. Countries with negative flows are "exporting" capital funds (e.g., financing deficits) and "importing" financial claims from net deficit countries.

III. FINANCIAL MARKETS AND THE BEHAVIOR OF OIL PRODUCERS

The previous section showed that financial markets allow oil-importing countries time to adjust to higher oil prices and enable them to offer a wider range of goods and claims on future goods in payment for oil whether or not these are directly acceptable by oil producers. This section focuses on the role financial considerations play in producers' output/pricing decisions.

The problem faced by each oil producer is analogous to the consumption/investment decision of an individual seeking to maximize his expected utility of consumption over time. The producer country must make three decisions:

1) How much oil to sell in the current period in the form of: (a) physical production; (b) financial claims issued against oil in the ground. The remaining unsold oil will be retained as an asset in the owner's portfolio.

2) How much to consume in the current period. The remainder of revenues, positive or negative, will be added to the investment portfolio.

3) How to allocate non-oil assets among domestic real investment and financial claims on other countries, both riskless and risky.

One major role of financial markets is to allow the producer to separate production and consumption decisions. In the absence of a capital market the owner of the oil cannot accumulate any claims on future consumption and thus must match consumption and production over time. This can be readily illustrated under an assumption of certainty in a two-period model.

If the oil producer is a cartel leader, he faces a downward sloping demand function for oil and will seek to equate marginal cost with marginal revenue over time. In such a world the producer may choose between two ways of allocating consumption over time. One is the market for oil, and the other is the market for financial claims. In the market for oil the owner faces a concave transformation curve. The rate of transformation of future consumption into present consumption (by selling one more barrel of oil) is changing over the production range.

Competitive financial markets, on the other hand, offer a constant rate of transformation—the market rate of interest. The two mechanisms for the allocation of consumption over time are depicted in Figure 1, below. The rate of production is determined by equating the rate of transformation in the oil market to the given market rate of interest. The actual consumption per period is determined by the owner's preference function. There is no portfolio allocation decision to be made in this certainty model, since there is only one investment asset. Further, the decision to sell claims against oil is identical to borrowing against future production since oil prices are known with certainty.

When uncertainty is introduced, a variety of investment assets is needed to gain insight into the production/investment decisions of the owner of the

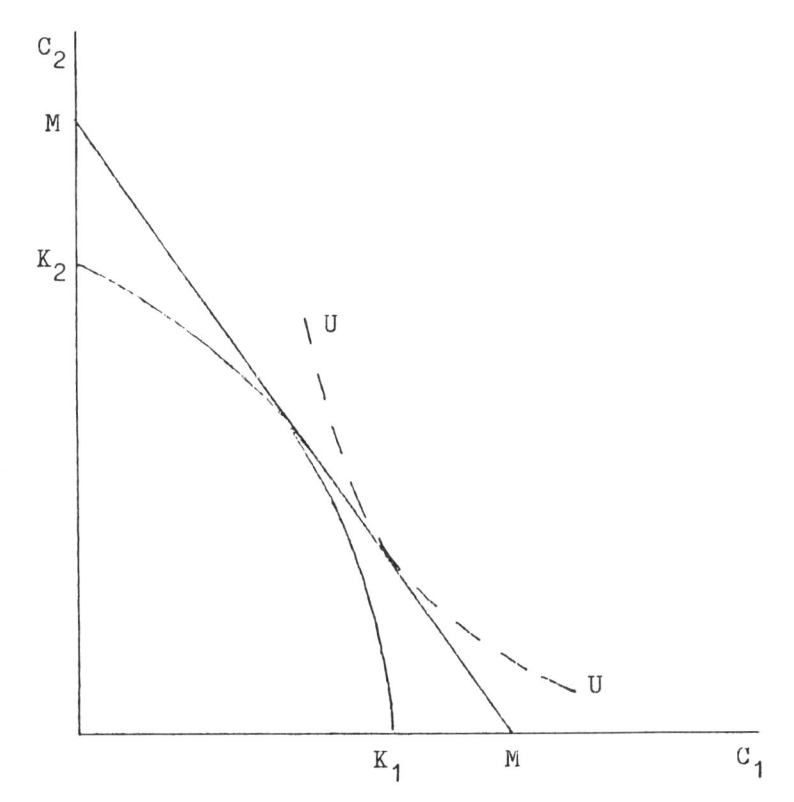

Figure 1. where:
    C_i axis measures consumption possibilities in period i
    $K_1 K_2$ is the oil-production possibility frontier.
    MM is the producer's budget line with constant slope as determined by the market rate of interest
    UU is the producer's preference curve

oil reserves. At a minimum, three types of assets must be considered. The first is a fund consisting of risky assets excluding oil in the ground (e.g., the world market portfolio of common stocks); the second is the oil itself (or, equivalently, financial assets whose value is linked to oil); and third is a riskless asset. Oil is a risky asset because of market uncertainties on both the demand and supply sides. Once the consumption decision has been made, the producer must decide how to allocate his holdings among these three assets. This can be viewed in the context of the single-period portfolio choice problem developed by Markowitz (4).[5] It involves selecting that combination of assets which maximizes expected utility, where both asset payoffs and the individual's utility are described in terms of the expected value and standard deviation of end-of-period wealth, $\bar{W}$ and σ_w, respectively.

The situation of the producer country in the absence of financial transactions is analogous to that of an individual who has no access to a capital market. As shown in Figure 2a, the frontier of potential investments will be a single point E, reflecting the endowment of oil reserves and other human and physical capital. By trading oil or claims linked to oil for other risky assets and/or riskless claims, utility can be increased in two ways. By lending, i.e., exchanging oil or risky claims linked to oil for riskless assets, the risk/return mix can be altered by moving along BL to B, as shown in Figure 2b. By diversifying risky holdings, i.e., trading oil or claims linked to oil for other risky assets which are less than perfectly correlated with the oil asset, the producer can move to point R on the frontier of risky opportunities D, as shown in Figure 2c. Point E lies below the frontier since it is highly concentrated in the oil asset and, as a result, reflects almost all of the risk of the oil asset even though much of this risk could be diversified away within the world economy. By both diversifying and altering the riskiness of the portfolio by lending, the producer can move to an overall optimum, 0, as shown in Figure 2d.[6]

Two factors limit the extent to which a producer can alter his portfolio. First, because of physical constraints and market considerations, he cannot exchange a large proportion of his oil holdings for financial assets in any particular time period. He could get around this constraint if he could sell arbitrary amounts of financial claims linked to oil, but such sales will be constrained by the "moral hazard" or "sovereign risk" associated with them. The source of this moral hazard is that the future value of the oil-linked claims is dependent on the producer's behavior. For example, the producer might renege on the contract to pay the claimholder when the oil eventually is sold, or he might no longer act within the cartel so as to maximize the value of the oil asset once he has sold his oil-linked claims.

The above discussion does not provide a solution to the general intertemporal production/investment problem for a producer with some degree of monopoly power, but it does make clear that financial considerations

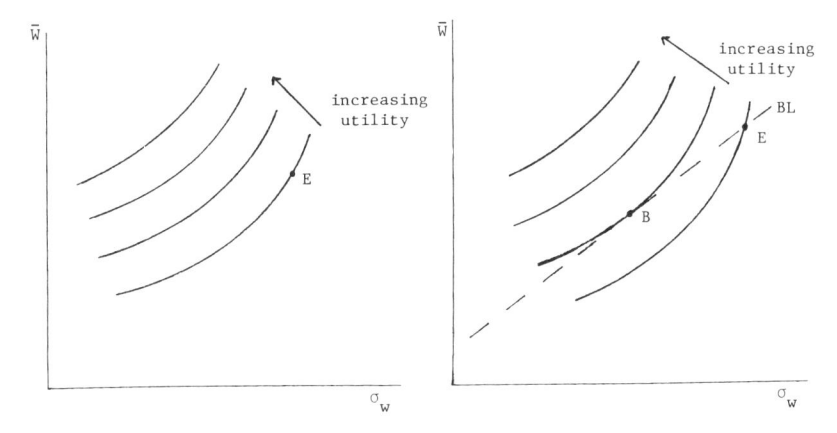

Figure 2a. Initial position of individual (country) without access to capital markets.

Figure 2b. Effects of riskless borrowing lending.

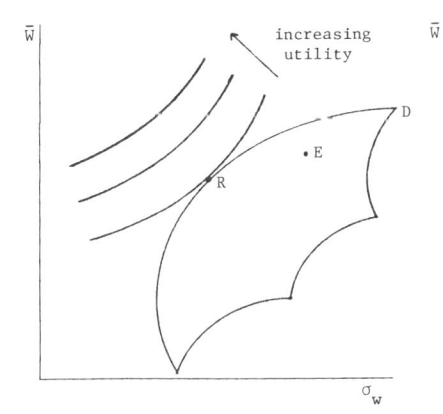

Figure 2c. Effect of diversifying risky portfolio.

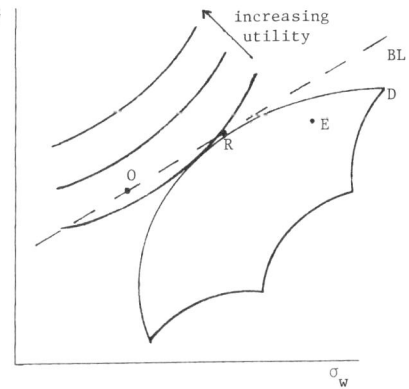

Figure 2d. Combined effects of borrowing, lending, and diversification.

Table 7. Financial investments of OPEC, 1974–1976.
(billions of dollars)

	1974	1975	1976
United States			
Treasury bonds and notes	} 6.0	2.0	4.2
Treasury bills		0.5	−1.0
Bank deposits	4.0	0.6	1.6
Other (equity, property)	1.0	6.9	6.7
Total	11.0	10.0	11.5
United Kingdom			
Government stocks	0.9	0.4	0.2
Treasury bills	2.7	−0.9	−1.2
Sterling deposits	1.7	0.2	−1.4
Other (inc. equity)	0.7	0.3	0.5
Foreign currency deposits	15.0	4.3	6.4
Total	21.0	4.3	4.5
Other Countries			
Bank deposits	9.0	5.0	5.5
Other investment	11.9	12.4	9.7
Total	20.9	17.4	15.2
International Organizations	3.5	4.0	2.0
All Financial Investment	56.4	35.7	33.2

Source: Bank of England.

come into play at several important points. Producers will take into account both the expected stream of revenues and the risk associated with those revenues in choosing among output/pricing programs. Their decisions will be conditioned by the extent that they can shift these risks to others through financial transactions in international financial markets. Since their ability to sell claims linked to oil will be constrained by considerations of sovereign risk, it is likely that they will seek to generate greater oil revenues than required for current consumption (i.e., a surplus on current account) in order to gradually shift to a more desirable portfolio with a less uncertain path of future consumption possibilities.

Table 7 shows the changing composition of OPEC financial holdings since the price rise. While transitory considerations undoubtedly influenced the size and composition of these holdings in early years, it appears that substantial external financial holdings represent part of a long-run production/ investment strategy. These financial holdings, along with massive investment in the domestic economy, lessen the concentration of the domestic portfolio in the oil asset. The changing composition of the holdings suggests that transitory factors no longer play a major role. They probably were the reason for the early (1974) concentration in riskless assets. However, by 1976 more investment is in risky securities such as equities and real estate.

IV. STRESS IN THE WORLD FINANCIAL MARKET—FEEDBACKS FROM CONSUMER TO PRODUCER BEHAVIOR

As was pointed out in section II above, the flow of oil to many countries in the period 1974–1976 was facilitated by multilateral financial transfers. This group includes all the non-OPEC LDCs and some of the weaker industrialized countries.

Although the world financial system was able to accommodate the demand for oil at roughly the same physical levels as in 1973, this accommodation created substantial financial stress. This stress was due to the fact that OPEC members, and in particular the Arabian peninsula countries, were willing to accept financial claims only if they had low risk, while many users of the funds, especially LDCs and the weaker industrialized countries, could only offer risky claims. This gap is bridged by financial intermediation in which individuals or financial institutions buy risky financial assets from the oil-importing countries and sell low-risk assets to OPEC members which have "surplus funds." The financial intermediaries, whether they are governments, international organizations or banks, assume the difference in risk. This intermediation function is rewarded by risk premiums, in the case of debt contracts the interest differential between creditor and debtor rates.

The scope of this kind of financial intermediation is quite impressive. The accumulated current account surplus of OPEC for the period 1974–1977 is $153.5 billion. According to recent data published by the Morgan Guaranty, the external debt of the non-OPEC LDCs has risen to $180 billion, of which $77 billion were lent by commercial banks. This amount is distributed between U.S. banks (about two-thirds) and non-U.S. banks (about one third). An approximate distribution of the total financing among the different sources is presented in Table 8.

Given the similarity of the total LDC debt and the OPEC surplus, it is tempting to attribute the deficits entirely to the increased cost of oil imports. This, however, fails to take into account other contributing factors. For example, attempts by industrialized countries to restore current account balance by restricting aggregate demand and/or imports also must have played a role. Nevertheless, it is reasonable to assume that there is a linkage between oil prices and financial stress.

Increased external debt implies an increased risk of default or rescheduling.

Table 8. The distribution of LDC external financing.

Source	Percent of total
Direct investment	12.0
Concessional or assistance loans	12.0
IMF credit	8.0
International bond issues	13.0
Bank credit	55.0
Total	100.0

Source: Morgan Guaranty, *World Financial Markets*, June 1977.

The repayment depends on the economic strength, in particular on the foreign exchange earning power, of the debtor as well as on its political decisions. Some measures of the ability of major borrowers to service their foreign obligations are shown in Table 9.

The price of oil is an important factor in the determination of the flows and the imbalances of world trade, especially in the short run. As such the price of oil is one of the underlying factors of the ability of the debtors to service and refinance their loans. Even without further specification it is clear that any further increases in the price of oil are likely to lead to new and heavier borrowing and hence increase the financial risk associated with both the existing and the new debt. The potential losers from default or from rescheduling are the intermediaries which sold time deposits and other low-risk assets to the major oil exporters and, if losses are substantial, holders

Table 9. External debt-related measures for major international borrowers.

Country	External debt end-1976 (billions of dollars)	Gross external debt as % of exports of goods and services	Real growth in external debt in % 1973–1976	Debt Service ratio 1976
Argentina	9.0	185	0[a]	40.9
Brazil	28.6	216	62	45.9
Finland	9.0	109	67	10.3
Korea	9.5	111	73	12.8
Greece	3.9	78	18	11.1
Mexico	27.6	361	103	31.7
Peru	4.4	226	61	27.9
Philippines	5.5	121	67	15.9
Taiwan	3.9	43	86	4.1
Turkey	5.7	128	33	9.9

Source: Morgan Guaranty, *World Financial Markets*, June 1977.
a = the zero growth for Argentina reflects mostly the market decision not to lend.

of claims against these intermediaries. Thus although OPEC countries use the international banking community to intermediate the risk, they also have a stake in its success or failure.

It would appear that the Arabian peninsula countries, which also are major holders of international financial claims, should take into account the impact of any price hike on the world financial system. As a result, they probably will seek to moderate price changes, although no definitive statements can be made without further specifying other elements of the producer decision. If OPEC gives in to pressures to finance LDC deficits directly, the linkage between financial factors and price/output decisions will be strengthened.

FOOTNOTES

*Senior Lecturer, Faculty of Management, Tel Aviv University, and Coordinator, Research Group in Economics and Management of Energy, Tel Aviv University; Associate Professor and Doctoral Candidate, respectively, Sloan School of Management, MIT. This paper draws on work done by the authors as part of the MIT World Oil Project, financed in part through NSF grant no. SIA75–00739.

1. The terms "paying" and "financing" oil were coined by Alexander (2).
2. See Alexander (2).
3. When bonds are risky, the existence of multilateral exchange of them in secondary markets will provide an additional advantage — it will allow increased diversification by individual portfolio holders across countries.
4. The derivation of equation (7) is given in an Appendix to Agmon, Lessard, and Paddock (1) which is available from the authors.
5. The portfolio choice problem is truly a simultaneous, intertemporal decision process. Production, consumption and investment allocation are related in a complex manner, particularly when a monopoly is involved, and closed form solutions are very difficult to obtain analytically. But much insight can be gained by first looking at a single-period portfolio decision problem where the production and consumption decisions are assumed to be made. For a rigorous, complete treatment of the individual's intertemporal consumption/investment decision, see Merton (5). The complexity of the intertemporal cartel solution, even when uncertainty and financial considerations are ignored, can be seen in Pindyck (6).
6. See Lessard (3) for further discussion of the portfolio problem faced by a commodity producer.

REFERENCES

1. Agmon, T., D. R. Lessard, and J. L. Paddock, "Accommodation in the International Capital Markets and the Recycling of Oil Funds," MIT Energy Lab Working Paper, 1976.
2. Alexander, S. S., *Paying for Energy: Report of the Twentieth Century Fund Task Force on the International Oil Crisis.* McGraw-Hill, New York, 1975.
3. Lessard, D. R., "Risk Efficient External Financing Strategies for Commodity Producing Countries," MIT Working Paper, July 1977.

4. Markowitz, H. M., "Portfolio Selection," *Journal of Finance* (March 1952).
5. Merton, R. C., "Optimum Consumption and Portfolio Rules in a Continuous-Time Framework," *Journal of Economic Theory* (December 1971).
6. Pindyck, R. S., "Gains to Producers from the Cartelization of Exhaustible Resources," forthcoming in *Review of Economics and Statistics*.

ADVANCES IN THE ECONOMICS OF ENERGY AND RESOURCES
A Research Annual

    Series Editor: Robert S. Pindyck, Sloan School of Management
                       Massachusetts Institute of Technology

Volume 2: The Production and Pricing of Energy Resources

Spring 1979	275 pages	Cloth	Institutions: $25.00
ISBN NUMBER 0-89232-079-6			Individuals: $12.50

CONTENTS: Alternative Methods of Oil Supply Forecasting, M. A. Adelman and Henry D. Jacoby, Massachusetts Institute of Technology. **A Basin Development Model of Oil Supply,** Paul L. Eckbo, Massachusetts Institute of Technology. **Estimating A Policy Model of U.S. Coal Supply,** Martin B. Zimmerman, Massachusetts Institute of Technology. **The Rate of Petroleum Exploration and Extraction,** Russell S. Uhler, University of British Columbia. **Uncertainty and the Optimal Supply Policy for an Exhaustible Resource,** Geoffrey Heal, Sussex University. **Search Strategies and Private Incentives for Resource Exploration,** Richard J. Gilbert, University of California—Berkeley. **Increasing Extraction Costs and Resource Prices,** Donald A. Hanson, Southern Methodist University. **Staving Off the Backstop: Dynamic Limit-Pricing with a Kinked Demand Curve,** Stephen W. Salant, Board of Governors of the Federal Reserve System. **ETA-MACRO: A Model of Energy-Economy Interactions,** Alan S. Manne, Stanford University. **The Bauxite Cartel in the New International Economic Order,** Harold J. Barnett, Washington University.

A 10 percent discount will be granted on all institutional standing orders placed directly with the publisher. Standing orders will be filled automatically upon publication and will continue until cancelled. Please indicate which volume Standing Order is to begin with.

JAI PRESS INC.
P.O. Box 1285
165 West Putnam Avenue
Greenwich, Connecticut 06830

(203) 661-7602   Cable Address: JAIPUBL.

RESEARCH IN PHILOSOPHY AND TECHNOLOGY
A Research Annual
Series Editor: Paul T. Durbin, Philosophy Department and Center for the Culture of Biomedicine and Science, University of Delaware.
Bibliography Editor: Carl Mitcham, St. Catharine College, St. Catharine, Kentucky.

OFFICIAL PUBLICATION OF THE PHILOSOPHY AND TECHNOLOGY GROUP

The series will serve three functions in the advancement of the philosophy of technology movement in American academic circles. Through its annual bibliographical update under the direction of Carl Mitcham, it will become the place to look for bibliographical leads, documentation, and all the other things a good bibliography serves for. It will serve as the outlet for the proceedings of a series of philosophy of technology conferences and symposia, with a major conference at least every other year. It will serve as a sort of substitute for a journal in the field, with submitted papers not intended for one of the conferences or symposia welcome at any time.

Volume 1. Published 1978   Cloth   400 Pages   Institutions: $28.50
ISBN NUMBER 0-89232-022-2   Individuals: $15.00

CONTENTS: Introduction to the Series. Introduction to Volume One.

Part 1—Method, Descriptive Framework, and a Practical Program for Philosophy of Technology: Culture and Technology, Joseph Margolis, Philosophy Department, Temple University. **The Problem of Scale in Human Life: A Framework for Analysis,** Robert E. McGinn, Values, Technology, and Society Program, Stanford University. **Technology, Mass Movements, and Rapid Social Change: A Program for the Future of Philosophy of Technology,** Joseph Agassi, Philosophy Department, Boston University and Tel Aviv University.

Part II—The University of Delaware Conference, 1975: Toward a Social Philosophy of Technology, Paul T. Durbin, Philosophy Department, Center for the Culture of Biomedicine and Science, University of Delaware. **The Explanation of Technology,** Albert Borgmann, Philosophy Department, University of Montana. **Values in Science,** Willis H. Truitt, Philosophy Department, University of South Florida. **Technology as Ideology,** Kai Nielsen, Philosophy Department, Brooklyn College and University of Calgary. **Humanization of Technology: Slogan or Ethical Imperative?** Edmund Byrne, Philosophy Department, Indiana University and Purdue University at Indianapolis. **What is Technology?** Robert E. McGinn, Values, Technology and Society Program, Stanford University. **Shifting from Physical to Social Technology,** Joseph Agassi, Philosophy Department, Boston University and Tel Aviv University. **The Cognitive Dimension of Technological Change,** Stanley R. Carpenter, Department of Social Sciences, Georgia Institute of Technology. **Types of Technology,** Carl Mitcham, St. Catharine College, St. Catharine, Ky.

Part III—Bibliographical Update: Philosophy of Technology, 1972-1974, Carl Mitcham.

Index.

Research in Philosophy and Technology

Volume 2. September 1979   Cloth   Ca. 425 pages   Institutions: $ 32.50
ISBN 0-89232-101-6   Individuals: $ 16.50

CONTENTS: Introduction to Volume Two: The International Cast of the Philosophy and Technology Movement.

Part I: EUROPEAN CONTRIBUTIONS. **Euthyphronics and the Problem of Adapting Technical Progress to Man,** *Jozef Banka, Katowice, Poland.* **Toward an Interdisciplinary and Pragmatic Philosophy of Technology,** *Hans Lenk and Gunter Ropohl, University of Karlsruhe.* **Fear and Insight in French Philosophy of Technology,** *Daniel Cerezuelle, Universite de Grenoble.*

Part II: CONFERENCE PAPERS, 1976-1977. **Freedom and Determinism in a Technological Setting,** *Albert Borgmann, University of Montana.* **The Normative Side of Technology,** *Edmund Byrne, Indiana University and Purdue University.* **Art in a Technological Society,** *Phillip Frandozzi, University of Montana.* **Marx, Machinery and Alienation,** *Bernard Gendron, University of Wisconsin - Milwaukee and Nancy Holmstrom, University of Wisconsin - Madison.* **Technological Culture and the End of Philosophy,** *Michael Zimmerman, Newcomb College, Tulane University (Comment by Robert McGinn, Bell Laboratories; Reply by Zimmerman).*

Part III: HISTORICO-PHILOSOPHICAL STUDIES. **The Concepts of 'Nature' and 'Technique' According to the Greeks,** *Wolfgang Schadewaldt, Universitat Tubingen.* **On the Nature of Nature,** *Jacob Klein, St. John's College, Annapolis.* **Documentation: Early Analyses of Machines in the French Intellectual Tradition,** *Alfred Espinas, Jacques Lafitte and Simone Weil.* **On the Antagonism Between Philosophy and Technology in Germany and Austria,** *Werner Koenne, Australian Elektrizitat Wirtschafts-Aktiengesellschaft, Vienna.* **Heidegger and Marcuse: Technology as Ideology,** *Michael Zimmerman, Newcomb College, Tulane University.*

Part IV: REVIEW AND BIBLIOGRAPHY. **Philosophy and Technology and the Verein Deutscher Ingenieure,** *Alois Hunting, VDI Wulfrath, West Germany.* **Philosophy of Technology in France: Overview and Bibliography, 1972-1977,** *Jean-Claude Beaune, Universite de Clermont.* **Hendrik van Riessen and Dutch Neo-Calvinist Philosophy of Technology, Hendrik van Riessen: Biography and Selected Bibliography,** *Donald Morton, Free University, Amsterdam.* **The Structure of Technology.** *Hendrik van Riessen, Free University, Amsterdam.* **Technology and Culture,** *Hendrik van Riessen, Free University, Amsterdam.* **Toward a Neo-Calvinist Philosophy of Technology: Review of E. Schuurman, Technology and Deliverance,** *Donald Morton, Free University, Amsterdam.* **Technology Assessment: A New Type of Science?** *Frederick A. Rossini, Georgia Institute of Technology.* **Supplementary Bibliography,** *Carl Mitcham and Jim Grote, St. Catherine College.* **Kenneth Sayre on Information-Theoretic Models of Mind,** *K. S. Shrader-Frechette, University of Louisville.*

APPENDIX. **Author Index for Current Bibliography in the Philosophy of Technology, 1973-1974, Research in Philosophy and Technology, Volume 1 (1978).**

A 10 percent discount will be granted on all institutional standing orders placed directly with the publisher. Standing orders will be filled automatically upon publication and will continue until cancelled. Please indicate which volume Standing Order is to begin with.

JAI PRESS INC., 165 West Putnam Avenue, P.O. Box 1285
Greenwich, Connecticut 06830.

Telephone: 203-661-7602   Cable Address: JAIPUBL

OTHER ANNUAL SERIES OF INTEREST FROM JAI PRESS INC.

Consulting Editor for Economics: Paul Uselding, University of Illinois

ADVANCES IN APPLIED MICRO-ECONOMICS
Series Editor: V. Kerry Smith, Resources for the Future, Washington, D.C.

ADVANCES IN ECONOMETRICS
Series Editors: R. L. Basmann, Texas A & M University, and George F. Rhodes, Colorado State University

ADVANCES IN ECONOMIC THEORY
Series Editor: David Levhari, The Hebrew University

ADVANCES IN THE ECONOMICS OF ENERGY AND RESOURCES
Series Editor: Robert S. Pindyck, Sloan School of Management, Massachusetts Institute of Technology

APPLICATIONS OF MANAGEMENT SCIENCE
Series Editor: Randall L. Schultz, Krannert Graduate School of Management, Purdue University

RESEARCH IN AGRICULTURAL ECONOMICS
Series Editor: Earl O. Heady, Director, The Center for Agricultural and Rural Development, Iowa State University

RESEARCH IN CORPORATE SOCIAL PERFORMANCE AND POLICY
Series Editor: Lee E. Preston, School of Management and Center for Policy Studies, State University of New York, Buffalo

RESEARCH IN ECONOMIC ANTHROPOLOGY
Series Editor: George Dalton, Northwestern University

RESEARCH IN ECONOMIC HISTORY
Series Editor: Paul Uselding, University of Illinois

RESEARCH IN EXPERIMENTAL ECONOMICS
Series Editor: Vernon L. Smith, College of Business and Public Administration, University of Arizona

RESEARCH IN FINANCE
Series Editor: Haim Levy, School of Business, The Hebrew University

RESEARCH IN HEALTH ECONOMICS
Series Editor: Richard M. Scheffler, University of North Carolina, Chapel Hill and the Institute of Medicine, National Academy of Sciences

RESEARCH IN HUMAN CAPITAL AND DEVELOPMENT
Series Editor: Ismail Sirageldin, The Johns Hopkins University

RESEARCH IN INTERNATIONAL BUSINESS AND FINANCE
Series Editor: Robert G. Hawkins, Graduate School of Business Administration, New York University

RESEARCH IN LABOR ECONOMICS
Series Editor: Ronald G. Ehrenberg, School of Industrial and Labor Relations, Cornell University

RESEARCH IN LAW AND ECONOMICS
Series Editor: Richard O. Zerbe, Jr., SMT Program, University of Washington

RESEARCH IN MARKETING
Series Editor: Jagdish N. Sheth, University of Illinois

RESEARCH IN ORGANIZATIONAL BEHAVIOR
Series Editors: Barry M. Staw, Graduate School of Management, Northwestern University, and Larry L. Cummings, Graduate School of Business, University of Wisconsin

RESEARCH IN PHILOSOPHY AND TECHNOLOGY
Series Editor: Paul T. Durbin, Center for the Culture of Biomedicine and Science, University of Delaware

RESEARCH IN POLITICAL ECONOMY
Series Editor: Paul Zarembka, State University of New York, Buffalo

RESEARCH IN POPULATION ECONOMICS
Series Editors: Julian L. Simon, University of Illinois, and Julie DaVanzo, The Rand Corporation

RESEARCH IN PUBLIC POLICY AND MANAGEMENT
Series Editors: Colin C. Blaydon, Institute of Policy Studies and Public Affairs, Duke University, and Steven Gilford, Chicago

ALL VOLUMES IN THESE ANNUAL SERIES ARE AVAILABLE AT INSTITUTIONAL AND INDIVIDUAL SUBSCRIPTION RATES. PLEASE WRITE FOR DETAILED BROCHURES ON EACH SERIES

A 10 percent discount will be granted on all institutional standing orders placed directly with the publisher. Standing orders will be filled automatically upon publication and will continue until cancelled. Please indicate which volume Standing Order is to begin with.

JAI PRESS INC.
P.O. Box 1285
165 West Putnam Avenue
Greenwich, Connecticut 06830

(203) 661-7602   Cable Address: JAIPUBL.

T. F. Yen Energy Sources
EDITOR

An International Interdisciplinary Journal of Science and Technology

Now in its third year of publication, *Energy Sources* has become a respected source of advanced information and sophisticated thinking about the wide range of problems and alternatives that comprise the planet's energy crisis.

The journal bridges gaps among scientists, engineers, and technologists involved in the development of new sources of energy into useful and efficient fuels. *Energy Sources* is a forum for members of several disciplines working toward a common goal: workable solutions to a worldwide, worsening, shortage of energy.

A sampling of recent articles includes:

- Prospects for Coal as a Direct Fuel and Its Potential Through Application of Liquefaction and Gasification Technology *(J.R. Bowen)*
- Oxidation of Lignite into Water-Soluble Organic Acids *(D.K. Young and T.F. Yen)*
- The Influence of the Properties of Coal on Their Conversion Into Clean Fuels *(A. Davis, W. Spackman, and P.H. Given)*
- Wind Power Feasibility *(J.P. LeBoff)*
- The Fischer Assay: Standard for the Oil Shale Industry *(R.N. Heistand)*
- Capital and Electric Production Costs for Geothermal Power Plants *(H.E. Klei and F. Maslan)*
- A Critique of the Nationwide 55 mph Speed Limit *(D. Rapp)*
- Hazardous and Toxic Air Pollutants *(M. Samfield)*

Energy Sources is published quarterly. Each volume contains approximately 400 pages. The subscription price for Volume 3 is $36.00. The subscription price for Volume 4 (beginning Fall, 1978) is $44.00. Personal subscriptions (payable by personal check only) are available at a 50% discount.

For subscriptions outside North America, please add $4.00 per volume for postage and handling.

Crane, Russak & Company, Inc.
347 Madison Avenue • New York 10017

Energy Systems *and* Policy

an international interdisciplinary journal

S. William Gouse, Jr.
EDITOR-IN-CHIEF

This new journal provides an international forum for examining large-scale energy system problems. It satisfies a long-felt need for a vehicle to present and discuss the complex multidisciplinary interactions that take place between physical science technology, economic, social and political sciences, international relations, aspirations of developing nations, and the inter-relationship between these disciplines and existing energy policy as well as what might be in the future. All aspects of energy systems are considered, from source to ultimate consumption.

Selected articles in early issues of ENERGY SYSTEMS AND POLICY included: *A Sulfur Emission Tax and the Electric Utility Industry; The Potential of Coal to Meet the Energy Crisis; A Program for Maximizing U.S. Energy Self-Sufficiency; Energy Rationing and Energy Conservation: Foundations for a Social Policy; Scenarios of Electric Utility Fuel Use in the United States, 1980 and 1990; Conservation Options for Air Transport; Discussion of Uranium Availability and the Breeder Decision; Elasticity of Demand for Gasoline;* and *Environmental Policies for Electricity Generation.*

ENERGY SYSTEMS AND POLICY is published quarterly. Each volume contains approximately 400 pages. The subscription price for Volume 2 is $36.00. The subscription price for Volume 3 (beginning Fall, 1978) is $44.00. Personal subscriptions (payable by personal check only) are available at a 50% discount.

For subscriptions outside North America, please add $4.00 per volume for postage and handling.

Crane, Russak & Company, Inc.
347 Madison Avenue, New York, N.Y. 10017

LAND ECONOMICS

A scholarly journal serving as a forum for dialogue between analysts and policy makers.

Land Economics **is devoted to the study of economic aspects of the entire spectrum of natural and environmental resources. It emphasizes conceptual and empirical work with direct relevance for public policy.**

A sample of recent articles:
"Analyzing the Marginal Cost of Water Supply," by *Ralph Turvey*
"Regulatory Rationing of Electricity Under a Supply Curtailment," by *Jan Paul Acton* and *Ragnild Mowill*
"Natural Resources Management and the Steady State," by *Oscar Burt* and *Ronald Cummings*
"A Study of the Impact of the Wetlands Easement Program on Agricultural Land Values," by *Ralph J. Brown*
"Impacts of Tax Alternatives on Forest Value and Investments," by *W. David Klemperer*
"The Relationship Between Firm and Fishery in Common Property Fisheries," by *Lee G. Anderson*
"Pricing by Rural Electric Cooperatives," by *John L. Mikesell* and *Patrick C. Mann*
"Urban Size and Structure and Expenditures for Gasoline," by *Charles T. Stewart, Jr.* and *James T. Bennett*
"Optimal Leasing Policy for Development of Outer Continental Shelf Hydrocarbon Resources," by *Dennis E. Logue, Richard Sweeney,* and *Thomas Willett*
"The Decline in Electric Utility Competition," by *Walter J. Primeaux, Jr.*
"Growth of Residential Consumption of Electricity," by *William Lockeretz*
"The Effects of Fuel Prices on Residential Appliance Choice," by *Martin Baughman* and *Paul Joskow*
"The Potential Consequences of Deregulation of Transportation," by *James C. Johnson* and *Donald V. Harper*
"Electricity Price Structures: Efficiency, Equity and the Composition of Demand," by *Sanford V. Berg* and *James P. Herden*

Editors: Daniel W. Bromley   Charles J. Cicchetti

Founded in 1925, *Land Economics* **is issued quarterly.**

Subscribe today or recommend a subscription to your library, department or reading room.

Subscription rates:
Institutions: $20/year (4 numbers)
Individuals (must prepay): $13/year
Please remit in U.S. funds.
Foreign postage: $2/year

Send orders and requests for back issue information to:
Journals Department EA
University of Wisconsin Press
P.O. Box 1379
Madison, Wisconsin 53701 U.S.A.